Sustainable Sanitation for All

Praise for this book

'CLTS was an unpredicted phenomenon that changed the way governments, civil society and external agencies approach improving sanitary conditions for the poor; and brought hope to a depressing era of neglect and stagnation in sanitation thinking. But it appeared CLTS had a fatal flaw in that the use of often hastily built household latrines doesn't always last. This timely book brings together experiences from Asia and Africa to examine how to sustain the transformed mind-set, the facilities triggered by CLTS and the new patterns of defecation behaviour, which changed age-old traditions, now made more treacherous by population growth. The book tackles the next frontier: how to utilize the power of CLTS to create permanent facilities and improved service levels. The volume captures experiences and analysis which sorely need to be understood and built upon if we are to induce the much-delayed sanitation revolution that transformed life in Europe.'

Piers Cross, Senior Advisor to Sanitation and Water for All, former Global Manager of the World Bank Water and Sanitation Program

'At last, after decades of neglect, the world seems to be waking up to the greatest challenge of the 21st century; sanitation for all. But, as this book points out, declaring millions of villages open defecation free is just a start, we need to maintain the gains, deal with the faecal sludge, resolve problems of menstrual and hand hygiene, and see sanitation businesses spread around the world. It's time for critical thinking, which is just what this book provides; a state of the art check-in on the problems that we face and the solutions that have been found around the world. Every sanitation practitioner, indeed anyone interested in sustainable approaches to public health, needs to read this thoughtful book.'

Val Curtis, Director of the Environmental Health Group at the London School of Hygiene & Tropical Medicine

'This book is a necessary and valuable addition to the sanitation literature, identifying what we have learned from 15 years of working on understanding community preferences, and addressing constraints in demand, supply and the enabling environment.'

Jan Willem Rosenboom, sanitation expert

'This book puts forward a mix of innovative thinking based on experience and evidence that is useful and relevant whether working with communities on programmes or with governments on policy.'

Sanjay Wijesekera, Chief of Water, Sanitation, and Hygiene, UNICEF

'This publication provides evidence on community-led total sanitation and it is essential we learn from it.'

Hilda Winarta, independent consultant, formerly Regional WaSH Specialist for Plan International Asia Regional Office

Sustainable Sanitation for All
Experiences, challenges, and innovations

Edited by Petra Bongartz,
Naomi Vernon and John Fox

PRACTICAL ACTION
Publishing

Practical Action Publishing Ltd
The Schumacher Centre,
Bourton on Dunsmore, Rugby,
Warwickshire, CV23 9QZ, UK
www.practicalactionpublishing.org

A catalogue record for this book is available from the British Library.

A catalogue record for this book has been requested from the Library of Congress.

ISBN 978-1-85339-927-5 Hardback
ISBN 978-1-85339-928-2 Paperback
ISBN 978-1-78044-927-2 Library Ebook
ISBN 978-1-78044-928-9 Ebook

Citation: Bongartz, P., Vernon, N., and Fox, J. (eds) (2016) *Sustainable Sanitation for All: Experiences, challenges, and innovations*, Rugby, UK: Practical Action Publishing, <http://dx.doi.org/10.3362/9781780449272>

Since 1974, Practical Action Publishing has published and disseminated books and information in support of international development work throughout the world. Practical Action Publishing is a trading name of Practical Action Publishing Ltd (Company Reg. No. 1159018), the wholly owned publishing company of Practical Action. Practical Action Publishing trades only in support of its parent charity objectives and any profits are covenanted back to Practical Action (Charity Reg. No. 247257, Group VAT Registration No. 880 9924 76).

This document has been financed by the Swedish International Development Cooperation Agency, Sida. Sida does not necessarily share the views expressed in this material. Responsibility for its contents rests entirely with the author.

Cover design by Mercer Design
Indexed by Elizabeth Ball
Printed in the United Kingdom
Reprinted in 2019

Contents

Figures, tables, and boxes

Figures

Tables

Boxes

About the editors

Petra Bongartz is the CLTS Knowledge Hub's Strategy, Communications and Networking Officer and has been working on CLTS for almost 10 years. Together with Robert Chambers she created the CLTS Knowledge Hub at IDS in 2009. Petra leads on the Hub's communication activities including the CLTS website, (co)facilitates workshops and develops and implements the Hub's strategy with the other Hub members. She is the co-editor of *Tales of Shit: CLTS in Africa*.

John Fox is a development communication consultant, journalist, and Managing Director, iDC, Nairobi. He was the lead author of the facilitator's resource pack, *Managing CLTS*, for Plan International Kenya in 2013.

Naomi Vernon is the Programme Officer for the CLTS Knowledge Hub at the Institute of Development Studies, where she has worked for nine years. She is also the lead editor and designer of the CLTS Knowledge Hub publication series *Frontiers of CLTS: Innovations and Insights*, and co-authored the issue 'CLTS and Sustainability: Taking Stock'.

Acronyms and abbreviations

BCC	Behaviour change communication
CATS	Community Approaches to Total Sanitation
CBO	Community-based organization
CHEW	Community Health Extension Workers
CHW/V	Community Health Workers/Volunteer
CLTS	Community-Led Total Sanitation
CHSA	Community Health Strategy Approach, Kenya
DFID	Department for International Development
DPHE	Department of Public Health Engineering
EcoSan	Ecological sanitation
FGD	Focus group discussions
FSM	Faecal sludge management
GIS	Geographic information system
GSF	Global Sanitation Fund
ICC	Inter-Agency Coordinating Committee
ICDDR,B	International Centre for Diarrhoeal Disease Research, Bangladesh
INGO	International non-governmental organization
JMP	Joint Monitoring Programme
KWAHO	Kenya Water for Health Organization
LGA	Local government authority
LSHTM	London School of Hygiene and Tropical Medicine
MDG	Millennium Development Goal
MHM	Menstrual hygiene management
MIS	Management information system
MoH	Ministry of Health
NGO	Non-governmental organization
OD	Open defecation
ODF	Open defecation free
PHAST	Participatory Hygiene and Sanitation Transformation
PhATS	Philippines Approach to Total Sanitation
PHO	Public Health Officer
PHT	Public Health Technicians
PIMS	Post-Implementation Monitoring Surveys
PM	Project manager
PO	Project Officers
PSU	Policy Support Unit
RALU	Rapid Action Learning Unit

SACOSAN	South Asian Conference on Sanitation
SDG	Sustainable Development Goal
SLTS	School-Led Total Sanitation
SNA	Social Network Analysis
SNT	Social Norms Theory
SSH4A	Sustainable Sanitation and Hygiene for All
STBM	Sanitasi Total Berbasis Masyarakat (Community-based Total Sanitation)
SWA	Sanitation and Water for All
TSSM	Total Sanitation and Sanitation Marketing
UN	United Nations
UNDP	United Nations Development Programme
UNICEF	United Nations International Children's Emergency Fund
VDC	Village Development Committee
VERC	Village Education Resource Centre
VIP	Ventilated pit latrine
WASH	Water, sanitation, and hygiene
WEDC	Water, Engineering and Development Centre
WHO	World Health Organization
WSP	Water and Sanitation Program
WSSCC	Water Supply and Sanitation Collaborative Council
ZOD	Zero Open Defecation

Acknowledgements

This book is the co-creation of many people. Right from its conception, it was a collective effort, of balancing different views and ways of working, of bringing diverse people, experiences, skills, and backgrounds to the table and into a productive relationship with each other. While the large number of people involved in putting together this book has at times made the process challenging, on the whole, it has made it an interesting, enjoyable, rich, and rewarding journey. In this way, perhaps it bears resemblance to the challenges as well as the unique momentum and energy of CLTS itself. We wish to personally thank the following people for their contributions in the ways of inspiration, knowledge, skill, and encouragement which helped to create this book:

Robert Chambers and Jamie Myers of the CLTS Knowledge Hub for their valuable insights, inputs, and hands-on involvement in all stages of the book.

Sue Cavill for her tireless support and hard work on so many fronts, including working with the authors, reviewing chapters, and giving incredibly useful feedback and making links to other sources of information.

John Fox for his help and inputs at the writeshop, as well as his editorial efforts.

In addition to the time, effort, knowledge, and skill that each of the authors poured into their chapter, we would like to highlight the learning journey and collaborative process we engaged in together. We appreciate the trust, patience, and goodwill that each of the authors showed during this long process of co-creation. We would like to express our gratitude to the many peer reviewers who offered their time and expertise in reading and giving constructive feedback on the chapters. We would also like to thank Matt Bond and Paul Tyndale-Biscoe for being part of the writeshop and their inputs into the entire process.

We are grateful to Plan Kenya for taking care of logistical arrangements and welcoming us to Kenya, and to the Lukenya Getaway for providing such a wonderful tranquil and inspiring setting for the writeshop, and taking care of our well-being for the duration of our stay.

We wish to thank Jan Boyes for the crucial role she played in copyediting the chapters of this book, and the support received throughout the process from Practical Action and Clare Tawney in particular. Big thanks also go to Barney Haward for bringing alive some of the concepts and ideas in the book through the illustrations he designed for us.

We thank the Swedish International Development Cooperation Agency (Sida) and our Programme Manager Johan Sundberg for their support of the CLTS Knowledge Hub which has made this book possible.

Last but not least, we wish to acknowledge that none of the experiences, learning, insights, and innovations described in this book would be conceivable without the many people in many places and in many roles who are working with commitment and determination to improve the well-being of the billions of women, men, and children currently suffering the consequences of a lack of adequate sanitation, be they Natural Leaders, Community Health Workers, government and NGO staff, donors, or researchers. And most importantly, the communities and people whose lives and experiences are at the heart of it all and provide the reason and the basis for the work described here.

Petra Bongartz and Naomi Vernon, CLTS Knowledge Hub
March 2016

Foreword

Robert Chambers

It is an honour and privilege to be invited to write a foreword to this book. By focusing on sustainability it resonates with the Sustainable Development Goals (SDGs) and breaks new ground on the frontiers of Community-Led Total Sanitation (CLTS). As a participant-observer-activist in the growth and spread of CLTS since its early days, and now as a team member in the CLTS Knowledge Hub at the Institute of Development Studies, Sussex, I have come to recognize sustainability as an overarching concern. As CLTS has gone rapidly to scale, it has come to impinge on almost every aspect of quality. There is no avoiding the many challenges it presents for policy and practice. Facing and overcoming these demands not dogma but continuous critical appraisal and questioning, a passion for realism, and commitment to our collective struggle to do better. It is for celebration that these shine through as the spirit animating the chapters in this book.

As an innovation CLTS was and remains remarkable. So too has been the scale and speed of its spread. It was pioneered in Bangladesh in early 2000 by Kamal Kar, who has subsequently been its major driver to become an international movement. After a decade and a half, it is now present in more than 60 countries, in over 20 of which it has been adopted as national policy for sanitation in rural areas. CLTS-related statistics tend to be inflated, but in 2016 a cautious estimate is that 20 to 30 million people, and possibly more, are living in communities which have with reasonable credibility been declared open defecation free (ODF); and that because of CLTS as many people again will have benefited through gaining access to toilets or cleaner environments in communities that are not yet ODF.

In recent years, though, in workshops, conferences, and elsewhere, practitioners and researchers have increasingly raised sustainability as the most burning issue facing CLTS. Research has repeatedly found slippage post-ODF, identifying institutional, physical, and social and behavioural dimensions, and raising acute challenges for policy and practice. At the same time, more and more evidence has accumulated of what can be done to enhance sustainability and minimize slippage in a whole variety of contexts.

In the earlier phases of CLTS, we had to hold firmly to the core revolutionary principles. Any compromise or qualification would have weakened resolution and undermined advocacy. Hardware subsidies to individual households had to be resisted at all costs. To persuade governments and NGOs to abolish these and rely on self-help for construction was an uphill task. At the same time, maintaining quality as CLTS went to scale exponentially demanded a strong focus on trainers, facilitators, and triggering and post-triggering activities. It was only as we entered a later phase with widespread feedback from post-ODF experience that sustainability surfaced as a pervasive challenge. Research showed disappointing, at times alarming, lapses back into open defecation. Handwashing with soap or ash was quite limited. Many issues were raised. The universality of some earlier principles came into question. Different contexts, conditions, and experiences indicated a need for more nuanced and varied understandings. Accumulating evidence showed both need and opportunity for consolidating and refining what had been learned. Earlier books on CLTS had concentrated on its potential and the processes leading to ODF. This is the first to focus on sustainability and its implications for policy and practice.

Concerns with sustainability have implications for almost all activities in the CLTS sequence, from pre-triggering onwards. This stands out again and again from the empirical evidence and analysis in the 18 contributions. These show just how much has been learned. Overall, we have learned to be more open-minded, context-specific, and nuanced in approach. We have learned that without losing its core essence, CLTS must be adapted and evolved to fit national and local conditions. We have learned the importance of an enabling environment. We have learned that formative research and more attention to pre-triggering can enhance eventual sustainability. We have learned that post-ODF engagement is vital and must be planned for from the start. We have learned about the need for a market with appropriate sanitary services and materials: this is important for sustainable toilets and for movement up the sanitation ladder. We have learned that in areas with dispersed settlements and/or poorly developed markets, external action may be needed to encourage or substitute for the private sector. We have learned that in closely knit communities there is potential for others to help those least able to build latrines for themselves. However, this ideal cannot be relied on generally and it is precisely the poorer and less able people who have the least sustainable latrines, are least able to maintain them, and bear the highest burden of disease and so are most likely to infect others when they revert to OD. Other forms of support for them may often be a priority. We have learned that for sustainability, as long as superstructure provides privacy, cover, and space, substructure matters more; and since it becomes invisible with use, it is vital that people in communities know what is needed and are able to supervise masons. We have learned that usage by all members of a household at all times cannot be taken for granted, and that partial usage is often hidden and can increase as pits fill: rural faecal sludge management can become a major problem. And the overarching lesson is that in campaigns, issues of sustainability need to be considered right from the outset.

These were not priorities in the early years of CLTS. As the evidence, experience, and analysis presented here show, all are now.

Some may fear that some of the nuances and qualifications implied will undermine the basic principles and key practices of CLTS, or weaken the case that can be put to governments for a no hardware subsidy approach. This should not be so. The poor progress in countries which persist with blanket hardware subsidies and standard designs – Burkina Faso and India for instance – compared with their neighbours who have abandoned such policies – speaks for itself. Far from diminishing its impact, innovations and adaptations should strengthen CLTS.

The range of practical experience and evidence presented here has taken me by surprise. There have been more significant innovations, and more is known, and known in a more context-sensitive, detailed, and nuanced way, than I had supposed. I cannot tell whether others will make similar discoveries. That said, it is evident throughout that there is a crying need for more innovation and for rapid action learning about field realities, and what works and what does not. Five areas that stand out from these pages are:

- How, without fuelling corruption or undermining self-help and CLTS, to provide effective targeted support to those least able to help themselves, so that no one is left behind.
- How to assure sustained changes in social norms and collective behaviour.
- When, how, and in what conditions to phase in sanitation marketing.
- How to achieve sustainability in difficult terrains, whether flood-prone, with high water tables, rocky, or other.
- How to adapt and apply CLTS in large communities which are diverse and/or conflicted.

For collecting, collating, and analysing so much well-evidenced experience the editors and authors deserve congratulations: they have done the sanitation sector a signal service. Over coming decades, the lessons documented and presented here should benefit many millions of marginalized and vulnerable people. But this depends on readers. My hope and plea is that many will engage with this book and be energized and inspired to take action: that all concerned policy-makers, practitioners, researchers, academics, activists, and others will read, digest, and take action on what is written here; and that they will not stop at that but find out more and share the lessons they learn. Let us strive for good and lasting outcomes, especially for those who are least able, marginalized and weak, and most likely to be left out and left behind. The efforts that have gone into this book will then bear the good fruit they deserve.

Robert Chambers
March 2016

CHAPTER 1
Going beyond open defecation free

Naomi Vernon and Petra Bongartz

Abstract

Sustainability is currently one of the key challenges in Community-Led Total Sanitation (CLTS) and wider water, sanitation, and hygiene (WASH) practice, subsuming issues such as behaviour change, equity and inclusion, physical sustainability and sanitation marketing, monitoring and verification, engagement of governments, NGOs and donors, particularly after open defecation free (ODF) status is reached. Achievement of ODF status is now recognized as only the first stage in a long process of change and sanitation improvement, with new challenges emerging every step of the way, such as how to stimulate progress up the sanitation ladder, how to ensure the poorest and marginalized are reached, or how to maintain and embed behaviour change. This chapter outlines the rationale and central themes of the book, highlighting key issues raised, the dimensions of sustainability that are addressed, and proposes ways forward if we are to achieve the ambitious aim of the Sustainable Development Goals (SDGs) of universal access to improved sanitation by 2030.

Keywords: SDGs, Sustainability, WASH, Sanitation ladder, Equity and inclusion, Financing, Behaviour change, Governments/leadership, Slippage

Introduction

Sustainability is one of the key words of our times, whether it is in terms of lifestyles, methods of production, energy, agriculture, or infrastructure. We need to look closely and critically at the ways in which we live, work, eat, and interact with our environment if we wish for life on the planet to be sustained for future generations. Sanitation is no exception. Initially, the challenge was to get sanitation onto the development agenda and make it a political and funding priority for governments, and a programming priority for NGOs and funders. Despite some real achievements and progress in some countries towards the Millennium Development Goal of reducing by half the proportion of people without access to adequate sanitation, there are still an alarmingly large number of people without access to the types of sanitation and hygiene facilities that they need to manage their basic bodily processes safely, with ease and dignity. In many countries, communities have made progress in achieving better sanitation in terms of becoming open defecation free (ODF) communities and/or upgrading facilities. However, recent experience and

http://dx.doi.org/10.3362/9781780449272.001

research has shown that current approaches and policies aimed at improving access and changing behaviour, have – and still do – fall short of doing so sustainably (Tyndale-Biscoe et al., 2013; UNICEF, 2014; Pasteur, 2014).

And yet, as recognized more and more by policy-makers, practitioners, and funders alike, the need to achieve sustainable sanitation for all is an urgent one: 2.4 billion people still use unimproved sanitation facilities, of whom 1 billion practise open defecation (OD). Nine out of 10 people defecating in the open live in rural areas (WHO/UNICEF, 2015). More research evidence has brought to light the many wide-ranging negative effects of a lack of, or inadequacy of, sanitation facilities. There is a growing understanding that sanitation impacts on many interrelated human rights (Musembi and Musyoki, 2016). The realization that 'shit stunts', that OD, faecally transmitted infections (FTIs), poverty, and undernutrition reinforce each other, is gradually being acknowledged (Humphrey, 2009; Chambers and von Medeazza, 2014; Quattri and Smets, 2014; Spears, 2014). Research is also showing that poor sanitation is related to psychological stress (Sahoo et al., 2015; Steinmann et al., 2015), and can increase women's vulnerabilities to water, sanitation, and hygiene (WASH)-related violence (House and Cavill, 2015). A lack of suitable facilities for menstrual hygiene management can result in girls regularly missing days at school (Roose et al., 2015). The growing recognition of the central role of sanitation for all aspects of human development has been mirrored in a UN General Assembly resolution which, in December 2015,[1] defined water and sanitation as two separate rights for the first time, as well as in the Sustainable Development Goals (SDGs), which include the ambitious aim of universal access to improved sanitation by 2030, with targets that include the elimination of OD (UN, 2015).

Many countries are making sanitation a political priority,[2] and some have set ambitious targets for creating ODF nations, some with detailed roadmaps of how to get there.[3] While the recognition of the huge potential of sanitation for improving health, wellbeing, and child development provide important fuel for the drive to sustainable sanitation for all, achieving this goal is going to need significant and rapid change within the sector, particularly in relation to reaching the poorest, where progress has been by far the slowest. The 2015 Joint Monitoring Programme (JMP) report predicts, 'At current rates of reduction, open defecation will not be eliminated among the poorest in rural areas by 2030' (WHO/UNICEF, 2015: 24). So the question now is, how do we harness the political momentum, commitments, money, promising innovations, and new technologies that have appeared in the sanitation landscape? We also need to ask, what will it take to turn them into effective long-term solutions?

The CLTS approach

Arguably one of the most promising approaches in sanitation in the last decade has been Community-Led Total Sanitation (CLTS), an innovative methodology for mobilizing communities to completely eliminate OD. It was pioneered in 2000 in Bangladesh by Kamal Kar together with VERC (Village Education Resource

Centre), a partner of WaterAid Bangladesh, while evaluating a traditionally subsidized sanitation programme. Communities are facilitated to conduct their own appraisal and analysis of OD and take their own action to become ODF. Merely providing toilets does not guarantee their use, nor does it result in improved sanitation and hygiene. CLTS focuses on the behavioural change needed to ensure real and sustainable improvements. One of the achievements of CLTS has been to change thinking about sanitation from a focus on individual households to whole communities becoming ODF, and from a focus on supplying hardware or technology to looking at how to create collective behaviour change. However, CLTS is not a silver bullet and much depends on the quality of training, facilitation, follow-up, and support, as well as on the social, political, cultural, and geographical context of its implementation.

CLTS has followed a similar trajectory to that of PRA (Participatory Rural Appraisal) from which it sprang:

> In the 1990s, PRA behaviours, approaches and methods, spread with astonishing speed, and were innovated, adopted, adapted and renamed. There was a great deal of bad practice as PRA was adopted by donors and governments and taken precipitately to scale. All of this has happened too with CLTS. There has been a lot of bad practice, often in good faith. CLTS triggering and follow-up require rather special aptitudes, behaviours and attitudes. Many second and third generation challenges have arisen. Maturity has been indicated by different emphases and by renaming. (CLTS Knowledge Hub, 2013)

Over the last 15 years the approach has evolved significantly, with various spin-offs emerging.[4] Alongside efforts to refine overall quality, this new landscape of CLTS at scale, in many cases led by national governments, brings with it new challenges. Foremost among them, and encompassing many of them, is sustainability. Research and programme experience highlighted throughout this book shows that we need to be open to further adaptation and flexibility if we are to achieve long-term sustainability. CLTS is increasingly being combined with other approaches such as sanitation marketing (Coombes, 2016, this book; Munkhondia et al., 2016, this book), and there is a growing awareness of the need for technical support and financing mechanisms to encourage progression up the sanitation ladder, particularly for the poorest.

The sustainability challenge

Acknowledging that CLTS operates within a complex and unequal world and is not a one-size-fits-all solution which will solve all global sanitation and wider societal problems, it nevertheless provides a good starting point. Programme experience has shown that there are a number of things which need to be in place for ODF status to be maintained, and for people to progress up the sanitation ladder. These are explored in this book. Recent studies on sustainability have pointed to the fact that progression up the sanitation ladder has been slow or non-existent, or that slippage from ODF status was common (Hanchett et al., 2011; WSP, 2011; Mukherjee et al., 2012; Tyndale-Biscoe et al., 2013; UNICEF, 2014). Many reasons for reversion have been identified, such as collapsing or disrepair of toilets caused, for example, by flooding, inability to afford ongoing costs of upgrading, repairs, or maintenance. Behaviour change not being sufficiently embedded can also lead to reversion (UNICEF, 2014). Future challenges such as climate change and increased conflict and displacement will only add to the uncertainty and challenge of sustainability.

Background to the book

This book emerged out of a desire to investigate in more depth the questions of a) how sustainable current CLTS practices and their outcomes are; and b) what makes CLTS and WASH sustainable. Over the last few years, the focus has gradually changed, from the target of reaching ODF status, to a realization that, in fact, this is just the first step on a long process of change and sanitation improvement. Achievement of ODF status is only the beginning; maintaining it is the real challenge: new households will form, others will break up; natural disasters will occur; pits will fill up; materials and structures will deteriorate; populations will migrate; leaders will move on; budgets will fluctuate.

Thus, the CLTS Knowledge Hub at the Institute of Development Studies is interested in exploring the emerging second and third generation problems, and in finding out if the initial progress and rush to change make sustainable ODF communities or not. Our first exploration of this topic led us to review the latest research on the subject and resulted in 'Sustainability and CLTS: Taking Stock' (Cavill et al., 2015), a synthesis of lessons from research and practice and a first attempt at defining the challenges and gaps. To take this one step further, we sent out a call for abstracts on the key themes identified in the synthesis, and convened a week-long writeshop with selected participants from a broad range of countries, institutions, and actors within the WASH sector, in Kenya in April 2015. During the week, the authors shared the intended focus of their chapters, discussed sustainability issues, exchanged experiences, fed into each other's chapters and received support in developing their writing.

The book maps out the landscape of sanitation sustainability as we currently know it from research, and on-the-ground experience, and it then takes a look at the different dimensions of sustainability that need to be considered. Drawing on a wide range of country and organizational experiences and the latest research, it asks what we know about what works, what are the major obstacles, as well as the most promising innovations and practical solutions, on the road to sustainable sanitation. It identifies common themes and success factors, as well as gaps in knowledge, and it suggests a future research agenda that will help to ensure that all these efforts really reach everyone and for good.

But as a starting point it is useful to consider and define what we mean by sustainability and to delineate the aspects we consider in this book.

What is sustainable/sustainability?

What do we mean by sustainability? In relation to CLTS, sustainability refers to whole communities and their achievement and maintenance of ODF status. Definitions for assessing ODF communities vary, but often include the following (Cavill et al., 2015):

- Eradication of open defecation in the community.
- Household toilets which are hygienic, provide the safe containment of faeces, offer privacy, with a lid on the defecation hole and a roof to protect.
- Use of sanitation by all household members and all in the community.
- A handwashing facility nearby with water, soap or ash, and evidence of regular use.

Some countries include additional elements, or a second stage (sometimes defined as ODF +), which may include (Cavill et al., 2015):

- Handwashing.
- Safe drinking water storage and handling.
- Food hygiene (elevated dish drying racks, covering of food).
- Grey water disposal.
- Solid waste management.
- Provision of institutional latrines in schools, markets and for passers-by.

Communities are verified as ODF, and are then certified, sometimes through a third party verification system (Sara, 2016, this book). Re-verification of ODF status is sometimes carried out to confirm if ODF status has been maintained. Statistics on sustainability, and indeed on ODF status, can be misleading, for example if the original verification was not rigorous enough (i.e. the community was not ODF to begin with), unprofessional, or if there are rewards for becoming, or verifying ODF status (CLTS Knowledge Hub, 2011; 2012). Re-verification is based on the assumption that a community was ODF in the first place, which may not always be the case (Tyndale-Biscoe et al., 2013; Cavill et al., 2015). In other situations, criteria for re-verification could differ from the original criteria for achieving ODF status. Whether, or how, a community can ever be truly certified as 100 per cent ODF, 100 per cent of the time, is also a critical question. What and how to measure is also crucial, counting toilets does not necessarily prove their actual use. With the inclusion of the elimination of OD in the SDG target (UN, 2015), country goals and targets may be able to be defined more in behavioural terms (Mukherjee, 2016, this book).

The three dimensions of sustainability

Three dimensions of sustainability have been identified (Cavill et al., 2015):

Enabling conditions: referring to institutions and processes, and including political priority and campaigns; programme quality, inclusiveness and intensity; and post-ODF follow-up.

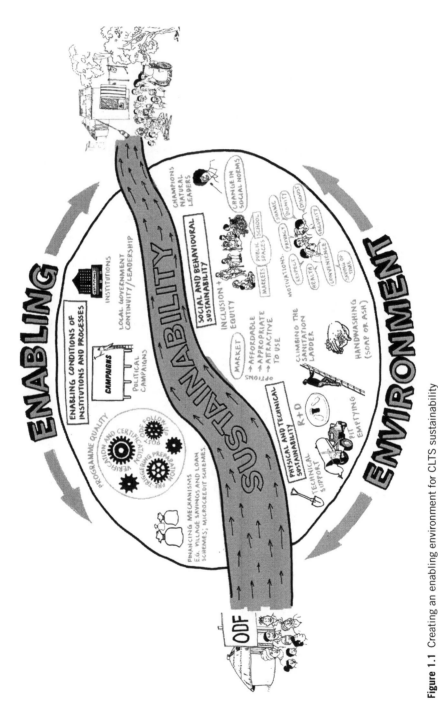

Figure 1.1 Creating an enabling environment for CLTS sustainability

Source: CLTS Knowledge Hub. Illustration by Barney Haward

Physical and technical sustainability: referring to physical conditions, structures, the sanitation ladder, the market, sanitation services.

Social and behavioural sustainability: referring to sustainable change in social and behavioural norms, motivations and preferences for OD, and dynamics within communities and cultures, including equity and inclusion, and meeting the varied needs of people.

Figure 1.1 elaborates on this in more depth.

Using these three dimensions, we identified priority areas for learning, which the book is broadly structured around: physical sustainability; post-ODF sustainability and monitoring; equity and inclusion; and social norms. The following section outlines the key issues identified by the chapters in the book according to these areas. However, the themes are of course all interconnected and support and reinforce each other.

Enabling conditions

Government engagement and public investment

Government leadership, commitment, and efficient public investment, have been shown as central to achieving sustained sanitation for all, and are subjects of many of the chapters in this book (e.g. Musyoki, 2016; Mukherjee, 2016; Thomas, 2016; Hanchett, 2016; Robinson and Gnilo, 2016, Chapter 9). Sector institutions and government systems are the only channels through which whole-country populations can be reached (Mukherjee, 2016, this book) and long-term follow-up can be provided. However, a lack of planning and investment for scaling-up is a challenge to sustainability, with ambitious targets potentially leading to compromises in quality, inclusion, and sustainability (Thomas, 2016, this book). For the SDG target to be met, better advocacy is needed from the development community to make the case to governments that investing in sanitation is cost-effective, with high returns due to the impact on health, education, dignity, security, and gender issues (Evans et al., 2004; Bartram, 2008; Trémolet and Mansour, 2013; Musyoki, 2016, this book). More and more evidence is emerging of the economic losses due to poor sanitation (Hutton et al., 2009; WSP, 2012; WHO, 2014; UN, 2014), and the terrible health impacts, such as malnutrition and stunting of children (Humphrey, 2009; Chambers and von Medeazza, 2014; Quattri and Smets, 2014; Spears, 2014). These are powerful advocacy messages. There are many initiatives to help stimulate increased government commitment, for example policy initiatives such as Sanitation and Water for All and the eThekwini Declaration, which call for greater public investment and high level political commitment. Regional sanitation conferences such as AfricaSan and SACOSAN and the resulting declarations also leverage political leadership on sanitation. National sanitation campaigns, which involve many stakeholders and sectors, for example in Bangladesh and Nepal, have proved successful (see Hanchett, 2016, this book; Regmi, 2016, this book).[5] However, more is needed to leverage long-term investment.

Due to its zero household subsidy approach, CLTS is often seen as a 'cheap option' and a way of governments shirking the responsibility of investing in sanitation; however, there are many costs, both short and long term, that are involved. But where and how to invest is critical. There are many cases of misguided investment in sanitation. For example, in India, despite decades of investment in construction of toilets, corruption, lack of demand, and an increase in population resulted in the number of rural households without toilets increasing by over 8 million between 2001 and 2011 (Hueso and Bell, 2013; Gupta et al., 2016, this book). Public investment in sanitation, and development of technology are only of use when they are locally appropriate, and 'based on what people want and are willing to use and maintain' (Evans et al., 2004: 3). Funding can help provide incentives to stimulate entrepreneurs to develop technologies which will meet the varied needs of households and individuals (Jenkins, 2004). Investing in training and capacity building, and developing coherent national strategies and plans which adopt goals defined in behavioural terms have proved successful in Laos PDR, Indonesia, and Vietnam (Mukherjee, 2016, this book). Establishing national strategies and integrating multiple stakeholders will help to ensure consistency in planning, funding, implementing, and monitoring of rural sanitation programmes across the country, and provide the structural framework for building institutional capacity and strong institutional environments (Hanchett, 2016, this book; Mukherjee, 2016, this book; Musyoki, 2016, this book; Regmi, 2016, this book). As a number of chapters outline, it is important that the mandate to carry out sanitation strategies is given to a specific department, such as the Ministry of Health, and sufficient budgets are allocated to carry out the strategy (see Hanchett, 2016, this book; Mukherjee, 2016, this book; Musyoki, 2016, this book). Ensuring that communities are engaged and are driving the process when CLTS goes to scale and becomes government policy is another challenge (Bongartz, 2014).

Establishing a national monitoring system to track progress and outcomes is a key element needed for sustainability (Mukherjee, 2016, this book). Many countries are starting to use web-based monitoring to do this (CLTS Knowledge Hub, 2013; Osbert et al., 2015). Monitoring, verification and certification of ODF status and beyond, are central in CLTS programming. Sara (2016, this book) outlines the certification process in Kenya, which uses a third party system, where certification is done by an external agency. Challenges in terms of cost and lack of capacity has led to the process being recently revised, with responsibility being devolved to the county level, and Master Certifiers being recruited to certify claims at the local level.

There are different challenges and opportunities for devolved governments such as Kenya (see Coombes, 2016, this book; Musyoki, 2016, this book; Sara, 2016, this book; Wamera, 2016, this book). County governments are closer to the community and are able to respond to and reflect local realities, but there is the potential for disparity and inequity across the country to creep in, particularly in terms of budget allocation for sanitation; again, evidence, data and advocacy are needed to leverage budgets. There is also still a reliance on non-governmental actors for funding and implementation (Crocker et al., 2015).

Programme quality and post-ODF follow-up

CLTS was initially seen as a low-cost, bottom-up approach, with many programmes ending at the certification of ODF status and with the belief that, once mobilized and empowered, communities would sustain their behaviours and take care of monitoring and follow-up themselves. However, it has become clear that ODF should not be seen as the destination, but a stage on the road to sustainable sanitation. Reversion and slippage are happening in many countries and there is little evidence of households climbing the sanitation ladder in CLTS communities. Recent experience has highlighted the importance of integrating post-ODF follow-up into programming from the outset (WSP, 2011; UNICEF, 2014; Cavill et al., 2015).

A number of chapters in this book outline innovations being trialled around the world to address the challenges of reversion, slippage and post-ODF follow-up. Robinson and Gnilo (2016a, this book) discuss the potential of the phased approach being trialled in the Philippines to lead to sustained progression up the sanitation ladder, breaking the process down into smaller, achievable stages, which rewards improved sanitation behaviour. Drawing on SNV's experience in Nepal, Regmi (2016, this book) illustrates the vital role that post-ODF activities play in successfully sustaining ODF status. The Nepali Government, together with other stakeholders, has developed a two-stage sanitation improvement approach to support communities and districts beyond the achievement of ODF to reach 'total sanitized village' status. To complement this, SNV has formulated a multi-strand post-ODF strategy, devised early detection processes to identify poorly maintained toilets or reversion to OD, and proposes a process to re-verify ODF status (SNV Nepal, 2012).

Continuity and commitment are essential to sustaining ODF status, and it is vital that, in keeping with CLTS principles, the community is engaged in post-ODF follow-up. To enable this, Musyoki (2016, this book) argues that funding levels allocated to national level activities as opposed to the community need revising: more funding needs to be made available to communities to carry out activities such as post-ODF and long-term monitoring and follow-up. Wamera (2016, this book) argues that existing social and administrative structures and groups within communities and government need to be identified in advance of implementation, and integrated into the process, in order for them to continue follow-up and embedding of the new social norm (see also Dooley et al., 2016, this book).

Physical and technical sustainability

Quality of toilets and reversion

Quality and durability of toilets are critical to long-term sustainability. Within CLTS, thinking is evolving from getting communities on the sanitation ladder, to a realization that poor quality toilets which collapse, or don't last long, can demotivate people from rebuilding and lead to reversion to OD; therefore, investment in better technology from the outset may be preferable. This will necessitate more technical input and assistance than initially recommended in CLTS. Research such as the Plan International study in four countries in Africa showed that people had constructed simple pit latrines, but that these often began to deteriorate, or collapse (Tyndale-Biscoe et al., 2013). Costs to rebuild may be too high (Thomas, 2014), or loss of trust may lead to reversion to OD (O'Connell, 2014; Beyene, 2016, this book). When toilets are dirty, they are quickly disused (Tyndale-Biscoe et al., 2013). In Bangladesh, pits are filling quickly (particularly the low-cost union-subsidized toilets for the poor), and there is leakage and breakage of low-cost, low-quality toilets, leading to the need for frequent rebuilding or reversion to OD if people cannot afford to repair them. The poorest people are often using unhygienic toilets, with no proper superstructure, and many are unable to own or maintain toilets without support from an external agency. Flooding causes pit latrines to overflow. Leaching of pit latrine contents in high water table areas is another problem (Hanchett, 2016, this book). These problems are echoed around the world (Beyene, 2016, this book; Coombes, 2016, this book; Munkhondia et al., 2016, this book; Thomas, 2016, this book). Context-appropriate technical designs are necessary, including guidance on issues such as pit depth, to ensure their safety (Coombes, 2016, this book; Munkhondia et al., 2016, this book).[6]

Improved and unimproved toilets and hygiene

Defining the criteria for a toilet that will provide health benefits is important, yet there is no set definition which all countries follow. Some countries use the benchmark of the JMP definition of whether a toilet is 'improved' or 'unimproved'. 'An improved sanitation facility is one that hygienically separates human excreta from human contact'.[7] Types of toilet which fall into this category include flush toilets, piped sewer systems, septic tanks, flush/pour flush to pit latrines, ventilated improved pit latrines (VIP), pit latrines with a slab and a lid, composting toilets. 'Unimproved' facilities include flush/pour flush to elsewhere, pit latrine without slabs or lids, buckets, hanging toilets or hanging latrines, shared sanitation, no facilities, or bush or field (OD). Moving from OD to an unimproved toilet has limited health gains (Quattri and Smets, 2014; WSP, 2014a and b). However, pit latrines can provide health benefits, as long as there is safe containment of faeces (e.g. with a slab and a lid), and the slab can be easily cleaned and maintained (Harvey and Mukosha, 2009; Reed, 2014; WHO, n.d.). Being able to wash the slab was cited in formative research in Kenya as something that respondents most wanted when asked to describe their ideal toilet (Coombes, 2016, this book). Design and construction are key to achieving an improved toilet, for example where there is poor design, pit latrines quickly start to deteriorate, collapse or need maintaining, as is discussed in the next section. Having adequate handwashing facilities is another element included in many countries' definitions for achieving ODF status, and is central to attaining health benefits. Without handwashing and other hygiene practices, communities can never become fully ODF, as CLTS aims to cut all faecal-oral contamination routes (Maulit, 2014).

While usually useful, definitions can be restrictive. For example, shared toilets are necessary in many contexts, particularly in urban environments (Hanchett, 2016, this book), for reasons of space, money, or convenience. However, they fall into the 'unimproved' category in the JMP classification, and thus would not count when verifying a community as ODF in some countries. There are potential problems surrounding the use of shared or communal toilets, such as: who is responsible for cleaning them and how often? (see Beyene, 2016, this book) Is there a charge to use them? Are they safe and hygienic? Can people with disabilities access them? Are there social barriers which mean some people can't use them? However, they should not be unilaterally rejected as unimproved. We need to find ways of making them work for those who need them.

Having definitions for what constitutes a 'quality' toilet is important; however, any definition has to be contextually defined. For example, in Kenya, formative research has shown that there is a lack of understanding of what constitutes an improved toilet, and why it's important (Coombes, 2016, this book). In addition, no guidance was given on the minimum standards required to provide health benefits, or advice on attributes to make it an 'improved' toilet, for example, having a slab that can easily be cleaned.

Movement up the sanitation ladder

Progression up the sanitation ladder is a central point of weakness in relation to sustainability of ODF status, as a number of the chapters in this book show (e.g. Munkhondia et al., 2016; Coombes, 2016; Hanchett, 2016; Robinson and Gnilo, 2016, Chapter 9). The earlier assumption that people will over time move up the sanitation ladder is proving inaccurate, particularly among poor and marginalized households (Ipsos Synovate, 2013; Thomas, 2014). A number of approaches for stimulating movement up the ladder are being explored, and there are a range of views as to what will help encourage community progression beyond the ODF outcome. Post-ODF follow-up, support and encouragement have been shown to help maintain ODF and support progression (Hanchett et al., 2011; Tyndale-Biscoe et al., 2013; UNICEF, 2014). Affordability has been identified as a key barrier to owning and maintaining a toilet and progressing up the sanitation ladder, particularly among the poorest (Jenkins and Scott, 2007; Whaley and Webster, 2011; Sara and Graham, 2014); without development of products which are affordable for everyone including the poorest, success will be limited. Development of suitable financing mechanisms, as discussed by Robinson and Gnilo (2016a and 2016b, this book) is also critical. Many people are willing to pay for a toilet, and there are a number of initiatives such as microfinance, credit schemes, and formal or informal loans being established. However, financing for the poorest must be a central part of any sanitation financing strategy. We also need to know more about the success of financing schemes, and if loans are in demand and being granted. Additionally, it is important to consult via formative research or user surveys, what households consider important and aspirational in terms of toilets (Devine and Kullmann, 2011; Coombes, 2016, this book).

There are many recent innovations which aim to stimulate progression up the sanitation ladder. Starting above the bottom rung may be one solution (Munkhondia et al., 2016, this book; Tyndale-Biscoe et al., 2013; Cavill et al., 2015). Evidence is emerging to show that in some cases toilets are being constructed which have a lifespan of only a few months, as they are built in unsuitable conditions such as sandy soils or high water tables (Phiri, 2010; Hanchett et al., 2011). Some programmes have found that, if people have the financial and technical options available, they would prefer to build a toilet in one effort, as opposed to upgrading regularly (Munkhondia et al., 2016, this book). There is also some evidence of the homogeneity of toilet designs following CLTS triggering, mainly based on existing local toilet types, which are not necessarily durable or meeting the needs of the household (Pedi and Sara, 2013; Coombes, 2016, this book). Sanitation marketing is increasingly being combined with CLTS to address this issue, providing households who can afford it with the ability to make an informed choice on the type of toilet they have. Coombes (2016, this book) discusses how the development of latrine guidelines in Kenya has been used as a starting point for integration of sanitation marketing and CLTS, and to provide a diverse range of options for households which will more closely align to their individual needs and help them to move up the sanitation ladder. Munkhondia et al. (2016, this book) highlight the importance of the development of supply chains (see also Thomas, 2014), skill-building for masons and entrepreneurs to provide low-cost, durable products, and use of local materials and knowledge in increasing access to sanitation and bringing down costs.

However, there are risks with this approach, as discussed by Munkhondia et al. (2016, this book), the right phasing of CLTS and sanitation marketing is critical to avoid undermining the behaviour change process, and this will likely differ according to context. The poorest or hardest-to-reach households may not be served unless there is some form of additional support, or very low cost option available to them (as is being trialled through participatory design) (Cole, 2013; 2015). Presenting informed choice materials to communities early on in the CLTS process can potentially lead to prescriptive options or a feeling that one particular brand or company is being promoted, which could undermine other potential local options and initiatives, or make people feel their own, more simple, but still 'improved' toilets are inadequate. Context-appropriate technical design is important (Sugden, 2003; WaterAid, nd), and needs will vary within a community (see Cavill et al., 2016, this book; Patkar, 2016, this book). When to introduce this type of material needs to be carefully considered; during triggering may be too early in the process. Harmonization of different activities, approaches, and organizations is also important (Munkhondia et al., 2016, this book).

A phased approach is another initiative being trialled to stimulate gradual progression beyond ODF status in the community, for example in the Philippines, (Robinson and Gnilo, 2016a, this book), and in Nepal (Regmi, 2016, this book). Higher levels of sanitation achievement are required at later phases. The central idea in this approach is that incentives are only given after each stage has been thoroughly verified; for example, after achieving ODF status. In the Philippines, financial mechanisms such as rebates and vouchers are also being set up to provide the poorest the means to progress up the sanitation ladder (again, after verified achievement of ODF status). This phased approach will likely take more effort and resources over a longer period of time, but may be more likely to embed behaviour change and take us beyond ODF achievement, and shows a potential solution for reaching the poorest people who are currently unserved.

Faecal sludge and pit management

Faecal sludge and pit management is essential to sustainability (Myers, 2016, this book), along with maintenance and cleaning. As people progress up the sanitation ladder, sub and superstructures will become more permanent (and less mobile), complex, and expensive. Emptying a filled pit is difficult for many people, and could result in reversion to OD. Fear of pits becoming full and the spiritually 'polluting' nature of faeces can also dissuade people from using them, or only using them occasionally (Myers, 2016, this book; Gupta et al., 2016, this book). In relation to the disposal or end use of sludge, a number of cases of 'postponed open defecation' have been discovered, when untreated faecal sludge is dumped into the environment (Myers, 2016, this book; Hanchett, 2016, this book). Safe containment of faeces in the pit (Myers, 2016, this book; Beyene, 2016, this book) and no groundwater contamination are critical to maintaining the health benefits of toilets. Sanitation marketing approaches will need to plan so that households either have access to affordable services or are able to deal with the sludge safely without assistance.

The role of pit emptiers, who are often stigmatized (Gupta et al. 2016, this book; Patkar, 2016, this book; Hanchett, 2016, this book; Myers, 2016, this book), must be addressed – they are often treated as outcasts of society, and exposed to dangerous working conditions. Changing this within a caste-based society such as India is beyond the scope of any one sanitation approach, programme, or project due to the deeply embedded complex socio-cultural dimensions of this stigmatization. It is vital that the sector and those working in it acknowledge and work towards mitigating the discrimination and exclusion of those who carry out this vital work.

Social and behavioural sustainability

Equity and inclusion: inequity of access

Alarmingly, the slowest rates of progress are among the poorest quintiles of society (WHO/UNICEF, 2015). The poorest and most marginalized often also have a high use of unhygienic, unimproved latrines (see Mukherjee, 2016, this book; Hanchett, 2016, this book), and reversion to OD has also been found to be higher (Robinson and Gnilo, 2016b, this book). Recent research in Uganda and Zambia indicates that a person who is older, disabled, or chronically ill is more likely to defecate in the open (Wilbur and Danquah, 2015; Cavill et al., 2016, this book). CLTS and WASH programmes are often not reaching these groups. Thomas (2016, this book) argues that this is likely to be an issue of planning, political prioritization, and inclusion, as opposed to purely an issue of financial resources. Understanding the barriers to access, and the underlying social dynamics and inequalities that operate in society is critical to developing inclusive programming (Cavill et al., 2016, this book; Gupta et al., 2016, this book; Patkar, 2016, this book; Regmi, 2016, this book; Bardosh, 2015). Without this, CLTS and other sanitation programmes could in fact reinforce these existing inequalities (Bardosh, 2015). People's realities, needs, and demands need to be listened to, and translated into policy and practice, with adequate budgets to achieve them (Patkar, 2016, this book). Many people have particular needs for their access to sanitation,[8] which can vary within a household, and change over the course of their lives (Cavill et al., 2016, this book; Patkar, 2016, this book). How these varied needs can be met needs to be considered and integrated into programming and policy at every level of the process. Meaningful engagement with, and participation of, different groups of people in all stages of the process is critical.

There is a growing body of research which investigates in more detail the barriers people with disabilities face in sanitation (Jones, 2015a and b; Wilbur et al., 2013). Efforts are being made to find practical ways in which CLTS can address these barriers and make each stage more inclusive, accessible, and sustainable (Cavill et al., 2016, this book). Patkar (2016, this book) describes projects that have consulted users whose needs are normally not considered, and delineates how the information is then used to influence policy agenda and decisions in order to design appropriate services.

When it comes to equity and inclusiveness of efforts, gender is of course a central consideration when addressing access. While constituting more than half of the world's population, women and girls are disproportionately affected by a lack of access to WASH (WHO/UNICEF, 2010; Cavill et al; Patkar, 2016, this book). Gender-related power dynamics and discrimination determine access. As Cavill et al. (2016, this book) describe, women also have increased WASH burdens; they are usually responsible for cleaning and maintenance of toilets, and have additional needs, for example relating to menstrual hygiene, pregnancy, and motherhood that have to be met. There is also evidence that ODF status is more likely to be sustained and embedded if women are central or lead the process (Adeyeye, 2011; Mahbub, 2011; Tyndale-Biscoe et al., 2013).

Financing for the poorest and marginalized

In recent years it has become clear that for too long, sanitation efforts were focused mainly on the 'low-hanging fruit', i.e. reaching those who were easy and quick to reach. The data illustrating the inequity of access (WHO/UNICEF, 2015) leads us to ask how to reach and improve the sanitation situation and lives of the poorest, most marginalized and disadvantaged. The issue of subsidy has long been controversial within CLTS (Kar, 2003; Kar and Bongartz, 2006; WSP, 2011; Chambers, 2015), but it is becoming increasingly evident that the poorest and most marginalized people will not necessarily be able to access sustained improved sanitation and climb the sanitation ladder without some form of external assistance. Robinson and Gnilo (2016b, this book) outline evidence for the need to integrate financing strategies for the poorest into programming, and draw on experience from the social protection sector, and recent innovations in the Philippines. They argue that effective sanitation finance is a key element for sustained progression up the sanitation ladder, and that it should be carefully designed, targeted, and delivered to reach the most vulnerable and marginalized people and communities, as well as encouraging continuous upgrading and improvement of sanitation services across the entire community.

How to identify the moment to introduce financial incentives to avoid undermining behaviour change, fraudulent reporting, and short-term incentives, are key concerns when designing a sanitation finance framework. We need to work out how to balance this assistance with embedding ODF behaviour change and the principle of home owner responsibility (Hanchett, 2016, this book). Robinson and Gnilo argue that integrating a financial framework with a phased approach (2016a and b, this book) will encourage regular and reliable monitoring of outcomes by both communities and local governments. How to identify the correct people for assistance is a vital question. In the past, finance has often been captured by non-poor households (Robinson, 2012). A number of countries have systems of identification. For example, in Bangladesh, large NGOs such as BRAC and Plan International have long-standing systems in place to provide for the poorest, with clear identification systems. We need to learn more from them to scale this up across countries. Robinson and Gnilo (2016b, this book) suggest that national poverty identification systems are used where available, and where they are not, objective targeting systems need to be established, with clear and verifiable criteria that can be checked, to ensure subsidies are not captured by non-poor households. Regmi (2016, this book), outlines the identification process in Nepal, where village WASH committees identify people within their community who need assistance, based on set criteria. In Cambodia, support was targeted to ID-poor 1 and 2 (using the Cambodian poverty targeting system) plus an additional group of so-called near poor (based on asset-ranking and additional questions) (Riviera et al., forthcoming).

Behaviour change and usage

Embedding behaviour change and new social norms is critical for sustainability. Partial usage, suggesting a lack of this embedding, is also emerging as a problem (Ashebir et al., 2013; Coffey et al., 2014a and b; Yimam et al 2015; Chambers and Myers, 2016), where not all members within a household use the toilet. Gupta et al. (2016, this book) discuss the role of caste and untouchability in India in limiting the success of sanitation campaigns, and how there is a need to understand and challenge embedded notions of purity and pollution. Communities with strong caste hierarchy, conflict and divisions have been found to have more OD than more homogeneous ones (Coffey et al., 2014a and b). As discussed by Cavill et al. (2016, this book), existing social inequalities and unequal power structures will hamper sanitation programmes – these need to promote a contrary social norm, where OD is no longer considered acceptable. In Bangladesh, the national sanitation campaign, which ran from 2003 to 2006, has been critical in its success, combining top-down government and bottom-up community mobilization strategies, and changing the mind-set of the population, so now in most parts of the country OD is not a socially acceptable practice (Hanchett, 2016, this book). Chambers and Myers (2016) argue that in order to stimulate a change in social norms, intense and provocative campaigns will be needed.

There are many reasons for preferences for OD, such as: social norms; taboos, beliefs and prohibitions; preferences and convenience; age and disability; gender and gender relations; pressure on use; full pits and fear of pits filling up; dirt, smell, disgust, fears and cleansing; or poor design, construction and subsequent lack of ownership (Chambers and Myers, 2016). Gupta et al. (2016, this book) describe how in India, research has uncovered an anxiety over the filling up of pit latrines, and an aversion to small pit latrines. Lack of knowledge about how long it will take for a pit latrine to fill up is widespread, even people who carry out health promotion in villages were found to have limited awareness. Cases of corruption, where pits are not dug properly or deeply enough also strengthen this perception. Pit emptying is frowned upon, as faeces are considered ritually polluting.

Dooley et al. (2016, this book) argue that we need a deeper understanding of existing norms and preferences for OD in order to change them. The UNICEF CATS evaluation (2014) highlighted a lack of understanding of the role expectations play in creating and embedding a new social norm. Social norms theory is now being integrated into UNICEF CATS programming, bringing in new elements, such as social network analysis at the pre-triggering stage to map out relationships between individuals and between groups and identify key influencers in all parts of society (i.e. include the poorest and marginalized) and gauge what structures already exist that could carry out post-ODF follow-up, and activities that embed behaviour change.

Natural Leaders

The importance of Natural Leaders and champions in CLTS sustainability and in encouraging and embedding behaviour change has been emphasized since the early days of CLTS. Many of the chapters in this book underline that it is vital to ask who they are and how they are identified. They are key at many stages of the process, from encouraging the community to become ODF after triggering, to long after ODF status has been achieved. Leaving Natural Leaders to emerge may sometimes result in people in existing positions of power taking the lead. While they can potentially be passionate and engaged, it shouldn't be assumed they are always the most appropriate people (Bardosh, 2015). They can also become gatekeepers and this can result in exclusion of more marginalized people within the society, who may not feel confident enough to step up, or may not be taken seriously if they do.

Understanding the motivations of and incentives for Natural Leaders, community health workers (CHWs), or Master Certifiers can help to make efforts more sustainable (Sara, 2016, this book; Wamera, 2016, this book). There is evidence to show that these groups and individuals can feel overburdened, or have conflicting responsibilities which mean they are unable or unwilling to carry on. Master Certifiers in Kenya are currently being recruited to certify ODF status of communities, yet they are not paid, and their travel and expenses are only sometimes covered (Sara, 2016, this book). CHWs in Kenya are changing from being unpaid volunteers to paid workers. However, there will be fewer of them, and it is not clear if all counties have the budget to pay for them. Ensuring suitable incentives (financial and non-financial, such as praise, recognition, or training) are in place to encourage and motivate people, and reward them for their essential work, has been shown to be central to success (Glenton et al., 2013; Kok et al., 2014).

Conclusion

We have come a long way in our thinking about CLTS, sanitation, and sustainability. Subjects that were rarely discussed even five years ago are now high up on people's agenda, such as: financing for the poorest; reality-checks on progress up the sanitation ladder; filling up of pits and management of faecal sludge; and reversion to OD. The sector needs to continue to look honestly at what is causing reversion to OD in some communities and how it can be stopped. Much more needs to be known about how ideas about social norms and sustainable behaviour change can be turned from theory into practice. The issue of subsidies, for years a taboo word within CLTS circles, is having to be revisited and re-conceived as we realize that the poorest and most vulnerable people are not being reached by current sanitation programming. And once the idea of targeted financial support is raised, further questions emerge. How to identify people in need of assistance, and how to ensure that assistance is not being captured by, or leading to, non-investment into sanitation by non-poor households. Sanitation marketing as an area of interest and expertise has grown, making available more information about consumer needs, aspirations, and appropriate affordable technologies. Nevertheless, the sector needs to know more about the optimal moment for introducing and combining it with CLTS activities, in order not to undermine behaviour change. However, more and more, we are beginning to see less of a separating out of these two approaches and more of a recognition that they speak to different aspects of sustainable sanitation and can in many instances work hand in hand. We still need to learn more about how to engage the private sector and encourage them to produce products which are affordable for the poorest; this may need initial government investment for research and development costs.

While we know that government leadership is crucial to sustainability, we have much to learn about how to carry out effective advocacy with policy-makers that further prioritizes sanitation, increases funding, builds capacity and creates long-term sanitation programmes that include sufficient follow-up, plans for monitoring and ongoing support for communities and the poorest to improve their sanitation situation. Activities aiming for sustainable sanitation need to be integrated with and supported by existing systems. Devolution, corruption, changing governments, and conflicting financial and staff commitments add further challenges into the mix. It is clear that governments cannot do this alone and so collaboration with and between different actors in and beyond the sector is essential. While a lot of focus has been on behaviour and mind-set changes in communities, there is an equal need to look at the mind-sets and behaviours in institutions and how these need to be challenged and changed to allow for sanitation to involve community participation and go beyond short-term fixes.

Similarly, it is clear that we need a better understanding of communities and their existing traditions, cultures, divisions, and structures at the pre-triggering stage. Equity and inclusion have always been a central part of the CLTS approach, but over the last few years, it has become obvious that we are still learning how to integrate it practically into every level of policy and programming, in order to ensure the poorest and marginalized are meaningfully consulted and considered. This is no doubt also true for the WASH sector at large. Understanding the motivations and incentives for Natural Leaders and groups such as CHWs and others carrying out CLTS activities on a long-term basis is also critical for sustainability.

There are still significant gaps in our learning, and more research on how to achieve and sustain sanitation for all is needed. At the end of the book, we highlight the key issues raised, and identify some priorities for research. The book is not exhaustive, and there are some significant gaps; for example, monitoring is not addressed in any depth. Consistent methods for implementation and monitoring across countries will be essential for scaling up and sustainability, and there are a number of web-based monitoring systems being developed to address this. What we monitor is also important, finding ways to monitor usage as opposed to counting toilets, or even counting ODF communities may be a way forward. Last but not least, monitoring that includes communities' own participation in what is being monitored and evaluation of the findings, is key to sustainable improvements. Slippage is another key issue; we need to know much more about what to do in communities where CLTS has failed, or when slippage from ODF status has been high. For example, should there be a re-triggering process? Who should take the lead in following up in these communities?

In addition to the unknowns, questions, and problems relating directly to sanitation itself, there are the challenges relating to the uncertain world we live in and the immense changes that are taking place on both national and global scales. Climate change is already directly impacting many countries. Environmental disasters, such as storms, earthquakes, droughts, floods, and the related problems of food and water shortages, destruction of homes, livelihoods, and displacement of huge numbers of people, are on the increase. While some aspects of the impact that climate change will have on humans and the planet can be forecast, calculated, and anticipated, there are many dimensions that we do not yet fully understand, and many ways in which, even if rapid and radical action were to be taken right now, the climate crisis' trajectory will not be stopped in time to prevent a major destructive impact. And of course this will have a knock-on effect on sanitation as on many other aspects of human life. Wars and conflicts, whether climate-related or not, are fuelling a rapidly growing refugee crisis of gigantic proportions, leading to millions of people being displaced and living in unsanitary conditions. In addition to these crises directly impacting human lives, livelihoods, and the circumstances in which sanitation and hygiene issues will play out, they will also affect funding streams, with funding being diverted away from longer-term sanitation efforts to immediate emergencies. All of this will likely affect the sustainability of sanitation projects and programmes.

Everything we have learnt throughout the process of creating this book points to the central importance of documenting, sharing experiences across countries, regions and organizations, learning from mistakes and innovations, and integrating this knowledge into policy and practice. Having platforms to share experiences honestly, and without fear is so important. Flexibility and openness will be required from institutions and donors to allow for ongoing learning and adjustments of course. Finding ways of addressing the many challenges in order to ensure sustainable sanitation for all is an urgent priority if we are to achieve the ambitious goal of sanitation for all by 2030. For as existing and continually emerging evidence suggests, good sanitation and hygiene is central to human wellbeing, mental and physical development, and thriving communities and nations.

About the authors

Naomi Vernon is the Programme Officer for the CLTS Knowledge Hub at the Institute of Development Studies, where she has worked for nine years. She is also the lead editor and designer of the CLTS Knowledge Hub publication series *Frontiers of CLTS: Innovations and Insights*, and co-authored the issue 'CLTS and Sustainability: Taking Stock'.

Petra Bongartz is the CLTS Knowledge Hub's Strategy, Communications and Networking Officer and has been working on CLTS for almost 10 years. Together with Robert Chambers she created the CLTS Knowledge Hub at IDS in 2009. Petra leads on the Hub's communication activities including the CLTS website, (co)facilitates workshops, and develops and implements the Hub's strategy with the other Hub members. She is the co-editor of *Tales of Shit: CLTS in Africa*.

Endnotes

1. See   http://www.exteriores.gob.es/Portal/en/SalaDePrensa/NotasdePrensa/ Paginas/2015_NOTAS_P/20151218_NOTA327.aspx [accessed 25 February 2016].
2. For example, Bangladesh (Hanchett, 2016, this book), Nepal (Regmi, 2016, this book); Kenya (Coombes; Musyoki; Sara; Wamera, 2016, this book); Indonesia, Laos PDR and Vietnam (Mukherjee, 2016, this book); India (Gupta et al., 2016, this book); and the Philippines (Robinson and Gnilo, 2016a, this book).
3. For example, Nepal has set a target of 2017; India: 2019; Madagascar: 2019; Kenya: 2020; Vietnam: 2025.
4. For example: CATS (Community Approaches to Total Sanitation) in UNI-CEF which is largely based on CLTS, School-Led Total Sanitation (several versions), Pakistan Approach to Total Sanitation (PATS), CLTSH (Community-led Total Sanitation and Hygiene, in Ethiopia), Women-Led Total Sanitation, Leader-Led Total Sanitation, and so on, and many names in national languages.
5. For a checklist of practical actions on campaigns, see Chambers, 2013.
6. Smaller pits tend to be more stable, and become self-supporting as they fill up over time; yet there are reports of pits as deep as 30 or 50 feet (Cavill et al., 2015). Digging a deep pit also costs a lot of money, leaving less available for the slab and superstructure. The slab is where people are most likely to come into contact with faeces, so it is more important than the depth of the pit in terms of hygiene and health benefits (Coombes, 2016, this book).
7. http://www.wssinfo.org/definitions-methods/watsan-categories/ [accessed 25 February 2016].

8. For example, people with disabilities, older people, the chronically sick, people with low income, and children.

References

Adeyeye, A. (2011) 'Gender and community-led total sanitation: a case study of Ekiti State, Nigeria', *Tropical Resources*, Bulletin of the Yale Tropical Resources Institute, 30: 18–27.

Ashebir, Y., Sharma, H.R., Alemu, A. and Kebede, G. (2013) 'Latrine use among rural households in Northern Ethiopia: a case study in Hawzien District, Tigray', *International Journal of Environmental Studies*, 70.4: 629–36 <http://dx.doi.org/10.1080/00207233.2013.835533>.

Bardosh, K. (2015) 'Achieving "total sanitation" in rural African geographies: poverty, participation and pit latrines in Eastern Zambia', *Geoforum*, 66: 53–63 <http://dx.doi.org/10.1016/j.geoforum.2015.09.004>.

Bartram, J. (2008) 'Sanitation is an investment with high economic returns', *UN Water Factsheet* 2, http://esa.un.org/iys/docs/IYS%20Advocacy%20 kit%20ENGLISH/Fact%20sheet%202.pdf [accessed 24 February 2016].

Beyene, H. (2016) 'Sanitation infrastructure sustainability challenges case study: Ethiopia', in P. Bongartz, N. Vernon and J. Fox (eds.) *Sustainable Sanitation for All: Experiences, Challenges, and Innovations*, Practical Action Publishing, Rugby.

Bongartz, P. (2014) 'CLTS in Africa: Trajectories, challenges and moving to scale', in P. Cross and Y. Coombes (eds) *Sanitation and Hygiene in Africa: Where do We Stand?* IWA Publishing, London and New York.

Cavill, S. with Chambers, R. and Vernon, N. (2015) 'Sustainability and CLTS: Taking stock', *Frontiers of CLTS: Innovations and Insights* 4, Institute of Development Studies, Brighton.

Cavill, S., Roose, S., Stephen, C. and Wilbur, J. (2016) 'Putting the hardest to reach at the heart of the SDGs', in P. Bongartz, N. Vernon and J. Fox (eds.) *Sustainable Sanitation for All: Experiences, Challenges, and Innovations*, Practical Action Publishing, Rugby.

Chambers, R. (2013) *CLTS Campaigns: A Checklist of 88 Practical Actions,* http:// www.communityledtotalsanitation.org/resource/clts-campaigns-checklist-88-practical-actions [accessed 24 February 2016].

Chambers, R. (2015) 'An open letter in response to the World Development Report 2015', CLTS website, http://www.communityledtotalsanitation.org/ blog/open-letter-response-world-development-report-2015 [accessed 24 February 2016].

Chambers, R. and von Medeazza, G. (2014) 'Reframing undernutrition: Faecally-transmitted infections and the 5 As', *IDS Working Paper* 450, Institute of Development Studies, Brighton.

Chambers, R. and Myers, J. (2016) 'Norms, knowledge and usage', *Frontiers of CLTS: Innovations and Insights* 7, Institute of Development Studies, Brighton.

CLTS Knowledge Hub (2011) *Lukenya Notes,* Brighton: IDS, http://www. communityledtotalsanitation.org/resource/lukenya-notes-taking-clts-scale-quality [accessed 24 February 2016].

CLTS Knowledge Hub (2012) *The Lilongwe Briefings*, Brighton: IDS, http://www. communityledtotalsanitation.org/resource/lilongwe-briefings-outputs-international-workshop-lilongwe [accessed 24 February 2016].

CLTS Knowledge Hub (2013) *CLTS Knowledge Hub Mission Statement*, unpublished paper, Institute of Development Studies, Brighton.

Coffey, D., Gupta, A., Hathi, P., Khurana, N., Spears, D., Srivastav, N. and Vyas, S. (2014a) 'Revealed preference for open defecation: evidence from a new survey in rural North India', *Economic & Political Weekly* 49.8: 43.

Coffey, D., Gupta, A., Hathi, P., Khurana, N., Spears, D., Srivastav, N. and Vyas, S. (2014b) 'The puzzle of widespread open defecation in rural India: evidence from new qualitative and quantitative data', Working Paper, R.I.C.E.

Cole, B. (2013) 'Participatory design development for sanitation', *Frontiers of CLTS* 1, Institute of Development Studies, Brighton.

Cole, B. (2015) 'Going beyond ODF: combining sanitation marketing with participatory approaches to sustain ODF communities in Malawi', *UNICEF Eastern and Southern Africa Sanitation and Hygiene Learning Series,* UNICEF, http://www.communityledtotalsanitation.org/sites/community ledtotalsanitation.org/files/GoingBeyondODF_CombiningSanMark_with_ ParticipatoryApproaches_Malawi.pdf [accessed 24 February 2016].

Coombes, Y. (2016) 'User centred latrine guidelines. Integrating CLTS with sanitation marketing: a case study from Kenya to promote informed choice', in P. Bongartz, N. Vernon and J. Fox (eds.) *Sustainable Sanitation for All: Experiences, Challenges, and Innovations*, Practical Action Publishing, Rugby.

Crocker, J., Bogle, J. and Rowe, E. (2015) *Community-led Total Sanitation Research Brief: Implementation Context in Kenya, Ghana, and Ethiopia*, The Water Institute, University of North Carolina, Chapel Hill.

Devine, J. and Kullmann, C. (2011) *Introductory Guide to Sanitation Marketing*, Water and Sanitation Program: Toolkit, World Bank, Washington, DC.

Dooley, T., Maule, L. and Gnilo, M. (2016) 'Using social norms theory to strengthen CATS impact and sustainability', in P. Bongartz, N. Vernon and J. Fox (eds.) *Sustainable Sanitation for All: Experiences, Challenges, and Innovations*, Practical Action Publishing, Rugby.

Evans, B., Hutton, G. and Haller, L. (2004) *Closing the Sanitation Gap - the Case for Better Public Funding of Sanitation and Hygiene*, http://www.ircwash.org/ sites/default/files/Evans-2004-Closing.pdf [accessed 24 February 2016].

Glenton, C., Colvin, C.J., Carlsen, B., Swartz, A., Lewin, S., Noyes, J. and Rashidian, A. (2013) 'Barriers and facilitators to the implementation of lay health worker programmes to improve access to maternal and child health: qualitative evidence synthesis', *The Cochrane Database of Systematic Reviews*, 10.10, CD010414 <http://dx.doi.org/10.1002/14651858.CD010414.pub2>.

Gupta, A., Coffey, D. and Spears, D. (2016) 'Purity, pollution, and untouchability: challenges affecting the adoption, use, and sustainability of sanitation programmes in rural India', in P. Bongartz, N. Vernon and J. Fox (eds.) *Sustainable Sanitation for All: Experiences, Challenges, and Innovations*, Practical Action Publishing, Rugby.

Hanchett, S. (2016) 'Sanitation in Bangladesh: revolution, evolution, and new challenges', in P. Bongartz, N. Vernon and J. Fox (eds.) *Sustainable Sanitation for All: Experiences, Challenges, and Innovations*, Practical Action Publishing, Rugby.

Hanchett, S., Krieger, L., Kahn, M.H., Kullmann, C. and Ahmed, R. (2011) *Long-Term Sustainability of Improved Sanitation in Rural Bangladesh*, Washington, DC: World Bank, http://www.wsp.org/sites/wsp.org/files/publications/ WSP-Sustainability-Sanitation-Bangladesh-Report.pdf   [accessed   25 February 2016].

Harvey, P.A. and Mukosha, L. (2009) *Community-Led Total Sanitation: Triggering Sustainable Development in Zambia*, paper presented at the 34th WEDC International Conference, Addis Ababa.

House, S. and Cavill, S. (2015) 'Making sanitation and hygiene safer: reducing vulnerabilities to violence' *Frontiers of CLTS: Innovations and Insights* 5, Institute of Development Studies, Brighton, http://www.communityledtotalsanitation. org/sites/communityledtotalsanitation.org/files/Frontiers_no5_Making_ Sanitation_and_Hygiene_Safer_0.pdf [accessed 24 February 2016].

Hueso, A. and Bell, B. (2013) 'An untold story of policy failure: the Total Sanitation Campaign in India', *Water Policy*, 15.6: 1001–17 <http://dx.doi. org/http://dx.doi.org/10.2166/wp.2013.032>.

Humphrey, J. (2009) 'Child undernutrition, tropical enteropathy, toilets and handwashing', *The Lancet* 374.9694: 1032–5 <http://dx.doi.org/10.1016/ S0140-6736(09)60950-8>.

Hutton, G., Rodriguez, U., Larsen, B., Leebouapao, L. and Voladet, S. (2009) *Economic Impacts of Sanitation in Lao PDR: A Five-Country Study Conducted in Cambodia, Indonesia, Lao PDR, The Philippines, and Vietnam*, Research Report, World Bank, Water and Sanitation Program – East Asia and Pacific.

Ipsos Synovate (2013) *Sanitation Formative Research – Quantitative Report*, Unpublished Report for Water and Sanitation Program, Kenya.

Jenkins, M. (2004) *Who Buys Latrines, Where and Why?* Field Note, Water and Sanitation Program: Washington DC, http://esa.un.org/iys/docs/san_lib_ docs/Who%20Buys%20Latrines.pdf [accessed 24 February 2016].

Jenkins. M. W. and Scott, B. (2007) 'Behavioral indicators of household decision-making and demand for sanitation and potential gains from social marketing in Ghana', *Social Science & Medicine* 64: 2427–2442 <http:// dx.doi.org/http://dx.doi.org/10.1016/j.socscimed.2007.03.010>.

Jones, H. (2015a) *Social Inclusion in Malawi WASH Project*, Research Report, Loughborough University, Loughborough.

Jones, H. (2015b) *CLTS+ triggering Rumphi District Malawi*, unpublished Research Report, Loughborough University, Loughborough.

Kar, K. (2003) *Subsidy or Self-Respect? Participatory Total Community Sanitation in Bangladesh*, IDS Working Paper 257, Institute of Development Studies, Brighton.

Kar, K. and Bongartz, P. (2006) *Some Recent Developments in Community-Led Total Sanitation: Latest Update to Subsidy or Self Respect,* supplement to IDS Working Paper 257, Institute of Development Studies, Brighton.

Kok, M.C., Dieleman, M., Taegtmeyer, M., Broerse, J.E., Kane, S.S., Ormel, H. and de Koning, K. A. (2014) 'Which intervention design factors influence performance of community health workers in low- and middle-income countries? A systematic review', *Health Policy and Planning*, <http://dx.doi. org/10.1093/heapol/czu126>.

Mahbub, A. (2011) 'Exploring the social dynamics of CLTS in Bangladesh: the inclusion of children, women and vulnerable people', in Mehta, L. and

Movik, S. (eds.) *Shit Matters: The Potential of Community-Led Total Sanitation*, Practical Action, Rugby.

Maulit, J.A. (2014) 'How to trigger for handwashing with soap', *Frontiers of CLTS: Innovations and Insights* 2, Institute of Development Studies, Brighton, http://www.communityledtotalsanitation.org/resources/frontiers/how-trigger-handwashing-soap [accessed 25 February 2016].

Mukherjee, N. (2016) 'Building environments to support sustainability of improved sanitation behaviours at scale: Levers of change in East Asia', in P. Bongartz, N. Vernon and J. Fox (eds.) *Sustainable Sanitation for All: Experiences, Challenges, and Innovations*, Practical Action Publishing, Rugby.

Mukherjee, N. with Robiarto, A., Effentrif, S. and Wartono, D. (2012) *Achieving and Sustaining Open Defecation Free Communities: Learning from East Java*, Washington DC: Water and Sanitation Program (WSP), www.communityledtotalsanitation.org/sites/communityledtotalsanitation.org/files/WSP_Indonesia_Action_Research_Report.pdf [accessed 25 February 2016].

Munkhondia, T., Simangolwa, W. and Zapico, A. (2016) 'CLTS and sanitation marketing: aspects to consider for a better integrated approach', in P. Bongartz, N. Vernon and J. Fox (eds.) *Sustainable Sanitation for All: Experiences, Challenges, and Innovations*, Practical Action, Rugby.

Musembi, C. and Musyoki, S. (2016) 'CLTS and the right to sanitation', *Frontiers of CLTS*, 8, Institute of Development Studies, Brighton.

Musyoki, S. (2016) 'Roles and responsibilities for post-ODF engagement: building an enabling institutional environment for CLTS sustainability', in P. Bongartz, N. Vernon and J. Fox (eds.) *Sustainable Sanitation for All: Experiences, Challenges, and Innovations*, Practical Action Publishing, Rugby.

Myers, J. (2016) 'The long-term safe management of rural shit', in P. Bongartz, N. Vernon and J. Fox (eds.) *Sustainable Sanitation for All: Experiences, Challenges, and Innovations,* Practical Action Publishing, Rugby.

O'Connell, K. (2014) *What Influences Open Defecation and Latrine Ownership in Rural Households? Findings from a Global Review*, Water and Sanitation Program Working Paper, World Bank, Washington DC, http://www.wsp.org/sites/wsp.org/files/publications/WSP-What-Influences-Open-Defecation-Global-Sanitation-Review.pdf [accessed 24 February 2016].

Osbert, N., Hoehne, A., Musonda, E., Manchikanti, S., Manangi, A. and Mboshya, P. (2015) 'Real-time monitoring of rural sanitation at scale in Zambia using mobile-to-web technologies', *UNICEF Eastern and Southern Africa Sanitation Learning Series*, http://www.communityledtotalsanitation.org/sites/communityledtotalsanitation.org/files/RealTimeMonitoringatScale_Zambia_Mobile2Web.pdf [accessed 24 February 2016].

Pasteur, K. (2014) *Improving CLTS from a Community Perspective in Indonesia*, Research Summary, CLTS Foundation, http://www.communityledtotalsanitation.org/sites/communityledtotalsanitation.org/files/CLTS_Research_Indonesia.pdf [accessed 24 February 2016].

Patkar, A. (2016) 'Leave no one behind: equality and non-discrimination in sanitation and hygiene', in P. Bongartz, N. Vernon and J. Fox (eds.) *Sustainable Sanitation for All: Experiences, Challenges, and Innovations*, Practical Action, Rugby.

Pedi, D. and Sara, L. (2013) *Sanitation Deep Dive*, unpublished report for IFC and the Water and Sanitation Program, World Bank: Washington DC.

Phiri, S. (2010) *TA MKanda CLTS Research: Summary*, Engineers without Borders, Canada, http://www.communityledtotalsanitation.org/sites/communityledtotalsanitation.org/files/Mkanda_research_revised.pdf [accessed 25 February 2016].

Quattri, M and Smets, S. (2014) *Lack of Community-Level Improved Sanitation Causes Stunting in Rural Villages of Lao PDR and Vietnam*, Paper, 37th WEDC International Conference, Hanoi.

Reed, B. (2014) *Simple Pit Latrines*, Water, Engineering and Development Centre, Loughborough University, Loughborough, http://wedc.lboro.ac.uk/resources/booklets/G025-Simple-pit-latrines-booklet.pdf [accessed 25 February 2016].

Regmi, A. (2016) 'Tools for embedding post-ODF sustainability: experiences from SNV Nepal', in P. Bongartz, N. Vernon and J. Fox (eds.) *Sustainable Sanitation for All: Experiences, Challenges, and Innovations*, Practical Action Publishing, Rugby.

Riviera, R., Joseph, G., Smets, S., Ljung, P., Nguyen, H., Um, S. and Chan, V. (forthcoming, 2016) *Understanding the Effect of Sanitation Marketing and Smart Subsidy Programs on Sanitation Uptake Among the Poor and Non-Poor in Cambodia*, Water and Sanitation Program, World Bank and East Meets West Foundation/ Thrive Networks, Washington DC.

Robinson, A. (2012) *Sanitation Finance in Rural Cambodia, Phnom Penh*, Report, Asian Development Bank and World Bank Water and Sanitation Program, Washington DC.

Robinson, A. and Gnilo, M. (2016a) 'Beyond ODF: A phased approach to rural sanitation development', in P. Bongartz, N. Vernon and J. Fox (eds.) *Sustainable Sanitation for All: Experiences, Challenges, and Innovations*, Practical Action Publishing, Rugby.

Robinson, A. and Gnilo, M. (2016b) 'Promoting choice: smart finance for rural sanitation development', in P. Bongartz, N. Vernon and J. Fox (eds.) *Sustainable Sanitation for All: Experiences, Challenges, and Innovations*, Practical Action Publishing, Rugby.

Roose, S., Rankin, T. and Cavill, S. (2015) 'Breaking the next taboo: Menstrual hygiene within CLTS', *Frontiers of CLTS: Innovations and Insights* 6, Institute of Development Studies, Brighton, http://www.communityledtotalsanitation.org/sites/communityledtotalsanitation.org/files/Frontiers_no6_MHM_0.pdf [accessed 24 February 2016].

Sahoo, K. C., Hulland, K. R. S., Carusoc, B. A., Swaina, R., Freemand, M. C., Panigrahie, P. and Dreibelbis, R. (2015) 'Sanitation-related psychosocial stress: a grounded theory study of women across the life-course in Odisha, India', *Social Science & Medicine*, 139: 80–9 <http://dx.doi.org/10.1016/j.socscimed.2015.06.031>.

Sara, L. (2016) 'Certification of open defecation-free status: emerging lessons from Kenya', in P. Bongartz, N. Vernon and J. Fox (eds.) *Sustainable Sanitation for All: Experiences, Challenges, and Innovations*, Practical Action, Rugby.

Sara, S. and Graham, J. (2014) 'Ending open defecation in rural Tanzania: which factors facilitate latrine adoption?' *International Journal of Environmental Research and Public Health*, 11: 9854–70 <http://dx.doi.org/10.3390/ijerph110909854>.

Steinmann, P., Juvekar, S., Hirve, S. and Weiss, M.G. (2015) *Coping Strategies to Deal with Inadequate WASH Facilities and Related Health Risks*, Research Briefing Note,

SHARE Research Consortium and Water Supply and Sanitation Collaborative Council (WSSCC), http://wsscc.org/wp-content/uploads/2015/09/Briefing_Note_1_2015_LoRes.pdf [accessed 24 February 2016].

SNV Nepal (2012) *Formative Research on Sanitation and Hygiene Behaviour in Kalikot, 2012/2013*, SNV Nepal, Kathmandu.

Spears, D. (2014) *The Nutritional Value of Toilets: Sanitation and International Variation in Height*, 2014 version, first circulated 2012, RICE Institute.

Sugden, S. (2003) *One Step Closer to Sustainable Sanitation: Experiences of an Ecological Sanitation Project in Malawi*, Water Aid, Lilongwe.

Thomas, A. (2014) 'Key findings of a sanitation supply chains study in Eastern and Southern Africa', *UNICEF Eastern and Southern Africa Sanitation and Hygiene Learning Series*, WASH Technical Brief, UNICEF, London, http://www.communityledtotalsanitation.org/sites/communityledtotalsanitation.org/files/Sanitation_Supply_Chains_ESAfrica.pdf [accessed 24 February 2016].

Thomas, A. (2016) 'Strengthening post ODF programming: reviewing lessons from sub-Saharan Africa', in P. Bongartz, N. Vernon and J. Fox (eds.) *Sustainable Sanitation for All: Experiences, Challenges, and Innovations*, Practical Action, Rugby.

Trémolet, S. and Mansour, G. (2013) *Evaluating the Effectiveness of Public Finance for Sanitation: A Synthesis Report*, WaterAid and SHARE, London.

Tyndale-Biscoe, P., Bond, M. and Kidd, R. (2013) *ODF Sustainability Study*, FH Designs and Plan International, http://www.communityledtotalsanitation.org/resource/odf-sustainability-study-plan [accessed 24 February 2016].

UN (2014) *Sanitation is a Good Economic Investment*, Fact Sheet 2, Sanitation for all-the drive to 2015 initiative, http://sanitationdrive2015.org/wp-content/uploads/2013/03/Planners-Guide-Fact-Sheet-2_English.pdf [accessed 24 February 2016].

UN (2015) *Sustainable Development Goals: Goal 6 Ensure Access to Water and Sanitation for All*, United Nations, Geneva, http://www.un.org/sustainabledevelopment/water-and-sanitation/ [accessed 24 February 2016].

UNICEF (2014) *Evaluation of the WASH Sector Strategy 'Community Approaches to Total Sanitation' (CATS)*, UNICEF, http://www.unicef.org/evaluation/files/Evaluation_of_the_WASH_Sector_Strategy_FINAL_VERSION_March_2014.pdf, [accessed 25 February 2016].

Wamera, E. (2016) 'Who is managing the post-ODF process in the community? A case study of Nambale sub-county in Western Kenya', in P. Bongartz, N. Vernon and J. Fox (eds.) *Sustainable Sanitation for All: Experiences, Challenges, and Innovations*, Practical Action, Rugby.

WaterAid (n.d.) *New Sanitation Technologies for Communities with Poor Soil*, WaterAid, Nigeria, http://www.sswm.info/library/54 [accessed 24 February 2016].

WHO (n.d.) *Simple Pit Latrines*, Fact Sheet 3.4, World Health Organization, Geneva, http://www.who.int/water_sanitation_health/hygiene/emergencies/fs3_4.pdf [accessed 24 February 2016].

WHO/UNICEF (2015) *Progress on Drinking Water and Sanitation: 2015 Update and MDG Assessment*, Joint Monitoring Programme (JMP), WHO/UNICEF, Geneva, www.wssinfo.org/fileadmin/user_upload/resources/JMP-Update-report-2015_English.pdf [accessed 24 February 2016].

WHO (2014) *The Health and Economic Cost of Poor Sanitation*, WHO in South-East Asia, New Delhi, http://www.searo.who.int/mediacentre/features/2014/

the-health-and-economic-cost-of-poor-sanitation/en/ [accessed 24 February 2016].

Whaley, L. and Webster, J. (2011) 'The effectiveness and sustainability of two demand-driven sanitation and hygiene approaches in Zimbabwe', *Journal of Water, Sanitation and Hygiene for Development*, 1.1: 20–36 <http://dx.doi.org/10.2166/washdev.2011.015>.

Wilbur, J., Jones, H., Gosling, L., Groce, N. and Challenger, E. (2013) *Undoing Inequity: Inclusive Water, Sanitation and Hygiene Programmes That Deliver for All in Uganda and Zambia*, Briefing Paper, 36th WEDC International Conference, Nakuru.

Wilbur, J. and Danquah, L. (2015) *Undoing Inequity: Water, Sanitation and Hygiene Programmes That Deliver for All in Uganda and Zambia – An Early Indication of Trends,* briefing paper, 38th WEDC International Conference, Loughborough University, Loughborough, http://wedc.lboro.ac.uk/resources/conference/38/Wilbur-2191.pdf [accessed 24 February 2016].

WSP (2011) *Factors Associated with Achieving and Sustaining Open Defecation Free Communities: Learning from East Java*, Water and Sanitation Program (WSP), Washington DC, http://www.communityledtotalsanitation.org/sites/communityledtotalsanitation.org/files/Factors_ODF_EastJava.pdf [accessed 24 February 2016].

WSP (2012) Africa Economics of Sanitation Initiative, Water and Sanitation Program (WSP), Washington DC, http://www.wsp.org/content/africa-economic-impacts-sanitation [accessed 24 February 2016].

WSP (2014a) Investing in the Next Generation: Children Grow Taller, and Smarter, in Rural Villages of Lao PDR where all Community Members use Improved Sanitation, WSP Research Brief, Water and Sanitation Program (WSP), Washington DC.

WSP (2014b) Investing in the Next Generation: Children Grow Taller, and Smarter, in Rural, Mountainous Villages of Vietnam where Community Members use Improved Sanitation, WSP Research Brief, Water and Sanitation Program (WSP), Washington DC.

Yimam, Y.T., Gelaye, K.A. and Chercos, D.H. (2014) 'Latrine utilization and associated factors among people living in rural areas of Denbia District, Northwest Ethiopia, 2013, a cross-sectional study', Pan African Medical Journal, 18.334 <http://dx.doi.org/10.11604/pamj.2014.18.334.4206>.

PART I: Mapping the territory

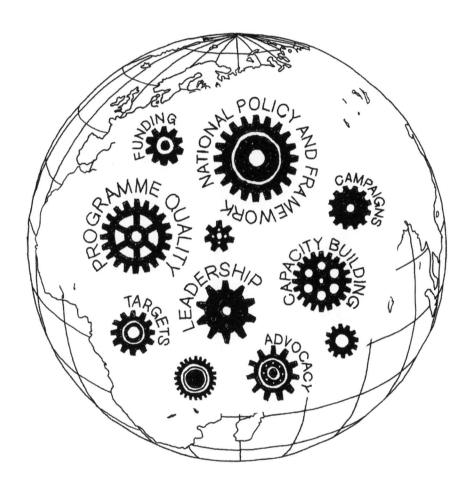

CHAPTER 2

Sanitation in Bangladesh: revolution, evolution, and new challenges

Suzanne Hanchett[1]

Abstract

Bangladesh is a hub of sanitation experimentation and model-building. It is internationally recognized as the place where CLTS first developed and succeeded in getting whole villages to declare themselves open defecation free (ODF). Such achievements rest on a broad foundation however. After briefly reviewing the history of sanitation promotion in rural Bangladesh, this chapter summarizes the most urgent issues and challenges related to sustaining the country's improvements in 2015. It concludes with some learning points of possible interest to other countries seeking to promote universal sanitation coverage.

Keywords: Bangladesh, Institutions, Collaboration, Policy, Subsidies, Shared toilets, Improved sanitation, Faecal sludge management

Context: leading up to a sanitation revolution

Intensive sanitation promotion in Bangladesh has a long and complicated history dating back to the 1960s. The Department of Public Health Engineering (DPHE) led by creating latrine production centres on the assumption that they would stimulate public interest. This approach did not succeed, however (Ahmed, 2011). A social mobilization for sanitation campaign, led by DPHE and the United Nations International Children's Emergency Fund (UNICEF) from 1988 to 1996, was the first attempt at large-scale change using participatory methods. Engagement of the NGO Forum for Drinking Water and Sanitation[2] made it also the first programme implemented jointly by government and NGOs. From the 1980s–1990s onward many approaches were tested and replicated by NGOs and others. For example, CARE's SAFE/SAFER programme continued for 10 years in south-eastern Bangladesh (1991 to 2001), producing public education materials for different social and ethnic groups and testing a no-subsidy approach. The most extensive campaigns and programmes have focused on changing household-level practices in rural areas.[3]

There was a government-led National Sanitation Campaign from 2003 to 2006. This was a remarkable campaign, one which set in motion a series of activities, some of which continue to this day. Led by a dedicated and detail-oriented government

http://dx.doi.org/10.3362/9781780449272.002

minister,[4] the campaign deployed a combination of top-down and bottom-up strategies. It gave the lowest level of government, the union *parishad* (council),[5] the responsibility for achieving 100 per cent household latrine coverage. Results were monitored by sub-district and district-level officers. Cross-visits among unions occurred. Sub-district administrators expected reports on sanitation progress at monthly meetings with the chairmen in their areas, and an unknown number still do so.

By 2006, a total of 526 unions (12 per cent of all unions) had achieved the '100 per cent' latrine coverage goal, 24 per cent with the help of NGOs and 76 per cent on their own. Most importantly, the mind-set of the population eventually changed to the point where most of the people in most parts of the country now think that open defecation (OD) is not a socially acceptable practice. Even now, local people and professionals alike speak of the National Sanitation Campaign as a 'revolutionary' experience, comparable in its importance to the nation's war of independence.

The studies

In 2009–2010 I led a study, on behalf of the World Bank, of 53 unions that reached the goal of 100 per cent household latrine coverage between 2003 and 2005. Four types of union-level organizations had managed to reach the 100 per cent goal: local government leaders only; NGOs following CLTS methods; single NGOs using non-CLTS approaches; or NGOs under contract with large donors (Danida or UNICEF). A survey covered 3,000 households of 50 unions. We did an in-depth study in 13 unions, five of which had been declared '100 per cent' after a CLTS process.[6] Unions were located in six different types of geographical areas. The study had generally positive findings. More than four and a half years after the Sanitation Campaign, 89.5 per cent of survey households were found to own or share a latrine that safely confined faeces (Hanchett et al., 2011).[7]

In February 2015 we interviewed 23 professionals in Dhaka about their views on how and why sanitation had progressed and the nature of present challenges.[8] In 2015 my team also did follow-up interviews and field visits, to see how some '100 per cent'/ODF unions were doing 10 or more years after the campaign ended. We were able to visit two of our former study unions. We spoke at length with 10 union chairmen about sanitation issues in their unions.[9]

Evolution: sustaining achievements

Our initial study and subsequent interviews demonstrate that Bangladesh's achievements in increasing household latrine use have resulted from a combination of social, political, and technical factors. These are:

- High-level policy commitment during the 2003–2006 campaign and the subsequent government's continuing willingness to communicate regularly with representatives of civil society organizations.

- Consistent support from development partners (bilateral and multilateral aid donors).
- Technical guidance from academic engineers.
- Several large-scale sanitation promotion programmes operating through-out the country for several years.
- The enthusiasm and pride of union council chairmen, and experience sharing among them.
- Ordinary people's determination to maintain village environments and enhance family status by setting up household latrines.

One other factor is women's energetic involvement in Bangladesh sanitation campaigns. There is general agreement that women are especially interested in household sanitation improvements. 'Women are more willing than men to talk in committees and so on. Those working outside the home – especially teachers and social workers – are most valuable. Women are much more interested in toilets than men are', says Milan Kanti Barua, of the BRAC water, sanitation, and hygiene (WASH) programme.

National-level dialogue supports local change activities. In Dhaka, the nation's capital, a number of committees, forums, dissemination workshops, and other occasions foster communication among a close community of experienced professionals representing both government and civil society. They have built a degree of consensus about what works, what does not, and why. There are debates and differences among them, of course, but the Dhaka network is a strong one. All organizations' sanitation approaches are constantly evolving, and there is much collaboration among them. A National Sanitation Task Force, chaired by the Secretary of the Local Government Division (part of the Ministry of Local Government, Rural Development and Cooperatives, MLGRD,C), continues to meet.

Policy documents offer frameworks, maps, and other information to guide sanitation-related activities of government administrators, union councils, and organizations implementing special projects. A Danida-funded Policy Support Unit (PSU), established within the Ministry of Local Government, Rural Development and Cooperatives, facilitates development of these documents and distributes them. Especially important are the Government's *National Sanitation Strategy*, its *Pro Poor Strategy for Water and Sanitation Sector in Bangladesh*, a *Sector Development Plan (2011–2015)*, and a *National Strategy for Water and Sanitation Hard to Reach Areas of Bangladesh 2012* (People's Republic of Bangladesh (GoB), 2005a, b, 2011, 2012).

The government has participated in an eight-country biennial South Asian Conference on Sanitation (SACOSAN) since it hosted the first one in 2003.[10] Presentations and commitments made at these conferences help to inform and motivate government officers to address sanitation issues. Bangladesh hosted the sixth SACOSAN conference in January 2016. This event has created a hopeful feeling among NGOs about the government's commitment to give sanitation improvement enhanced priority in the future.

The Bangladesh sanitation sector benefits from some national routines established during the 2003–2006 campaign. October is now celebrated as National Sanitation Month throughout the country. According to most reports, there is close cooperation between governmental and non-governmental organizations each October, when the country's larger NGOs and district or sub-district-level officials jointly organize rallies and meetings.

Other widespread changes have occurred. The school curriculum raises children's awareness of the importance of latrines. There are now thousands of trained volunteers working to discourage OD in their villages. Neighbours complain about bad smells from others' latrines, even in some remote areas. The movement has developed its own momentum.

Some union council chairmen use funds allocated through the nation's Annual Development Programme to buy latrines for their constituents. They are supposed to give poor households sets of three concrete rings and one slab for installation of simple pit latrines. But there is no precise information on how many of these sets have been distributed or who actually receives them. Although there are (or were) some required steps to identify really poor households, chairmen may or may not follow formal procedures. As elected officials, they are under pressure to meet demands of their constituents to the extent that resources allow.

Scaling-up

Expanded sanitation programming in Bangladesh has been characterized by a combination of governmental, non-governmental, and commercial activities. Although control of the government changed in 2006 from one political party to another, the new government allowed certain activities to continue, albeit with less fanfare.

Though guided in a general way by policy documents, the Bangladesh scaling-up process is not a uniform one. Rather, different agencies, organizations, or coalitions follow distinct approaches. Priorities are determined in free-ranging discussions and debates among sector professionals, and there are differences among stakeholders. At the national level, all-important dialogue between government and civil society representatives has continued. While some, but not all, sub-district administrators continue to hold chairmen accountable for sanitation improvements, recognition through '100 per cent' awards was discontinued when the National Campaign ended.[11] District administrators continue to support National Sanitation Month events, often with the help of large NGOs.

Several very large sanitation projects were critical to sustaining momentum for national change after the National Campaign ended. The largest programmes have been implemented by BRAC, WaterAid and its 23 partner organizations, the Hygiene, Sanitation and Water Supply Project (HYSAWA) Fund, DPHE-UNICEF, and Danida. These projects have covered from 9 to 53 districts each, hiring thousands of field workers and reaching estimated populations of 3 to 39 million (Hanchett, forthcoming).

The National Campaign supported and subsidized formation of private latrine production businesses, some of which continued and expanded after 2006. As demand for latrine supplies expanded, businesses began to appear in most sub-district headquarters towns and in some union centres as well. Sanitation marketing, discussed below, is one way to encourage growth of businesses and offer choices to consumers.

CLTS strategies and scale

The Community-Led Total Sanitation (CLTS) approach was first developed in Bangladesh in the rural working areas of the Village Education Resource Centre (VERC), an NGO affiliated with WaterAid, Bangladesh. This approach is based on a participatory concept of sustainable development and the assumption that effective control of faecal-oral disease transmission requires change at the total community level. No household-level subsidies are provided; rather, families figure out ways to install latrines with their own resources. Specific techniques of 'ignition' and 'triggering' proceed until whole communities 'declare' themselves to be ODF, and these are well-known by now.

CLTS is not the only approach used to promote latrine use in Bangladesh, but it is quite influential, even outside the WaterAid network that first adopted it. As news spread about its efficacy, other organizations adopted CLTS concepts and techniques, often changing them in the process. A variety of 'total sanitation' strategies have thus emerged. In 2004, a project named Dishari began to scale-up the approach to the level of a total union, putting the union chairman and council in charge of the ignition and triggering process, and funding a staff position to look after sanitation issues inside the union office.[12] From 2003 to the present, Plan has implemented two programmes placing WASH facilitators inside union offices to look after water and sanitation issues. Plan's most recent 'Government-led Total Sanitation' programme operates in 81 unions of eight different sub-districts. Plan also operates its programme at scale in some sub-districts (*upazilas*). UNICEF created a programme called School-led Total Sanitation (SLTS), which gave schools the local leadership role.[13]

Those organizations not using CLTS still embrace participatory change methods, such as formation of village groups. Such methods strive to develop a sense of ownership among populations and community responsibility for behaviour change, as does CLTS. The largest organization using such alternative methods is BRAC.

Regarding programming scale, most CLTS programmes focus on transforming rural neighbourhoods or villages to ODF status, but the premier CLTS innovator, VERC, declared a whole sub-district to be ODF in 2004 or 2005, according to VERC managers. Moving beyond the most localized rural settlements, another Bangladesh NGO, Unnayan Shahojogy Team (UST), also affiliated with WaterAid, forms ward development management committees to conduct ward-based sanitation promotion. WaterAid Bangladesh is using the same approach in climate-vulnerable areas in the coastal belt.

Data on household latrine coverage

The government carried out a baseline survey in 2003, before the National Campaign started. This survey found 33 per cent of all households using 'hygienic latrines',[14] 25 per cent using 'unhygienic' types, and 42 per cent resorting to OD (GoB, 2005a).

The current status varies depending on what definition of a satisfactory latrine is used. The Joint Monitoring Programme's (JMP) most recent national survey data indicate that approximately 85 per cent of Bangladesh households in 2015 are using latrines that would meet the JMP 'improved' standard, if the question of sharing were set aside (WHO/UNICEF, 2015). Sources counting what the government calls 'hygienic' latrines (limited to no more than two sharing households and having intact water-seals or other tight covers) find percentages around 50 to 60 per cent. This is an increase from the 33 per cent found in the government's 2003 baseline survey, but not sufficient to meet the Millennium Development Goal of 100 per cent coverage by 2015 (BBS and UNICEF, 2010; BRAC Research and Evaluation Division, 2013). The main problem with meeting the government's standard is that people break water-seals so as not to need much water for flushing. If the intact water-seal requirement were excluded, the basic latrine coverage rate would rise to around 89 per cent (GoB, 2011). Table 2.1 summarizes some information from recent surveys.

With regard to the accuracy or usefulness of available data, 7 of the 23 professionals we met in Dhaka in 2015 expressed concern about the current state of sanitation monitoring. Two representatives of the PSU, Md. Mohsin and Md. Abdur Rauf, told us, 'There is not any solid data. The JMP is based on secondary data. The last government survey was done in 2003. A new survey is needed.'

One recent national sample hygiene survey was conducted in 2014 by the International Centre for Diarrhoeal Disease Research, Bangladesh (ICDDR,B), WaterAid, and the Policy Support Unit. This survey collected information on latrines and handwashing facilities, not only in households, but also in schools, hospitals, and restaurants. Including shared toilets, 86 per cent of households were found to have satisfactory types, and 13 per cent used either hang latrines (less than 1 per cent), open pits (3 per cent), latrines flushing to open spaces (8 per cent), or no latrines (2 per cent) (ICDDR,B et al., 2014).

The data in Table 2.1 are not all comparable, but they give a general picture of current household latrine coverage. These various surveys suggest that approximately 6–15 per cent of households are continuing to defecate either in the open or in uncovered spaces.

Positive trends in child health

Bangladesh reached its Millennium Development Goal to reduce under-5 child mortality by 2015. Between 1993 and 2014 the rate declined by 65 per cent, from 133 per 1000 live births to just 46 (GoB, 2015). During this same period latrine use almost doubled (from around 30 per cent to almost 60 per cent), using the JMP's 'improved' definition. While diarrhoeal disease is not the only cause of child deaths, it always has been a substantial contributor. And increased latrine use surely has contributed to this positive result.

Table 2.1 Recent Bangladesh surveys on latrine coverage

Information source	Survey year	Survey area	Household latrines (%)	Latrine category/OD
WHO/UNICEF (2015)	2015	National sample survey	61	Improved
			28	Unimproved because shared
			11	Other unimproved (10%) and OD (total: 1%, rural: 2%, urban <1%)
ICDDR,B, WaterAid, and PSU (2014)	2014	National sample survey	86	Sanitary pit, septic tank system, or piped sewer system connection, individual or shared
			11+	Flush to open space, open pit, or hang latrine
			2	No toilet
Akter et al. (2015)	2014	Sample survey by BRAC Research and Evaluation Division		
		BRAC intervention areas (WASH-I,-II,-III)*	74.7	Sanitary latrine: hygienic (GoB definition)+shared
			19.7	Ring & slab latrine without water-seal
			5.6	Uncovered pit and OD
		Comparison areas	44.1	Sanitary latrine: hygienic (GoB)+ shared
			40.9	Ring & slab latrine without water-seal
			15.0	Uncovered pit and OD

*Final evaluation study of completed project

Child stunting, related to malnutrition, also is associated with faecally transmitted diseases, as the intestines are affected in ways that make it difficult for the body to absorb nutrients. Stunting of children declined from 65 per cent to 36 per cent during this same period,[15] but stunting remains at an unacceptably high level, according to WHO standards.

Climbing the sanitation ladder

Enclosures and basic pit latrines

When sanitation specialists describe the steps needed to make improvements, the first one mentioned is the move away from OD to some kind of 'fixed-place' arrangement. OD was common along village pathways or railroad tracks, in bamboo groves, and under trees with above-ground roots. Fifty-eight per cent of households had already made the move to some kind of 'fixed-place' defecation before the 2003 Sanitation Campaign began. A popular, 'unhygienic' arrangement was to put a plastic or other fence around a small patch of ground at the edge of a rural compound, where family members could defecate on the open earth. As a region with many waterways, Bangladesh's sanitation problems included numerous 'hanging latrines' extending over rivers and canals, especially in the southern, coastal belt region. Or elevated 'hanging latrines' were constructed out of wood, or even bricks and concrete, with faeces dropping into household ponds or onto bare earth.

The next step, now achieved by the majority of the population, is to confine faeces in some kind of pit. A simple pit with a crude cover, for example, is called *gorto paikhana*. For poor people in many of our study areas, the low-cost or free (from the union *parishad*) concrete ring and slab system is common. If it is the typical, union-subsidized three-ring system, it is only 1.5 metres deep. A latrine pit of this type fills up quickly, and there often are problems of leakage and breakage, as low-quality concrete is likely to be used. In CLTS-influenced areas, and in others, a variety of locally invented pit latrine types are still found.

Non-poor households – and some poor ones as well – are upgrading their three-ring and slab systems to five or more rings, thus increasing the depth of the pit. Offset pits are considered relatively easy to clean, and twin-pit systems allow filled-up pits to decompose while a family uses the second pit (see Ahmed and Rahman, 2010). Vent pipes are common in these upgraded types.[16] Relatively affluent families in rural areas may have septic systems and attached bathrooms.

Flooding during the monsoon season can cause pit latrine contents to overflow. One solution to this problem is to build latrines on raised platforms. Most homes are built on raised plinths to prevent water entry during normal floods. Poorer families, however, often consider building a raised latrine platform to be unaffordable.[17] Latrines in *char* and *haor* areas[18] are especially vulnerable to flood damage, so they must be built on elevated platforms.

In a 2015 visit to a relatively remote union in Barisal District, Banaripara sub-district, we found that consumers have begun to demand improved quality concrete (made with a special type of sand and more cement than usual) for the manufacture of latrine rings and slabs, so that their facilities will not easily crack or break. Latrine sellers are responding to this demand.

As their experience with latrines goes on, many families improve the housing for their facilities as well as the rings and slabs. Crude (*kacca*) walls of leaves, jute bags, or plastic sheets may be the first enclosures erected. The next step is a tin shed. The most desirable housing is a brick wall (known as a pucca structure). Roofs provide protection from storm damage, so adding a roof is an important step.[19]

Union chairmen interviewed in 2015 all commented on the need to improve standards of household latrine maintenance and cleanliness. Breakage is a general problem, and poor households cannot always afford to make repairs or replace broken rings and slabs. Others may not be sufficiently motivated to do so. In one union formerly covered by a CLTS programme, the chairman told us that the poorest people are still using simple pit latrines without concrete rings and covering the squat-holes with plastic sheets.

Sanitation marketing

The World Bank's Water and Sanitation Program (WSP), together with some partner organizations, is starting up a programme to support small-scale entrepreneurs wishing to develop and market new latrines and other products.[20] Capacity development and financial support for entrepreneurs are parts of this programme. Small-scale sanitation entrepreneurs receive three days of training on how to produce and market newly developed options, with practical demonstrations.

Latrine manufacturers and sellers need credit, in order to offer instalment payment plans to their customers. The micro-credit organization, Association for Social Advancement (ASA), provided loans to 300 entrepreneurs within the six months prior to February 2015, and ASA was working to introduce sanitation loans in 24 districts.

Sanitation marketing is most suitable to consumers with increased incomes and an interest in using their money to upgrade latrine facilities. Several of the professionals we met told us that rural poverty in Bangladesh is declining. One reason for this trend is that the garments industry is attracting large numbers of unskilled workers, so daily pay for agricultural labourers is increasing. Remittances from family members working abroad also contribute to the income of poor households. Some undetermined number use their larger incomes to upgrade their latrines. Poverty, however, has not disappeared; the issue will continue to be relevant in future years.

Technical innovations

The widespread pour-flush, water-sealed latrine requires 1 or 2 litres of water to flush properly. To save themselves the trouble of arranging a sufficient supply of water near the latrine, many owners break the water-seal.[21] A newly invented, low cost, plastic slab model (SaTo-pan, from American Standard Co.) is rapidly gaining popularity, because faeces can slip into the pit without any need to flush with much water. A weighted flap closes as soon as the faeces drop down (see Figure 2.1).The plastic pan has the added advantage of being light weight and thus easily portable. According to Sayedur Rahman, of UST, some union chairmen in river islands (*chars*) are distributing these items to their community members.

Leaching out of latrine pit contents is a common problem, especially in high water table areas. One solution to this problem is to create a sand envelope around the sides and the bottom of the pit, to filter the liquid and reduce risk of bacterial contamination of ground water. WASHplus is currently testing the efficacy of this technology in a small study with the ICDDR,B.

In 2015, in a remote union of Banaripara sub-district, we found that a buffer wall had been erected to prevent water pollution by blocking the flow of any leaked pit contents from a row of privately owned latrines set alongside

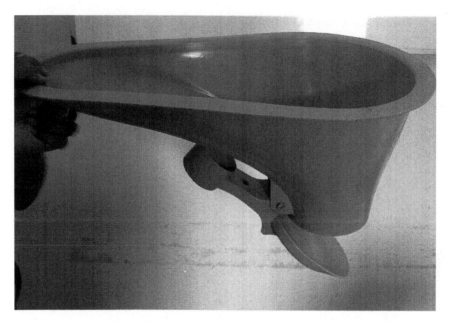

Figure 2.1 American Standard SaTo-pan sanitary toilet pan

a village canal. A local leader – formerly a DPHE-Danida sanitation committee member and now an elected union council ward representative – explained:

> I try to spread good ideas among the neighbourhoods (*para*) in my ward. For example, we still set latrines alongside the canal and the road. But these are very different from the old types of hanging latrines or crude (*kacca*) structures. These are ring-slab latrines. Sometimes it is difficult to stop leakage. I found one latrine owner had created a buffer wall, so that if there was leakage it would be stopped. I advised others to create these walls, and now everyone in my ward does it.[22]

At least two organizations are known to be working on 'eco-san' latrine designs: UNICEF and Bangladesh Rural Academy for Development (BARD, in Comilla). UNICEF is promoting 11 different models, ranging in price from Tk.5,000 to 20,000 (US$60–250). These latrines separate urine from faeces and thus accelerate the drying-up of faecal matter.

Faecal matter also dries up in the twin-pit latrine system. Disposal and use of this composted material are still subjects of experiment and debate. Several experts we met in Dhaka said that some people, but not all, are willing to use the material to fertilize food crops, especially winter vegetables. Concerns about the perceived spiritually and physically 'polluting' nature of human faeces, however, remain an obstacle to full acceptance of using human waste to fertilize food crops in South Asian countries.

Figure 2.2. A tree grove used for OD in 2010 (top) had a household latrine built in it by 2015 (bottom). Location: Banaripara sub-district, Barisal District (Photo credits: Anwar Islam)

An interesting innovation we found in Banaripara sub-district was the placement of latrines in formerly preferred OD locations. In one remote southern union, moving along canals that were formerly lined with hanging latrines, we saw that all had been replaced with ring-slab sets. In a larger, more centrally located union of the same sub-district, we re-visited three or four bamboo groves or other 'jungle' areas used in 2010 for OD and found five years later that families had built latrines in those places (see Figure 2.2).

Challenges: Bangladesh's unfinished business

Discussing the current state of Bangladesh sanitation with representatives of 14 organizations in early 2015, we found most agreeing that the problem of OD is more or less solved, but that important problems still require urgent attention. Rokeya Ahmed from the WSP said, 'CLTS was good for ODF. ODF is done now. Now something more is needed'. The people we met emphasized five current sanitation priorities in Bangladesh: quality of existing latrines; hard-to-reach areas; faecal sludge management; urban squatter settlements; and hygiene.

Quality and sustainability of existing latrines

Seven of the Dhaka professionals we met expressed concern about the poor quality of many household latrines now in use. This problem is especially relevant for poor families, who may not have the means to improve or replace rings and slabs when they break, or to clean out pits when they fill up.

Hard-to-reach areas

There are still some regions of Bangladesh where sanitation programmes have had only minimal effects to date. These include sandbar islands (*chars*), areas called *haors*, which are deeply flooded for six months of every year, parts of the Chittagong Hill Tracts, and other areas, depending on a combination of social and physical factors, plus vulnerability to extreme weather events. The PSU has formed a Hard-to-Reach Thematic Group, in order to disseminate information about these areas and encourage organizations to work in them.

Faecal sludge management

Reflecting a broad consensus among sanitation professionals, Md. Wali Ullah, Director of the Sanitation Secretariat, told us, 'Faecal sludge management is a burning issue'. Hasin Jahan, formerly of WaterAid Bangladesh, said,

> The whole sector should now plan for the second generation sanitation problem – faecal sludge management. We installed thousands of pit la-trines without asking about either faecal sludge or environmental pol-lution. Our mind-set wasn't aligned to the truths. We never appreciated how important these things were.

She continued, 'We need to search the whole stool chain, from collection to re-use'.

Cleaning out filled-up pits is a constant problem. If they have space, families may just cover a filled-up pit and shift their latrine to a different location.[23] Others bargain with pit cleaners, who are available in increasing numbers nowadays, to get their pits cleaned at a cost of Tk.100–200 (US$1–2) per ring, depending on the width of the pit. However, union chairmen we interviewed in 2015 mentioned that poor families sometimes clean out their own pits.

In rural areas pit cleaning usually is done with buckets, spades, and ropes, although there have been experiments with mechanical pumps here and there. Waste is either buried in new holes, diverted through pipes to new holes, or dumped in canals or onto fields. There are no statistical data on rural sludge disposal practices.

Professor Mujibur Rahman, of ITN-BUET, commented on urban problems, 'the picture behind the success is really challenging. I have been trying to tell the government people, if 5,000 litres of faecal sludge is being dumped openly [in municipal areas], then 5,000 people are doing open defecation'. He praised the country's achievements in rural sanitation, however, because so many people are now 'thinking of latrines'. A regulatory framework for sludge management is being developed under a government initiative led by Professor Mujibur Rahman in 2015.

Faecal Sludge Management conferences, three of which (FSM-I,-II,-III) have been funded thus far by the Bill & Melinda Gates Foundation. They are influencing opinion among Bangladesh sanitation professionals.

Urban squatter settlements

Known as *bastis*, large squatter settlements can be found in almost all Bangladesh cities and towns. Four of the professionals we met in 2015 agreed that, 'Sanitation for the urban poor is the biggest challenge because of poor drainage and maintenance issues', as Md. Masud Hassan of VERC, put it. Latrines in *bastis* are generally shared by multiple households because of space constraints, and they often are managed by hired caretakers. According to Sayedur Rahman of UST, female caretakers are needed in these situations, to ensure the safety of female users.

Several municipalities are working on sanitation in *bastis*, some with the help of large NGOs, such as DSK, Practical Action, or the NGO Forum for Public Health. Dhaka's Water and Sanitation Authority (DWASA) has formed a new Low Income Communities Department. Nonetheless, the professionals we met agree that this problem is extremely serious and that latrine sharing arrangements are essential to solving it.[24]

Hygiene

Training on handwashing with soap, domestic water management, hygienic food preparation and storage, and solid waste disposal are standard parts of all organizations' sanitation programmes, with each organization devising its own approach.[25] All are striving to improve their hygiene education techniques by introducing methods such as hands-on demonstrations and training of local volunteers.

Nowadays, increased attention is being paid to the hygiene issue of placement of latrines far from drinking water sources. And the problem of keeping household latrines clean continues to be a challenge in many places, including those with high percentages of 'improved' or 'hygienic' types.[26]

We found a newly added emphasis on menstrual hygiene in our 2015 Dhaka conversations. As most sanitation specialists now recognize, problems associated with menstrual hygiene can obstruct, or even stop, adolescent girls' educational progress, unless their schools' facilities are set up to help meet this need. Emerging from the shadows, this issue has received increasing attention in recent years. According to Milan Kanti Barua, BRAC-WASH organizes sub-district conferences for adolescent girls, in order to 'give them a chance to speak up about menstruation and menstrual hygiene'. PSU staff members mentioned recently conducting 18 district-level dissemination workshops on personal hygiene, food hygiene, and menstrual hygiene.

Subsidy issues

The Bangladesh sanitation sector has tried out a full range of approaches to subsidizing sanitation facilities, from the zero-subsidy system of CLTS and earlier programmes, through partial subsidies, on to union chairmen simply giving rings and slab sets to households. Experiments with subsidies continue to evolve, as many organizations strive to expand or improve latrine coverage, especially among poor households. 'About subsidies, it is important to ask, "Subsidy for whom?". People who own motorcycles or cell phones do not need subsidies. Give subsidies only after achieving 70–80 per cent latrine coverage. Free latrines otherwise will not be used.' This is the advice of Md. Masud Hassan, of VERC.

There is a broad consensus among the sanitation professionals and others we met in 2015 that subsidies can do harm as well as good. As many observers of CLTS programmes have noted, *not* subsidizing latrine installation forces people to think about the whole-village health and environmental advantages latrines offer. Not subsidizing latrine installation can thus motivate people to invest their own time, energy, and money in equipment which they probably will feel responsible to use and maintain.

Expecting subsidies can delay personal action. One middle-class man we met in Barisal District in 2015, for example, said he had been promised a free ring-slab set by an NGO after the devastating Sidr cyclone of 2007. He waited three or four years but never received one.

> If they had not misled me [he said], I would have bought a latrine myself. I carried the shame for a long time because my household had no latrine. This hurt me a lot. Now I have a three-ring and slab set, a whole latrine that I set up in 2014 without help from anyone. I am proud of that.

The Bangladesh experience, like that of many other countries, has shown that simply giving latrines to people will not change their defecation habits unless they are motivated (personally and group-wise) to use latrines. A well-meaning union chairman we interviewed in 2015 stopped giving away free latrines. After spending Tk.100,000 (US$1,300) to distribute many free latrines to poor villagers, he found that, 'most of the latrines we constructed remained unused. People preferred to buy their own, better quality and larger ones'.[27]

An important issue related to ODF sustainability is the situation of the very poor. There is no doubt that truly poor households cannot own, maintain, or upgrade latrines without some kind of financial support. This is a point of general agreement among almost all those we interviewed in 2015. One chairman of a union that became ODF under the government-only approach told us in 2015 that his union provides funds to poor households to cover pit cleaning expenses.

It is especially interesting that union chairmen and NGOs in five CLTS unions we recently contacted are now subsidizing latrine installations or distributing free ring-slab sets to poor households. CLTS approaches established a general sense of local pride in being ODF, but some subsidy measures are considered necessary to maintain the situation.

Poor households receive help with acquiring latrines from both governmental and non-governmental programmes. During the national campaign the government authorized use of up to 20 per cent of each sub-district's Annual Development Programme funds for this purpose. This allocation has continued, but less consistently than before 2006. BRAC's Targeting Ultra-Poor (TUP) programme fully supports sanitation for 'ultra-poor' households as part of its 'sustainable livelihoods' strategy. TUP either gives them latrines or arranges for free latrines to be provided from other sources as an essential health maintenance measure. Eligibility to 'graduate out' of the ultra-poor status is carefully computed according to multiple criteria.[28]

The programmatic challenges are, first, to identify those who truly require subsidies and, second, to arrange financial assistance in ways that encourage a sense of self-help and homeowner responsibility, as Robinson and Gnilo discuss elsewhere in this book (Robinson and Gnilo, 2016). The identification process is considered effective, but it is not 100 per cent perfect. Poor households are identified by union council chairmen and members from voting lists. If NGOs work in an area, they may assist with preparation of lists in that area. Female-headed households and persons eligible for government support (widows, elderly, or disabled) also often qualify. Lists may be checked for accuracy, especially in areas covered by the larger-scale water and sanitation programmes.

Flexible financing is helpful to poor households wanting new or upgraded latrines. Plan International has started offering financial support of a new type. 'We designed a new model of offset-pit latrine with five rings', explained

Md. Zillur Rahman in a recent conversation. 'The total cost is Tk.3,000–4,500 (US$45–52). We give hard-core poor Tk.2,300 toward the cost. They pay the rest in instalments. They can afford this. Some people are adding more rings.'

An important point to keep in mind when addressing the needs of the poorest households is their heterogeneity. Female household heads, disabled people, and marginalized ethnic or occupational groups must overcome multiple social and economic obstacles to livelihood improvement.

Some learning points

Government and community involvement

Bangladesh is a centralized state. Unions and sub-districts have very little independence, either financially or administratively. So central government policies are likely to drive future change. Thus far, responsibility within the central government rests primarily with the MLGRD,C. The DPHE, part of MLGRD,C, has been officially responsible for implementing most government-led water supply and sanitation projects outside of municipalities or city corporations. DPHE is an engineering organization, not one with strong health education or community mobilization expertise (Matrix, 1993; Pendley and Ahmad, 2009). UNICEF's WASH Section has partnered with DPHE since 1990, and UNICEF (or earlier, the NGO Forum) has tended to handle the 'software' aspect of sanitation programming. Formation of the Policy Support Unit in 2006 created an alternative knowledge hub within MLGRD,C but outside of DPHE.

The Ministries of Health and Education have the non-engineering expertise and the field-level staff to help move sanitation forward in a sustainable manner. But until now health has not been much involved in sanitation programming or promotion. Education, however, has done its part with curriculum changes and school-level programmes. Inter-ministerial efforts and communication need improvement, if the country is to face the sanitation challenges ahead.

One learning point from the generally successful Sanitation Campaign of 2003–2006 was the value of combining government directives with initiatives to support community mobilization. 'For a sanitation campaign to succeed, it has to come from the head of government. Our sanitation started from the top. We did it both ways: top-down and bottom-up'. says Md. Monirul Alam, of UNICEF. Community people need to understand the health benefits of hygienic latrine use. Processes such as CLTS definitely help to change all-important social norms. But governmental authority is needed to guide and sustain full-scale change.

The union is an appropriate administrative level for capacity-building in Bangladesh, according to many of those we interviewed. 'Union councils have statutory responsibility. Our learning point was: it works. Many thought that the union would misappropriate funds or not supervise their WASH facilitators properly. But they are working nicely in 81 unions now', says Md. Zillur Rahman, of Plan International Bangladesh. Open defecation is now down to 3 per cent.

The credit for this mainly goes to the union *parishads*, according to Md. Nurul Osman, of the HYSAWA Fund. The union council represents a larger and more diverse population than India's village *panchayat*. Being rather large, however, it has the advantage of making visible changes in environmental practice and testing various approaches in different environments.

Role of NGOs

NGOs are a prominent part of the Bangladesh sanitation scene. Some are huge and have implemented large-scale sanitation programmes. Most of the 10 union chairmen we recently interviewed expressed appreciation for the help their unions had received from NGOs in becoming ODF and solving follow-up problems, but two mentioned that NGOs may withdraw at any time. Governmental officers or departments, weak or strong, do not have that option. The learning point here is that NGOs cannot replace governmental institutions. It is only government that has the authority and full-scale responsibility – and some steady revenue stream, however limited – to protect public health by sustaining 100 per cent latrine usage. A distinctive feature of the Bangladesh sanitation sector is the existence of opportunities for regular communication between NGO leaders and government officers.

Tailored approaches

While not as geographically or culturally diverse as India, Bangladesh does have plenty of diversity. 'When installing latrines, we must consider geographical conditions, disaster risk, and water availability', according to Rozina Hoque, of BRAC-TUP. 'Tailor the approach to different geographical and cultural situations', says Rokeya Ahmed, of the World Bank Water and Sanitation Program. Experience has shown that different areas require different approaches, both technical and social. This is another argument in favour of community mobilization strategies.

Latrine sharing

It is becoming increasingly clear that some residential arrangements demand multi-household latrine sharing. Though problematic for cleaning and other reasons, latrines shared by joint family members are normal in this part of the world. Even in rural areas there can be settlements almost as congested as urban squatter settlements, where some kind of community latrine arrangement is needed. Rather than rejecting these as 'unimproved', the international community should study ways to make them work for the people who need them.

Monitoring

An important gap in the Bangladesh situation is the lack of routine monitoring of sanitation coverage or quality. As happened during the National Campaign and in CLTS programme areas, monitoring of *total communities'* facilities and practices is needed, not just individual household latrine coverage. At the individual household level, monitoring should track who actually does or does not *use* the available latrines and people's motivations for use or non-use. Latrines' maintenance (cleanliness) is as important as their physical presence. And a satisfactory survey should cover latrines in institutions, especially schools, clinics, and hospitals as well as those in homes.

The government seems too ready to accept the Joint Monitoring Programme's 2015 report of 'one per cent [total national] OD', as if this means the sanitation job is finished (UNICEF and WHO, 2015: 56). One per cent is a positive finding, but it is not helpful to focus on this news instead of arranging to monitor the country's sanitation status properly and regularly.

Ensuring continuity

The most important learning point 10 years after the Sanitation Campaign is: **sanitation improvement is a continual process**. It is never finished. New households are formed, and new houses are built. Floods and cyclones come. Concrete breaks. Rats eat bamboo pit liners. Pits fill up. Migrant labourers come in large numbers to help with the harvest. There will always be new problems to solve, new leaders to educate. The Bangladesh experience has shown that declaring thousands of villages to be ODF is just the beginning.

Conclusions

Our 2015 discussions with people at all levels of Bangladesh society reveal both pride in sanitation achievements and concern about meeting future challenges. A combination of approaches – subsidies, non-subsidies, micro-credit, sanitation market improvements, programming at various scales, motivating of individuals and groups – has resulted in a majority of households using latrines rather than defecating openly. Policy documents have created frameworks to guide activities in diverse areas. Issues such as quality, faecal sludge removal, and appropriate subsidies for very poor households remain, however. Hard-to-reach geographical areas lag behind the rest of the country. As a review by Professor Mujibur Rahman (2009) has pointed out, failing to address present challenges will threaten the sustainability of achievements.

Unique characteristics of the Bangladesh sanitation situation include the focus on its local government institution (the union), a long history of NGO-sponsored community mobilization, the willingness of government to work with NGOs, and high population density. Donor involvement has been a regular feature of the sanitation scene for more than three decades. It is a relatively small country, the size of only one of India's states. All of these special conditions and characteristics have supported its achievements to date.

The transitions and challenges occurring in 2016 are daunting, to be sure, but the country has faced larger ones in the past. Moving away from OD was the biggest challenge. This achievement was psychological, cultural, and also political. Introducing and maintaining sewer systems, however, will involve substantial expense. Upgrading household latrines in rural areas also costs money. Donors' interests will shift away from sanitation to urgent matters such as climate change, so new revenue sources will be needed.

There is by now a well-established network of professionals working on the critical issues of the day, and the general population is committed to maintaining public health through latrine use. It seems likely that the next challenges will be met, considering the Bangladesh sanitation sector's intellectual and organizational strengths.

About the author

Dr Suzanne Hanchett is an applied anthropologist with a PhD from Columbia University. She is a partner in the consulting firm, Planning Alternatives for Change, and a Research Associate with the Center for Political Ecology in Santa Cruz, California, USA. Her work has mainly focused on Bangladesh where she has carried out programme evaluations for major NGOs as well as research related to arsenic, gender, water, and sanitation.

Notes

1. Five associates contributed substantially to this report, and to the research on which it is based: Tofazzel Hossain Monju, Mohidul Hoque Khan, Anwar Islam, Shireen Akhter, and Kazi Rozana Akhter.
2. The organization's name has been changed since then to the NGO Forum for Public Health.
3. The population of Bangladesh is estimated to be approximately 70 per cent rural.
4. Abdul Mannan Bhuiyan (1943–2010), Minister of Local Government, Rural Development, and Cooperatives (MLGRD,C).
5. A union *parishad*/council (UP) represents a population of 20,000–50,000. Each union is divided into nine wards, each of which has an elected representative. Three women additionally are elected to the council, each woman representing three of the nine wards. There is a separately elected UP chairman representing the whole union. A union has numerous distinct, named, villages and neighbourhoods. In 2001 there were 4,484 unions in Bangladesh.
6. The in-depth study involved a small team of three researchers holding focus group discussions, key informant interviews, and making structured observations in multiple union locations for a period of approximately one week. Three villages were sampled randomly from each union for survey and in-depth study, one near the union council headquarters, one moderately distant, and one remote. Ten of the 50 unions covered by this study had become ODF after a CLTS process.
7. This study was conducted under contract with The Manoff Group.

8. In February 2015 we met with 23 staff members of 14 organizations, who kindly took time to share their experience and views with us. The organizations were: BRAC-WASH (Milan Kanti Barua), BRAC-TUP (Rozina Hoque, Md. Abdullahil Baquee, Sagarika Indu, and Arunava Saha); the HYSAWA Fund (Md. Nurul Osman); ITN-BUET/International Training Network Centre, Bangladesh University of Engineering and Technology (Professor Dr Mujibur Rahman); Plan International Bangladesh (Md. Zillur Rahman); Policy Support Unit/PSU (Md. Mohsin and Md. Abdur Rauf); Practical Action (Engr. Dipok Chandra Roy); Sanitation Secretariat (Engr. Md. Wali Ullah); UNICEF (Md. Monirul Alam and Syed Adnan Ibna Hakim); UST (Md. Sayedur Rahman, Shah Md. Anowar Kamal, and Dr Hamidul Haque); VERC (Md. Masud Hassan); WASHplus/FHI360 (Kathrin Tegenfeldt and Md. Faruqe Hussain); WaterAid Bangladesh (Hasin Jahan and Mujtaba Mahbub Morshed); and the World Bank Water and Sanitation Program (Rokeya Ahmed).
9. Eight interviews were done in multiple telephone conversations and two were done in personal visits.
10. The first conference was funded entirely by outside donors. The Government of Bangladesh has contributed substantial funds to SACOSANs since then.
11. There are 488 sub-districts (*upazilas,* formerly *thanas*) in Bangladesh. Each sub-district has around 10 unions. A sub-district administrator (Upazila Nirbahi Officer, or UNO) coordinates the activities of various governmental departments and hosts a monthly meeting that includes all union chairmen. Since 2010 there also are elected sub-district chairmen, vice-chairs, and councils. At the time of writing of this chapter, the respective roles and responsibilities of UNOs and sub-district chairmen are still being sorted out.
12. Dishari was a joint endeavour of Dhaka Ahsania Mission, Plan Bangladesh, WaterAid Bangladesh, and the World Bank Water and Sanitation Program.
13. Howes et al. (2011) review and compare expansion of CLTS and some related programmes in Bangladesh.
14. The government's definition of 'hygienic latrine', in contrast to the JMP definition of 'improved latrine', includes latrines shared by no more than two households (up to 10 people), and which confine faeces in pits or septic tanks, but only if their covers/slabs are closed by intact water-seals or flaps (GoB, 2005a).
15. Information from UNICEF Bangladesh WASH Section, September 2015.
16. In our 2010 survey of 50 ODF unions we found 25 per cent of household latrines to have vent pipes in good condition, and approximately half had nets on them to prevent entry by insects.
17. In our 2010 survey of household latrines of 50 unions we found 30 per cent to be elevated above the level of the homestead yard.
18. *Chars* are sandbar islands; *haors*, are low-elevation areas deeply flooded for approximately six months of every year.

19. In the 2010 survey of household latrines in 50 unions, we found 52 per cent of the enclosures to have roofs.
20. At the time of our February 2015 meeting, the piloting phase of this programme had been completed.
21. In our 2010 survey we found 45.2 per cent of all latrines with slabs to have no water-seal, a broken water-seal, or no other flap or cover sealing the hole in the slab (Hanchett et al., 2011).
22. Tofazzel Hossain Monju notes, February 2015.
23. They might or might not upgrade their latrine model when they shift. Poor people tend to replace it with the same type.
24. Christine Sijbesma's study, *Financing Models for the Urban Poor* (2011), systematically reviews the global experience in seeking economic solutions to these types of problem.
25. In our 2010 survey of household latrines in 50 ODF unions, we found 84 per cent to have handwashing stations. Water was available at 74 per cent of them, and soap was observed at 30 per cent (source: World Bank WSP database, used for Hanchett et al., 2011).
26. In our 2010 survey of household latrines in 50 unions, we found 44.3 per cent of all improved/shared latrines to be clean, meaning no faeces visible on the floor, pan, or water-seal, and the pit not leaking profusely (Hanchett et al., 2011).
27. This union had been declared ODF under the government-only approach. The chairman at the time was enthusiastic about promoting hygienic latrine use, as is his successor.
28. No self-reported food deficit for one year, multiple sources of income, homes with solid roofs, ownership of livestock or poultry, kitchen gardens, cash savings, no child marriage, school-age children going to school, couples using family planning, and use of a sanitary latrine and clean drinking water (BRAC, n.d. and 2013).

References

Ahmed, M.F. and Rahman, Md. M. (2010) *Water Supply and Sanitation; Rural and Low Income Urban Communities*, ITN-Bangladesh, Centre for Water Supply and Waste Management, BUET, Dhaka.

Ahmed, S.A. (2011) 'Community-led total sanitation in Bangladesh: chronicles of a people's movement', in L. Mehta and S. Movik (eds.) *Shit Matters; The Potential of Community-led Total Sanitation,* pp. 25–37, Practical Action Publishing, Rugby.

Akter, T., Jhohura, F.T., Chowdhury, T.R., Akter, F., Mistry, S.K. and Rahman, M. (2015) *The Status of Household WASH Behaviors in Rural Bangladesh* (draft), BRAC, Research and Evaluation Division, Dhaka.

Bangladesh Bureau of Statistics/BBS and UNICEF (2010) *Progotir Pathey. Monitoring the Situation of Children and Women; Multiple Indicator Cluster Survey 2009. Volume 1: Technical Report*, Government of Bangladesh, Dhaka.

BRAC, Research and Evaluation Division (RED) (2013) *Achievements of BRAC Water, Sanitation and Hygiene Programme Towards Millennium Development Goals and Beyond*, BRAC, Research Monograph Series No. 60, BRAC, Dhaka.

BRAC (2013) 'An end in sight for ultra-poverty: scaling up BRAC's graduation model for the poorest', *BRAC Briefing Note No. 1: Ending Extreme Poverty*, BRAC, Dhaka.

BRAC (n.d.) *Breaking the Cycle of Poverty; Can We Eradicate Extreme Poverty for the Next Generation?* (Brochure), BRAC, Dhaka.

People's Republic of Bangladesh (GoB) (2005a) *National Sanitation Strategy*, Ministry of Local Government, Rural Development and Cooperatives, Dhaka.

GoB (2005b) *Pro Poor Strategy for Water and Sanitation Sector in Bangladesh*, Ministry of Local Government, Rural Development and Cooperatives, Local Government Division, Unit for Policy Implementation (UPI), Dhaka.

GoB (2011) *Sector Development Plan (FY 2011–25) Water Supply and Sanitation Sector in Bangladesh*, Ministry of Local Government, Rural Development and Cooperatives, Dhaka.

GoB (2012) *National Strategy for Water and Sanitation Hard to Reach Areas Bangladesh 2012*, Ministry of Local Government, Rural Development and Cooperatives, Local Government Division, Policy Support Unit, Dhaka.

GoB (2015) *Millennium Development Goals; Bangladesh Progress Report 2015*,General Economics Division, Bangladesh Planning Commission, Dhaka.

Hanchett, S. (forthcoming) *Sanitation in Bangladesh: Past Learning and Future Opportunities*, Report submitted to UNICEF, WASH Section, UNICEF, Dhaka.

Hanchett, S., Krieger, L., Kullman, C. and Ahmed, R. (2011) *Long-Term Sustainability of Improved Sanitation in Rural Bangladesh*, World Bank, Water and Sanitation Program, Washington, DC.

Howes, M., Huda, E. and Naser, A. (2011) 'NGOs and the implementation of CLTS in Bangladesh: selected case studies', in L. Mehta and S. Movik (eds.) *Shit Matters; The Potential of Community-led Total Sanitation*, pp. 53–69, Practical Action Publishing, Rugby.

ICDDR,B, WaterAid Bangladesh, and Policy Support Unit of MLGRD,C (2014) *Bangladesh National Hygiene Baseline Survey; Preliminary Report*, Dhaka.

Matrix Consultants and Associated Consulting Engineers (BD) Ltd (1993) *Report on an Organizational Study of the Department of Public Health Engineering July–October 1993*, DPHE and UNICEF, Dhaka.

Pendley, C.J. and Ahmad, A.J. (2009) *Learning from Experience; Lessons from Implementing Water Supply, Sanitation and Hygiene Promotion Activities in the Coastal Belt of Bangladesh*, Royal Danish Embassy, Dhaka.

Rahman, Md. M. (2009) *Sanitation Sector and Gap Analysis: Bangladesh*, Water Supply and Sanitation Collaborative Council, Global Sanitation Fund, Geneva.

Robinson, A. and Gnilo, M. (2016) 'Beyond ODF: a phased approach to rural sanitation development', Chapter 9 in P. Bongartz, N. Vernon and J. Fox (eds.) *Sustainable Sanitation for All: Experiences, Challenges, and Innovations*, Practical Action Publishing, Rugby.

Sijbesma, C. (2011) *Sanitation Financing Models for the Urban Poor*, The Hague: International Water and Sanitation Centre, Thematic Overview Paper, No. 25, http://www.irc.nl/top25 [accessed 13 January 2016].

World Health Organization (WHO) and UNICEF (2015) *25 Years Progress on Sanitation and Drinking Water; 2015 Update and MDG Assessment*, WHO Joint Monitoring Programme, Geneva.

CHAPTER 3

Building environments to support sustainability of improved sanitation behaviours at scale: levers of change in East Asia

Nilanjana Mukherjee

with contributions from Viengsamay Vongkhamsao, Minh Thi Hien Nguyen and Hang Diem Nguyen

Abstract

Research evidence from many countries has established direct links between poor sanitation practices in communities and measurable stunting in children. The elimination of both open defecation (OD) and the usage of unhygienic latrines is now being recognized as necessary for a country's human resources to develop to their full potential. The Sustainable Development Goal challenge for the rural sanitation sector is therefore defined in terms of sanitation behaviour change by whole communities, at countrywide scale, within time spans as short as 5 to 15 years. This chapter presents learning about building supportive policy environments and institutional practices for catalysing sustainable collective sanitation behaviour change at scale. This includes scaling up the use of improved sanitation by all, along with improving the availability of affordable sanitation for all, to help rural communities achieve 'open defecation free' (ODF)[1] status that is sustained over the long-term. This chapter traces how a set of sector change-inducing levers were used to build enabling environments for rural sanitation in Lao PDR, Vietnam, and Indonesia over the period 2007–2015[2].

Keywords: Sustainability, Scaling up, Behaviour change, Enabling environment, East Asia, Change levers

Scalability and sustainability of sanitation behaviour change

Sanitation behaviour change at scale, by whole communities, within years rather than decades, and the sustainability of that change, have all become global imperatives.

Irrefutable research evidence is emerging from different countries that poor sanitation, particularly open defecation (OD) by community members, is causally linked to measurable stunting in children (Spears, 2013; WSP, 2014a; Quattri et al., 2014). The physical and cognitive development losses suffered

http://dx.doi.org/10.3362/9781780449272.003

by these children are often irreversible. No country can afford such a drain on its human resources. It is increasingly being recognized by policy-makers that the elimination of OD and other unhygienic practices in communities is necessary, to protect the physical and intellectual growth potential of children growing up therein.

There is a need, then, for the development of institutional environments and practices that can support collective behaviour change in relation to sanitation, to enable community-based processes like Community-Led Total Sanitation (CLTS) to be applied on a country-wide scale, along with fostering the growth of local markets offering improved sanitation services affordable by all.

CLTS began its meteoric impact on the rural sanitation sector, spreading steadily across continents at the start of the current millennium. It continues to evolve in terms of its capacity to catalyse rapid sanitation behaviour change at a scale hitherto unprecedented. However, several years after CLTS spread across continents policy-makers and sector professionals are seeking answers to questions about the sustainability of these behaviour changes. Research in a number of countries has revealed insights into what helps and what hinders the achievement of sustainable behaviour change, though some of the findings may well be country and situation-specific (Hanchett et al., 2011; Mukherjee et al., 2012; Tyndale-Biscoe et al., 2013). The search for generalizable influencing factors has not been limited to CLTS interventions. The scope of research and the learning related to successful scaling-up now spans a wide range of influencing factors, complementary approaches and programme environments, all of which need to be managed in a synchronized manner along with research on CLTS, for understanding what could make optimal impact on population-wide sanitation behaviours.

What is important is that the learning is utilized and internalized by sector institutions and government systems, as these are the only channels through which whole-country populations can be reached. With the goal being defined as achieving improved sanitation behaviours by whole populations it will be necessary for sector institutions and government systems to answer a number of key questions related to where to intervene, with what inputs, at what levels, through what channels, and in what sequence. This chapter explores these questions using experiences from Lao PDR, Vietnam, and Indonesia.[3] It draws on:

- The development of sector operational guidelines and sector capacity building strategies for rural sanitation in Lao PDR and Vietnam, during the period 2011–15.
- Pathways adopted in Indonesia for scaling-up rural sanitation learning from the Total Sanitation and Sanitation Marketing (TSSM) project 2007–10 in East Java to all provinces, and the resulting updates during 2011–15.

These experiences are used to identify several strategic and interconnected change levers used within each country. The change levers were applicable across the three countries, with comparable results in terms of sector transformation, even though the levers grappled with diverse country contexts and generated country-specific learning and solutions. It is plausible that they are applicable globally for sector development. The change levers are:

- Defining sector goals in terms of collective behaviour change, to generate accountability in sector systems for achieving them.
- Establishing a national monitoring system to track progress and outcomes in behavioural terms.
- Formulating a theory of change as the basis for identifying the programme methodology, roles, and responsibilities.
- Building institutional capacity to facilitate collective behaviour change at scale.
- Securing sustained funding for programme processes and human resources.
- Establishing efficient institutional learning and sharing mechanisms.

Country rural sanitation profiles: pre-scaling up

Systematic scaling-up of rural sanitation interventions began around 2010–11 in Laos and Vietnam, and several years earlier in Indonesia. The following country profiles reflect the timeline differentials in starting up. The progress achieved thereafter till the end of 2015 in each country, the paths taken, and the learning gained in the process are described in the next section on the levers of change.

Lao PDR

In 2010, Lao PDR was a country of 6.2 million of which 70 per cent were rural. One of the poorest countries in East Asia, UNDP's 2010 Human Development Index ranked it as 122nd out of 169 countries (UNDP, 2010) and 139th out of 187 countries in 2013 (UNDP, 2013). Poverty was, and continues to be, predominantly a rural phenomenon. Eighty-four per cent of the country's poor live in villages. The Joint Monitoring Programme (JMP) 2012 figures indicated that by 2011 Lao PDR's household access to improved sanitation had already progressed beyond the Millennium Development Goal (MDG) target of 54 per cent and reached 62 per cent (WHO/UNICEF, 2012). However, that figure represented mostly urban access growth, and growth of 'self-supplied' sanitation rather than programme achievements.

The extent of inequity in access to improved sanitation was extreme. The 2012 Lao Social Indicators Survey revealed that while 99 per cent of households of the richest quintile had access, only 12.7 per cent for the poorest quintile did so (Government of Lao PDR et al., 2012). Access to improved sanitation was 51.2 per cent among rural households with road access, but only 22.5 per cent among those without road access. While central and northern regions had achieved 68 per cent and 61 per cent access rates respectively, the southern region lagged far behind with only 35 per cent access.

Meanwhile, estimated economic losses due to poor sanitation were costing up to 5.6 per cent of the country's GDP annually or US$193 million (Hutton et al., 2009). Even that did not adequately highlight the human development losses: almost 49 per cent of rural children and 61 per cent of the poorest children were found to be stunted in 2011. That the stunting figures were 20 per cent for the richest children and 27 per cent for urban children only illustrated how poor sanitation environments harmed all, across social and economic boundaries (Government of Lao PDR et al., 2012).

In 2010 there were a number of obstacles to be overcome in scaling up rural sanitation:

- Sanitation was a low priority on the national development agenda, and allocated little programme capacity.
- The nodal national agency, Nam Saat (the National Centre for Environmental Health and Water Supply), had a low profile within the Ministry of Health.
- There was no national programme vehicle or policy for rural sanitation. Consequently, the national government's budget and personnel allocations for rural water, sanitation, and hygiene (WASH) were minimal. Local government funding for rural sanitation was little or none.
- Formal mechanisms for sector coordination were lacking, while capital investment was financed externally, mainly from foreign aid (Giltner et al., 2010). The country was divided up into a series of donor projects, using a variety of approaches in the same or different provinces. Individual donors designed projects of their choice in bilateral consultation with the national government.
- The availability of sanitation products and services in rural areas was not known, but was estimated to be limited. There was no market assessment information available.

By 2011 a number of opportunities had been identified. These were:

- A new WASH Strategy for Lao PDR[4] was nearing completion, with UNICEF support.
- Positive experience and lessons had become available from CLTS pilots in two southern provinces during 2009–11.
- An agreement had been reached by major funding partners to adopt CLTS as a programme approach and to discontinue household subsidies.
- Government exposure to sanitation marketing approaches used in Cambodia and Indonesia had helped spark new thinking about what might be possible in Lao PDR.

- There was a willingness within the government and key funding partners to field-trial CLTS complemented by a sanitation marketing approach which had shown promising results in Asia and Africa.
- The country had set itself the economic development goal of exiting 'least developed country status' by 2020.
- An informal Technical Working Group established in 2009, involving all sector funding supporters, had begun to serve as an unofficial sector coordination mechanism.

By the end of 2015, much had changed in Lao PDR. Now there is a uniform national programme methodology guiding all rural sanitation interventions. In order to generate sustainable institutional capacity to apply the methodology across Laos, a capacity building framework and plan have been developed and are being implemented. Rural sanitation has gained political importance with the government's Sanitation and Water for All (SWA) commitment to reduce OD. Methods to monitor collective behaviour change have been standardized. Funding has been earmarked for rural sanitation within national programmes for poverty reduction and child malnutrition prevention. Sanitation marketing efforts to reach the poorest with affordable products are being developed in different donor-funded project areas, based on the government's countrywide formative research and supply chain assessments. Government-led sector coordination mechanisms are formally established and functioning.

Vietnam

The sanitation sector situation in 2010–11 in Vietnam was atypical by developing world standards. Home to a population of 87.8 million (Government of Vietnam, 2011), Vietnam has remained overwhelmingly rural (nearly 70 per cent of the population in 2010–11) and is characterized by great geographic and ethnic diversity. At a time when most countries were preoccupied with reducing the percentage of populations defecating in the open, Vietnam had achieved a steep 12 per cent annual decline in open defecators since 1990, and by 2011 only 3 per cent of the population practised OD (WHO/UNICEF, 2013). However:

- While household access to improved sanitation had grown to 56 per cent, the poorest two quintiles did not gain much.
- The 44 per cent that lacked access were poor, rural, mostly ethnic minorities for whom OD is culturally acceptable, and often linked to livelihood activities such as domestic animal breeding and agriculture.
- The population pockets without access were mostly in the mountainous areas far from markets and in flood-prone coastal plains where hanging latrines over fish-breeding ponds are the norm.
- During 1990–2012 the percentage of households using unimproved latrines did not decline – in fact, it grew from 26 per cent to 30 per cent.

The main sector programme was the Third National Target Programme for Rural Water Supply and Sanitation (NTP3), operational from 2011 to 2015 with the following features:

- There was overall coordination by the Ministry of Rural Development (MARD).
- The Ministry of Health (MoH) had responsibility for rural sanitation, but all funding for behaviour change interventions, capacity building, supervision, and monitoring remained under MARD management.
- In the early years of the NTP3, the methodologies used were still conventional ones and not tailored to changing behaviours in the population pockets identified above.

Vietnam has been searching for strategies to reach the unreached population groups which are still proving extremely resistant to desired behaviour changes. Meanwhile, children growing up in communities where unimproved sanitation is practised have been losing on average 3.7 cm of height and parallel cognitive development quotient, compared with children in communities where all households are using improved sanitation (Quattri et al., 2014).

By end-2015, rural household access to hygienic latrines had grown to 64 per cent, and several other milestones were reached. National guidelines to plan and implement rural sanitation have been launched by the MoH, and a sector capacity building strategy developed, based on them. Following the Government's SWA commitments for universal access by 2030 and an open defecation free (ODF) Vietnam by 2025, an ODF definition and verification system have been established by the MoH, tailored to the Vietnam-specific situation of little OD but wide usage of unhygienic latrines. A province-scale learning initiative is testing innovations to grow pro-poor sanitation markets and consumer demand for hygienic latrines in remote rural pockets. Funding has been committed in two new national WASH projects for scaling-up access to hygienic sanitation in targeted poor rural and ethnic minority-inhabited areas who have low sanitation access. The MoH has the mandate to manage and implement the sanitation and hygiene components in both projects.

Indonesia

Spread over more than 17,000 islands, Indonesia had a population of 239 million in 2010, of whom 110 million still lacked access to improved sanitation (WHO/UNICEF, 2012). The 2013 JMP Update reported that in 2011 more than 58 million still practised OD, nearly 42 million of whom lived in rural areas (WHO/UNICEF, 2013). The costs to the country from poor sanitation practices were amounting to US$6.3 bn annually at 2006 prices, equivalent to 2.3 per cent of its GDP (Hutton et al., 2009).

For several decades, rural sanitation efforts in Indonesia had focused on improving access to basic sanitation using hardware subsidies and hygiene education. The approach proved to be ineffective, highlighting the size of the challenge:

- Rural household access to improved sanitation grew at less than 1 per cent per annum from 1985 to 2006, reaching only 20.6 per cent in 2006.
- With less than 10 years to 2015, the rural MDG target of 56 per cent seemed well beyond reach.

Policy-makers and sector administrators were anxiously searching for new directions when two promising new approaches emerged on the global scene, stirring up powerful winds of change in Indonesia. Exposure to CLTS and sanitation marketing in Bangladesh, India, and Vietnam provided hope and impetus to new rural sanitation thinking and experimentation in Indonesia during 2005–06, and the unprecedented success of the new approaches led to the MoH declaring CLTS as its national approach for rural sanitation in 2006, along with handwashing with soap.

By 2007, Indonesia was the first country in East Asia to embark on a new rural sanitation initiative at scale, combining CLTS and sanitation marketing with strengthening enabling policy and institutional environments. This was the Total Sanitation and Sanitation Marketing (TSSM) project covering all of East Java, a province of 37.5 million people. After several decades of stagnation, the rural sanitation scene began to change radically.

- TSSM signalled a complete break away from past subsidy-based approaches, and offered only a nine month window of technical assistance to local governments interested in becoming ODF districts.
- Four years later, by the end of TSSM, 2,200 communities had been verified as ODF, and more than 1.4 million people had gained access to improved sanitation over the baseline of 2007, with 100 per cent of the sanitation improvements being financed by rural households themselves.
- Within a year of TSSM implementation, the first national Sanitasi Total Berbasis Masyarakat or Community-based Total Sanitation (STBM) strategy was launched in 2008 as the Health Minister's Decree, officially discontinuing government subsidies for household latrines and identifying five key hygiene behaviour changes (the '5 pillars of STBM'), the first of which was eliminating OD.
- In 2014 it was replaced by the Health Minister's Decree 3/2014, establishing STBM as the national strategy, and providing operational guidelines for planning, implementing, and monitoring rural sanitation interventions.
- With changes in programme approaches, Indonesia's rural sanitation access growth rate has accelerated from less than 1 per cent in the years before 2006 to 3.4 per cent per annum during 2007–13.
- Rural access to improved sanitation more than doubled in seven years: from 20 per cent in 2006 to 44 per cent households in 2013 (BPS Indonesia, 2014).

From 2011 onwards, after TSSM closed, the learning gained is being applied in almost all of 34 Indonesian provinces through national systems for sector knowledge management, outcome monitoring, institutional capacity building, and support for the growth of pro-poor sanitation markets. How this progress has unfolded is described in the next section.

Levers of change for sustainability at scale

This section identifies six strategic and interconnected levers of change that can be operated when promoting sanitation sector transformation and working for sustainability at scale. They are illustrated by drawing on the experience of scaling up rural sanitation programmes nationally in the three countries, from the starting points described in the previous section.

Lever 1: Goals defined in terms of collective and equitable behaviour change for accountability in sector systems

As long as programme planners are held accountable for targets like the number of toilets built and the percentage of households having toilets, they may well ignore, or only pay lip service to, behaviour change objectives. Even today, monitoring systems in the majority of countries demand only sanitation coverage data; namely, data on the physical presence of household and institutional toilets. However, institutional accountabilities can be turned around once national goals are reset in terms of collective community behaviour change. An example of such a goal could be a targeted percentage of communities, villages, communes, or districts becoming ODF by a specified date. The definition of ODF would spell out the behaviour changes desired, i.e. elimination of both OD and unimproved sanitation usage, possibly along with handwashing at critical times. Targets can then be set for collective behaviour-changing interventions by sector institutions. Programme performance monitoring then must track numbers and percentages of communities intervened in, and verify the achievement of ODF outcomes, in addition to household access to toilets. The MDG targets for increasing only the access to sanitation caused the behavioural focus of sanitation programmes to be neglected. Now that the Sustainable Development Goal (SDG) targets include the elimination of OD (UNDP, 2015), country governments may be more willing to adopt goals defined in behavioural terms, and accept accountability for progress towards them.

In Indonesia, the national rural sanitation goal was first set in collective behaviour terms as *Indonesia ODF 2014*, in the National Medium Term Development (MTD) Plan 2010–14. Although unrealistic and unachieved, the 2014 ODF target served to highlight what it will take to push collective behaviour changes on a nationwide scale. A definition of ODF status and ODF verification guidelines, first applied in East Java by the TSSM project in 2008, were adopted for national use by the MoH in 2011. Later, verification guidelines were expanded to cover the remaining rungs of the STBM behaviour change ladder up to 'Total Sanitation' (see Figure 3.1), and launched nationally in 2013 (MoH, 2013).

The 2015–19 MTD Plan has now set the goal as universal access by 2019. It has become evident that the 11 per cent annual access growth rate required to achieve such a goal will require a lot more than 'business as usual'. While funding levels and channels of intervention are being greatly stepped up, sector monitoring systems continue to track and publicize both access gains and ODF achievements by villages, sub-districts, and districts. The verification procedure provides for sustainability checks every two years and even allows for ODF status to be revoked when communities are found to have slipped (MoH, 2013).

In 2014, the Government of Vietnam made a high-level SWA commitment, for the country to be ODF by 2025, and universal access to be achieved by 2030. Subsequently, a collective behaviour change focus is being developed through making 'village-wide and commune-wide sanitation improvement' the performance target, proposing mechanisms to verify collective behaviour change outcomes uniformly, and rewarding commune leadership for outcomes. Although some provinces had already instituted their own ODF definitions and piloted ODF verification processes, until 2015 there was no recognition of 'ODF status' within government policy and legislation. After the SWA commitment, external funding partners are now working with the MoH on uniform national criteria for ODF and a standardized ODF verification process.

Lao PDR does not yet have a national rural sanitation goal in terms of collective behaviour change. But at the 2014 High Level Meetings on Sanitation and Water for All (SWA), the government made a commitment to reduce OD from 52 per cent to 35 per cent by 2016, and to develop a comprehensive national sanitation policy by 2016. The commitment to OD reduction can be seen as a first step towards developing accountability on the part of the government for behaviour change goals. The monitoring system reflects progress in this direction. The multiple ODF verification processes used in different projects have now been consolidated and one ODF verification process standardized by the MoH for national use.[5]

Box 3.1 Key learning 1: redefinition of goals catalyses all other changes

Defining goals in collective behaviour change terms is ideally the place to start as it can set the remaining levers in motion. However, real life sector situations in countries are not always conducive to allowing ideal entry point choices. Change influencers have to start working with whichever of the change levers provides the opportunity. From that platform they can open up other fronts, engaging and building consensus with country sector stakeholders in the process.

In addition to behaviour change, accountability for equity and inclusion in outcomes needs to be integrated into goals and tracked by sector monitoring systems. Macro-scale target definitions need to take into account country-specific regional disparities and unserved groups.

Vietnam is currently using geographic information system (GIS) mapping for concentrations of poor populations and overlaying them with mapping of access to sanitation, as well as mapping of the prevalence of child malnutrition. The results are eye-opening, and are determining priority target areas for national programmes. Monitoring systems for sanitation improvement are being redefined to ask for data disaggregated by unserved ethnic minority populations versus total populations.

Lao PDR is integrating CLTS and other sanitation behaviour change interventions into national-scale programmes addressing poverty and malnutrition. The forthcoming Health Governance and Nutrition Project will support the adoption of ODF as a new requirement for villages to achieve 'Model Healthy Village' status. This will greatly help establish collective sanitation behaviour change as a necessary condition for improving child health and nutrition. In addition, the Poverty Reduction Fund targeting the poor in remote rural areas of four provinces has integrated CLTS with its community-driven development process.

Indonesia continues to target the poorest households through pro-poor sanitation market development. Through *Asosiasi Pengelola dan Pemberdayaan Sanitasi Indonesia* (APPSANI), an association of sanitation producers and sellers, local entrepreneurs are being trained and mentored in setting up and growing their rural sanitation business by capitalizing on the consumer base at the bottom of the pyramid, where most households lack improved sanitation. Public sector banks have been drawn into the effort, in providing capital credit to entrepreneurs so that they can offer improved latrines to poor consumers on instalment credit.

Lever 2: Establishing a national monitoring system to track progress and outcomes in behavioural terms

Goals defined in population behaviour change terms mean little unless progress towards them is measurable. Monitoring indicators must be defined unambiguously and simultaneously with goal setting. However, since many projects have already been using CLTS and verifying ODF outcomes in a variety of ways in developing countries, building stakeholder consensus for nationally applicable indicators and methods can be a politically sensitive exercise and fraught with inordinate delays. To find the most workable and sustainable solutions, national governments have to take the lead in analysing sector needs with key stakeholders, and complete the process of developing a behaviour-focused sector monitoring system, tailored to the country's context.

Most countries in Africa, and some in Asia, started out in 2009–10 by defining ODF in terms such as, 'all community households using some kind of latrine rather than defecating in the open environment'. Problems with such a definition became evident after a few years of using it.[6] Many households continued using unimproved and unhygienic latrines; people failed to upgrade to hygienic latrines; many unimproved latrines collapsed and were not rebuilt; smelly unimproved latrines built after triggering turned people away from the notion of latrines and back to OD at some distance from homes. Most importantly, the continued use of unimproved latrines meant that there was no large-scale positive health impact. This was borne out by the evidence from studies in East and South Asia that linked child stunting with poor sanitation – unimproved latrine use and OD. The Government of Indonesia was the exception, having decided as early as 2008 in the TSSM project that East Java communities would be certified as ODF only when, besides other conditions, '100 per cent community households are using only improved latrines for all excreta disposal including the disposal of infant faeces' (STBM, 2010). This was later included among national criteria for ODF.

Until 2015, Vietnam had not instituted a national definition for ODF because the practice of OD had been almost eliminated, having declined to below 5 per cent of the population by 2010. However, in the perspective of the research linking the use of unhygienic latrines and child stunting, an approach aimed at achieving ODF villages and communes has been specifically included in Vietnam's Capacity Building Strategy for rural sanitation (MoH, 2015). Accordingly, 'village-wide and commune-wide sanitation improvement' have been incorporated as programme performance targets. During 2015, the major funding partners came together to review the experience with the MoH, to identify standard criteria and a verification procedure for ODF, tailored to the Vietnam situation wherein there is little real OD and high usage of unhygienic latrines. The MoH will apply the ODF verification process nationwide after the NTP3 ends, in 2015.

Developing nationally applicable indicators for the elimination of OD is also the opportunity to outline a country's vision for higher levels of hygiene behaviour change, by moving up the behaviour change ladder – and to define how that movement will be verified. The example of the 'hygiene and sanitation behaviour change ladder' from Indonesia, shown in Figure 3.1, covering five key hygiene behaviour changes (Five Pillars of STBM) is a case in point.

Box 3.2 Key learning 2: a country's definition of 'ODF' drives the outcomes it achieves

The quality and sustainability of community-level behaviour change outcomes depend greatly on what conditions are accepted as ODF in a country. The most useful definition of ODF would reflect the rural population's capacity and aspirations for change, the country government's vision about the level of sanitation behaviour change envisaged by target dates, and the capacity to manage data related to sanitation behaviour change on a national scale.

Figure 3.1 Community Behaviour Change Ladder envisaged by STBM (Indonesia)

Source: STBM Verification Guidebook, Ministry of Health, Government of Indonesia, 2013

Note: The five pillars of STBM (five key hygiene behaviours) are: stopping OD; handwashing with soap at critical times; safe food and drinking water handling; safe household solid waste disposal; and safe household liquid waste disposal

Manual monitoring systems become impractical and unsustainable at scale. In Indonesia, the TSSM experience quickly exposed the limitations of manual systems when the programme scaled-up even in a single province. Since cell phone penetration was high in rural Java, a cell phone-based monitoring system was trialled in East Java in 2010 and expanded to all districts by 2012. Valuable lessons were learned about what it would take to scale-up nationwide.

The system has now rolled out in all 34 provinces. By December 2015, the STBM website maintaining the web-based Management Information System (MIS) was reporting real-time data updates from 69,130 out of 80,276 villages. Data entry is done through mobile phones by trained community health centre staff. Data reported include ODF claims, ODF achievements, numbers of households using improved sanitation, sharing latrines, and defecating in the open. Access to the data is public through the STBM website, which also provides graphic translations of data and comparisons across districts and provinces. While the national STBM Secretariat channelled technical guidance from international funding partners for the roll-out, local governments in Indonesia invested substantially in staff capacity building, to be able to participate in the web-based monitoring system.[7]

Lever 3: Formulating a theory of change as a basis for programme methodology, roles and responsibilities

That the quality of CLTS processes is fundamental for achieving sustained community-level outcomes is widely accepted, but that is only part of the story. When planning for sustainability at scale, the scope of the process must go well beyond CLTS *per se* and far beyond the community level. It needs to cover whole provinces, districts, and sub-districts, depending on the degree of decentralization of governance. For rural sanitation outcomes at scale, all key stakeholders (government staff, political leaders, external funding partners, implementation supporters) for rural sanitation at different levels need to have a shared understanding of:

- Programme objectives (the kind and extent of population behaviour change desired).
- The theory of change for the desired outcomes to be achieved.
- Key programme components (demand creation, supply improvement, enabling environment building).
- Implementation approaches (e.g. CLTS, expanding sanitation product and financing options for the poor, whether to use subsidies for household sanitation).
- The sequence and phasing of activities.
- Roles and responsibilities at each level.

The pre-CLTS era theory of change assumed that people defecate in the open only because they lack awareness of latrines and the health hazards of OD, and that poor households cannot build their own latrines unassisted. The principal approach therefore was to provide free or subsidized latrines to a few, along with health education messages for all. The expectation was that the rest would be stimulated to build and use latrines. We now know that such interventions failed, and millions of development dollars were wasted.

Post-CLTS, it has become possible to envisage behaviour change by whole communities, and even scaling-up that drives change rapidly across countries. Fresh insights have emerged from formative research into drivers of population sanitation behaviour,[8] identifying new kinds of interventions to catalyse collective behaviour change. But these approaches were unfamiliar to sector institutions accustomed to doling out subsidized latrine packages and instructions on how to build latrines. A new theory of change had to be understood and accepted by sector managers and implementers. Figure 3.2 summarizes the basics of the new theory of change that has been progressively adopted by many countries in recent years, starting with Indonesia, India, and Tanzania, where the Total Sanitation and Sanitation Marketing (TSSM) project introduced it during 2007–2010.[9]

TSSM project's Causal Logic – later developed into WSP's Theory of Change for Scaling Up Rural Sanitation globally

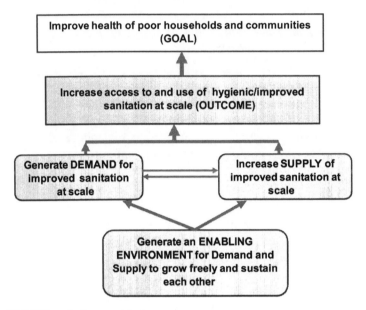

Figure 3.2 TSSM project's causal logic

Source: Author's own

The process of adoption of a theory of change is as important as the theory itself. In Lao PDR, as an initial step to scaling up rural sanitation, the WASH strategy draft prepared by a consultant in 2011 was reviewed with sector stakeholders in mid-2012, and made more explicit for rural sanitation. A theory of change and related programme components were added and it was finally issued by the MoH in 2012 as the National Plan of Action for Rural Water Supply, Sanitation and Hygiene (NPA) 2012–15.

The Lao PDR experience demonstrates how important it is that key concepts are defined, understood and agreed by sector stakeholders collectively. Once the new rural sanitation theory of change was defined in the NPA, the government urged donor partners who were funding almost all rural sanitation interventions in Laos through their various projects, to agree on a common programme implementation process. Initial dialogues in 2012 quickly revealed that people held very diverse views, and project-specific perceptions, about basic concepts relevant for the scaling-up process. It took several stakeholder workshops to get concepts defined and their implications discussed by stakeholder groups. They tussled with questions such as:

- What exactly is 'demand' for improved sanitation? Why is it necessary to work on demand creation?

- Why do the government and donor partners need to do anything on the supply side?
- What happens if they don't?
- What is an enabling environment? How does it make a difference?
- What comes first: demand creation, supply improvement, building an enabling environment, and why?
- How should interventions be sequenced at national and sub-national levels in the Lao PDR context?

The process of stakeholder consensus building culminated in the Government of Lao PDR's *Operational Program Guidelines for Scaling Up Rural Sanitation* being adopted by the MoH in 2013. The three-pronged intervention framework built into the NPA (the same as the *Demand – Supply – Enabling Environment* triangle at the base of Figure 3.2) provided the foundation for stakeholder dialogues. All rural sanitation interventions in Lao PDR are now required to follow the 2013 guidelines. It is expected to change the fragmented nature of sector support so far practised by many different agencies, by requiring consistent methods for implementation and monitoring, both of which are essential for scaling-up.

In Vietnam, the MoH utilized the National Target Program platform to redefine a rural sanitation theory of change and translate it into the *Guidelines for Planning and Implementation of Rural Sanitation Programmes*, launched in 2014 (Government of Vietnam, 2014). These were the result of an analysis of past programme approaches and a consultative process involving all sector funding partners, and provincial and district-level implementers. Programme components were identified for demand generation, supply improvement, enabling environment building, knowledge generation, and learning, reflecting a similar theory of change. And institutional roles and responsibilities for planning, implementing, and monitoring were redefined accordingly, with stakeholder consensus building during 2012 and 2013.

Indonesia was in fact the first East Asian country to translate such a theory of change into practice through the TSSM project in East Java in 2007, and scale it up to other provinces starting in 2011. This is the framework upon which its *Sanitasi Total Berbasis Masyarakat Programme Operational Guideline*[10] is modelled for districts and provinces. The programme identified the sequence of preparatory and implementation activities at these levels, synchronizing supply improvement activities with activities for demand creation and strengthening the enabling environment. The original TSSM project's methodology was refined, based on a market research study by Nielsen Indonesia in 2009 and a participatory action research evaluation of TSSM in 2010 by 80 communities in East Java (Mukherjee et al., 2012). The Nielsen study led to the development of an appropriate marketing strategy to reach poorer consumers with affordable sanitation options of their choice. By 2015, the market development effort was unfolding across multiple provinces, with training and support to sanitation entrepreneurs

(Pedi and Kamasan, forthcoming); with 150 sanitation entrepreneurs, including 24 female entrepreneurs, already active in five provinces after being trained in promoting and delivering a range of affordable improved sanitation options. Following the 2010 action research recommendations, new provinces starting districtwide ODF programmes are first building local sanitation suppliers' capacity to do this, before starting to raise consumer demand using CLTS.

Once a common sector language has been developed among stakeholders, a meaningful dialogue begins. A logical and feasible sequence of activities can then be identified, along with responsibilities for carrying them out at each administrative level. In all three countries, the end result has been national operational guidelines for their rural sanitation programmes. The guidelines are now serving as powerful instruments for ensuring consistency in planning, funding, implementing, and monitoring of rural sanitation programmes across the country. They also provide the structural framework for building institutional capacity. This is a process that has taken between 12 and 18 months in each of the countries.

Box 3.3 Key learning 3: adoption of a new sector theory of change needs to be a collective learning process

Translating the theory of change into a country-specific programme implementation process is a strategic opportunity for sector reform. When carried out using participatory analysis and consensus building with stakeholder groups, this activity becomes a transformational collective learning experience. It begins by developing a shared understanding of basic concepts and definitions in country-specific context and terminology, such as 'OD', 'ODF', 'improved and unimproved sanitation', 'demand' and 'demand creation', 'supply improvement', 'enabling environment building', 'progress and outcome indicators', etc.

Lever 4: Building institutional capacity to facilitate collective behaviour change at scale

Before the spread of CLTS, institutional capacity for rural sanitation typically meant the capacity for the distribution of subsidy packages to selected households, delivering health education messages to all, providing construction advice, and reporting the number of the subsidy recipients. Skills training for using behaviour change interventions such as CLTS, other participatory methods, and behaviour change communication (BCC) was typically provided only to specially recruited animators and community volunteers by NGOs in donor-funded projects on a small and pilot scale. When projects ended, the trained personnel dispersed and were often lost to the sector.

Now that sector goals and monitoring indicators have begun to be set in terms of population behaviour change, demand is growing for re-skilling members of sector institutions. CLTS trainers are in great demand across countries and continents because staff training is seen as the easiest and most obvious solution when desired programme results are not achieved. However, training without contextualization can be wasteful and the skills built easily lost from the system. For example, those trained in CLTS methods may never apply them because they lack budgets to implement triggering or follow-up activities. Those who received training may not have institutional roles and functions for community outreach activities. Or they have competing responsibilities more important for their careers or salaries, and so they lack incentives to apply CLTS skills.

A critically important issue that is often overlooked is that institutional capacity building for sustainable outcomes needs to cover facilitation of the entire collective change process. Triggering is now widely recognized as only the first step. Sector outreach staff need to have both training and incentives for seeing the change process through, with a clearly structured and fully resourced follow-up support process, including the provision of reliable technical advice on sanitation improvement options and facilitation of access to supplies if necessary.

Sector capacity building at country scale is not at all a one-off exercise. For sustained support to the sector, capacity building services need to be institutionalized by national governments, with cost recovery mechanisms, and they should be provided in response to demand from local governments.

Figure 3.3 shows the capacity development framework identified for Lao PDR, based on the 2013 Operational Guidelines and a capacity needs assessment. This framework guides the country's sector Capacity Building Strategy and Action plan, which were adopted by the government for implementation at the national, provincial, and local levels in 2014.

Implementation of the plan has begun in two provinces, with World Bank support. As part of the plan to create skilled rural sanitation workers of the future, training modules on CLTS and sanitation marketing are now being integrated into Vientiane's University of Health and Sciences diploma course in environmental health, which is essential for technical staff of Nam Saat (the MoH department responsible for rural water and sanitation). In addition, the MoH has decided to update and align university curricula of public health degrees and diploma courses with current rural sanitation sector realities. Topics like CLTS, sanitation marketing, and operational guidelines for rural sanitation are being included in the curriculum for students of environmental hygiene and Associate Degree on Public Health.

Vietnam has developed a sector Capacity Building Strategy and Plan (MoH, 2015) based on a needs assessment in eight provinces during 2014. This strategy, along with advocacy and financing strategies, addresses a number of key issues: a definition of goals in behavioural terms; formulation of indicators to measure the desired behaviour changes; recommendations for adopting a

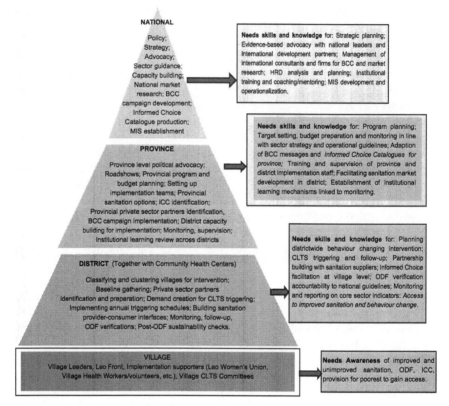

Figure 3.3 Capacity Development Framework and Action Plan for Rural Sanitation in Lao PDR
Source: Vongkhamsao and Weitz, 2015

commune-wide approach for sanitation improvement and collective behaviour change; preparation of advocacy packages directed at funding decision-makers in provinces; and preparation of capacity building programmes to be delivered through the MoH's four regional resource institutes.

Indonesia has advanced furthest in this direction among East Asian countries. As reported by WSP Indonesia in early 2015:

> Formal curricula focusing on sanitation have been introduced at 30 government health schools (which train health outreach staff) as part of a plan to substantially ramp up human resources to implement the national sanitation strategy. Five training modules (about demand creation, supply improvement, and enabling programme environment building), and distance learning courses, have been developed and accredited by the government. Once someone completes training they receive a certificate that is recorded with the MoH's Human Resource Office's database for career advancement. (Setiawan and Weitz, 2015)

Strategic choices were made in Indonesia during 2011–15 to fully integrate sector capacity building into MoH systems and institutions for human resource development. As described in a recent WSP report (World Bank, 2015) technical collaboration was established with the existing MoH unit mandated for delivering institutional capacity building, the Agency for Development and Empowerment of Human Resources. Separate capacity building streams were developed to target sector professionals with accredited and certified STBM training programmes that could be delivered through in-service channels. Simultaneously, career advancement-related incentives were built into career development pathways for sector staff, so that they would actively seek, qualify for, and successfully complete the STBM training curricula. Pre-service training programmes have integrated STBM modules into 24 government run, and four privately run, health polytechnics. In addition, interactive e-learning STBM modules reach out to a wider group of professionals and academics, both within and outside health service institutions.

Box 3.4 Key learning 4: building sector capacity at scale is a matter of building systems to equip present and future staff to deliver selected programme approaches with quality

For institutional capacity to be sustained, capacity building must be synchronized with the programme methodology embedded in sector operational guidelines, which clarify staff roles and responsibilities at each level of the programme process, delineating the skills required at each level.

In addition, staff capacity development needs to be linked to incentives such as career advancement and salary increments, through human resource management systems.

Lever 5: Securing sustained funding for programme processes and human resources

Sustained programme funding is the kind that comes from annual budgets, of both national and local governments. In many developing countries rural sanitation has traditionally been a neglected issue, with little political priority, and therefore little or no budget support. External funding partners have tended to cover costs of rural sanitation programme activities, while governments provided a limited number of staff salaries. Under such conditions, programme sustainability is not feasible. Change influencers are thus forced to focus on political advocacy to raise the sector's profile with funding decision-makers. In this regard, the research linking poor sanitation with stunting of children is proving to be a powerful advocacy message, one that makes politicians not only uncomfortable but also accountable.

Systematic scale-up in each country invariably began with strategic advocacy with national and local leaders and funding decision-makers, who are often politicians. Advocacy efforts combined: a) quantified research evidence about the impact of poor sanitation on the country's economic and human development; b) the country's sanitation challenge described in terms of high-profile targets like MDGs, SDGs or SWA commitments, and its implications for national economic and human development goals; and c) exposure to in-country rural sanitation innovations at a scale relevant for the country's size. Mass media were found to be powerful allies in this effort. Once rural sanitation was accepted as a government priority local and national leaderships found novel ways to gather and sustain support for scaling up.

In Lao PDR, the national government-led process that produced the national Operational Guidelines for Scaling-Up Rural Sanitation in 2013 set an important precedent. It was the first time that various donor agencies had collaborated technically and financially to support the same final product owned by the national government. The issue-based stakeholder collaboration was extended to joint funding by several donor partners of two country-wide formative and market research studies commissioned by the government during 2013–14, to build an evidence-based foundation for designing rural sanitation interventions in Laos. This was in complete contrast to the limited focus of many different project-specific approaches of the past.

Since Lao PDR's current National Plan of Action for WASH ends in 2015, and no large-scale sector programme is yet in sight, alternative means of harnessing funding and human resources for rural sanitation for 2015–20 have been identified in other countrywide programmes. Evidence-based advocacy with decision-makers and exposure visits for them to already piloted in-country innovations (CLTS and sanitation marketing) made this possible. CLTS is now being integrated with the community-driven development approach of the World Bank-supported Poverty Reduction Fund (PRF), which has a strong presence in remote rural areas where sanitation access is typically very low. The new high profile multi-sectoral nutrition programme for 2016–20 has recognized WASH improvements and CLTS approaches as priorities for addressing child malnutrition. The programme has capacities to take community-based sanitation interventions to scale. The MoH plans to equip staff and facilitators of PRF and nutrition programmes with the tools and skills to support community sanitation behaviour change. All donor agencies that will help build capacity for rural sanitation interventions within the nutrition programme are committed to do so in line with the 2013 Operational Guidelines and MoH-approved standards of CLTS facilitator training.

In Vietnam, fund sources are being identified for operationalizing the new sector Capacity Building Plan, subsequent to Vietnam's SWA commitment to be an ODF nation by 2025. The plan's recommendations have been built into the US$200 million World Bank credit (approved in November 2015) covering 21 provinces in the northern mountains and central highland regions, the Results-based Scaling up Rural Sanitation and Water Supply Program (abbreviated as P4R). It is expected to improve access to water supply and hygienic sanitation for over 5 million people living in the poorest rural and mountainous areas of Vietnam, where 75 per cent of the ethnic minorities live. These population groups represent 75 per cent of the country's poorest, with a high prevalence of stunting among children under five and some of the lowest levels of access to hygienic sanitation. The MoH is mandated to manage fully the sanitation and hygiene components of the programme. These include: creating demand for improved sanitation at-scale; intensive behaviour change communication from national to commune-level; developing local sanitation supply chains in the covered provinces; and capacity building of frontline workers in villages.

In Indonesia, the field-tested STBM approach and the national goal of 'universal access by 2019' have catalysed dedicated fund flows for redoubling programme efforts. STBM approaches are mandatory in all projects for rural WASH. These include the World Bank-supported PAMSIMAS[11] 1 and 2 during 2011–16, which are covering 32 of the 34 Indonesian provinces. Apart from large-scale national projects, it is the operational budgets of the 9,600 community health centres that are driving rural sanitation interventions in Indonesia. To accelerate ODF achievements, in 2013 the MoH officially instructed all community health centres to support at least one CLTS-triggered village in their command areas with interventions to help them become ODF (without external assistance to households – STBM explicitly disallows sanitation subsidies to households).

Box 3.5 Key learning 5: sustained budget support for rural sanitation can be elicited through strategically crafted and targeted political advocacy

Eliciting adequate national and local fund flows for rural sanitation is highly possible once it can be demonstrated that supporting rural sanitation can be politically advantageous.

To accomplish this it is necessary to invest in strategic advocacy campaigns which are designed professionally and delivered through well-planned media mixes, targeting funding decision-makers.

Lever 6: Establishing efficient institutional learning and sharing mechanisms

No country has yet discovered fail-proof ways of scaling-up rural sanitation rapidly and sustainably, reaching the poorest populations effectively, and ensuring sustainable impact on public health and well-being. Every country's dynamic socio-economic, cultural, and political contexts create incredibly complex environments, where what works and what makes for sustainable outcomes must continually be learned afresh and improved upon. When sustainable outcomes at scale is the goal, rural sanitation programmes cannot afford to be designed without a learning strategy, integrated with programme implementation. Paradoxically, while large-scale institutional systems are most in need of continual learning, they are also typical bureaucracies that are rarely open to learning. Unfortunately, the larger the scale and cultural diversity, the greater the need for rapid institutional learning and, typically, the lower the institutional propensity to adjust approaches.

Building capacity for scaling-up is largely a matter of building an enabling policy for the sector. As argued above, and as illustrated in Figure 3.4, it is possible to identify a logical starting point and a sequence in which such policies should be developed. But sector situations vary greatly, and pathways are not uniform, as illustrated by the three country case studies. Arguably, the only common principle is that there should at least be an identified institutional arrangement with responsibility and authority for managing the country's rural sanitation sector. Without this basic foundation, sustainable scaling up cannot be envisaged.

In Lao PDR, two early innovator provinces that demonstrated successful CLTS pilots, are serving as learning laboratories for scaling up. Champasak and Sekong provinces have the best CLTS trainers, who assist the MoH's national training efforts. With World Bank assistance, both provinces have engaged the private sector in the development and marketing of affordable sanitation options. Action research on the efficacy of different outcome-based incentives for ODF achievements is also under way in these provinces, which will inform the much-awaited sector financing strategy.

In Vietnam, to support the scaling up of new approaches, the northern, mountainous province of Hoa Binh is serving as a learning laboratory. It has a high concentration of ethnic minorities and poorest population groups where many children are vulnerable to stunting. Supply chain assessments, operational research, and piloting carried out in Hoa Binh in 2014 has resulted in the development of an evidence-based *Provincial Strategy for Rural Sanitation Behaviour Change and Market Strengthening*, to be implemented during 2015–2020. Its execution will help assess the effectiveness and feasibility of cost-efficient BCC campaigns targeting ethnic minority pockets to address their practices of disposal and use of human excreta for livelihood-related purposes. This will be the core BCC strategy to be rolled out through the new $200 million P4R programme in 21 provinces of the Northern Mountains and Central Highlands. Another similar strategy is under preparation for the Mekong region.

Also in Indonesia, the starting point for scaling up was a learning initiative launched in 2007 covering a province of 37 million people, the TSSM project in East Java. TSSM was explicitly designed as a learning laboratory large enough in scale to be able to influence the country of a population of 230 million. Twenty-eight out of East Java's 29 district governments chose to participate in TSSM, using their own funds and human resources. By the end of TSSM, all local governments in East Java were implementing multi-year strategic sanitation plans using the new approaches, with their own funding and with personnel trained through TSSM. Household access to improved sanitation in East Java grew at rates several times the national average during the years 2007–11 and the trend continues. By early 2015, four of East Java's districts had been certified as ODF without any government subsidy. That the learning laboratory in East Java has demonstrated adequate 'proof of concept' is evident in the national STBM strategy's holistic adoption of its programming tools, monitoring innovations, and capacity building interventions.

The TSSM project introduced non-fiscal incentives to make the analysis and sharing of learning attractive to local government personnel. Individuals who contributed valuable lessons, about failures as well as successes, were voted for and received annual Learning Champion awards. Innovators were recognized publicly and supported in sharing their 'know-how' across districts. Annual inter-district Stakeholder Learning Reviews were introduced to bring together district teams for comparing progress, analysing implementation experiences, and sharing lessons learned. The provincial Health Department added rural sanitation performance benchmarking to an existing annual evaluation of district governance quality, conducted by East Java's biggest media network, the Java Post. The annual Jawa Pos Institut Pro-Otonomi (JPIP) award, given to 1 district out of 29, is coveted by district heads (*Bupatis*), who are elected politicians.

When TSSM closed in 2010, provincial and district governments in East Java identified a number of institutional funding sources (not utilized until then) to support learning and sharing. From 2011 onwards, these mechanisms are being sustained by a range of local government budgets in East Java. Four new provinces that have adopted the STBM methodology have begun to institute similar mechanisms with government funding.

At the national level, learning and knowledge-sharing is managed through the STBM Secretariat, set up in 2012 and staffed by MoH personnel. All donor agencies now channel their support for sector information and knowledge-sharing through the Secretariat. It maintains the web-based monitoring system, updated through registered cell phones of Sanitarians (health personnel) in nearly 9,600 community health centres across the country. The Secretariat also maintains the STBM website for knowledge-sharing with local governments and the public at large. Access to sector information is public on the website.

This key learning is summarized in Figure 3.4, which shows a logical sequence for strengthening enabling policy and institutional environments for rural sanitation in any country. However, as explained earlier, pathways to change do not always follow this sequence.

The box at the base of Figure 3.4 traces the country-specific variations that unfolded in the process to illustrate that pathways to building enabling environments vary greatly with country contexts, and depend on the Change Lever/s available to work with at the start of the scaling up process.

Box 3.6 Key learning 6: efficient institutional learning mechanisms and a learning-focused implementation culture are essential to achieving and sustaining desired outcomes at scale

Opportunities to strengthen a country's enabling policy and institutional environment (EE) rarely arise in the desired logical order. Sector change influencers have to enter where opportunities arise in the process and work simultaneously forward and backward from the entry point, to help build a stable foundation for sector transformation.

The key is to build simultaneously institutional mechanisms to harvest the learning generated by the process of strengthening the EE, in ways that ensure ownership and internalization of the learning by sector institutions and policy-makers.

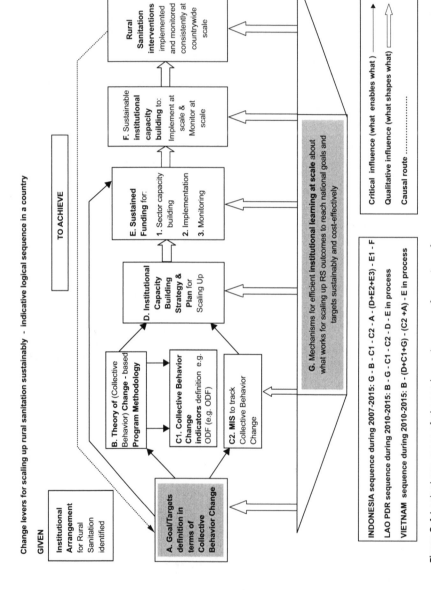

Figure 3.4 Logical sequence of change levers to engage for sector reform

Source: Author's own

Box 3.7 Summary of key learnings

1. Defining programme goals in collective behaviour change terms is the logical place to start since it can set the remaining levers in motion. However, opportunities to strengthen a country's enabling environment rarely arise in the desired logical order.
2. The quality and sustainability of community-level behaviour change outcomes depend greatly on what conditions are accepted as ODF in a country.
3. Translating the theory of change into a country specific programme implementation process is a strategic opportunity for sector reform.
4. For institutional capacity to be sustained, capacity building must be synchronized with the programme methodology, covering the entire collective change process from triggering change, to structured follow-up support to ODF achievement and sustainability checks thereafter.
5. Eliciting adequate national and local fund flows for rural sanitation is highly possible once it can be demonstrated that supporting rural sanitation can be politically advantageous.
6. While strengthening enabling environments, a key requirement is to simultaneously build institutional learning mechanisms that can capture learning generated by the process, in ways that ensure ownership and internalization of the learning by policymakers and sector institutions.

An agenda for SDG-era learning

The rural sanitation sector has progressed rapidly and changed extensively in all three countries in the few years before 2015. While the sequence of changes has been similar in all of them, Indonesia began the process several years before Laos and Vietnam. The results are evident in its national scale systems for monitoring, capacity building, and sector learning, and in the fund flows from both national and local governments earmarked for rural sanitation. These features are indicative of sustainable changes in institutional practice, and they provide reason to hope that similar progress will soon be visible in Vietnam and Lao PDR, where the process is taking less time because the Indonesian experience has provided rich learning about what has worked and what has not. However, much remains to be learned, and learned afresh, in each country, due to socio-cultural, economic, and geo-physical variations in the contexts of rural sanitation.

In all countries scaling-up rural sanitation, research and institutional learning could now focus on the following issues and questions.

Equity and inclusion: How effective are the current operational strategies for equity and inclusion? Are the poorest being reached with services of their choice? Are they able to find affordable options in sanitation products and services and in financing them?

Integration with programmes for impact on human resource potential: What are effective approaches to integrate sanitation and hygiene in programmes to improve maternal and child health and development, education, sustainable livelihoods, and environmental protection?

Scaling-up supply capacity for equity in outcomes: What strategies are viable at scale for building private sector capacity and interest in delivering products and services for the poorest population quintiles?

Financing rural sanitation interventions: What methods work best with influencing decision-makers in local governments who allocate funding for development programmes? How effective are current advocacy campaigns and strategies in eliciting their support for rural sanitation?

Building and sustaining capacity for performance: How to best incentivize rural sanitation performance by individuals and implementing units? How can talent from academic streams relevant for rural sanitation – technology, social development, communication, environmental management, marketing and business development, and public health – be attracted and retained?

Institutionalization of monitoring-linked programme improvement: How can institutional analysis of monitoring data by implementers for improving programme effectiveness be inculcated?

About the author

Dr Nilanjana Mukherjee, World Bank Water and Sanitation Program (WSP), 1996–2015. Nilanjana Mukherjee has worked with country governments of India, Indonesia, Lao PDR, Cambodia, Philippines, Mongolia and Vietnam on WASH policy formulation, sustainability, and equity. From 2006 to date she has focused on developing national strategies and institutional capacities for scaling up rural sanitation programmes in Indonesia, Lao PDR, and Vietnam. She currently works as an independent international consultant.

Endnotes

1. Or 'living environments free of faecal contamination', as emphasized in Vietnam where OD is negligible.
2,3. The experiences reported in this paper relate to work carried out as part of the World Bank Water and Sanitation Program's (WSP's) global Scaling Up Rural Sanitation and Hygiene (SURSH) project, by WSP country teams and consultants working with national and local governments, as well as external sector funding partners in the respective countries.
4. Now called the National Plan of Action on Rural Water Supply, Sanitation and Hygiene for Lao PDR 2012–15.
5. The ODF verification process is spelt out in the *Handbook on CLTS in Lao PDR and Trainers' Guide on CLTS in Lao PDR* issued by the Ministry of Health, Government of Lao PDR, 2013. The process is included in the Ministry of Health's *Operational Program Guidelines for Scaling Up Rural Sanitation, 2013*.

6. Subsequently most countries have revised their ODF protocols, and now have much more elaborate criteria, and even several steps to become ODF. For details see Thomas and Bevan (2013).
7. For the monitoring system development and operationalization story see Mukherjee et al. (2011) and WSP (2014b).
8. See examples in a multi-study review by O'Connell (2014).
9. By 2015 this theory of change for rural sanitation has spread to 18 Asian, African, and Latin American countries through WSP's global SURSH initiative.
10. Regulation No. 3 of 2014 of the Ministry of Health of the Republic of Indonesia, concerning Community Based Total Sanitation.Ministry of Health of the Republic of Indonesia, 2014.
11. Penyediaan Air Minum dan Sanitasi berbasis Masyarakat (Safe Water Supply and Community-based Sanitation) project, Indonesia.

References

Badan Pusat Statistik, Statistics Centre (BPS) (2014) *Statistik Indonesia 2014*, Government of Indonesia, Jakarta.

Giltner, S., Dutton, P. and Kouangpalath, P. (2010) *Lao PDR Sanitation and Hygiene Financing Study*, Water and Sanitation Program, World Bank, Washington DC.

Government of Lao PDR, Ministry of Health and Lao Statistics Bureau (2012) *Lao Social Indicator Survey (LSIS) 2011–12*, Government of Lao PDR, Vientiane, https://dhsprogram.com/pubs/pdf/FR268/FR268.pdf [accessed 18 January 2016].

Government of Vietnam (2011) *Population and Employment Statistics in 2011*, General Statistics Office of Vietnam, Ha Noi, http://www.gso.gov.vn/default_en.aspx?tabid=467 [accessed 18 January 2016].

Government of Vietnam (2014) *Guideline for the Planning and Implementation of Rural Sanitation Programs: RWSS National Target Program 2012– 2015*, Health Environment Management Agency (VIHEMA), Ministry of Health.

Hanchett, S., Krieger, L., Kahn, M.H., Kullmann, C. and Ahmed, R. (2011) *Long-Term Sustainability of Improved Sanitation in Rural Bangladesh*, Water and Sanitation Program Working Paper 8, World Bank, Washington DC, https://openknowledge.worldbank.org/handle/10986/17347 [accessed 18 January 2016].

Hutton, G., Rodriguez, U., Larsen, B., Leebouapao, L. and Voladet, S. (2009) *Economic Impacts of Sanitation in Lao PDR: A Five-Country Study Conducted in Cambodia, Indonesia, Lao PDR, The Philippines, and Vietnam*, Research Report, Water and Sanitation Program East Asia and Pacific research report series, World Bank Group, Jakarta.

Ministry of Health (MoH) (2013) Republic of Indonesia, *Buku Saku Verikasi Sanitasi Total Berbasis Masyarakat* (Community-based Total Sanitation Verification Booklet), Directorate of Environmental Health, Jakarta.

MoH (2015) Government of Vietnam. *Capacity Building Strategy for Health System in Planning and Implementing Rural sanitation for the Period 2015–2020 and Vision to 2015*, Health Environment Management Agency (VIHEMA), Ministry of Health, Hanoi.

Mukherjee, N., Wartono D. and Robiarto, A. (2011) *Managing the Flow of Monitoring Information to Improve Rural Sanitation in East Java*, Water and Sanitation Program Working Paper, World Bank, Washington DC, http://www.wsp.org/sites/wsp.org/files/publications/WSP-Monitoring-Information-TSSM.pdf [accessed 18 January 2016].

Mukherjee, N. with Robiarto, A., Effentrif, S. and Wartono, D. (2012) *Achieving and Sustaining Open Defecation Free Communities: Learning from East Java*, Water and Sanitation Program Research Report, Word Bank, Washington DC, http://www.communityledtotalsanitation.org/sites/communityledtotalsanitation.org/files/WSP_Indonesia_Action_Research_Report.pdf [accessed 18 January 2016].

Neilson Indonesia (2009) *Total Sanitation and Sanitation Marketing Research Report*, Water and Sanitation Program, World Bank: Washington DC

O'Connell, K. (2014) *What Influences Open Defecation and Latrine Ownership in Rural Households? Findings from a Global Review*, Water and Sanitation Program Working Paper, World Bank, Washington DC, www.wsp.org/sites/wsp.org/files/publications/WSP-What-Influences-Open-Defecation-Global-Sanitation-Review.pdf [accessed 18 January 2016].

Pedi, D. and Kamasan, A. (forthcoming) *Sanitation Market Transformation in Indonesia: Designing Viable Business Models*, Water and Sanitation Program Field Note, World Bank, Washington, DC.

Quattri, M., Smets, S. and Nguyen, M. (2014) *Investing in the Next Generation: Children Grow Taller and Smarter, in Rural, Mountainous Villages of Vietnam Where Community Members Use Improved Sanitation*, Water and Sanitation Research Brief, World Bank, Washington, DC.

Setiawan, D. and Weitz, A. (2015) *How Transformational Changes in Rural Sanitation Service Delivery in Indonesia Accelerated* Access, The Water Blog 11 February, The World Bank, http://blogs.worldbank.org/water/how-transformational-changes-rural-sanitation-service-delivery-indonesia-accelerated-access [accessed 18 January 2016].

Spears, D. (2013) *The Nutritional Value of Toilets: How much Variation in Child Height can Sanitation Explain?* Working Paper, Research Institute for Compassionate Economics (RICE) http://riceinstitute.org/research/the-nutritional-value-of-toilets-how-much-international-variation-in-child-height-can-sanitation-explain/ [accessed 25 January 2016].

STBM (2010) *Panduan Verifikasi ODF di Komunitas* (Guideline for Verification of ODF in Communities), STBM/TSSM Leaflet, Sekretariat STBM, Jakarta, http://www.stbm-indonesia.org/files/Verifikasi%20ODF_Final%20March%205_pocketsize.pdf [accessed 19 January 2016].

Thomas, A. and Bevan, J. (2013) *Developing and Monitoring Protocol for the Elimination of Open Defecation in sub-Saharan Africa*, ODF Protocol, UNICEF, http://www.communityledtotalsanitation.org/sites/communityledtotalsanitation.org/files/Thomas_and_Bevan_Elimination_of_open_defecation_SSA.pdf [accessed 19 January 2016].

Tyndale-Biscoe, P., Bond, M. and Kidd, R. (2013) *ODF Sustainability Study*, FH Designs and Plan International, www.communityledtotalsanitation.org/resource/odf-sustainability-study-plan [accessed 19 January 2016].

UNDP (2010) *Human Development Report 2010. The Real Wealth of Nations: Pathways to Human Development*, United Nations Development Programme, New York NY.

UNDP (2013) *Human Development Report 2013. The Rise of the South: Human Progress in a Diverse World*, United Nations Development Programme, New York NY.

UNDP (2015) 'Goal 6: Ensure access to water and sanitation for all', Sustainable Development Goals, UNDP, http://www.un.org/sustainabledevelopment/water-and-sanitation [accessed 19 January 2016].

Vongkhamsao, V. and Weitz, A. (2015) *Strengthening Water Supply, Sanitation and Hygiene Sector Coordination in Lao PDR: Supporting Sector Reform for Scaling Up Rural Sanitation* – synthesis report. World Bank Working Paper, Report No: ACS12445, Washington, DC.

WHO/UNICEF (2012) *Progress on Drinking Water and Sanitation: 2012 Update*, WHO/UNICEF JMP, http://www.wssinfo.org/fileadmin/user_upload/resources/JMP-report-2012-en.pdf [accessed 19 January 2016].

WHO/UNICEF (2013) *Progress on Drinking Water and Sanitation: 2013 Update*, WHO/UNICEF JMP, http://www.wssinfo.org/fileadmin/user_upload/resources/JMPreport2013.pdf [accessed 19 January 2016].

WSP (2014a) *Investing in the Next Generation: Children Grow Taller and Smarter in Rural Villages in Lao PDR, Where All Community Members Use Improved Sanitation*, Water and Sanitation Program, Research Brief, World Bank, Washington, DC.

WSP (2014b) *Scaling Up Indonesia's Rural Sanitation Mobile Monitoring System Nationally*, Water and Sanitation Program Learning Note, World Bank, Washington, DC, http://wsp.org/sites/wsp.org/files/publications/WSP-Indonesia-Mobile-Monitoring.pdf [accessed 19 January 2016].

World Bank (2015) *Institutionalization of Rural Sanitation Capacity Building in Indonesia*, World Bank, Washington, DC, https://openknowledge.worldbank.org/handle/10986/22087 [accessed 19 January 2016].

CHAPTER 4

Strengthening post-ODF programming: reviewing lessons from sub-Saharan Africa

Ann Thomas

Abstract

Over 30,000 'open defecation free' or ODF communities exist across sub-Saharan Africa as a result of Community-Led Total Sanitation (CLTS) implementation. Country evaluations suggest that most ODF communities gradually 'slip' back to OD at an average rate of 10 per cent per year, suggesting significant losses over time. What is the nature of the support required to sustain ODF communities and what is known about slippage and mitigating programme innovations? This chapter discusses variations in implementation models as well as innovations in programming that have evolved in response to a limited private sector engagement in rural sub-Saharan Africa and the need to support ODF communities. The chapter also covers the issues of political prioritization of sanitation, the creation of an enabling environment, and the effective use of planning tools to allow CLTS to scale from a community approach to a national strategy for sanitation.

Keywords: Open defecation, ODF protocol, Sanitation, Sustainability, Rural sanitation, Scaling up, sub-Saharan Africa

Introduction

UNICEF piloted Community-Led Total Sanitation (CLTS) in Zambia in 2007, to help stop open defecation (OD) in rural communities. Quick results – communities mobilized and toilet construction – led local authorities to quickly scale the approach. Since then, CLTS spread to over 30 countries on the continent, which adopted CLTS as a primary strategy against rural OD. Over 30,000 'Open Defecation Free' or ODF communities (UNICEF, 2014a) now exist resulting from these efforts across sub-Saharan Africa. Country evaluations suggest that most ODF communities gradually 'slip' back to OD at an average rate of 10 per cent per year, suggesting significant losses over time. This chapter focuses on the nature of the support required, beginning with insights on slippage and programme design innovations from UNICEF's rural sanitation programming in the continent. The chapter then discusses the issue of political prioritization of sanitation, enabling environment, and the effective use of planning tools to allow CLTS to scale from a community approach to a national strategy for sanitation.

http://dx.doi.org/10.3362/9781780449272.004

Sustainability and slippage

Figure 4.1 shows a typical CLTS programme trajectory: triggering leading to sustained facilities and behaviours, and possibly other positive improvements with certification and beyond. Figure 4.2 shows the results from sustainability checks in Mozambique in 2013, which revealed a 10 per cent annual slippage rate in ODF communities. Over time, slippage can be significant, with a five year horizon leading to a 50 per cent return to OD behaviour. Slippage of this magnitude, confirmed by other studies (Tyndale-Biscoe et al., 2013) which seem to suggest similar results across the continent, indicates that ODF outcomes are not stable and require further inputs to continue on the intended trajectory.

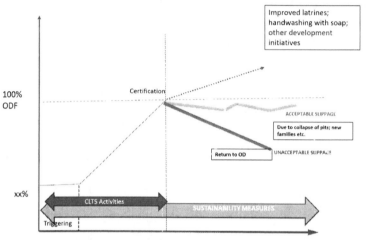

Figure 4.1 Timeline to ODF in a typical sanitation project cycle
Source: UNICEF, 2013

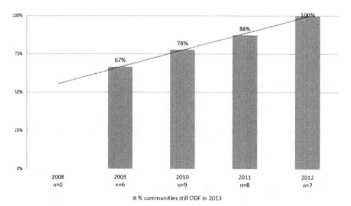

Figure 4.2 Percentage of communities in Mozambique that had been declared ODF in the previous five years that remained ODF in 2013
Source: UNICEF Mozambique sustainability check 2013

In discussing sustainability and slippage, it's useful to understand what happens after a typical CLTS intervention. Beyond certification or beyond ODF, most communities are left on their own to improve and sustain their sanitation facilities and behaviours. Programmes typically are designed with ODF as a specific end target yet there is an expectation that the trajectory keeps moving upward (much as in Figure 4.1) toward other development gains (i.e. handwashing, general community cleanliness etc.). The reality is that construction with temporary building materials (grass, sticks, mud), low building standards (such as unlined pits, unstable squatting areas) or climate extremes (heavy rain, flooding) can confound even the best efforts to maintain ODF behaviours. Kenya's recent ODF sustainability study showed that technical issues relating to toilet construction were the primary cause of slippage in ODF communities two years post-ODF (Singh and Balfour, 2015b). So the need to upgrade and improve toilets for durability in places where services and materials are hard to come by, which is a fairly common phenomenon in rural sub-Saharan Africa, leaves communities at a serious disadvantage for improving their toilets.

Technical considerations aside, a failure to ensure sustainability of behaviours, or rather to instil a lasting social norm, has also been identified as an issue affecting sustainability of outcomes (Maule, 2013). UNICEF Kenya's ODF sustainability study showed a strong correlation between social cohesion factors and retention of ODF behaviours two years after certification but it also showed that, where children were not included as part of the sensitization and norm-building activities, children were a defining variable in post-ODF slippage (Singh and Balfour, 2015b). Post-ODF monitoring, or lack thereof, is often blamed as a primary reason for sustained ODF status. Yet, a series of studies related to a national CLTS programme in Mali with limited post-ODF monitoring and high sustainability of ODF suggest otherwise. Clearly, further studies are needed to understand more systematically what impacts sustainability.

Post-ODF: emerging best practice in social norms development

The quality of facilitation and engagement with local leadership are critical factors in how well communities are mobilized and incentivized to maintain behaviours. Several countries, particularly those where remote, traditional communities are reluctant to adopt new behaviours, are turning more to the support of local authorities and community outreach mechanisms to strengthen CLTS. Similarly, countries with large-scale programmes are looking to leverage the support and influence of powerful traditional leaders to improve the performance of CLTS programmes.

Leveraging local leadership

In Zambia and Malawi, local chiefs still command enormous respect and exercise power over their constituencies. Ensuring buy-in for CLTS from these traditional authorities has provided strong support in both countries to ensure that communities are receptive to facilitators, to lead enforcement and follow-up of ODF status within the communities. The chiefs are able to reinforce the new 'normal' and make it acceptable to the local communities in a more meaningful and lasting way than is possible through either non-governmental organizations (NGO) or local government support teams. Further, the chiefs are able to work with the government in lobbying for resources and advocating for further investment in sanitation. However, it is important to avoid situations where people with existing power within the community drive the process, and local social-political contexts and relations are considered when champions or natural leaders are identified (Bardosh, 2015). Natural leaders, or 'key influencers' should be selected from all sections of the community (see Dooley et al., 2016, this book; Wamera, 2016, this book). This will help to ensure poorer and marginalized sections of the community are not excluded from the process.

Social norms from theory to action in Madagascar

In Madagascar, social norms theory has been translated into practical action on the ground to help move isolated, traditional communities from OD to ODF. 'Institutional triggering' is one example of a systematized process by which networks of influence are mapped and key influential stakeholders in districts are met and convinced of the CLTS approach prior to triggering communities. Public declarations or 'Shit Festivals' are a second. Public declarations and plans following the intent to abandon the behaviour of OD are used to hold communities accountable for their commitment by other villages and observers to the process. Finally, value deliberations are applied one village at a time, introducing customary laws (or dinas) that can support the upholding of the new social norm. The advantages of this changing behaviour include health benefits and savings in health costs (Gaya et al., 2015).

Specific inclusion of children in norm-building activities

Kenya's experience suggests that children are an important element in maintaining ODF within a community and, as such, that they should be specifically targeted both in mobilization activities (i.e. through the school and community) as well as technically speaking, in terms of toilet solutions that suit small children (Singh and Balfour, 2015b).

Post-ODF: emerging best practice in technical support and monitoring

Sanitation marketing is typically the programming option of choice to upgrade toilets. Sanitation marketing relies on development of more appropriately designed toilets, engagement of the private sector and better insight into consumer motivations. In many regions of the continent it is simply unfeasible *in the short-term* to consider that the private sector will develop business models to serve remote, disparate populations. The sector, particularly in rural areas, suffers from fragmentation, overpriced and inappropriate products, and physical inaccessibility. Affordable products are in short supply across sub-Saharan Africa, and this would be perhaps a solid medium-term venture for the development community to help stimulate the proliferation of the products and their eventual distribution much in the same way that the generic vaccines business was greatly supported (see Coombes, 2016, this book). For the short-term, more immediate solutions to support communities are evolving with less reliance on the private sector as described below.

Participatory design as part of a hybrid approach to sanitation marketing

In countries such as Malawi the high cost of cement in rural areas means that communities might have to rebuild mud-based toilets annually after rainy seasons. This presents an opportunity for relapse or 'slippage' to OD behaviours. From a programming perspective, this annual cycle has driven a process of participatory design targeted at filling the knowledge and capacity gaps for local government and entrepreneurs in durable and low-cost toilet design. This process ensures users participate in creating and selecting sanitation technologies that are appropriate and affordable for them (Cole, 2013, 2015). Furthermore, Malawi uses a hybrid sanitation marketing approach, integrating participatory design and sanitation marketing principles to create a market for low-cost, durable, and locally available products.

Community coaches

In Madagascar, where rural communities can be so physically isolated that business development is unlikely to be successful, communities are supported for a longer period post-ODF to develop improved toilets through the training and support of community coaches. The coaches are well versed in the construction of durable designs and are able to support communities in developing solid toilets from the initiation of CLTS triggering visits through to post-ODF periods. The coaches come from within the communities, and generally they are already the voluntary community health workers, so the support itself is local and easily accessible. They themselves are then provided with a mentor coach who reviews the quality of toilet construction and is able to support capacity development as needed.

Triggering and follow-up by community health workers (CHWs)

In Ethiopia and Malawi, paid community health workers are being trained to support toilet upgrading. Malawi's health workers are paid by local government and accountable to a set of villages, enabling them to provide a continuity of support; they are also a channel to local government for accessing further resources where needed. In Ethiopia, the health workers are part of a highly structured workforce for which training modules are developed related to supporting, not only CLTS, but also sanitation marketing methods. This approach suggests better sustainability and scalability through government resourced and led programming compared with other approaches (see Box 4.1).

Integration of ODF indicators as part of routine health monitoring at district level

In Somalia, where district health programming is still in a development phase, ODF indicators have been integrated as part of routine health monitoring, allowing districts to leverage minimal staffing structures and ensure the prioritization of sanitation as part of basic health programming.

Box 4.1 Comparison of CLTS implementation models in sub-Saharan Africa

There is great variety in how CLTS programmes are implemented in sub-Saharan Africa. At the triggering and community support level, some programmes rely heavily on unpaid natural leaders, some programmes pay natural leaders, some rely on paid NGO support to communities, and others leverage paid community health workers. Understanding which models work best and are most cost-effective under what circumstances remains to be fully understood. A few lessons based on UNICEF's work in Eastern and Southern Africa, include:

- The NGO model in Mozambique which used NGO staff to lead triggering and monitoring efforts initially yielded results. However, several years later sustainability reports showed a gradual loss of ODF status and further that the political buy-in needed to continue to scale the approach did not exist either at rural or national levels. The approach was considered expensive for the results delivered. The programme had set up parallel monitoring and support mechanisms at the rural level and did not leverage existing government resources of the health sector or local authorities to increase comprehension and support for the programme.

- In Zambia, local champions have been selected to provide support and monitoring of communities. The 'professionalization' of these champions refers to training and results based payments (i.e. phone credits) intended to help keep the champions motivated and sustain support to communities on a national scale. This approach is relatively recent and its merit will be tested when external funding is lifted.

- In Malawi, health workers are paid by local government and accountable to a set of villages, enabling them to provide a continuity of support; they are also a channel to local government for accessing further resources where needed. In Ethiopia, the health workers are part of a highly structured workforce for which training modules are developed related to supporting not only CLTS but also sanitation marketing methods. A dedicated health worker, available and accountable, who makes sanitation a health priority is a strong asset for a community. They should be identified at the pre-triggering stage, and could potentially continue post-ODF follow-up as part of their existing role (see Wamera, 2016, this book). In the few countries that have well-structured paid health worker programmes, this model shows great potential for scalability.

- In Somalia, NGOs work with fledgling institutions to support local communities and structures in maintaining ODF. A central theme in this case has been one of leveraging minimal resources at community, government, and NGO levels in a difficult context. One innovation here has been the inclusion of ODF as a health indicator to be monitored by local health workers. In this case, NGOs, government, and communities have worked together to find solutions for sustained monitoring and support.

The question of which model works best is yet to be answered but certainly as the examples above illustrate, there are clues as to the right direction and getting the mix right in each context. The implementation experience in Eastern and Southern Africa provides rich learning for good programme design and for which further evaluation and comparison of costs and outcomes is needed.

Political prioritization and equity

In the last 15 years, OD has declined across sub-Saharan Africa by a quarter. However, as countries become more middle income, it's not a given that OD will improve for the bottom wealth quintile. Joint Monitoring Programme (JMP) data over a 17 year period (1995–2012) suggests that countries like Ethiopia and Mali, classified as least developed countries (LDCs), are making positive improvements in OD reduction for their poorest through investments in national sanitation programmes (WHO/UNICEF, 2015). Ethiopia made impressive gains for the WASH sector, by placing water supply at the core of its development agenda, reaching its Millennium Development Goal for water supply from 14 per cent to 57 per cent access to safe water supply between 1990 and 2015. Although water supply was the primary target, sanitation benefited from WASH being on the national agenda. There was an increase in improved sanitation from 3 per cent to 28 per cent and OD rates dropped from 93 per cent to 45 per cent (UNICEF, 2014b).

However, governments in countries such as Kenya, Cameroon, and Ghana, classified as middle income countries (MICs), are not having the same impact on their rural poor as Ethiopia, despite having national sanitation programmes. Ethiopia's annual rate of OD reduction exceeds that of more developed and well-resourced countries in sub-Saharan Africa. But what explains Ethiopia's success compared to its neighbours in the continent? Namibia provides some insight as to why some populations do not develop in tandem with the rest of the country. The apartheid system, introduced into Namibia in 1964 under South African rule, left deep social and economic divides in Namibian society. A large country with a small population, Namibia has only a tiny proportion of the population that enjoys considerable wealth and access to resources. The rest of the population, generally rural, lives in poverty. Rural WASH access rates reflect this socio-economic division. Rural OD rates are high while urban improved sanitation rates are fairly high. The implication is that the majority of Namibians live with extremely high levels of OD and regular cholera outbreaks, second only to South Sudan (see Table 4.1), despite Namibia being a middle income country. Namibia illustrates the fact that poorly progressing OD rates can be the signal for larger issues of inclusion, political prioritization, and planning, while Ethiopia illustrates that rapid change is possible with political prioritization in lesser developed countries.

Ensuring quality of large-scale elimination of OD: the next frontier

Countries such as Kenya, Zambia, Ethiopia, and Malawi have declared national ODF targets, with CLTS as the primary vehicle for eliminating OD. No country has managed to achieve a national ODF target, although the declaration (and in many cases failure to achieve) of targets have led in some cases to national self-reflection and a galvanizing of the sanitation sector. It has also shed light on sloppy monitoring and data collection methods. Overall, one of the interesting side products of setting and failure to achieve

Table 4.1. Similarities and differences in sanitation access rates Namibia and South Sudan 2011-2015

Country	Year	Urban		Rural	
		Total Improved (%)	Open Defecation (%)	Total Improved (%)	Open Defecation (%)
Namibia	2011	55.5	18.9	15.7	74.5
	2012	55.2	19.2	16.0	74.2
	2013	55.0	19.6	16.3	73.9
	2014	54.7	19.9	16.6	73.5
	2015	54.5	20.3	16.8	73.2
South Sudan	2011	16.4	49.8	4.5	79.2
	2012	16.4	49.8	4.5	79.2
	2013	16.4	49.8	4.5	79.2
	2014	16.4	49.8	4.5	79.2
	2015	16.4	49.8	4.5	79.2

Source: wssinfo.org, accessed 18 August 2015

ODF national targets has been the more rigorous analysis of planning and investment for scale-up that have underpinned the efforts and a closer look at costing and resources required to achieve scale. Countries are increasingly interested in tools that allow them to systematically consider the human and financial resources, political buy-in and leadership, and effective monitoring and coordination that are needed to develop an effective national sanitation programme (Wijesekera and Thomas, 2015).

Providing meaningful metrics for CLTS at a mass scale is critical for evaluating and improving performance of these programmes. This goes beyond measuring ODF communities. Since CLTS requires significant investment into building political capital and leadership within government, achievements in this domain need also to be measured and considered as part of success or failure of a programme. Monitoring implementation outcomes without monitoring institutional outcomes (e.g. political will, financing etc.) would provide an incomplete picture of the national programme.

Fortunately, several tools are emerging to support an articulation of both enabling environment and implementation progress and sustainability. Although far from meeting all the needs of the sector, they represent tools which can be useful to the practitioner or government official in taking stock of progress and gaps in a national programme. Learning how to use and improve on these needs to be part of the sanitation professionals' new skillset. Following is a discussion of a selection of tools and how and when they are best used.

Microplanning

Kenya recently underwent an exercise in microplanning led by UNICEF (Singh and Balfour, 2015a). This was an in-depth study looking at how a national-level policy and targets for ODF translated to implementation at the county level. Each county was comprehensively assessed in terms of human, political, and financial resources that would enable effective roll-out at sub-national level (county level). The exercise revealed serious shortcomings in budget allocation, training, and partnerships development (see Figure 4.3), to support effective scaling-up of CLTS across the country. Effectively, it also showed serious shortcomings in political buy-in at the county level, along with failures to adequately resource the national roadmap from both a financial and capacity perspective (see Musyoki, 2016, this book and Wamera, 2016, this book).

The micro-plan provides accurate financial figures needed at the county level to reach ODF and, as such, it provides a basic orientation for counties interested in truly taking on the approach. It also is an opportunity to raise the profile of sanitation within countries and counties. The tool could also be developed further to factor in post-ODF costs (Wamera, 2016, this book).

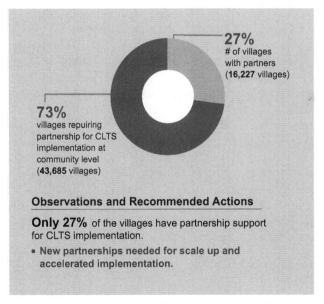

27%
# of villages
with partners
(**16,227** villages)

73%
villages repuiring
partnership for CLTS
implementation at
community level
(**43,685** villages)

Observations and Recommended Actions

Only 27% of the villages have partnership support
for CLTS implementation.

• **New partnerships needed for scale up and
  accelerated implementation.**

Figure 4.3 Review of partnerships required for CLTS implementation in Kakamega County, Kenya
Source: Singh and Balfour, 2015a

Sustainability checks

Initially intended for water supply, sustainability checks (see Figure 4.4 for an example) have now been applied in the context of sanitation in countries

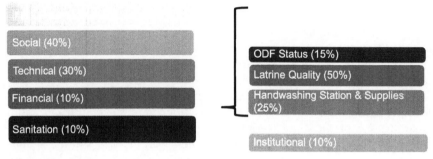

Figure 4.4 Sustainability Check Framework, Mozambique
Source: UNICEF PowerPoint presentation

such as Mozambique, Rwanda, Malawi, and Zambia (Godfrey et al., 2009; Schweitzer et al., 2014). They are designed to support better understanding of how sanitation behaviours and facilities are maintained over time. They are a performance-oriented tool, undergoing continual adjustment to better reflect the complexity of the sanitation sector.

CLTS Rapid Appraisal Protocol (CRAP)

The CRAP tool (an extract of which is shown in Table 4.2), currently being tested and developed by UNICEF and the CLTS Foundation, will seek to provide support to countries undergoing a rapid expansion of CLTS programmes and those interested in ensuring quality in the scale-up process. A five to seven day participatory process, CRAP aims to support national governments in reflecting on the programmes and where adjustments may be needed to support effective scaling. The tool explores six pillars of CLTS programmes at the national, sub-national, and community level, as detailed in Table 4.2. Each pillar has two to three indicators at each level that cumulatively give a sense of where constraints may lie within the context of a national programme and helps to stimulate self-reflection by key stakeholders. The methodology for CRAP is largely focused on focus group discussions, key information interviews, and plenary debate intended to support self-directed dialogue rather than an extractive process of external-led evaluation.

Table 4.2. CLTS Rapid Appraisal Protocol (CRAP) dashboard

Pillars	Key questions at national and sub-national levels
Policy, roadmap and directives	**Is there strategy and political buy-in to drive CLTS?**
	Is CLTS in the national sanitation policy along with requisite directives/guidelines?
	Is there a national roadmap with target, timelines, and milestones?
	Is there a clear lead ministry for rural sanitation?
	Is there a regional roadmap/plan with target, timelines, and milestones?

Table 4.2. CLTS Rapid Appraisal Protocol (CRAP) dashboard

Financial planning and budgeting	**Is financial planning and resourcing of CLTS adequate/realistic?**
	Is there a government budget line for national rural sanitation programming?
	Does the budget allocated at national level correlate to national rollout/roadmap plan?
	Is the budget allocation for rural sanitation used for CLTS activities?
	Is there a sub-national/regional plan consistent with the national plan?
	Is the sub-national/regional budget for sanitation sufficient to fund planned CLTS activities?
CLTS protocol	**Is there one agreed CLTS protocol applied consistently nation-wide?**
	Is there one national ODF protocol that has been endorsed by the national government?
	Does the protocol cover all relevant aspects including post-ODF aspects?
	Is the protocol followed by all CLTS partners in country?
	Is the national protocol (verification/certification/definition) well understood and adopted by the sub-national/regional authorities?
	Is there a clear, scalable, and accountable (i.e. third party or some such) verification and certification process in play at this level?
Partnerships, capacity, and leadership	**Are there sufficient partnerships, capacity and leadership to sustain the programme?**
	Are sufficient partnerships in place at national level to reach targeted communities across the country with CLTS?
	Is there any functional coordination mechanism among various partners to share resource/capacity?
	Are master trainers in place with requisite training materials/guidelines at national level to support training efforts?
	Is there a sufficient number of trained master facilitators to support CLTS implementation?
Monitoring and coordination	**How is information captured and used for programmatic coordination?**
	Is there a comprehensive and functional monitoring system linking local-regional-national information?
	Is there consistency between the data collected and the national CLTS protocol?
	Is monitoring data fed back into coordination platforms/other levels as applicable/available?
	Are monitoring indicators consistent with national CLTS protocol?

(Continue)

Table 4.2. CLTS Rapid Appraisal Protocol (CRAP) dashboard (*Continued*)

Post-ODF sustainability	**Are mechanisms in place to ensure sustainability of behaviours and facilities post-ODF?**
	Is post-ODF sustainability addressed as part of national ODF strategies?
	Are national level efforts being made to engage the private (formal/informal) sector in sanitation?
	Is there an institutional capacity building mechanism to support post-ODF research?
	Is there a mechanism for engagement of the private (formal/informal) sector?
	Is there an institutional system to support and monitor post-ODF actions?
	Is a process/system of participatory technology development, institutional capacity building?

Box 4.2. Issues for community-level interaction for CLTS

Policy to practice

- In the perception of community leaders, do local government authorities understand the importance of CLTS and do they ever mention achieving national ODF objectives?
- Do community leaders understand the shift from toilet construction to collective behaviour change?

CLTS protocol

- Is there a clear understanding of CLTS process and protocol by the facilitation teams?
- Is the average time between triggering to ODF under three months?
- Are communities aware of options of safe sanitation and able to access relevant information?

Partnership, capacity, and leadership

- Do target villages have assigned trained facilitators (ratio)?
- Are there formal mechanisms to engage Natural Leaders in the scaling up process?
- Are community leaders aware of the CLTS programme and do they understand its importance?
- Have traditional/clan/religious leaders been leveraged to support rollout?

Monitoring

- Is there a community-led monitoring and verification system in place to collect and feed local data into the regional/national monitoring system?
- Is there clear comprehension of monitoring requirements by the frontline staff?

Post-ODF action

- Is there evidence of leveraging collective action to move up the sanitation ladder and other development benefits?
- Is there capacity building, access to skills/information/materials and low cost design or products to support improved sanitation?
- Is there a process for engagement of traditional authorities to support/enforce ODF as a social norm?
- Is there a system of post-ODF monitoring and support system for upgrading?

Source: Kar et al., forthcoming

Final thoughts: lessons to strengthen sustainability

CLTS has evolved from a community mobilization approach for sanitation into the most widely adopted strategy of national rural sanitation programmes globally. With this shift, from method to policy, comes a need to build out the approach to address core issues of sustainability: budgeting, programme design, equity and inclusion among others, to truly go to scale with quality.

We have learned that CLTS, done well, works for changing behaviours and achieving sanitation outcomes better than any other approach the sector has seen. It's also clear that sustaining behaviours is difficult and most programmes lose out on their initial efforts by not investing more resources into the factors that will ultimately sustain both behaviours and structures. *Often these factors imply complementing interventions – beyond CLTS – that will sustain behaviour change; a contextual application of interventions needed on both the demand and supply side of sanitation.* Understanding these factors and systematically applying the knowledge into programmes is a sector priority.

Putting it all together at a meaningful scale with the right investments in capacity building, local leadership, coordination, and strategy is the ultimate goal. Sector diagnostic tools are a step in the direction towards understanding what makes CLTS work at scale, and their use is becoming more ubiquitous as countries look for more evidence-based ways of making policy and decisions for the sector.

The following chapters in this book will address these dimensions with more specific cases and insights from around the world.

About the author

Ann Thomas is UNICEF's Sanitation and Hygiene Adviser in Eastern and Southern Africa based in Nairobi, Kenya. She has more than 15 years of global experience working on issues of water, sanitation, and hygiene with UNICEF, World Bank, WSP, Oxfam, and the International Development Research Centre (IDRC).

Endnote

1. Study on willingness to pay for sanitation in CLTS villages, University of South Florida, 2011–2012 (100 households in six villages surveyed 1.5 to 2 years after CLTS triggering) (Meeks, 2012); impact evaluation of CLTS, University of La Plata/PEP network, 2011–2014 (60 intervention villages and 60 control villages surveyed before implementation and again one year after the end of programme operation, between five and 20 months after ODF certification) (Alzua et al., 2015); impact evaluation of WASH in schools, Emory University, 2011–2014 (100 intervention schools and 100 control schools surveyed before, during, and after implementation, for some schools up to 25 months after they had benefitted from the CLTS+SLTS triggering session) (Trinies et al., 2015).

References

Alzua, M.L., Pickering, A., Djebbari, H., Lopez, C., Cardenas, J., Lopera, M., Osbert, N. and Coulibaly, M. (2015) *Final report: Impact evaluation of community-led total sanitation (CLTS) in rural Mali*, University of La Plata/PEP network, www.communityledtotalsanitation.org/resource/impact-evaluation-clts-rural-mali [accessed 18 February 2016].

Bardosh, K. (2015) 'Achieving "total sanitation" in rural African geographies: poverty, participation and pit latrines in eastern Zambia', *Geoforum*, 66: 53–63 <http://dx.doi.org/10.1016/j.geoforum.2015.09.004>.

Cole, B. (2013) 'Participatory design development for sanitation', *Frontiers of CLTS*, 1, Institute of Development Studies, Brighton, www.community ledtotalsanitation.org/sites/communityledtotalsanitation.org/files/media/Frontiers_of_CLTS_Issue1_PartDesign_0.pdf [accessed 18 February 2016].

Cole, B. (2015) 'Going beyond ODF: combining sanitation marketing with participatory approaches to sustain ODF communities in Malawi', *Eastern and Southern Africa Sanitation and Hygiene Learning Series*, UNICEF, New York NY, www.communityledtotalsanitation.org/sites/communityledtotalsanitation.org/files/GoingBeyondODF_CombiningSanMark_with_Participatory Approaches_Malawi.pdf [accessed 18 February 2016].

Coombes, Y. (2016) 'User centred latrine guidelines. Integrating CLTS with sanitation marketing: a case study from Kenya to promote informed choice', in P. Bongartz, N. Vernon and J. Fox (eds.) *Sustainable Sanitation for All: Experiences, Challenges, and Innovations*, Practical Action, Rugby.

Dooley, T., Maule, L. and Gnilo, M. (2016) 'Using social norms theory to strengthen CATS impact and sustainability', in P. Bongartz, N. Vernon and J. Fox (eds.) *Sustainable Sanitation for All: Experiences, Challenges, and Innovations*, Practical Action, Rugby.

Gaya, S., Balfour, N. and Thomas, A. (2015) 'Using social norms theory to strengthen CLTS in southern Madagascar', *Eastern and Southern Africa Sanitation and Hygiene Learning Series*, UNICEF, New York NY.

Godfrey, S., Freitas, M., Muianga, A., Amaro, M., Fernadez, P. and Sousa Mosies, L. (2009) *Sustainability Check: A Monitoring Tool for the Sustainability of Rural Water Supplies*, 34th WEDC International Conference, Addis Ababa, http://wedc.lboro.ac.uk/resources/conference/34/Godfrey_S_-_719.pdf [accessed 18 February 2016].

Kar, K., Pradhan, S.K., Thomas, A., Harvey, P. and Prabhakaran, P. (forthcoming) *CLTS Rapid Appraisal Protocol (CRAP): A Tool for Rapid Assessment of the Practice of CLTS at Scale*, UNICEF ESARO, Nairobi.

Maule, L. (2013) *Using Social Norms Theory to Strengthen UNICEF's CATS Programmes*, UNICEF, New York NY, www.sas.upenn.edu/ppe/Events/uniconf_2013/documents/Maule.Louise_FinalPaper_UsingSocial NormsTheorytoStrengthenUNICEFsCATSProgrammes.pdf [accessed 18 February 2016].

Meeks, J. (2012) *Willingness-to-Pay for Maintenance and Improvements to Existing Sanitation Infrastructure: Assessing Community-Led Total Sanitation in Mopti, Mali*, MA thesis, University of South Florida, Tampa, FL.

Musyoki, S. (2016) 'Roles and responsibilities for post-ODF engagement: building an enabling institutional environment for CLTS sustainability', in P. Bongartz, N. Vernon and J. Fox (eds.) *Sustainable Sanitation for All: Experiences, Challenges, and Innovations*, Practical Action, Rugby.

Singh, S. and Balfour, N. (2015a) 'Micro-planning for CLTS: Experience from Kenya', *Eastern and Southern Africa Sanitation and Hygiene Learning Series*, UNICEF, New York NY, www.communityledtotalsanitation.org/resource/ micro-planning-clts-experience-kenya [accessed 18 February 2016].

Singh, S. and Balfour, N. (2015b) *Sustainability and Impact of ODF Practices in Kenya*, Eastern and Southern Africa Sanitation and Hygiene Learning Series, UNICEF, New York NY.

Schweitzer, R., Grayson, C. and Lockwood, H. (2014) *Mapping of WASH Sustainability Tools*, Working Paper 10, IRC, The Hague, Netherlands, www.ircwash. org/sites/default/files/triple-s_wp10mappingofwashsustainabilitytools.pdf [accessed 18 February 2016].

Trinies, V., Ghulamali, S. and Freeman, M. (2015) *Dubai Cares Water, Sanitation and Hygiene (WASH) in Schools Initiative in Mali (DCIM)*, Emory University, Atlanta.

Tyndale-Biscoe, P., Bond, M. and Kidd, R. (2013) *ODF Sustainability Study*, FH Designs and Plan International, www.communityledtotalsanitation.org/ resource/odf-sustainability-study-plan [accessed 18 February 2016].

UNICEF (2014a) *Evaluation of the WASH Sector Strategy 'Community Approaches to Total Sanitation' (CATS)*, UNICEF, New York NY, www.unicef.org/evaluation/ files/Evaluation_of_the_WASH_Sector_Strategy_FINAL_VERSION_ March_2014.pdf [accessed 18 February 2016].

UNICEF (2014b) *UNICEF Sanitation Priority Country Factsheet Ethiopia 2014*, UNICEF, http://www.unicef.org/ethiopia/Ethiopia_Fact_Sheet_Jan_2014._ final.pdf [accessed 24 February 2016].

Wamera, E. (2016) 'Who is managing the post-ODF process in the community? A case study of Nambale sub-county in Western Kenya', in P. Bongartz, N. Vernon and J. Fox (eds.) *Sustainable Sanitation for All: Experiences, Challenges, and Innovations*, Practical Action, Rugby.

WHO/UNICEF (2015) *Progress on Drinking Water and Sanitation: 2015 Update and MDG Assessment*, Joint Monitoring Programme (JMP), UNICEF/WHO, Geneva, www.wssinfo.org/fileadmin/user_upload/resources/JMP-Update-report-2015_English.pdf [accessed 18 February 2016].

Wijesekera, S. and Thomas, A. (2015) 'Taking stock: reaching the bottom billion: beyond open defecation', *Waterlines*, 34(3): 206–9 <http://dx.doi. org/10.3362/1756-3488.2015.020>.

PART II: Physical sustainability

CHAPTER 5

CLTS and sanitation marketing: aspects to consider for a better integrated approach

Twitty Munkhondia, Warren Mukelabai Simangolwa and Alfonso Zapico Maceda[1]

Abstract

This chapter draws on experiences of three large sanitation programmes in Malawi, Tanzania, and Zambia, and discusses eight aspects to consider when integrating Community-Led Total Sanitation (CLTS) and sanitation marketing: phasing; affordability; financing; the supply chain; masons and entrepreneurs; informed choice; technology; and monitoring. Working out the optimal moment to phase sanitation marketing and CLTS to ensure that community initiative and the behaviour change process is not stifled by imposing inappropriate or unaffordable designs, is still part of our emerging learning. The chapter discusses programme experiences, where progression up the sanitation ladder has been slow, with many households remaining with basic, unimproved toilets. Identified in all the programmes was the need to develop low-cost, durable, and acceptable products that respond to the needs of all.

Keywords: Sanitation ladder, Sanitation marketing, Sanitation supply chains, Sanitation financing, Masons and entrepreneurs, Informed choice materials

Introduction

Post-ODF (open defecation free status), there is an assumption that households will climb the sanitation ladder and upgrade their toilet over time; however there is no guarantee this will happen (Thomas, 2014). Post-triggering, gains made in behaviour change and demand for sanitation facilities can be undone by lack of timely support and information on appropriate toilet technology (Coombes, 2016, this book). Consequently, it is not uncommon to find households working hard to construct pit toilets that will only have a life span of a few months because they are built in unsuitable conditions such as sandy soil or high water table areas with frequent flooding (Phiri, 2010; Hanchett et al., 2011). Poor construction and materials are a significant factor in the decision to abandon toilets (Cavill et al., 2015): households with access to technical support are more likely to maintain their toilets (Tyndale-Biscoe et al., 2013). When toilets collapse, costs to rebuild may be too high, and people may

http://dx.doi.org/10.3362/9781780449272.005

revert to OD (Thomas, 2014). Negative perceptions and a loss of trust in toilets can also reduce motivation to re-build (O'Connell, 2014). Context-appropriate technical design is therefore required (Sugden, 2003; WaterAid, n.d.).

Ensuring that households have easy and convenient access to materials and parts is another key challenge in moving up the sanitation ladder. Supply chains are often fragmented, and the 'last mile' consumers (i.e. the poorest or most isolated communities) tend not to have access. Missing 'are the skills and activities to transform these materials into a product or service for the rural poor' (Thomas, 2014: 3). Poor, marginalized or hard-to-reach people are often not able to afford the sanitation products available, since prices for materials are driven up by high transportation costs and lack of competition, and even when financing options are established, such as vouchers or microfinance loans, often the poorest will not meet the criteria to be approved for a loan (Jenkins and Pedi, n.d.).

A successful approach will consider and integrate the aspects outlined in Figure 5.1.

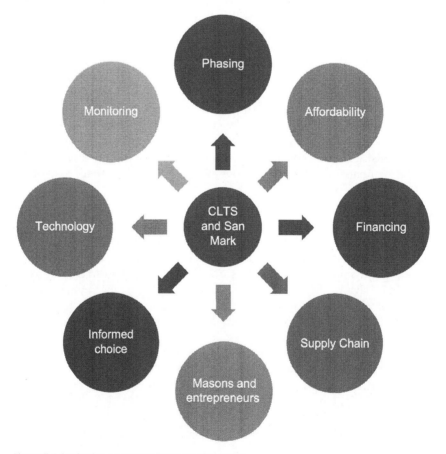

Figure 5.1 Sanitation marketing integrated approach
Source: Author's own

Figure 5.1 shows eight aspects to consider when integrating Community-Led Total Sanitation (CLTS) and sanitation marketing; these are explored in turn in this chapter. Working out when to phase in which one, and what the optimal order is, is still part of our emerging learning. However, this chapter aims to set out current experience based on the learning from three scaled-up sanitation programmes: the Accelerated Sanitation and Hygiene Promotion Programme (ASHPP) in Malawi; the Usafi wa Mazingira Tanzania programme (UMATA) (both programmes funded by the Global Sanitation Fund, GSF); and SNV's Department for International Development (DFID) funded Sustainable Sanitation and Hygiene for All (SSH4A) results-based programme and its water, sanitation, and hygiene (WASH) sector partnerships in Zambia. These are countries where large parts of the rural population use traditional toilets and where sanitation actors are grappling with how to promote ODF sustainability and at the same time support households to move up the sanitation ladder. Experience in these settings suggests that the timely introduction of context-specific sanitation marketing can speed up the household's ability to climb the sanitation ladder (Kappauf, 2011; GSF, 2014). The programmes are described in more detail in Box 5.1.

Box 5.1 Scaled-up sanitation programme descriptions

The work described in this chapter relates principally to three sanitation programmes:

UMATA 'Usafi wa Mazingira Tanzania', funded by the Water Supply and Sanitation Collaborative Council (WSSCC) through the GSF, is one of the first initiatives of sanitation at scale, which was designed to strengthen the Tanzanian National Sanitation Campaign. Its first phase was implemented since the last quarter of 2013 until April 2016 in three districts of Dodoma Region, Bahi, Chamwino, and Kongwa. Sanitation marketing, CLTS, and microfinance are developed at the same time. In Kongwa, ONGAWA is in charge of sanitation marketing, with Lay Volunteers International Association (LVIA) as a local partner. Research about sanitation technologies is key and is supported and conducted by the Polytechnic University of Madrid in partnership with Ardhi University.

Plan International Malawi serves as Executing Agency for the **Accelerated Sanitation and Hygiene Practices Programme (ASHPP)**, a five year initiative supported by the WSSCC through the Global Sanitation Fund (GSF). Through sub grantees, ASHPP has been running since December 2010 and it aims to reach out to up to 1.06 million people by the end of 2015, applying CLTS and sanitation marketing approaches. Over 60 per cent of the people in the targeted districts of Rumphi, Nkhotakota, Ntchisi, Balaka, Phalombe, and Chikhwawa are living in an ODF environment.

SNV Zambia has been implementing the DFID-funded Sustainable **Sanitation and Hygiene for All (SSH4A)** Results Programme since April 2014. Its goal is to improve access to sanitation and promote good hygiene practices especially handwashing with soap. The targets are:
By the end of 2015:

- 250,000 people reached through hygiene promotion
- 230,000 people gain access to sanitation

By the end of 2017:

- 115,000 people further improve their sanitation facilities to the Joint Monitoring Programme (JMP) benchmark
- 80,000 people practise handwashing with soap

Sanitation market development was implemented in two phases – prior to and soon after sanitation demand creation.

The rest of this chapter describes the eight aspects to consider for integration of CLTS and sanitation marketing based on the learning from these three programmes.

Phasing

There is a need for more evidence on the optimal moment for sequencing sanitation marketing. Is it before, during, or after triggering? At follow-up meetings? After ODF achievement? As market research, product, and business model development, and the creation of marketing and supply chain strategies, all require substantial time, recent experiences suggest that these initial steps of the sanitation marketing component should start before sanitation demand creation and CLTS triggering (Hanchett et al., 2011; WSP, 2011; Kappauf, 2011; Pedi and Jenkins, n.d.; Pedi and Kamasan, forthcoming, 2016).

A WaterAid study in Nigeria recommends introducing sanitation marketing a year after the initial CLTS intervention to help people upgrade facilities and move up the sanitation ladder (Robinson, 2009). However there are also examples of countries where households have skipped up the sanitation ladder, moving directly to improved sanitation. Experiences in Uganda found that implementing sanitation marketing straight after ODF achievement was more successful, as it didn't undermine use of local materials, and initiative, training of masons, and market analysis was initiated beforehand (Nabalema, 2011).

In Malawi, a participatory design approach to sanitation marketing was successfully trialled by UNICEF, aligned with the philosophy of CLTS, drawing on local knowledge and experience to design toilets (Cole, 2015). ASHPP projects in Malawi conduct CLTS activities alongside forming linkages between small-scale sanitation providers and village banks to enable rural households to access improved sanitation. In Tanzania, artisans are present during triggering sessions and introduced to the community, and are available to answer any questions they have at that stage.

Introducing sanitation marketing to communities years after the initial CLTS triggering proved unsuccessful, with households sticking with basic, unimproved toilets. For example, the first sanitation programme developed at scale in Tanzania was piloted by the Water and Sanitation Program (WSP) in 10 districts, combining CLTS and sanitation marketing and using the Total Sanitation and Sanitation Marketing (TSSM) methodology, and was not as successful as expected (Briceño et al., 2015). Constraints on uptake included limited availability of hardware materials creating bottlenecks in the process. In Malawi (2010–2015), ASHPP targeted 180,000 households accessing improved sanitation and introduced sanitation marketing two or three years after conducting CLTS triggering. But after four years of implementation only 29,933 households accessed improved sanitation (GSF, 2014).

In Malawi, the importance of basic sanitation is emphasized in the National Sanitation Policy (MoIWD, 2008: 1) and the priority for the elimination of open defecation is set out in the ODF strategy (Malawi Government, 2011).

However, improvement of existing toilets is a major concern. Despite the fact that simple pit toilets built after triggering can meet hygienic criteria if properly constructed and maintained (Harvey and Mukosha, 2009; Reed, 2014; WHO, n.d.), there is evidence that the health gains in moving from OD to unimproved simple pit toilets are limited (Quattri and Smets, 2014; WSP, 2014a and b).[2] There is some evidence to show that projects where CLTS is blended with sanitation marketing have proven effective in stopping OD and moving households up the sanitation ladder (Devine and Kullmann, 2011; Cole, 2015). ASHPP project experience suggests that some people do not want to build another toilet or upgrade after sanitation marketing is introduced at a later stage. Households thought building a simple pit toilet was the ultimate end, only to be told later to further improve or upgrade their toilets when sanitation marketing was introduced a year or so later. If they have the financial resources and knowledge of technical local options available, they would prefer to build an improved toilet straight away (GSF, 2014). In addition, households would prefer to build a new toilet rather than upgrading an existing one that is partially filled in with excreta. 'I would rather build a new toilet than upgrade the same toilet, because I do not want to see shit in the pit and also touch dirty parts of the latrine' (John Mkandawire, Rumphi District). As such, project staff have been asked to market all sanitation options during CLTS implementation so that households are able to make informed decisions (GSF, 2014; SNV, 2014a, b), as opposed to waiting until ODF status is reached.

This all implies that starting above the bottom rung of the sanitation ladder may be beneficial, in addition to a focus on continuous upgrading and maintaining.

Affordability

Affordability is a key determinant for moving up the sanitation ladder (Whaley and Webster, 2011). Toilet costs are affected by the number of people willing to buy them – fewer people will lead to an increase in the cost – which then results in even fewer people being able to afford them. High costs, or competing priorities for limited household funds, are repeatedly given as main reasons for not having a toilet, even if people would like one (Jenkins and Scott, 2007; Whaley and Webster, 2011; Sara and Graham, 2014; Cole, 2015). Upgrading existing toilets can also be unaffordable or else people may be unwilling to pay (Whaley and Webster 2011; Sara and Graham, 2014). And rebuilding a toilet every year after flooding or collapse is expensive and unsustainable (SNV, 2015a).

Experience to date shows that the poorest and most marginalized people in a community are rarely able to afford to buy the goods without some form of assistance (SNV, 2014b). They are also most likely to revert to OD or remain on the lowest rung of the sanitation ladder. Ensuring they are able to move up the ladder and avoid reversion to OD is critical to sustaining ODF communities (see Robinson and Gnilo, 2016a, this book).

In Tanzania, when ONGAWA[3] conducted a survey at the beginning of the programme, one of the questions asked was 'How much can you afford to spend on a toilet?' (Muñoz, 2014). The average price of a toilet is around TZS250,000 (approximately US$125) but half of the respondents stated an amount between TZS20,000 and 50,000 (see Figure 5.2). This reveals the importance of developing low-cost solutions for the market to be sustainable.

In Zambia, SNV (2014a) did a supply chain analysis at the beginning of the programme, which included a review of affordability of existing sanitation options. In the study seven sanitation options were identified, with costs ranging from ZMK485.71 (US$77.00) to ZMK3,840.10 (US$609.00). The average annual cash incomes of households averaged at ZMK2,580 (US$350) (Table 5.1), which means that even the cheapest option was not largely affordable to consumers. Hence improving affordability through supply chain interventions and microfinance became a priority for the programme.

What a household can afford varies within districts in Zambia. SNV (2014a) found that if households are near the district centre they tend to opt for more expensive sanitation options. Households in and near district centres have a larger disposable income than those far away. Furthermore, the high cost of transportation and the poor state of feeder roads for remote communities limit them to the most basic of toilet options.

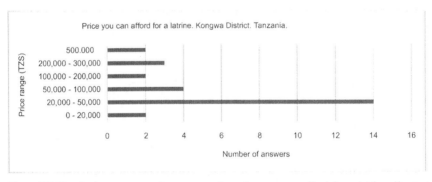

Figure 5.2 Results from a research survey on the price you can afford for a latrine, Kongwa District, Tanzania

Source: Muñoz, 2014

Table 5.1 Average annual household incomes in Zambia, 2014

District	Average annual household income (ZMK)
Luwingu	2,340 (US$371)
Mporokoso	2,280 (US$362)
Mungwi	2,580 (US$409)
Kasama – Rural	3,120 (US$495)

Financing

Sanitation marketing strategies should include a financing component. Research has shown that some (wealthier) rural households would be willing to borrow to buy a toilet, and would prefer to pay in instalments (Perez et al., 2012; Shah et al., 2013). However, access to financial services is a critical constraint. In villages, households, traders, and transporters have to travel long distances to access financial services. Financial institutions do not reach many villages due to high transaction costs and perceptions of the 'high risk' of lending to poorer customers.

In Zambia, credit schemes have been initiated by members of local cooperative societies and women's clubs. For example, in Chanda Mwamba village, Lukulu ward of Kasama district, there are two registered cooperatives promoting saving and lending schemes among the local people (SNV, 2014a). In Zambia, SNV is exploring formal and informal finance mechanisms with the National Savings and Credit Bank, Kasama Christian Community Centre, and the Ministry of Community Development.

In Nkhotakota, Malawi, rural women have acquired improved toilets through village-level sanitation financing mechanisms. Village banks have been established to help members procure toilet slabs and other materials to enable them move up the sanitation ladder. Although it does not leave out men, the initiative strategically empowers women, widows, and the economically weak, and allows them to access better sanitation facilities.

It is critical to integrate financing mechanisms to reach the poorest and most marginalized people within communities. They will often not meet the criteria for lending demanded from financial institutions, and there is often a reluctance to get into debt or be burdened with a loan they may not be able to repay. Community-initiated schemes will also likely be beyond their reach. Potential ways of establishing financing mechanisms to reach the poorest such as rewards, targeted subsidies, rebates, and vouchers are explored by Robinson and Gnilo (2016b, this book).

Supply chains

Good technical innovations will be unsustainable and can fail to scale up if there are not suitable supply chains in place. Lack of transport can limit access and also supply (Perez et al., 2012). Transportation of sanitation products is typically provided by trucks, bicycles, or ox carts (SNV, 2014a). Poor road conditions can lead to cement slabs breaking and an increase in cost in remote and rural areas (Thomas, 2014). In the UMATA project area in Tanzania, the price of 50 kg of cement was around US$8, but transportation costs added a minimum of US$1 if the location was near the hardware shop (Thomas, 2014). Some cheap sanitation accessories such as the plastic 'P-traps' piece were found to be 50 per cent more expensive in rural areas than in main towns like Dodoma or Dar es Salaam, mainly because of the transportation fees and the lack of competitors there. In Malawi, there are many cases where slabs are cast on site, making it easier and cheaper for the household.

The SNV-developed SAFI[4] toilet proved very popular. However, the slow development of local supply chains is a major constraint to meeting the high demand for the product (Kome, 2015). The provision of the SAFI-latrine rests on a systematic supply chain business model. A review of SAFI-latrine market penetration in Kenya and Tanzania found that it was not affordability, but rather the sales capacity of the entrepreneurs that holds back SAFI-latrine sales. The SAFI-latrine is in retrospect perceived as a 'significant investment in home improvement' for the household rather than a 'fast moving consumer product' (WR Partnership, 2015). Roll-out depends on development of sales capacity for sanitation entrepreneurs.

Once business communities have been identified in the district, their capital investment is channelled to identify trained masons, who act as extended business chain actors for the businessman. The business investment has many ripple effects that include sustainable marketing from the business community and systematic monitoring.

Masons and entrepreneurs

Training masons and entrepreneurs within communities has had mixed results. Not every mason can be an entrepreneur; different skill sets are needed. In Malawi, people with a background in masonry and who currently own a small business were more successful (Cole, 2015). The UMATA project has identified the level of demand for sanitation facilities along with the ability for masons and entrepreneurs to make a sufficient profit as crucial to their decision to remain in the sanitation business. Experiences such as these show that a more complex model will be needed, which draws on local skills, resources, and contexts.

Improving local sanitation options and services is important. Masons often have good ideas of appropriate toilet options using locally available building materials. Indigenous local knowledge must be used in designing options so that they are tailored to fit the affordability and durability needs of the consumer. Participatory design has been trialled in Malawi, where stakeholders design very low-cost toilets using easily available local resources, costing US$6–30, depending on the provision of materials and the ability of customers to pay (Cole, 2013, 2015). As the market develops, masons and entrepreneurs can create economies of scale as their average cost of production will be reduced with the increased number of units produced.

In Zambia, the Technical Education, Vocational and Entrepreneurship Training Authority (TEVETA) is revising its building course Level III to include masonry. TEVETA has been training masons in the districts where UNICEF and SNV are operating. This is intended to enhance the sustainability of technologies, as trade schools adopt them into their curriculum. The district councils in Zambia provide the legal enforcements for standards and quality of service delivery in conjunction with ward and district mason and artisan associations.

In Tanzania, the approach applied by the UMATA Programme combines the training of masons and entrepreneurs with more intensive and specialized knowledge transfer. Six experienced masons and entrepreneurs were selected to follow a 'Training of Trainers' (ToT) course, conducted by a consultant with the guidance of the project manager (PM) and project officers (PO).[5] The participants were especially skilled at construction and sanitation technologies, but they lacked some knowledge about entrepreneurship. An ONGAWA project officer and a member representing the team of ToTs, attended the modules 'Business Model and Plan in Sustainable Sanitation' and 'Running a Sanitation Business' of an EU funded training programme called 'Entrepreneurship, Community Planning and Appropriate Technologies in Sustainable Sanitation'.[6] The aim of the training was to make the trainers capable of providing technical advice to masons and entrepreneurs within the community. This knowledge transfer to community-based resources was a way of providing long-term sustainability for the project as they will remain in the area after implementation finishes.

In Malawi, under the ASHPP, entrepreneurs were identified by their community. However, this tended to result in the selection of inappropriate individuals with no interest in sanitation and with no entrepreneurial skills. In Chikwawa district, 202 masons were trained through a project, but only 10 per cent remained active after four years of implementation. Community members often selected relatives on the basis that they may get some benefits from the project. In Balaka, training individuals from a business background on sanitation marketing was more successful. However, care should be taken not to train an excessive number of entrepreneurs in one community, which can flood the market and reduce profit margins (GSF, 2014).

The ASHPP also conducts training in business management to hone the skills and impart knowledge that enable entrepreneurs to sustain sanitation businesses and continue to serve their communities. The ASHPP uses existing structures that include government extension workers, Area Development Committees (ADCs), Village Development Committees (VDCs), District Coordinating Teams (DCTs), and market committees to implement its activities. Such an approach avoids the creation of parallel programme implementation structures and ensures continuity and sustainability of activities even after programme funding stops.

There are many efforts to provide credit to households, but comparatively few to provide credit or financing facilities to the masons, suppliers, entrepreneurs, and the local private sector (Perez et al., 2012) (i.e. in Zambia; SNV, 2014a). Affordability of materials is an obstacle once the masons are trained and the demand has been triggered. Access to finance helps to ensure sanitation entrepreneurs are able to sustain the supply of improved sanitation products and services, and enable them to have diversity of choice in products and services. It also helps develop the supply chain, which is a key constraint to scaling up in rural areas.

Materials to inform choice

Households need the knowledge to make informed choices about the ways to construct the most suitable and affordable toilets and handwashing stations, the life span and durability of the toilet options, as well as their cleaning or emptying needs. Households can then discuss and analyse options with other members of their family and community. Similarly, masons should have the relevant information to build a toilet that lasts and functions as intended and responds to people's needs and budgets.

In Tanzania, a catalogue of affordable sanitation products and local innovations has been developed by the 'Water and Sanitation Systems for Development Cooperation Group' (GCSASD) of the Polytechnic University of Madrid in collaboration with ONGAWA and the Ardhi University to help to link CLTS with sanitation marketing. The need for a catalogue was clearly identified during the initial triggering sessions as households frequently demanded detailed explanations and information about different sanitation options from the masons. The less experienced masons lacked a tool that could help them in those situations, and a catalogue could serve as a technical reference for their work as well.[7]

In Zambia, in compiling its informed choice materials, SNV held focus group discussions with:

- Masons and bricklayers with experience in constructing rural toilets who highlighted the importance of understanding the soil of the village before construction; the construction materials available; for example if cement needs to be transported or burnt bricks fetched or made to construct brick-dome toilets.
- Community members to ascertain their preferences, needs, aspirations, and the concerns of rural communities.
- Chiefs who have promoted various innovations in their chiefdoms. Chief Muporokoso, from Mporokoso district, for example, has put up several demonstration toilets at his palace.
- District Water, Sanitation, Health Education (D-WASHE) officials, who attended a workshop to generate innovative ideas for developing locally specific informed choice materials, as well as to develop plans to distribute and disseminate these materials.

All the materials have been translated into Bemba, the major language spoken in Mporokoso, Luwingu, Kasama, and Mungwi districts. Where appropriate, details on cost have been included for intended users. Traditional leaders have been included as key stakeholders in the dissemination of this information.

In Malawi, learning materials have been developed for masons and entrepreneurs, aimed to enhance their skills to provide user-friendly improved sanitation facilities and hygiene practices on a sustainable basis.

Technical innovations and solutions to fit local contexts

It is essential for toilet designs to be appropriate for local contexts. Without this, scaling-up could quickly stall. A few examples of locally appropriate technology in Malawi, Tanzania, and Zambia are presented in this section, including options for handwashing and adaptations for disabled and elderly people.

1. *Ecological sanitation (Eco-san)*: Eco-san technology was introduced in Malawi along the lakeshore areas of the Traditional Authority Mwamlowe in Rumphi district through a careful blending of sanitation marketing and CLTS. In the past, the area used to continuously shift between OD and ODF status due to regular toilet collapses in sandy and other unstable soils (Sugden, 2003; Munkhondia, 2013). Eco-san technologies provided a clear way up the sanitation ladder. With the Eco-san toilets, the Traditional Authority Mwamlowe in northern Malawi has been able to sustain ODF.

2. *Traditional pour flush*: In Kongwa, Tanzania, there is only one functional water point for every 1,200 people (WPM, 2014). Water scarcity makes it essential to design technological options that need less water. The 'pour flush' toilet uses a raised plastered brick platform with a pipe on a slight slope connecting it with the off-site pit (see Figure 5.3). There is no water seal and it requires just 300–400 ml of water per use.[8]

Figure 5.3 Traditional pour flush toilet
Source: Esteban-Zazo et al., 2014

3. *The SAFI-latrine*: This innovation meets consumer aspirations of durability, safety, acceptability, and affordability (SNV, 2015a; see Figure 5.4). It makes use of toilet parts that can be easily moved and transported by ox-carts and bicycles. As the toilet parts are movable, households that relocate to another plot can still use their old toilet parts. Further, the SAFI-latrine can be used as bathing shelters, thus reducing resources to be spent on constructing a separate shelter. The one-off investment in a SAFI-latrine has long-term extended benefits. However, as previously discussed, the supply chain is still under development to take this innovation to scale.

4. *Slab for disabled and non-disabled users*: Developing low-cost practical solutions for people with disabilities and the elderly is vital (Wilbur and Jones, 2014). In Zambia, private sector actors involved in the provision of technology options, ideal for people living with disabilities, pregnant women, children, and the elderly, have partnered with SNV to enhance availability of appropriate market-based sanitation options, such as Toilet Yanga.[9] In Tanzania, applied research came up with a slab that brings together a drop hole with a foot rest and a separated second drop hole with a raised structure[10] for people with disabilities. Figure 5.5 shows it during the development phase.

Figure 5.4 SAFI-latrine

Source: SNV Zambia

Figure 5.5 Slab for disabled and non-disabled people, Kongwa, Tanzania
Source: Ana Esteban Zazo et al., 2014

5. *Ash for handwashing*: Handwashing with soap is a parameter in defining the adequacy of a toilet in Zambia and in many other countries.[11]
   In Zambia, communities in the SSH4A results programme mix water
   and ash and use the resulting product for handwashing. This prevents
   ash placed in open vessels from dissolving when it is raining. As a
   marketing strategy, the masons provide a handwashing station as a
   bonus when a consumer seeks their services and products. In Kongwa,
   Tanzania, where water scarcity is also high, handwashing with ash has
   been promoted as an alternative to handwashing with soap.

Monitoring

Monitoring the success of programmes that merge sanitation marketing with
CLTS is essential. We need to know more about what works, and what does
not, and as quickly as possible.

The Ministry of Local Government and Housing (MLGH) conducts
sanitation monitoring in Zambia, with the support of UNICEF (Osbert et al.,
2015). These organizations have developed a monitoring system based on
DHIS 2[12] to capture data on sanitation and hygiene activities. DHIS 2 is a web-
based system that provides real-time sanitation information for planning,
monitoring, and decision making at district, provincial, and national levels,
by providing an automated feedback on data from village level up to national

level through SMS.[13] While the sanitation marketing interface is still being developed and piloted for DHIS 2, SNV Zambia has developed a sanitation marketing web-based monitoring tool used to develop appropriate market-based interventions in real time. Indicators include profitability, toilet and soils types, annual household cash incomes, sources for purchasing expenditures, and sanitation supply chain business development. This ensures timely and appropriate interventions in areas of need.

In Tanzania, one of the key operational challenges has been to coordinate the implementation of sanitation marketing and CLTS, as they were carried out by different organizations. Local government authorities (LGAs), sanitation marketing and CLTS project managers are involved in monthly one-day joint planning sessions to plan 'triggering sessions', together with the activities in the other components. This has improved the effectiveness of those activities and the impact of sanitation marketing significantly. LGAs (from the Health Department mainly) were also able to share learning on the earlier failures found when previous triggering sessions were conducted in a former project in some villages of the district[14] and the logistics needed to reach each sub-village. For example, some sub-villages cover a vast and mountainous geographical area, and two triggering sessions were needed. LGAs monitor and evaluate the performance of masons and entrepreneurs. Village or ward executive officers verify the monthly data registered by the Community Own Resource Person (CORPs). The official reporting channels facilitate coordination. The Regional Health Officer has created registers (A4 size books) to monitor a set of indicators on a three-monthly basis including, for example, toilet type, presence and use of a handwashing facility. Data was initially collected by the village health workers at sub-village level, and then compiled in steps: village, ward, district, and region. Although valuable, this information is not enough to evaluate the sustainability of sanitation marketing measures: whether the mason and entrepreneur selected remain active in the sanitation business, and if not, why not.

Conclusion

This chapter has discussed eight aspects to consider in order to better integrate CLTS and sanitation marketing within sanitation programmes, based on learning from the programmes in Tanzania, Zambia, and Malawi. We still have much to learn on when to phase each one in, and what the ideal order is. Sustainable access to sanitation for rural communities demands strategies that allow for products and services that respond to consumer needs and aspirations. Financing strategies (such as microfinance) need to be developed to ensure all households can climb the sanitation ladder so that the poorest are not left on the bottom rung, or revert to OD. Participatory design processes based on local knowledge show potential to develop low-cost, durable, and acceptable products that respond to the needs of all, including people with disabilities and the elderly. Understanding local markets and their limitations is also key to the development of successful supply chains.

We need to know more about the optimal time to phase sanitation marketing with CLTS, and it is vital that experiences, successes, and failures are monitored, documented, and shared widely. More research and continued learning is needed to do this. Formative research is needed in advance of implementation to identify evidence on current practices, the factors that influence these practices, the current supply, and the types of sanitation products and services needed (Devine and Kullmann, 2011; SNV, 2015b).

Moving up the sanitation ladder should not necessarily be viewed as a step-by-step process; sanitation marketing provides the opportunity to rise to any level of the sanitation ladder depending on affordability and willingness to pay. Getting the delicate balance right to ensure that community initiative and the behaviour change process are not stifled by imposing prescriptive, inappropriate, or unaffordable designs early on in the CLTS process is central to achieving long-term sustainability.

About the authors

Twitty Munkhondia, Plan International. Twitty carried out research in Malawi on moving up the sanitation ladder funded by the Global Sanitation Fund (GSF).
Warren Mukelabai Simangolwa, SNV Netherlands Development Organisation. Warren, a WASH Market Specialist, has led efforts in reinvigorating WASH markets with cutting-edge WASH market interventions for profitability, sustainability, and scalability.
Alfonso Zapico Maceda, ONGAWA Engineering for Human Development. Alfonso was the Programme Manager Adviser for Sanitation Marketing in the first phase of UMATA (Usafi wa Mazingira Tanzania) programme in Kongwa District.

Endnotes

1. The contributions to the Tanzania related aspects of this chapter are based on the teamwork of ONGAWA's Technical Adviser David Muñoz Cifuentes, Researcher Ana Esteban Zazo, and Professor José Antonio Mancebo Piqueras, from the Polytechnic University of Madrid, and Alfonso Zapico.
2. WHO define an 'unimproved' pit latrine as one without a slab or platform, or an open pit. Pit latrines with a slab or covered pit, or ventilated improved pit (VIP) latrines are both defined as 'improved' http://www.who.int/water_sanitation_health/monitoring/jmp2012/key_terms/en/ [accessed 29 January 2016].
3. ONGAWA: Engineering for Human Development, http://www.ongawa.org/en/ [accessed 29 January 2016].
4. Kiswahili for 'clean'.
5. ONGAWA conducted 194 personal interviews of artisans in 22 different wards. Selection criteria included: they should know how to read and write; must have completed standard VII or more; they should belong to the respective village/ward and not expect to move from that village/ward; they should be self-disciplined and respected by the community.

6. Organized by ACRA in collaboration with International Centre for Water Management Services (CEWAS), University of Natural Resources and Life Sciences, Vienna (BOKU), Research Laboratory on Appropriate Technologies for Environmental Management in resource-limited Countries (CeT-Amb), and Maji na Maendeleo Dodoma (MAMADO).
7. http://issuu.com/ana_ezazo/docs/catalogue_english/1 [accessed 29 January 2016].
8. Normal pour flush with common P-trap needs around 2 litres for a full flush.
9. https://www.facebook.com/pages/Toilet-Yanga-Limited/592504520854328?fref=ts
10. Non-disabled people generally prefer non-raised platforms in rural areas of East Africa.
11. Other criteria are a smooth cleanable floor, a super-structure which provides privacy, and a lid for the pit hole.
12. https://www.dhis2.org/ [accessed 29 January 2016].
13. Short Message Service.
14. Under a Health Promotion and Systems Strengthening (HPSS) project funded by the Swiss Agency for Development and Cooperation (SDC).

References

Briceño, B., Coville, A. and Martinez, S. (2015) *Promoting Handwashing and Sanitation: Evidence from a Large-Scale Randomized Trial in Rural Tanzania*, Water Global Practice Group & Development Research Group Impact Evaluation Team, World Bank, January.

Cavill, S. with Chambers, R. and Vernon, N. (2015) 'Sustainability and CLTS: Taking stock', *Frontiers of CLTS: Innovations and Insights* 4, Institute of Development Studies, Brighton.

Cole, B. (2013) 'Participatory design development for sanitation', *Frontiers of CLTS: Innovations and Insights* 1, Institute of Development Studies, Brighton.

Cole, B. (2015) 'Going Beyond ODF: Combining Sanitation Marketing with Participatory Approaches to Sustain ODF Communities in Malawi', *Eastern and Southern Africa Sanitation and Hygiene Learning Series*, UNICEF, New York NY, http://www.communityledtotalsanitation.org/sites/communityledtotalsanitation.org/files/GoingBeyondODF_CombiningSanMark_with_ParticipatoryApproaches_Malawi.pdf [accessed 28 January 2016].

Coombes, Y. (2016) 'User centred latrine guidelines. Integrating CLTS with sanitation marketing: a case study from Kenya to promote informed choice', in P. Bongartz, N. Vernon and J. Fox (eds.) *Sustainable Sanitation for All: Experiences, Challenges, and Innovations*, Practical Action Publishing, Rugby.

Devine, J. and Kullmann, C. (2011) *Introductory Guide to Sanitation Marketing*, Water and Sanitation Program: Toolkit, World Bank, Washington DC.

Esteban-Zazo, A., Mancebo-Piqueras, J.A. and Zapico, A. (2014) *Affordable Sanitation Products, Choo Bora na Mazingira Safi*, Kongwa District, Dodoma,

Universidad Politécnica de Madrid, Madrid, http://issuu.com/ana_ezazo/docs/catalogue_english/1 [accessed 28 January 2016].

Hanchett, S., Krieger, L., Kahn, M.H., Kullmann, C. and Ahmed, R. (2011) *Long-Term Sustainability of Improved Sanitation in Rural Bangladesh*, World Bank, Washington DC, https://openknowledge.worldbank.org/handle/10986/17347 [accessed 28 January 2016].

Harvey, P.A. and Mukosha, L. (2009) *Community-Led Total Sanitation: Triggering Sustainable Development in Zambia*, paper presented at the 34th WEDC International Conference, Addis Ababa, Ethiopia.

Global Sanitation Fund (GSF) (2014) *Annual Narrative Progress Report*, Global Sanitation Fund.

Jenkins, M. and Pedi, D. (n.d.) *Equity in Sanitation Marketing: How Can We Support the Market to Reach the Poorest?* Guidance Note 8, UNICEF Sanitation Marketing Learning Series, http://www.unicef.org/wash/files/Guidance_Note_8_-_Reaching_the_Poor.pdf [accessed 28 January 2016].

Jenkins. M. W. and Scott, B. (2007) 'Behavioral indicators of household decision-making and demand for sanitation and potential gains from social marketing in Ghana', *Social Science & Medicine* 64, 2427–42 <http://dx.doi.org/10.1016/j.socscimed.2007.03.010>.

Kappauf, L. (2011) *Opportunities and Constraints for a more Sustainable Sanitation through Sanitation marketing in Malawi, Case study for Mzimba and Lilongwe districts*, MSc thesis, Loughborough University, Loughborough.

Kome, A. (2015) *CLTS and Sustainability*, webinar presentation, IDS webinar, http://www.communityledtotalsanitation.org/sites/community ledtotalsanitation.org/files/Presentation_SSH4A_sustainability.pdf [accessed 28 January 2016].

Malawi Government (2011) *Open Defecation Free Strategy*, Ministry of Agriculture, Irrigation and Water Development, Lilongwe, http://www.sanitationmonitoringtoolkit.com/images/SMTdocuments/12_ODF%20Malawi%20Strategy%20_2011_2015.pdf [accessed 28 January 2016].

Ministry of Irrigation Water and Development (MoIWD) (2008) *National Sanitation Policy*, Government of Malawi, Ministry of Water and Development, Lilongwe.

Muñoz, D. (2014) *Analysis of Sanitation Demand and Supply Quick Research*, ONGAWA, Madrid.

Munkhondia, T. (2013) 'On the road to sustainable sanitation: an overview of lessons learned in a sanitation programme in Malawi', *Waterlines*, 32(1): 50–7 <http://dx.doi.org/10.3362/1756-3488.2013.005>.

Nabalema, C. (2011) *The Phasing of CLTS and Sanitation Marketing in Uganda*, CLTS one pager, Institute of Development Studies, Brighton, http://www.communityledtotalsanitation.org/resource/phasing-clts-and-sanitation-marketing-uganda [accessed 28 January 2016].

Osbert, N., Hoehne, A., Musonda, E., Manchikanti, S., Manangi, A. and Mboshya, P. (2015) 'Real-time monitoring of rural sanitation at scale in Zambia using mobile-to-web technologies', *Eastern and Southern Africa Sanitation Learning Series*, UNICEF, New York NY, http://www.communityledtotalsanitation.org/sites/community ledtotalsanitation.org/files/RealTimeMonitoringatScale_Zambia_Mobile2Web.pdf [accessed 28 January 2016].

O'Connell, K. (2014) *What Influences Open Defecation and Latrine Ownership in Rural Households?: Findings from a Global Review*, Water and Sanitation Program Working Paper, World Bank, Washington DC, http://documents. worldbank.org/curated/en/2014/08/20134123/scaling-up-rural-sanitation-influences-open-defecation-latrine-ownership-rural-households-findings-global-review [accessed 28 January 2016].

Pedi, D. and Jenkins, M. (n.d.) 'Sanitation marketing and CATS: How do we link approaches?', Guidance Note 10, *UNICEF Sanitation Marketing Learning Series*, UNICEF, New York NY, http://documents.worldbank.org/curated/en/2014/08/20134123/scaling-up-rural-sanitation-influences-open-defecation-latrine-ownership-rural-households-findings-global-review [accessed 28 January 2016].

Pedi, D. and Kamasan, A. (forthcoming, 2016) *Sanitation Market Transformation in Indonesia: Designing Viable Business Models*, Water and Sanitation Program Field Note, World Bank, Washington, DC.

Perez, E. with Cardosi, J., Coombes, Y., Devine, J., Grossman, A., Kullmann, C., Kumar, A., Mukherjee, N., Prakash, M., Robiarto, A., Setiawan, D., Singh, U. and Wartono, D. (2012) *What Does It Take to Scale Up Rural Sanitation?*, Water and Sanitation Program Working Paper, World Bank, Washington, DC.

Phiri, S. (2010) *TA MKanda CLTS Research: Summary*, Engineers Without Borders Canada, Toronto, http://www.communityledtotalsanitation.org/sites/communityledtotalsanitation.org/files/Mkanda_research_revised.pdf [accessed 28 January 2016].

Quattri, M and Smets, S. (2014) *Lack of Community-Level Improved Sanitation Causes Stunting in Rural Villages of Lao PDR and Vietnam*, paper presented at the 37th WEDC International Conference, Hanoi.

Reed, B. (2014) *Simple Pit Latrines*, Water, Engineering and Development Centre, Loughborough, http://wedc.lboro.ac.uk/resources/booklets/G025-Simple-pit-latrines-booklet.pdf [accessed 28 January 2016].

Robinson, A. (2009) *Sustainability and Equity Aspects of Total Sanitation, Programmes: A Study of Recent WaterAid-Supported Programmes in Nigeria*, WaterAid, London, www.communityledtotalsanitation.org/sites/communityledtotalsanitation.org/files/Nigeria_CLTS_synthesis_report.pdf [accessed 28 January 2016].

Robinson, A. and Gnilo, M. (2016a) 'Beyond ODF: a phased approach to rural sanitation development', in P. Bongartz, N. Vernon and J. Fox (eds.) *Sustainable Sanitation for All: Experiences, Challenges, and Innovations*, Practical Action Publishing, Rugby.

Robinson, A. and Gnilo, M. (2016b) 'Promoting choice: Smart finance for rural sanitation development', in P. Bongartz, N. Vernon and J. Fox (eds.) *Sustainable Sanitation for All: Experiences, Challenges, and Innovations*, Practical Action Publishing, Rugby.

Sara, S. and Graham, J. (2014) 'Ending open defecation in rural Tanzania: which factors facilitate latrine adoption?' *International Journal of Environmental Research and Public Health*, 11: 9854–70 <http://dx.doi.org/10.3390/ijerph110909854>.

Shah, N.B., Shirrell, S., Fraker, A., Wang, P., and Wang, E. (2013) *Understanding Willingness to Pay for Sanitary Latrines in Rural Cambodia: Findings from Four*

Field Experiments Of iDE Cambodia's Sanitation Marketing Program, Study Report, Idinsight.

SNV (2014a) *Sanitation and Hygiene Supply Chain Study Report*, SNV Zambia, http://www.communityledtotalsanitation.org/resource/sanitation-supply-chain-study-kasama-mungwi-luwingu-and-mporokos [accessed 1 February 2016].

SNV (2014b) *The Informed Choice for the Elderly and Disabled Report*, SNV Zambia, http://www.communityledtotalsanitation.org/resource/report-informed-choice-materials-incorporating-disabled-and-elderly-snv-zambia [accessed 1 February 2016].

SNV (2015a) *Connect*, SNV, The Hague, http://updates.snvworld.org/intranet/presentations/SNV-Connect-2015/files/basic-html/page20.html [accessed 29 January 2016].

SNV (2015b) *The Sanitation and Hygiene Consumer Demand Study*, SNV Zambia, http://www.communityledtotalsanitation.org/resource/sanitation-and-hygiene-consumer-study-snv-zambia [accessed 1 February 2016].

Sugden, S. (2003) *One Step Closer to Sustainable Sanitation: Experiences of an Ecological Sanitation Project in Malawi*, WaterAid, Lilongwe.

Thomas, A. (2014) 'Key Findings of a Sanitation Supply Chains Study in Eastern and Southern Africa', *UNICEF Eastern and Southern Africa Sanitation and Hygiene Learning Series*, UNICEF, New York NY, http://www.communityledtotalsanitation.org/sites/communityledtotalsanitation.org/files/Sanitation_Supply_Chains_ESAfrica.pdf [accessed 29 January 2016].

Tyndale-Biscoe, P., Bond, M. and Kidd, R. (2013) *ODF Sustainability Study*, FH Designs and Plan International, www.communityledtotalsanitation.org/resource/odf-sustainability-study-plan [accessed 29 January 2016].

Whaley, L. and Webster. J. (2011) 'The effectiveness and sustainability of two demand-driven sanitation and hygiene approaches in Zimbabwe', *Journal of Water, Sanitation and Hygiene for Development*, 1(1): 20–36 <http://dx.doi.org/10.2166/washdev.2011.015>.

WHO (n.d.) *Simple Pit Latrines*, World Health Organization, Geneva, http://www.who.int/water_sanitation_health/hygiene/emergencies/fs3_4.pdf [accessed 29 January 2016].

WaterAid (n.d.) *New Sanitation Technologies for Communities with Poor Soil*, WaterAid, Nigeria, http://www.sswm.info/library/54 [accessed 29 January 2016].

Wilbur, J. and Jones, H. (2014) 'Disability: making CLTS fully inclusive', *Frontiers of CLTS: Innovations and Insights* 3, Institute of Development Studies, Brighton, http://www.communityledtotalsanitation.org/resources/frontiers/disability-making-clts-fully-inclusive [accessed 29 January 2016].

WPM (2014) *Water Point Mapping in Tanzania*, WPMS Tanzania, http://wpm.maji.go.tz/ [accessed 239 January 2016].

WR Partnership (2015) *WR Partnership, Kenya and Tanzania SAFIm SNV, Discovery Report*, internal document, December 2015.

WSP (2011) *Factors Associated with Achieving and Sustaining Open Defecation Free Communities: Learning from East Java*, Research Brief, Water and Sanitation Program (WSP), Washington, DC, www.wsp.org/sites/wsp.org/files/publications/WSP-Factors-Achieving-ODF-East-Java.pdf [accessed 29 January 2016].

WSP (2014a) *Investing in the Next Generation: Children Grow Taller, and Smarter, in Rural Villages of Lao PDR where all Community Members use Improved Sanitation*, WSP Research Brief, WSP, Washington, DC.

WSP (2014b) *Investing in the Next Generation: Children Grow Taller, and Smarter, in Rural, Mountainous Villages of Vietnam where Community Members use Improved Sanitation*, WSP Research Brief, Washington, DC.

CHAPTER 6

User-centred latrine guidelines – integrating CLTS with sanitation marketing: a case study from Kenya to promote informed choice

Yolande Coombes[1]

Abstract

There is increased attention on how to integrate Community-Led Total Sanitation (CLTS) and sanitation marketing to support households with informed choice for building more sustainable latrines from the outset. In Kenya, the development of simplified latrine guidelines has been a first step in integrating the two approaches, in an attempt to build more diversified latrine types which better suit the needs of individual households, and which optimize latrine cost-effectiveness according to different household's income levels. Simple latrine guidelines are being used as a support tool for health workers, private sector implementers, and community health workers. Households can review latrine options following CLTS triggering, allowing them, if they wish, to leverage the more improved supply chain products developed as part of sanitation marketing.

Keywords: Sanitation marketing, CLTS sustainability, Improved latrines, Latrine guidelines, Informed choice, Kenya

Introduction

In Kenya, as in many other countries, sanitation stakeholders are now asking at which point sanitation marketing (focusing on both supply and demand) should be introduced to follow on from Community-Led Total Sanitation (CLTS) so as to optimize both self-help and sustainability (Cavill et al., 2015). Should they be introduced together or used selectively or sequentially depending on the issues and coverage within a county (see Munkhondia et al., 2016, this book)? Kenya has recently devolved sanitation services to local government with the creation of 47 counties. Devolution was introduced to allow for more tailored responses and service delivery to the different local contexts at county level. Sanitation is no different, for example a county like Nyeri has 99.3 per cent latrine coverage (of which 60 per cent are shared or unimproved) and therefore CLTS as an approach would not be cost-effective. Conversely a county such as Kwale with 52 per cent open defecation (OD)

http://dx.doi.org/10.3362/9781780449272.006

might be better with a CLTS approach sequentially followed by sanitation marketing. A county such as Migori, which has 33 per cent OD and 40 per cent unimproved sanitation, probably needs a parallel CLTS and sanitation marketing approach (Ministry of Health/WSP, 2014).

It is likely that we do not have sufficient evidence to know what the optimum combination and sequence of CLTS and sanitation marketing is, but as Munkhondia et al. (2016, this book) point out, the approach of first conducting CLTS and introducing sanitation marketing at a later stage may not always be an effective one since it can lead to households getting stuck or being satisfied with basic latrines which cannot last long and tend to limit health benefits. We do know, however, that building a strong enabling environment for both CLTS and sanitation marketing interventions is crucial (Perez et al., 2012). Typically, sanitation marketing interventions are more resource intensive than CLTS, if both adequate at-scale demand creation and supply chain strengthening activities involving private and public sector are to be developed. They also take considerable time to roll out in a comprehensive manner, given the specific enabling environment development needed for the private sector to engage in rural sanitation product development and business models for the poor. Within the sector, there has often been a division between CLTS and sanitation marketing approaches, but more recently implementers are not viewing them as either/or approaches, but are looking to see how to integrate CLTS and sanitation marketing from the outset, in order to support households in building more sustainable latrines in a comparatively more cost-effective way the first time they build. Could this integration pave the way for CLTS and sanitation marketing activities that build on the strengths of each other and address the challenges levied by the proponents of each of these approaches against the other? In Kenya, the development of simplified latrine guidelines has been a first step in integrating the two approaches, in an attempt to build more diversified latrine types which better suit the needs of individual households, and which maximize the resources available to them so that they can, where possible, jump up the sanitation ladder, missing a few rungs on the way.

In Kenya, the Ministry of Health (MoH) advocates for both CLTS and sanitation marketing. The idea of latrine guidelines is not to replace sanitation marketing activities, nor to undermine CLTS. Furthermore, the idea is not to roll out CLTS, latrine guidelines, and sanitation marketing as a linear process. The hypothesis is that all these approaches are complementary and are different ways of 'cracking the same nut'.

As CLTS programmes have scaled across Kenya (and globally), there has been increasing emphasis on how to sustain CLTS results. The concern is with how communities and households achieve and maintain their open defecation free (ODF) status, both in terms of the new behaviours they have adopted, but also in terms of the conditions of the new facilities that they are using, without slipping back to OD behaviours. Sanitation practitioners have noted an implicit expectation that households will continue to climb the 'sanitation ladder' by investing in higher levels of technology which will give them increased health benefits as well as other functional (comfort, convenience) and emotional (status, dignity) benefits. In Kenya, formative research (Ipsos Synovate, 2013) noted that few communities have continued to move up the sanitation ladder following the initial triggering and building of first, basic latrines as part of CLTS activities. Additionally there is a high degree of satisfaction with unimproved latrines, with households citing no intention to improve. In order to increase the behaviour of continuous upgrading people need to be dissatisfied with their current latrine. As a result, the MoH has introduced a national improved sanitation campaign[2] as part of broader sanitation marketing activities in the country, designed to generate demand for improved sanitation latrines of a higher quality (compared with those usually built as a result of CLTS). This campaign is designed to be integrated with existing CLTS activities.

The MoH in Kenya developed a roadmap to make Kenya ODF by 2013. By the end of 2013, only two sub-counties had been declared ODF, and none of the 47 counties had achieved that status, although Busia County is close but has yet to be verified (see Wamera, 2016, this book). By 2014, 3,886 villages (7 per cent) had been declared ODF, 2,518 had been verified, and 1,960 certified.[3] Increased focus on becoming ODF and a revision to the roadmap has seen renewed efforts by counties to achieve ODF status. In addition, in 2014, with support from UNICEF, counties completed a micro-planning exercise to map out and cost what it would take to become ODF. UNICEF estimate that KES1.5 bn (US$16.6 m) will be required to achieve 100 per cent ODF status in the country, with an average of US$35,000 per county. The cost of training, follow-up, and administration is about KES5,584,900 (US$62,000) per county but more than 70 per cent of counties have completed the CLTS training in full, although many will need to do refresher training which has not been budgeted for (Singh and Balfour, 2015).

In comparison, the demand creation campaign for improved sanitation that is being rolled out by government as part of the sanitation marketing activities is expensive. Depending on the channels used it is approximately US$30,000–60,000 to execute the campaign for three months in a given county, but this does not guarantee exposure to all communities/households. The more expensive roll-out of the campaign includes inter-personal communication in a sub-set of sub-county locations. The primary aim of the improved sanitation campaign is to move people to more sustainable latrines (thus saving households money in the long-term because they will not be re-building their latrine so frequently, leading to a reduction in lifecycle cost compared with annual costs). In addition, economic studies of sanitation have demonstrated increased cost-benefits with more durable latrines (Hutton, 2012). There is a second objective of targeting resistant or hard-to-reach communities who may have been unsuccessfully triggered as part of CLTS activities. Many counties have not budgeted for the campaign, so it is unlikely to be rolled out in every county in the near future. Counties are very dependent on international non-governmental organizations

(INGO), donors, and civil society budgets for campaign activities. Few budget for such activities within the County Integrated Development Plan. Kenya has recently devolved, and counties are still in their infancy in terms of planning and budgeting comprehensively. The focus still tends to be project based. Work by the Kenya Water and Sanitation Network (KEWASNET), the SNV Netherlands Development Organization, the Water and Sanitation Program of the World Bank (WSP), Red Cross, and UNICEF through the guidance of the National MoH is now focused on helping counties to better budget for a more comprehensive approach to sanitation. In the meantime, the campaign is being rolled out by partners through local government, and counties are reporting increases in improved latrines, which can be verified by the sale of latrine slabs which have increased substantially in these counties.[4]

Challenges with 'CLTS-designed' latrines

During the course of formative research[5] to inform a large-scale, market-based approach in Kenya, a number of key observations were made:

Homogeneity in latrine designs

In their research, Pedi and Sara (2013) found a high number of communities across the country where the same latrine design is used throughout (both improved and unimproved latrines). It seems there is little variation or innovation in latrine designs within individual communities. Respondents indicated that this was because, following CLTS, latrine designs were copied from those households with an existing latrine or were based on the advice of natural leaders and/or community health workers/volunteers (CHW/CHVs). These leaders and workers often have limited experience of different latrine types and so their advice and guidance is based on what they know or have seen. Although this may not be a problem for some, and might be a useful way to scale access to latrines (by having a simple design that all can follow), it may also mean that households are not building latrines that address their specific needs or requirements, or that meet their aspirations. They may also be investing in a less sustainable latrine design which they will be forced to re-build, or repair more frequently, or which they may not continue to use, because it does not meet their needs in terms of privacy, odour, or ease of use.

Inadequate technical specifications

The research found some common technical problems, in particular, inappropriate pit depth. The average depth, as indicated from the quantitative sample, was 30 ft (9 m). In qualitative data collection, respondents cited pit depths of 50 ft (15 m) and even 80 ft (24.5 m). Contrary to CLTS guidance (that no significant cost should be involved in building a latrine), most respondents had paid someone to dig their pits paying an average of KSH250 per foot (US$3) in areas of good soil, and up to KSH1,000 per foot in rocky areas (US$12), thus paying as much as US$360 for the pit to be dug (almost 70 per cent of annual income for households in the bottom 40 per cent of earners in Kenya). Since pit depths are typically too deep, many households are using too large a proportion of their available resources when they invest in a latrine. This leaves less investment for the slab and superstructure. The slab is where they are most likely to come into contact with faeces, where people have failed to position themselves over the squat hole correctly, which was a common problem raised in the formative research report, especially among children.

Other findings with regard to technical specifications were that most households with latrines have pits which are typically 3 feet (1 m) by 4 feet (1.2 m) in width/length and rectangular in shape. Respondents wrongly thought that round pits are more likely to collapse than square ones. As expected, superstructure materials tended to be consistent with materials used for the house, or of a lesser quality. It was rare to find a more substantial superstructure, except in areas where latrines had been subsidized.

Lack of understanding of what constitutes an improved latrine and why it is important

Few households were aware of the importance of a lid on the latrine, or what the attributes of an improved latrine are, in both CLTS and non-CLTS communities. In the quantitative survey only 10 per cent of households had a lid on their latrine slab. This, apart from in ventilated pit latrines (VIPs), is considered one of the most important aspects of an improved latrine, because it prevents flies from entering and exiting the latrine, and thus stops flies contaminating food and fingers with excrement (Chavasse et al., 1999).

Poor quality design and construction

Recent qualitative research (Ipsos Synovate, 2013) in some of the areas which first adopted CLTS approaches in Kenya, as well as data gathered from the quantitative formative research for the market-based approach, show that there is a high number of latrines which are not being used due to collapse of pits or disrepair of slab or superstructure. In some cases this is because households have failed to maintain them (superstructure disrepair), in others it is because of poor design and construction methods (slab and pit collapse).

In Kenya, most of the focus of CLTS has been on building a latrine and not on providing guidance on the minimum standards in order to provide health benefits or advice about the attributes of a latrine that means it can be considered 'improved'. So, for example, having a slab that can be cleaned is important for health benefits when faeces have not been fully contained in the pit and are left on the slab. Permanent foot rests designed on many slabs encourage users to position their feet on the foot rests, but because of differences in leg length, the user may not be directly over the squat hole which means excreta ends up on the slab. In fact, being able to wash the slab was cited in the research as something that respondents most wanted when asked to describe their ideal latrine. Yet this issue appeared not to have been discussed during CLTS implementation.

Existing 'first-generation' latrine guidelines

There are a number of latrine guideline manuals that have been promoted by various agencies and NGOs over the years. Most counties have some type of latrine options catalogue, though most are quite long and few are under 20 pages.[6] These manuals have been developed for a variety of reasons:

- To provide choice for consumers.
- To provide technical specifications for masons or builders.
- As a technical resource for local government officers as a follow-up to the training they have received.

The guidelines often cover a variety of soil types and situations, for example, rocky soils, sandy soils, and high water tables. The existing guidelines for Kenya were developed by sanitary and civil engineers more than 20 years ago, and the cost of most latrine options presented in the manual are beyond the reach of most rural poor households (Government of Kenya, 1987). In addition, they do not take into account ease of emptying (see Myers, 2016, this book). Generally, latrine guidelines are not used with communities that have been triggered using the CLTS methodology, as this is seen to go against the self-help principles of the CLTS approach, and also because the designs are beyond the budget of most households.

In Kenya, some public health officers (PHO) and technicians note that the training they received on latrine standards during their diploma focused on high end technologies such as VIP latrines and water-borne systems, with insufficient information on low-cost latrines and appropriate technologies for difficult soil conditions. The current curriculum for PHO diploma training does contain modules on both low-cost and more advanced sanitation technologies, but it is difficult to see from the curriculum description the detail of what is covered by each module (Hickling, 2013). In addition, prior to 2015, all PHOs and technicians were not being routinely trained on CLTS as part of their diploma. This has been recognized as an oversight and rectified by the Association of Public Health Officers, who are in the process of strengthening the curricula to take into account both CLTS and sanitation marketing approaches.

A further challenge with the existing latrine guidelines is that they are long. The Kenya guidelines extend to more than 50 pages of close-typed text with few drawings and illustrations. The manual in Kenya is not unique. Across the board, countries' long latrine manuals lead to potential problems:

- The cost of producing the manuals is high.
- They are often general and not customized to particular country situations, nor written in the appropriate language.
- They are large and heavy to carry for use in the field.
- Most are printed on normal paper, which reduces their shelf life when used in the field as the paper tears, or cannot withstand getting wet.
- They are often too complex for front-line staff such as CHWs and Natural Leaders who are the ones interacting with households and providing advice on latrine construction, especially following CLTS.

In order to address some of these barriers, it was decided to develop and test a simpler set of latrine guidelines. Testing and revisions took approximately four months. In addition, given that work had already been carried out on developing the supply side for the work on market-based approaches, it was felt that simplified latrine guidelines might be a way to expand the demand for these products provided by the private sector because they would reach a larger group of households than the commercial marketing and demand campaigns.

Simplified latrine guidance

Given the problems relating to the lengthy guidelines in Kenya, coupled with the evidence of homogeneity in latrine designs and inadequate technical specifications, particularly on pit depth, the MoH in Kenya, working with partners FHI 360, Population Services Kenya, and WSP, embarked on a project to develop some simple job-aids to provide uniform information for front-line staff, in order to assist them in providing guidance to newly triggered households and communities.

The first step was to achieve some consensus about pit depth. We could find no academic studies or references with hard evidence to support specific maximum pit depths (though they do exist for minimum depths). We carried out consultations with sanitary engineers, academics, and sanitation specialists around the globe, to see if we could build consensus on pit depth guidelines. The consensus we arrived at was a maximum pit depth of 1.5 metres above the wet season's water table, as a cut-off, which is of course location specific (in the case of difficult soil or rock conditions).

Following the discussion on pit depth guidelines, it became apparent that Kenya needed to develop a definition for an improved latrine. This process was led by the MoH's policy and research technical working group (TWG) for sanitation whose members are drawn from the ministry, donors, partner agencies, NGOs, and research institutions. A definition of improved sanitation was arrived at which builds on the Joint Monitoring Programme of the World Health Organization and UNICEF (JMP) definition (see Box 6.1).

Box 6.1 Kenya Ministry of Health definition of improved sanitation

An improved facility hygienically separates human excreta from human contact which includes:

  a. Flush/pour to:
    • Piped sewer system
    • Septic tank
    • Pit latrine
  b. Ventilated improved pit (VIP) latrine
  c. Composting toilet

In addition, an improved facility MUST HAVE the following features:

    • Latrine floor/slab should be raised, smooth and impervious, for it to be easily cleaned;
    • It should have no cracks;
    • It should slope towards the squat hole to facilitate draining;
    • It should have a well-fitting lid that does not allow flies into the pit;
    • The superstructure should offer maximum privacy, with a roof to prevent rain entering;
    • It should be at least 40 m from water sources and with a pit depth at a minimum of 1.5 m above the highest ground water levels.

In urban/peri-urban areas, the facility should be embedded in a functioning sanitation system, where the excreta from the toilet is properly stored, transported, treated, disposed, or re-used in a manner which is not hazardous to human health and not detrimental to the environment.

Using this definition developed by the TWG and the MoH, several iterations of the latrine guidelines were tested. Starting off as a two-sided (one page) laminated card (Ministry of Health, 2015), the tool was pre-tested with a number of different community health staff, including CHWs, public health technicians (PHT), PHOs, Community Health Extension Workers (CHEW), and Natural Leaders from communities carrying out CLTS.

The materials were pre-tested to:

1. Learn whether the guidance referred to as 'job aids' by local government were likely to significantly contribute to the ODF rural Kenya roadmap campaign objective of making the country ODF.
2. Assess whether the messages used were clear, understandable, informative, and practical for front-line CLTS implementers.
3. Learn whether the format/design of the materials is convenient, visually appealing, and appropriate for use by CLTS implementers.

A series of focus group discussions and key informant interviews were carried out in areas where CLTS had been carried out and in areas where it has yet to be implemented in Migori, Nakuru, and Baringo counties in Kenya.

In all the sites, the government officers and volunteers had a similar understanding and interpretation of the tool. However, there were differences about how the tool could be used. In non-CLTS sites, the only avenues that government officers have for using the job aid are during community dialogue meetings, home visits, schools and health facility visits. They would have to organize these specifically. However, those in CLTS sites immediately identified that the tool could be used for post-triggering follow-up, and some felt they could use it with communities which had failed to ignite properly following triggering, as the job aids provided a different entry point for further discussion and conversations with communities. Volunteers indicated that they could use the material during their regular community dialogue/action days.

In earlier versions of the tool, it was not obvious that the job aid was to help households make informed choices/assess options while choosing a latrine rather than to provide step-by-step guidance on how to build. However, government officers found that the materials were very useful in their day-to-day work in advising households on latrine construction. They felt it made their work easier, because the job aid provided a focal point with which to have a conversation, and also prompted them to cover all aspects of latrine design. In the counties where the tools were pre-tested, the staff have continued to use them prior to national roll-out. In the field testing areas, although a household survey was not done, the PHOs reported an increased variety of latrine designs. Based on the pre-test and results, national staff from the MoH decided to roll out the guidelines nationally.

The pre-test found that volunteers, unlike the government officers, wanted a different (slightly less technical) version of the tool. It has been developed in two formats, in both English and Kiswahili. Each version is either a short booklet or poster which covers key information on pit depth and lining, slab choice and superstructure. And both outline the pros and cons of all options and link them to the improved sanitation campaign (see Figure 6.1 for an example of the Volunteers English tool). The tools are now being printed and distributed to every county in Kenya by the MoH and have been shared at the Interagency Coordination Committee by the MoH to ensure partners who are implementing either CLTS or sanitation marketing activities use these guidelines. A recent addition is that the tools are being used by sales agents for private sector sanitation solutions.

Conclusions

Carrying out this exercise, we learned that:

- Without guidance, some people build a less sustainable latrine than they can afford, or put the majority of their investment into aspects of the latrine which are unnecessary.
- Latrine choice is not just a factor of how much money a household has, it also depends on their experience of different latrines, the availability of local materials, and knowledge/ideas on how to construct a latrine to maximize health benefit, and to meet aspirations and needs.

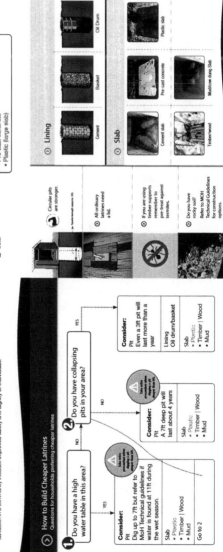

Figure 6.1 Guidelines to help households choose a latrine

Source: Ministry of Health, Kenya

- However, price is important. Given the fluctuation in prices of products, components (cement, iron sheets), and labour over time and in different geographic locations, we did not provide prices on the guidance but indicated which were cheaper and which more expensive. PHOs and PHTs are able to give better price indications to communities at the time of construction.
- Providing simple guidance in field testing led to some households building a longer-lasting sustainable latrine or purchasing latrine components immediately after CLTS triggering.
- The guidance is also used as part of sanitation marketing activities focused on the behaviour of upgrading a latrine.
- It was also established that if volunteers and government officers are going to be involved in CLTS follow-up, they appreciate having tools and job aids to facilitate their discussions and support the guidance they are providing.
- Traditional latrine manuals are too detailed and complex for this cadre of staff and for the majority of households. What is important is that the guidance should be short, portable, made from card or laminated to last, and should not be overly didactic about latrine choice, in order to fit with both CLTS and market-based approaches.
- It is important that the guidelines cover latrine options that are made from locally available materials (as advocated by CLTS) as well as options for purchase or construction by masons, which require a more developed supply chain (sanitation marketing).

Next steps

As mentioned above, the simple latrine guidelines are being rolled out at scale in Kenya. The next step is to evaluate whether areas which are using these tools during CLTS and for follow-up end up building more sustainable latrines, and are less likely to slip back to OD following the disrepair or collapse of their latrines. The MoH plans to follow this as part of the data collection being done with the MIS system for sanitation which is being developed. In addition, with the advent of the Sustainable Development Goals and the need to look at the whole chain for sanitation, as pointed out by Myers (2016, this book), the guidelines will need to be extended to cover safe removal of excreta from filled latrines, and incorporate the costs of emptying into the calculations in terms of life time cost.

Despite the benefits of simple guidelines, there is still a need for more detailed guidance for some difficult terrains, for example, places with loose soils, high water tables, and rocky soils. But during our testing we found that these households could be referred to the government officers or other technical specialists such as builders by volunteers. This advice about seeking technical advice has been added to the final version of the tools.

The reason this initiative is working in Kenya is because CLTS has been rolled out to more counties (almost all 47) than sanitation marketing (less than 10). The products for the supply chain for sanitation marketing are easily available, so the latrine guidelines provide an opportunity for households to view other options if they want to build a more sustainable latrine following triggering, allowing them to leverage the more developed supply chain and products, which have been developed for market-based approaches. Thus they are a supplement to both CLTS and sanitation marketing approaches, and they are not a substitute for either of them. Their aim is to provide consistency and to aid integration.[7]

About the author

Dr Yolande Coombes, World Bank. Yolande worked on a programme to support the Government of Kenya to scale up access to sanitation while working with the Water and Sanitation Program of the World Bank until 2015.

Endnotes

1. With thanks to the Ministry of Health (MoH), USAID's WASHplus, FHI 360 and Population Services Kenya, who worked on this initiative.
2. See http://www.pskenya.org/index.php?id=209 or http://www.wash-cltskenya.or.ke/
3. There are 57,841 villages in total.
4. For more information see http://www.wash-cltskenya.or.ke/
5. This includes a national representative quantitative questionnaire, focus group discussions, household observations, and interviews.
6. For example, Afghanistan (USAID, 2010) and Bhutan (Royal Government of Bhutan, 2012; Shaw, 2014).
7. See also Munkhondia et al., 2016, this book, and http://www.wash-cltskenya.or.ke/

References

Cavill, S. with Chambers, R. and Vernon, N. (2015) 'Sustainability and CLTS: taking stock', *Frontiers of CLTS: Innovations and Insights* 4, Institute of Development Studies, Brighton.

Chavasse, D.C., Shier, R.P., Murphy, O.A., Huttly, S.R., Cousens, S.N. and Akhtar, T. (1999) 'Impact of fly control on childhood diarrhoea in Pakistan: community-randomised trial', *The Lancet*, 353(9146): 22–5 <http://dx.doi.org/10.1016/S0140-6736(98)03366-2>.

Government of Kenya (1987) *Sanitation Field Manual for Kenya*, supported by UNDP and World Bank, Environmental Health Division, Ministry of Health, Nairobi.

Hickling, S. (2013) *Capacity Mapping for Rural Sanitation in Kenya*, unpublished report, Water and Sanitation Program, Nairobi.

Hutton, G. (2012) *Economics of Sanitation*, World Bank, Water and Sanitation Program, Washington, DC.

Ipsos Synovate (2013) *Sanitation Formative Research – Quantitative Report*, unpublished report for Water and Sanitation Program, Nairobi.

Ministry of Health (2015) *Choosing a Latrine, a Guide for CLTS Implementers at the Household Level*, MoH, Nairobi.

Ministry of Health/Water and Sanitation Program (2014) 'Sanitation county fact sheets', http://www.wsp.org/sites/wsp.org/files/publications/WSP-Kenya-47-County-Sanitation-Profiles-2014.pdf [accessed 25 January 2016].

Munkhondia, T., Simangolwa, W. and Zapico, A. (2016) 'CLTS and sanitation marketing: aspects to consider for a better integrated approach', in P. Bongartz, N. Vernon and J. Fox (eds.) *Sustainable Sanitation for All: Experiences, Challenges, and Innovations*, Practical Action, Rugby.

Myers, J. (2016) 'The long-term safe management of rural shit', in P. Bongartz, N. Vernon and J. Fox (eds.) *Sustainable Sanitation for All: Experiences, Challenges, and Innovations in Community-Led Total Sanitation*, Practical Action Publishing, Rugby.

Pedi, D. and Sara, L. (2013) *Sanitation Deep Dive*, unpublished report for IFC and the Water and Sanitation Program, World Bank, Washington, DC.

Perez, E. with Cardosi, J., Coombes, Y., Devine, J., Grossman, A., Kullmann, C., Kumar, A., Mukherjee, N., Prakash, M., Robiarto, A., Setiawan, D., Singh, U. and Wartono, D. (2012) *What Does It Take to Scale Up Rural Sanitation?* Water and Sanitation Program Working Paper, World Bank, Washington, DC.

Royal Government of Bhutan (2012) 'Training manual for toilet construction, Rural Sanitation & Hygiene Programme', Public Health Engineering Division, SNV Bhutan, Thimphu.

Shaw, R. (2014) *A Collection of Contemporary Latrine Designs*, EOOS and WEDC, Loughborough.

Singh, S. and Balfour, N. (2015) 'Micro-planning for CLTS: experience from Kenya', *Eastern and Southern Africa Sanitation and Hygiene Learning Series*, UNICEF, New York NY, www.communityledtotalsanitation.org/resource/micro-planning-clts-experience-kenya [accessed 25 January 2016].

USAID (2010) *Sustainable Water Supply and Sanitation (SWSS) Project Latrine and Sanitation Options Manual*, USAID, Washington DC.

Wamera, E. (2016) 'Who is managing the post-ODF process in the community? A case study of Nambale sub-county in Western Kenya', in P. Bongartz, N. Vernon and J. Fox (eds.) *Sustainable Sanitation for All: Experiences, Challenges, and Innovations*, Practical Action Publishing, Rugby.

CHAPTER 7

Sanitation infrastructure sustainability challenges case study: Ethiopia

Hunachew Beyene

Abstract

This chapter is based on the findings of a cross-sectional study which investigated the high rate of reversion to open defecation (OD) in Sidama, southern Ethiopia. Collapsing toilets, and the lack of availability of durable and affordable toilet options and materials for construction on the market were identified as key reasons for this reversion. The study identified the importance of formative research to identify community needs, financial capabilities, and availability of sanitation technologies, and encouraging successful local innovations as key lessons for sustainability of open defecation free (ODF) status.

Keywords: Latrine sustainability, Sanitation technology, Open defecation, Pit latrine, Pit collapse, Ethiopia

Methodology

A cross-sectional study carried out in June to July 2013 in Sidama, southern Ethiopia assessed the sanitation infrastructure sustainability challenges in eight kebeles (the smallest administrative unit in the country), four from ODF (open defecation free) and four from non-ODF kebeles. The ODF kebeles had been declared ODF between five months to two years previously. A total of 1,677 households, 49.7 per cent from ODF and 50.3 per cent from non-ODF kebeles were selected. Household data was collected through questionnaires and observations. In addition, eight focus group discussions (FGDs) were held in each kebele, with 8–12 participants in each group.

Findings

Quantitative data

In ODF villages, nearly 80 per cent of households had a toilet, in non-ODF villages the figure was only 59 per cent. The number of functional toilets was approximately 75 per cent in ODF and 55 per cent in non-ODF communities meaning 25 per cent in ODF communities were still practising OD. Thirty per cent of toilets in ODF and 22 per cent in non-ODF villages did not have

http://dx.doi.org/10.3362/9781780449272.007

a proper soil slab. Fifty-eight per cent of toilets in ODF and 55 per cent of toilets in non-ODF kebeles had superstructures. In addition, 20 per cent of the toilets were flood-prone, and more than 39 per cent of the toilets were not considered hygienic.

Qualitative data

Various challenges to use were revealed. One of the main challenges was durability, with collapse of pit latrines shortly after construction. One respondent said:

> Temporarily, people construct their toilet by using any available material, mainly using eucalyptus tree logs 'Terb'. This does not last long as it decomposes easily ... the soil applied on the logs facilitates the decomposition. Therefore, within a year, it falls down. Mainly in the rainy season rain just falls on it as there is no rain protection [superstructure].

Durability affected confidence in using the toilets, 'because of fear of collapse, people defecate near the toilets...' Availability and affordability were also key challenges. There was agreement among participants that due to population increases and a reduction in forest cover, strong wood is either not available, or it is prohibited to cut the trees down. Consequently, they had to buy a stronger locally available wood ('kench') to make a toilet slab or a proper superstructure. However, 'kench' is not affordable for many of the families. One respondent said:

> ... for my own household, I can construct the toilet in a good way so that I can use it as long as possible. But, that will be done when I have money and able to buy the good quality woods. We don't afford to buy them as one kench costs 20 birr (US$1).

Another respondent said, 'Grass is not available in the environment that can be used to cover the roof... We apply leaves, and when the leaves, dry and fall on the ground it becomes open'.

Communal toilets are even more problematic. In addition to the lack of strong wood, there is also the fact that there is no one responsible for them. One respondent mentioned, 'Once when I was using a communal toilet, my leg entered the hole because ... the superstructure collapsed'.

To combat the issue of durability some households have used locally carved stone slabs, which are resistant to decomposition and more durable. These local innovations should be supported and encouraged.

Even when families had financial resources to construct good quality toilets, more durable materials were not easily available in the market or the surrounding area. The current Community-Led Total Sanitation approach encourages households to construct using locally available materials with no infrastructure options given, and no consideration of financial capabilities. Most toilet owners (94 per cent) were interested in improved toilet options and some said they would need partial or full government support. However, 64 per cent mentioned they would be able to afford to buy new sanitation technologies.

Key lessons learnt

- A lack of appropriate locally available and affordable options means some facilities do not fulfil the requirements needed to climb onto the first rung of the sanitation ladder.
- Formative research should be used to identify community needs, financial capabilities, and availability of sanitation technologies.
- Government and NGOs should promote appropriate simple, affordable, and sustainable options that can be applicable to different geographic locations and are resilient to the environment and suitable to local soil conditions.
- Different options for different socio-economic conditions should also be promoted.
- Post-triggering, professionals should support communities choosing an appropriate location and assist in the construction of good pit latrines with locally available materials.
- Local innovations that have proven to be successful, such as the locally carved stones, should also be encouraged and supported.
- If the cutting of trees goes against the law, the government or other stakeholders need to provide other options.

About the author

Hunachew Beyene is an employee of Hawassa University and is currently working on his PhD. He has been teaching Environmental Health courses such as on-site sanitation, and conducted research focusing on the effect of sanitation interventions on diarrhoeal disease, intestinal parasites, and trachoma in southern Ethiopia.

CHAPTER 8

The long-term safe management of rural shit

Jamie Myers

Abstract

Community-Led Total Sanitation (CLTS) has led to millions of pit latrines being built in rural communities across the world. However, pits or tanks filling up is emerging as a challenge to the open defecation free (ODF) status of some of these communities. Households or individuals may revert back to open defecation (OD) if digging a new pit is problematic or emptying services are not available or too expensive. Furthermore, fear of pits becoming full can dissuade people from using toilets. Services for emptying are often inadequate and can result in unsafe and indiscriminate dumping of pit content into the environment. This chapter explores this problem, which has the potential to become more pressing with time as more and more pits begin to fill, and presents potential options for tackling this challenge. It includes specific recommendations for CLTS practice that will help ensure rural shit is contained and managed safely and hygienically.

Keywords: Faecal Sludge Management, Rural sanitation, On-site sanitation, Health, Environment

Introduction

Bad rural pit latrine management, including pit emptying, has serious health and environmental risks (Evans et al., 2015). Most outcomes of Community-Led Total Sanitation (CLTS) programmes lead to households creating on-site sanitation solutions. Whether the outcome is a pit latrine or a septic tank, faeces are not directly taken away by sewage systems but remain contained, hopefully hygienically, in the ground below the toilet facility.

Faecal Sludge Management (FSM) encompasses the storage, collection, transport, treatment, and safe end use or disposal of faecal sludge (Strande et al., 2014). Discussions around FSM have not been ignored, but are usually confined to urban environments where higher population densities mean the poor disposal of sludge will have a higher impact on health. The 3rd International FSM Conference held in 2015 had only one presentation focusing on rural sludge. Last year saw the publication of *Faecal Sludge Management: Systems Approach for Implementation and Operation*. It argued for the need to first determine the final disposal options of sludge (Strande et al., 2014). It also suggested that all members of the community must properly manage faecal sludge to ensure

http://dx.doi.org/10.3362/9781780449272.008

public health benefits (Strande et al., 2014), something that may resonate with those familiar with the CLTS approach. However, the focus of the book was exclusively urban. By using an FSM lens, focusing on safe and hygienic storage, collection and transportation (where appropriate), and disposal or end-use, various issues that challenge the sustainable and safe confinement of rural shit begin to appear.

This chapter argues for the need for CLTS and other rural programmes to consider what will happen when pits begin filling up. It is an attempt to convince practitioners and policy-makers of the need to consider the safe confinement of shit permanently in rural environments as an issue needing attention from the start.

The problem: a mountain out of a molehill?

Why has FSM been given such little attention? Is it not a serious problem? Are most rural pits new additions to households and not yet full? Is it assumed that new pits are always dug?

When pits in rural areas are filling or full there are four options:

- Stop using and dig another pit.
- Empty the pit.
- Use sparingly.
- Abandon and revert to open defecation (OD) (Chambers and Myers, 2016).

Emptying pits can be expensive. In rural Laos, the average cost of emptying a pit is US$50. Households that were unable to afford this reverted back to OD (Opel and Cheuasongkham, 2015). In Cambodia, it has also been noted that there is an increased risk of reversion back to OD by households who can't afford pit emptying services (Wood, 2011).

Digging a new pit can be difficult where there is little space or the soil type, topography, or hydrogeology makes this process difficult and expensive. In Zambia, where pits are generally abandoned when full and a new latrine is then constructed, those with small compounds are running out of space (SNV Zambia, 2014). Furthermore, it is generally only viable when the superstructure is moveable (Tilley et al., 2014). Consequently, this option is not always feasible.

Recently we have seen an increased interest in combining CLTS and sanitation marketing (see Coombes, 2016, this book; Munkhondia et al., 2016, this book). As households invest more in both the substructure and the superstructure, moving towards the middle rung of the sanitation ladder, digging a new pit becomes more and more difficult. Soil slabs can be made again relatively cheaply, concrete slabs can be moved but pits lined with concrete rings or bricks and superstructures made from bricks and stones are difficult to transfer to new pits. Once pits fill up, households are faced with the question of what to do next. The World Bank's Water and Sanitation Program (WSP) 'Introductory Guide to Sanitation Marketing' recommends that masons should be trained in services, including proper sludge management (Devine and Kullman, 2011). However, a recent review of 22 rural sanitation supply studies commissioned by WSP found that there was little innovation in aftersales services such as maintenance, repairs, waste removal, and management once a pit or tank reaches capacity (Dumpert and Perez, 2015).

In Bangladesh, the evaluation of the BRAC water, sanitation, and hygiene (WASH) programme identified pit emptying and the safe final disposal of the sludge as a major 'second generation' challenge (BRAC, 2014). In addition, Chapter 2 on Bangladesh (Hanchett, 2016, this book) showed that because the country is so close to ODF the major challenge now is the problem of faecal sludge, in both rural and urban environments. It highlights the concerns of WASH professionals who described the installation of pit latrines across the country without considering what to do with the faecal sludge as a major problem (Hanchett, 2016, this book). The same problem has also been identified in Kerala, India, where latrine coverage is 96 per cent (Samuel, 2013).

In addition, the fear of having to empty pits can dissuade people from using toilets. In rural northern India, people strive for deep, large pits that will not have to be emptied in their lifetime (Coffey et al., 2015; Shah et al., 2013). The availability and perceived affordability of pit emptying services has also been noted as a key issue in sustaining latrine usage and subsequently ODF communities in Bangladesh (Hanchett et al., 2011).

Problems along the sanitation chain

Sanitation services need to be thought out throughout the entire sanitation chain (Verhagen and Carrasco, 2013). Using the FSM chain (storage, collection and transportation, and end-use and disposal) to frame practices in rural areas can help further expose the importance of the issue.

> ATTENTION! It is important to note here the FSM does not always mean collection. The emptying, transportation, and disposal of sludge from pit latrines can pose a significant health risk alongside organizational difficulties (Water Research Commission, 2007). Covering pits and digging new ones can also be a safe and hygienic FSM option.

Storage

Human excreta needs to be contained and stored safely. Safe confinement means a slab that seals the pit and prevents rodents and flies from entering. Storage is where CLTS has focused; however problems have still occurred. Data collected in southern Ethiopia found that 30 per cent of slabs in ODF villages where CLTS interventions had taken place contained openings additional to the squat hole (Beyene, 2016, this book). In addition, personal experience from visiting CLTS villages in Uganda has highlighted a similar problem:

slabs made from wood with large gaps between the boards. Consequently, although there is no longer shit in fields where children play, slabs are not adequately sealed and vectors are able to move in and out of the pit, enabling the continuation of faecal-oral pathways.

There are different perspectives on the dangers associated with contamination of groundwater from pit latrines. WASH professionals have been accused of being irrational as health risks are usually lower than anticipated (Sugden, 2006). In the majority of cases, contamination of groundwater is not a serious concern and most on-site latrines separate latrine content from drinking water sources (Cave and Kolsky, 1999). However, baseline data collected by SNV in Ghana, Nepal, and Tanzania found that pit latrines were in danger of contaminating groundwater (SNV Ghana, 2014; SNV Nepal, 2014; SNV Tanzania, 2014). Although contamination risks may be low, alternative water sources in rural areas may be limited, making contamination very costly (Howard et al., 2014). Methods of reducing the risk of contamination include: increasing the distance between latrines and water points; moving the water point higher than the latrine; using a drier form of toilet; and increasing the vertical separation between the bottom of the pit and the water table (Sugden, 2006).

Collection and transportation (where appropriate)

As mentioned above, there are certain instances when emptying and desludging may be an appropriate action, where digging a new pit is not possible due to space or soil type or the substructure or superstructure is not easily movable. Those providing this service are often not well protected. In Bangladesh, sweepers often do not use either gloves or protective clothing, thus coming into direct contact with sludge (Evans et al., 2015). Furthermore, Aashish Gupta et al.'s contribution to this book shows the social stigma associated with *dalit* communities who traditionally deal with human waste (Gupta et al., 2016, this book).

Disposal or end use (where appropriate)

Untreated faecal sludge is very dangerous and highly pathogenic, and direct contact should be avoided (Tilley et al., 2014). Despite this it is common for sludge to be disposed of in the sea, rivers, ponds, lakes, and onto land (Pickford and Shaw, 1999). A report published by IRC noted, 'In rural areas, it is becoming increasingly clear that when pit latrines are emptied, the sludge is dumped indiscriminately, leading to what may be labelled as "postponed open-defecation"' (Verhagen and Carrasco, 2013: 6).

In Ghana, SNV found that in 53.1 per cent of cases excreta had been emptied into a hole on the compound and just left open (SNV Ghana, 2014). In Laos, as official dumping sites are too expensive for the private sector, raw sludge is placed in roadside ditches, canals, and open water bodies with no objection from government or the public (Opel and Cheuasongkham, 2015). In Cambodia, sludge from pits is often put into neighbouring padi fields

(Wood, 2011). In Vietnam, even in urban areas untreated sludge is dumped into the environment (PSI Vietnam, 2014).

Safe and hygienic FSM can help not just sustain ODF communities but also sustain the removal of faeces from **everybody's** environment permanently.

Ways forward?

All major organizations working in WASH were contacted for this chapter; however it emerged that there is little programmatic experience. Below are examples of work happening across the world on pit latrine management and FSM.

Measuring

The saying 'what gets measured gets managed' seems appropriate here. The rate at which pits fill up, what happens after, and how this affects sustainability is something we know little about. The Joint Monitoring Programme 2014 Report suggests measuring 'the percentage of people who use a basic sanitation facility and whose excreta are safely transported to a designated disposal/treatment site or treated *in situ* before being reused or returned to the environment' to measure access to safely managed sanitation services (WHO and UNICEF, 2014). Having this information is an important first step.

As part of Plan's Pan Africa CLTS Programme participating countries were required to count the number of full pits. The data suggests that 3,000 toilets had filled up, approximately 1 per cent of the total constructed. However, it was also noted that the data was fairly unreliable (Robinson, 2014) and what happened afterwards was not measured.

In SNV's Sustainable Sanitation and Hygiene Results Programme, participating countries all included FSM emptying and collection as a sustainability indicator. A score of 0 to 4 is given depending on the system in place (SNV Zambia, 2014):

> 0 – no on-site storage;
> 1 – storage but no emptying;
> 2 – unsafe emptying;
> 3 – partially safe emptying and collection;
> 4 – safe emptying and collection.

At WaterAid, Post-Implementation Monitoring Surveys (PIMS) are used to assess the sustainability of their programmes. A range of different questions about water, sanitation, and hygiene are asked, including what will happen once the pit is full. Each country is supposed to conduct one small-scale PIMS each year, surveying a limited part of a WaterAid supported intervention. One country from each of the four different regions WaterAid work in are supposed to conduct a large-scale PIMS, meaning it covers all the interventions.

Researchers at the University of North Carolina are developing and piloting ways that international organizations and countries are able to estimate the fraction of human excreta unsafely returned to the environment to establish at what points along the sanitation chain this happens. More information about the project titled *Unsafe Return of Human Excreta to the Environment* can be found on the Water Institute's project page.[1]

Certification criteria

The phased sanitation framework introduced in the Philippines by UNICEF (Robinson and Gnilo, 2016, Chapter 9, this book) has three stages of certification. In the second phase, Sustainable Sanitation Barangay, toilets must have sustainable designs which include the potential for safe emptying or replacement of the pit or septic tank (UNICEF Philippines, 2013).

Emptying technologies

There are a number of different technologies that are either manually operated or fully mechanized. However, these technologies do not help answer the question of what happens to the sludge after it has been removed. One is the Gulper, a manually operated pump that can be connected to pits via a pipe. The user raises and lowers a handle which pumps the sludge out of the pit. It has been used in urban areas but has also been tested in remote areas (Cranfield University et al., 2011).

For a range of different semi and fully mechanized technologies see Mikhael et al. (2014) and WASTE et al. (2015).

Transfer stations

Transfer stations act as a primary collection point. Those using manual or small technologies can empty into transfer stations which can then be collected by larger vacuum trucks and taken to treatment facilities. They have been used in urban areas where even the travel times to and from treatment or disposal sites can be too great for sludge collection to be economically viable. Establishing multiple transfer stations across cities should decrease the risk of illegal dumping as well promote the emptying market (Tilley et al., 2014). Despite built-in inefficiency, the shit having to be handled twice, they may be viable in rural areas where indiscriminate dumping is a problem. For more details on transfer stations in an urban environment see Mukheibir (2015).

Combining FSM services with sanitation marketing

Indonesian truck-based emptying services for pits and septic tanks are already worth an estimated US$100 m per year. There, 90 one-stop-shop (OSS) sanitation entrepreneurs offering a single enterprise for products and services have been set up. They offer a range of different product options, delivery of products, installation, flexible payment options, and bulk purchase discounts. In addition, and most importantly for FSM and sustainability of infrastructure, some also provide after-sales services including maintenance. It is reported that between one (Pedi and Kamsan, forthcoming) and several (Budi Dar-mawan, personal communication) also offer desludging services. Although this number is disappointing, it is reported that many OSSs have built a strong customer base and are starting to see the potential of providing FSM services. Questions still remain regarding ways to encourage more to provide this ser-vice and what will happen further down the sludge chain (Pedi and Kamsan, forthcoming).

Ecological Sanitation (EcoSan)

Where appropriate, EcoSan could be a viable option. EcoSan comprises a range of technology options that promote the use of human excreta as a resource. The fact that households are able to manage their own sludge can be either positive or negative. A huge benefit, other than the reuse in agriculture, is that households are less reliant on others. However, households can also be unhappy about the extra burden being placed on them and there are many cultural barriers to the handling and reuse of excreta.

Different options include:

- **The Arborloo:** A shallow pit is dug and covered with a simple super-structure. Dried leaves are added to the bottom of the pit and a concrete slab is placed over the pit. After use, a mix of ash, soil and/or wood is added. Household rubbish should not be thrown in the pit. Before the pit is full the slab is removed and the pit filled up with soil and a tree planted (CSR, 2009). Arborloos are low cost and easy to make (Morgan, 2004). However, they require an adequate amount of space and old pits cannot be reused (Tilley et al. 2014). In addition, they are unsuitable in areas with a high water table.
- **Urine Diverting Dry Toilets (UDDT):** UDDTs are waterless with the urine and faeces being separated at the source and stored apart. UDDTs require less space yet have relatively high construction, operation, and maintenance costs (Nilsson et al., 2011).
- **Twin Pits:** A two pit model is currently being promoted in India as part of the Swachh Bharat Mission and has been promoted in Bangladesh by BRAC since 2008. The two pits are used in rotation. Once one pit is full it is left so that the content degrades into organic fertilizer. The other pit is then used. Sludge, once composted and therefore safe, can be emptied manually.

Tigers and worms: a way forward?

The Tiger Toilet is an onsite sanitation system that uses worms to change fresh faeces into vermicompost. A bedding layer made from locally available material acts as a filter with effluent infiltrating the soil below. Unlike other options it reduces the frequency of emptying. Through field tests in India, developers have estimated that it would require emptying after approximately five years. Vermicompost is produced which is dry and soil-like and easy and safe to empty (Furlong et al., 2015).

The vermifilter below the ground is connected to a pour-flush toilet. The water seal provides a superior system to current traditional pit latrine options giving it the potential to be an aspirational product with similar benefits of a septic tank but with better waste treatment and at a considerably lower cost (Furlong et al., 2015).[2]

Challenges to safe rural pit management services

There are various challenges to safe rural pit management in rural areas. Increased distances to towns where FSM services may be located raises the costs of safe and hygienic emptying. Treatment and disposal facilities are also more likely to be further away, increasing prices and encouraging dumping. Furthermore, market-based solutions are only viable where communities see there is a problem. In West Bengal it has been noted there is little to no dissatisfaction with dumping sludge (Sugden, 2015), while in Laos there is limited awareness about the health issues associated with the unsafe disposal of sludge (Opel and Cheuasongkham, 2015). Indiscriminate dumping in Laos does not trigger complaints from governments or communities (Opel and Cheuasongkham, 2015). Dispersed populations in rural areas also makes it more difficult to regulate and enforce laws (Sugden, 2015) even in areas where governments are keen to take action.

Even for those wanting to make a career out of pit emptying, the social costs can be heavy (Sudgen, 2013). For example, in India the lowest castes are seen as both permanently polluted as well as polluting to others. Those who clean human faeces are considered the most polluted. This link to pollution is often used to justify continued oppression. Those who do this job are the most socially excluded (see Gupta et al., 2016, this book; Coffey et al., 2015). It is important that any FSM system does not lead to those dealing with shit also being treated like shit.

Recommendations and ways forward

- It is important not to overload the triggering process and dilute the communities' realization that they are eating each other's shit (Roose et al., 2015). However, actions with the community can be taken in the post-triggering phase where different latrine options are being considered.
- Follow-up could include facilitated discussions about fill-up rates, options once pit latrines have filled up and raising awareness about the health and environmental risks involved in the indiscriminate dumping of faecal sludge.

- Finding the appropriate timing for introducing any pit management/ FSM component to a project is an area of formative research. Further thinking and discussion is needed about whether pit management should be incorporated into post-triggering or post-ODF follow-up.
- FSM options must be user-friendly. Following in the tradition of CLTS, communities should participate in discussions surrounding what happens when pit latrines fill up. Should new pits be dug or should they be emptied and disposed of safely? Consumer preferences, including costs, need to be discussed and considered. Any discussion around toilet options should include how technologies affect pit management. Those working in FSM could learn from CLTS practitioners about participatory methods.
- Beyond the technological, social considerations are needed, especially in South Asia, where there is the risk that pit management/FSM service providers could be ostracized.

Conclusions

Using an FSM lens, assessing all parts of the chain is helpful to identify problems and suggest areas where inventions are needed to sustain the safe containment or removal of faeces from pits or tanks and the environment. This also includes safe storage of faeces while pits are filling up. An increase in interest in sanitation marketing that focuses on hardware components will exacerbate the problem. It is essential that households who invest in more permanent and less mobile sub- and superstructures have affordable services available or are able to deal with the sludge safely without assistance. There are many opportunities within the CLTS process post-triggering and post-ODF that can help. However, developing FSM services is riddled with problems and additional support from those outside the community will be necessary in most cases including government and the private sector.

About the author

Jamie Myers is the CLTS Knowledge Hub's Research Officer. Based at the Institute of Development Studies, he works on CLTS and CLTS-related activities across the world with a particular interest in post-triggering and post-ODF processes. He is the co-author of *Frontiers of CLTS: Innovations and Insights* 'Norms, Knowledge and Usage'.

Endnotes

1. http://waterinstitute.unc.edu/research/current-projects/unsafe-return/
2. For more information contact Dr Claire Furlong c.furlong@lboro.ac.uk.

References

Beyene, H. (2016) 'Sanitation infrastructure sustainability challenges case study: Ethiopia', in P. Bongartz, N. Vernon and J. Fox (eds.) *Sustainable Sanitation for All: Experiences, Challenges, and Innovations*, Practical Action Publishing, Rugby.

BRAC (2014) *Faecal Sludge Management – 1*, BRAC Water Sanitation and Hygiene Programme, Dhaka, http://www.ircwash.org/sites/default/files/brac_wash_faecal_sludge_management_dec_2014.pdf [accessed 25 January 2016].

Cave, B. and Kolsky, P. (1999) *Groundwater, Latrines and Health*, WELL Resource Centre, http://www.lboro.ac.uk/orgs/well/resources/well-studies/full-reports-pdf/task0163.pdf [accessed 28 January 2016].

Chambers, R. and Myers, J. (2016) 'Norms, knowledge and usage', *Frontiers of CLTS: Innovations and Insights* 7, Institute of Development Studies, Brighton.

Coffey, D., Gupta, A., Payal, H., Spears, D., Srivastav, N. and Vyas, S. (2015) *Culture and Health Transition: Understanding Sanitation Behaviour in Rural North India*, International Growth Centre Working Paper, IGC, London, http://www.theigc.org/wp-content/uploads/2015/04/Coffey-et-al-2015-Working-Paper.pdf [accessed 25 January 2016].

Coombes, Y. (2016) 'User centred latrine guidelines. Integrating CLTS with sanitation marketing: a case study from Kenya to promote informed choice', in P. Bongartz, N. Vernon and J. Fox (eds.) *Sustainable Sanitation for All: Experiences, Challenges, and Innovations*, Practical Action Publishing, Rugby.

Cranfield University, SKAT, WaterAid and IRC (2011) *Africa Wide Water, Sanitation and Hygiene Technology Review*, WASHTech Deliverable 2.1, Cranfield University, Cranfield, https://washtechafrica.files.wordpress.com/2011/04/washtech_wp2-1_africa_wide_water_sanitation_hygiene_technology_review.pdf [accessed 25 January 2016].

CSR (2009) *Innovations in Water and Sanitation: The ArborLoo Latrine*, http://www.medbox.org/key-resources/innovations-in-water-and-sanitation-promoting-ecological-sanitation-in-ethiopia-through-the-arborloo-latrine/preview?q [accessed 28 January 2016].

Devine, J. and Kullmann, C. (2011) *Introductory Guide to Sanitation Marketing*, Water and Sanitation Programme: Toolkit, WSP/The World Bank, Washington, DC.

Dumpert, J. and Perez, E. (2015) 'Going beyond masons training: enabling, facilitating, and engaging rural sanitation markets for the base of the pyramid', *Waterlines*, 34.3: 210–226 <http://dx.doi.org/10.3362/1756-3488.2015.021>.

Evans, B., Fletcher, L.A., Camargo-Valero, M.A., Balasubramanya, S., Rao, C.K., Fernando, S., Ahmed, R., Habib, A., Asad, N.S.M., Rahman, M.M., Kabir, K.B. and Emon, M.H. (2015) *VesV - Value at the end of the Sanitation Value Chain*, University of Leeds, Leeds, http://www.ircwash.org/sites/default/files/vesv_final_report_30-mar-2015_macv_-_amended.pdf [accessed 25 January 2016].

Furlong, C., Gibson, W.T., Templeton, M.R., Taillade, M., Kassam, F., Crabb, G., Goodsell, R., McQuilkin, J., Oak, A., Thakar, G., Kodgire, M. and Patankar, R. (2015) 'The development of an onsite sanitation system based on vermifiltration: the "tiger toilet"', *Journal of Water Sanitation and Hygiene for Development*, 5(4): 614–9 <http://dx.doi.org/10.2166/washdev.2015.167>.

Gupta, A., Coffey, D. and Spears, D. (2016) 'Purity, pollution, and untouchability: challenges affecting the adoption, use, and sustainability of sanitation programmes in rural India', in P. Bongartz, N. Vernon and J. Fox (eds.) *Sustainable Sanitation for All: Experiences, Challenges, and Innovations*, Practical Action, Rugby.

Hanchett, S. (2016) 'Sanitation in Bangladesh: revolution, evolution, and new challenges', in P. Bongartz, N. Vernon and J. Fox (eds.) *Sustainable Sanitation for All: Experiences, Challenges, and Innovations*, Practical Action, Rugby.

Hanchett, S., Krieger, L., Kahn, M.H., Kullmannn, C. and Ahmed, R. (2011) *Long-Term Sustainability of Improved Sanitation in Rural Bangladesh*, World Bank, Washington, DC, https://openknowledge.worldbank.org/handle/10986/17347 [accessed 28 January 2016].

Howard, G., Reed, B., McChesney, D. and Taylor, R. (2014) 'Human excreta and sanitation: control and protection', in O. Schmoll, G. Howard, J. Chilton and I. Chorus (eds.), *Protecting Groundwater for Health: Managing the Quality of Drinking-Water Sources*, World Health Organization, IWA Publishing, London.

Mikhael, G., Robbins, D.M., Ramsay, J.E. and Mbéguérém, M. (2014) 'Methods and means for collection and transport of faecal sludge', Chapter 4 in D. Brdjenovic, M. Ronteltap and L. Strande (eds) *Fecal Sludge Management: Systems Approach for Implementation and Management*, IWA Publishing, London   http://www.eawag.ch/fileadmin/Domain1/Abteilungen/sandec/publikationen/EWM/Book/FSM_Ch04_Collection_and_Transport.pdf [accessed 26 January 2016].

Munkhondia, T., Simangolwa, W. and Zapico, A. (2016) 'CLTS and sanitation marketing: aspects to consider for a better integrated approach', in P. Bongartz, N. Vernon and J. Fox (eds.), *Sustainable Sanitation for All: Experiences, Challenges, and Innovations*, Rugby: Practical Action Publishing.

Morgan, P. (2004) *The Arborloo Book: How to Make a Simple Pit Toilet and Grow Trees or Make Humus for the Garden*, Stockholm Environment Institute, Stockholm.

Mukheibir, P. (2015) *Learning Paper: Septage Transfer Stations*, prepared for SNV Netherlands Development Organisation by Institute for Sustainable Futures, University of Technology Sydney, Sydney, http://forum.susana.org/media/kunena/attachments/1609/SNVISFSeptagetransferstationslearningpaper-draftJune.pdf [accessed 26 January 2016].

Nilsson, Å., Cross, P., Robinson, A., Alvetag, T., Bara, A., Quiroga, T. and Yun, L. (2011) *Evaluation of EcoSanRes Programme*, Phase 2 (personal communication).

Opel, A., and Cheuasongkham, P. (2015) *Faecal Sludge Management Services in Rural Laos: Critical Gaps and Important Ways Forward*, 3rd Faecal Sludge Management Conference, Hanoi, Vietnam.

Pedi, D. and Kamsan, A. (forthcoming 2016) *Sanitation Market Transformation in Indonesia: Designing Viable Business Models*, Water and Sanitation Program, World Bank, Washington, DC.

Pickford, J. and Shaw, R. (1999) 'Emptying pit latrines, Technical Brief No. 54', in R. Shaw (ed.) *Running Water: More Technical Briefs on Health, Water and Sanitation*, IT Publications, London.

PSI Vietnam (2014) *Rural Sanitation Rapid Market Scan Report*, PSI, Vietnam, http://www.psi.org/wp-content/uploads/2014/11/Sanitation-Market-Scan-Final-rev-2.pdf [accessed 26 January 2016].

Robinson, A. (2014) *Plan Pan African CLTS Program Benchmarking Summary Report*: Q5 June 2014, unpublished (personal communication).

Robinson, A. and Gnilo, M. (2016) 'Beyond ODF: a phased approach to rural sanitation development', Chapter 9 in P. Bongartz, N. Vernon and J. Fox (eds.) *Sustainable Sanitation for All: Experiences, Challenges, and Innovations*, Practical Action Publishing, Rugby.

Roose, S., Rankin, T. and Cavill, S. (2015) 'Breaking the next taboo: menstrual hygiene within CLTS', *Frontiers of CLTS: Innovations and Insights* 6, Institute of Development Studies, Brighton.

Samuel, S. (2013) *Septage: Kerala's Looming Sanitation Challenge*, The Water Blog, World Bank, http://blogs.worldbank.org/water/septage-kerala-s-looming-sanitation-challenge [accessed 7 September 2015].

Shah, A., Thathachari, J., Agarwai, R. and Karamchandani, A. (2013) *A Market Led, Evidence Based Approach to Rural Sanitation*, White Paper prepared by Monitor Inclusive Markets on behalf of The Bill and Melinda Gates Foundation, DTTIPL, India, http://www.gramalaya.in/pdf/Market_Led_Approach_to_Rural_Sanitation.pdf [accessed 26 January 2016].

SNV Ghana (2014) *Sustainable Sanitation and Hygiene for All Results Programme*, Baseline Survey Report, Ghana, DFID Sustainable Sanitation and Hygiene for all Results Programme, http://snv-website-2015.live.dpdk.com/public/cms/sites/default/files/explore/download/p1-gh-1_baseline_report_ghana_0.pdf [accessed 26 January 2016].

SNV Nepal (2014) *Sustainable Sanitation and Hygiene for All Results Programme*, Nepal Baseline Report, SNV, Kathmandu, (unpublished).

SNV Tanzania (2014) *Sanitation Baseline Results for Karatu, Babati, Geita, Kwimba, and Chato Districts in Tanzania*, SNV Smart Development Works, http://snv-website-2015.live.dpdk.com/public/cms/sites/default/files/explore/download/p1-tz-1_baseline_report_tanzania.pdf [accessed 26 January 2016].

SNV Zambia (2014) *Zambia Country Baseline Report: Sustainable Sanitation and Hygiene for All Results Programme*, SNV, (unpublished).

Strande, L., Ronteltap, M. and Brdjanovic, D. (2014) *Faecal Sludge Management: Systems Approach for Implementation and Operation*, IWA Publishing, London.

Sugden, S. (2006) *The Microbiological Contamination of Water Supplies*, WELL Resource Centre, http://www.lboro.ac.uk/orgs/well/resources/fact-sheets/fact-sheets-htm/Contamination.htm [accessed 28 January 2016].

Sugden, S. (2013) 'The importance of understanding the market when designing pit-emptying devices', *Waterlines*, 32(3): 200–212 <http://dx.doi.org/10.3362/1756-3488.2013.021>.

Sugden, S. (2015) *Rural FSM Development in West Bengal*, unpublished.

Tilley, E., Ulrich, L., Lüthi, C., Reymond, P. and Zurbrügg, C. (2014) *Compendium of Sanitation Systems and Technologies*, Eawag, Dübendorf.

UNICEF Philippines (2013) 'Development of a multi-stakeholder implementation strategy for scaling up rural sanitation: Final Report', (unpublished), UNICEF, Philippines.

Verhagen, J. and Carrasco, M. (2013) *Full-Chain Sanitation Services that Last: Non-sewered Sanitation Services*, IRC, The Hague.

WASTE, Netherlands Red Cross and the International Federation of Red Cross and Red Crescent Societies (2015) *Testing and Developing of Desludging Units for Emptying Pit Latrines and Septic Tanks*, WASTE/IFRC/ESP, http://www.speedkits.eu/sites/www.speedkits.eu/files/Elaborate%20report%20field%20testing%20pit%20emptying%20Blantyre.pdf [accessed 26 January 2016].

Water Research Commission (2007) *Design and Operation Requirement to Optimize the Life Span of VIP Toilets: Outcome of WRC Project 1630*, WRC, South Africa, http://www.susana.org/_resources/documents/default/2-253-wrc-2007-optimize-life-span-vip-en.pdf [accessed 26 January 2016].

WHO and UNICEF (2014) *Progress on Drinking Water and Sanitation*, 2014 Update, WHO/UNICEF, Geneva, http://www.unicef.org/gambia/Progress_on_ drinking_water_and_sanitation_2014_update.pdf [accessed 26 January 2016].

Wood, J. (2011) 'The quest for sustainable sanitation in Cambodia', in *What Happens When the Pit is Full?* Report of FSM Seminar, Durban, 14–15 March 2011, Water Information Network, South Africa/Water Research Council, http://www.ecosanres.org/pdf_files/WhatHappensWhenThePitIsFullFSM SeminarReportSouthAfricaNodeMarch2011.pdf [accessed 26 January 2016].

PART III: Post-ODF engagement and monitoring

CHAPTER 9

Beyond ODF: a phased approach to rural sanitation development

Andrew Robinson and Michael Gnilo

Abstract

Community-Led Total Sanitation (CLTS) has proved a powerful approach for triggering open defecation free (ODF) communities, but there is increasing evidence that the sustainability of these collective sanitation outcomes is fragile, and that the most critical households in terms of health benefits – disadvantaged groups with the highest disease burden – are often the first to revert to open defecation (OD). A phased approach to rural sanitation development encourages community progression beyond the ODF outcome to higher levels of service that incorporate other critical sanitation outcomes: institutional sanitation, improved handwashing with soap, solid and liquid waste management, and safe water management. Each phase sets gradually higher targets for collective sanitation outcomes, with carefully designed verification criteria and sustainability checks on previous outcomes. Achievement of the first ODF outcome is taken as proof of genuine demand and behaviour change, after which targeted support is provided to poor and vulnerable households that might otherwise struggle to achieve better sanitation and hygiene.

Keywords: Phased approach, Rural sanitation, Sustainability, Philippines, Handwashing with soap, Policy

Why is the phased approach relevant to rural sanitation development?

This chapter outlines a phased approach to rural sanitation development that has been developed and implemented by UNICEF in the Philippines (Robinson, 2012, 2013). The phased approach was developed in late 2013, shortly before Super-Typhoon Yolanda hit the central Philippines, and was subsequently adapted for use in the large post-typhoon recovery programme.

The phased approach has since been tested, refined, and scaled-up in both UNICEF development and UNICEF emergency programmes in five different areas of the Philippines. Within two years of introducing the approach, around 600 open defecation free (ODF) communities (known as Zero Open Defecation, ZOD barangays, in the Philippines) have been verified in these areas, and the first group of ZOD communities is currently being verified for the second grade, G2 Sustainable Sanitation barangays.

http://dx.doi.org/10.3362/9781780449272.009

It is still early days for the phased approach, and too soon for evidence that the approach has been effective in taking communities beyond ODF to the higher and more sustainable levels of environmental sanitation that most people want to see. But the feedback has been very positive. Prior to 2013, only 50 ZOD communities had been achieved in the Philippines in the five years since Community-Led Total Sanitation (CLTS) was first introduced. The ZOD success rate has now dramatically increased and spread, in large part due to the greater ZOD and post-ZOD incentives created by the phased approach. The phased approach sets sanitation and hygiene outcomes for each phase, and encourages implementers to find the best way to achieve these outcomes given their local context, resources, and capacity. Significant learning and innovation has arisen from this outcome-based approach, and the visible results have encouraged large investments by local governments that were previously reluctant to invest in rural sanitation and hygiene. Most importantly, the approach makes sense to lots of people, as it solves many of their concerns about the sustainability and long-term equity of the CLTS approach, with an easily understood framework for progress beyond ODF. Support for the phased approach has grown rapidly in the Philippines, with entire municipalities (district equivalents) verified as 100 per cent ZOD, and now vying with each other to become the first municipalities to reach the higher outcome levels.

As such, the phased approach to rural sanitation development is presented as a promising approach supported by growing evidence from the Philippines, with several other countries already adopting similar phased approaches based on their own experience and thinking. Further time and research will be required to provide firm evidence of the long-term effectiveness of the approach, but it is presented in the hope that its aims and strategies resonate with those looking for solutions to the sustainability and long-term equity challenges of rural sanitation development.

This chapter has been split into two. The first, here, outlines the phased approach to rural sanitation development, and the second, Chapter 14, explains the sanitation finance approaches that were developed to support and accelerate the achievement of the different levels of collective sanitation outcomes set by the phased approach.

What is the challenge?

Post-ODF engagement remains challenging. Despite recognition of the importance of follow-up to, and monitoring of, the sustainability of the new sanitation facilities and practices generated by successful CLTS interventions, few projects or local governments allocate the budget, resources, and capacity needed for long-term support. NGOs often struggle to support ever-growing numbers of triggered and ODF communities, and local governments are rarely ready to take on the longer-term support role. All too often, the ODF gains prove fragile, with disadvantaged households in poor communities often the first to revert to open defecation (OD).[4]

A related challenge is demand for higher levels of sanitation service. CLTS can be effective in creating an intensive drive to build simple toilets from local materials. While most households are proud of their new sanitation facilities, and many work hard to maintain and repair their toilets, some are not happy with CLTS toilets and aspire to higher levels of service, while others build facilities that are unlikely to stand the test of time, which limits government buy-in to the CLTS approach.

Government stakeholders in developing countries, particularly those from infrastructure and engineering backgrounds, are often dissatisfied with these low-cost CLTS toilets. Sustainability studies by WSP (Hanchett et al., 2011), UNICEF (Kunthy and Catalla, 2009), Plan International (Tyndale-Biscoe et al., 2013), WaterAid (Robinson, 2009) and others raise concerns about the durability and hygiene of low-cost toilets, and the risk that badly built or unhygienic home-made toilets may create, rather than alleviate, public health hazards (by bringing the pathogens and risk of contamination closer to the home). Engineers often suggest that more expensive concrete slabs and ceramic pans would be a better and more economical solution over the long term, despite limited evidence that these more costly alternatives provide comparably higher health or other benefits.

Greater scrutiny of CLTS sustainability has also raised concerns about the equity of sanitation outcomes over time. One of the main strengths of the CLTS approach is that everyone has to be reached to achieve an ODF community, which means that even the poorest and most vulnerable have to stop OD and start using a toilet. However, sustainability studies show that previously ODF communities in even the best performing CLTS programmes report some reversion to OD over time.

The extent of this OD reversion often varies significantly. In 2012, a UNICEF regional CLTS review in the East Asia and Pacific region (UNICEF, 2013) compiled the results from seven sustainability studies in Africa and Asia, which found that OD reversion rates varied from 10 to 57 per cent. The disadvantaged groups within CLTS communities are often the first to revert to OD (Robinson, 2015) due to a number of factors, ranging from the construction of less robust or durable facilities, larger household sizes, social marginalization or exclusion, to – sometimes – the use of facilities subsidized or constructed by others in the community, which can lead to lower commitment to sustaining the collective behaviour change or ODF outcome.

The phased approach to sanitation development discussed in this chapter attempts to tackle three areas of weakness: through provision of a structure for post-ODF engagement; through the encouragement of higher levels of sanitation and hygiene service, including management of solid and liquid wastes; and through recognition that disadvantaged households often need external support to build and use more durable and hygienic sanitation facilities.

Why a phased approach?

The phased approach aims to protect the ODF process, but also introduces incentives to progress beyond ODF status to broader environmental sanitation outcomes. Additional sanitation finance is provided in the later stages, to accelerate progress and reward improved sanitation behaviour. However, it is conditioned on community commitment to sanitation and hygiene improvement as evidenced by verification of ODF status, and it is carefully targeted to those most in need of assistance to build and use durable and hygienic sanitation facilities.

Importantly, the ODF phase is achieved without the use of direct financial assistance,[5] which means that effective demand creation and behaviour change are required, while making sure that local sanitation markets are not skewed or undermined by supply-driven project activities or large hardware subsidies.

In the second stage, the good sanitation behaviour associated with ODF status is rewarded by additional finance and support to assist the community to develop more durable and hygienic facilities, improve school and institutional sanitation facilities,[6] and encourage routine handwashing with soap.

Poor and vulnerable households, who may be able to build simple toilets using local materials during the ODF phase (sometimes with assistance from other members of the community, particularly if they lack sufficient labour to dig pits and construct toilets), often lack the resources or market access required to upgrade their facilities and develop more durable and attractive toilets.

The provision of carefully targeted assistance to these households during the second phase, while encouraging household choice and ownership, increases the chances of the entire community upgrading to the more durable, hygienic, and user-friendly sanitation facilities that are likely to encourage sustainable use and maintenance (see Box 9.1).

The final phase aims to move the community from sustainable sanitation, which focuses on safe excreta disposal and handwashing with soap, to a broader 'total sanitation' status that includes solid and liquid waste management, safe management of animal excreta, and the protection and testing of water supplies.

The phased approach is designed to break sanitation and hygiene development down into smaller and more manageable chunks, with simple messages and goals that are relatively easy to measure and achieve. The multiple phases provide visible and relatively easy achievements, which encourage communities, local governments, and implementing agencies to continue their efforts, and allow regular sustainability checks. Previously targeted outcomes, such as ODF, are checked at each subsequent stage as part of the enhanced verification process. The approach provides a robust and flexible framework for sustainability monitoring, with gradually higher and broader criteria introduced at each stage as local capacity and understanding

---

Box 9.1 Action Contre le Faim (ACF), Philippines

In 2013, ACF implemented a CLTS project in the southern Philippines with support from UNICEF. The project was implemented in a post-conflict area in Mindanao, mostly in poor, remote, and marginalized communities.

ACF utilized a two-stage process, focusing on the successful achievement of ODF status by the community in the first stage, followed by the provision of subsidized latrine components (latrine pans, p-traps and pipework) in a second stage to encourage households to build more permanent and durable facilities. Following verification of ODF status, ACF facilitated the selection and purchase of components for toilet upgrading, providing free transport and subsidizing some of the standard materials, but requiring the households to choose what sort of toilet they wanted (based on information on different options, costs, advantages, and disadvantages) and pay for higher costs associated with more expensive options.

This household choice resulted in a range of different latrine models. A rapid review by UNICEF in mid-2013 encountered non-upgraded 'gallon' designs,[8] plastic pour-flush pans, ceramic pour-flush pans, and ceramic pedestal pour-flush pans. Significantly, almost every household had made some effort to upgrade and improve their toilet during the second phase, with the result that the upgraded facilities were more hygienic and user-friendly, and more valued by the users. UNICEF[9] estimated that for every US$1 invested by ACF, households invested US$0.50–2.50 (depending on the context and preferred toilet model).

Evidence of the adoption of several different latrine models (reflecting individual preferences) suggests good participation in the process, and ownership of the facilities, thus increasing the chances of sustainable and beneficial outcomes. This ACF model underpinned the development of a phased implementation strategy for rural sanitation in the Philippines, variants of which are now being used by UNICEF in both its development and emergency programmes.

Source: Robinson (2013)

---

of the approach improves. Wherever possible, monitoring and financing are provided by local governments and communities, with the aim of developing systems and activities that are within their long-term capacity and resources.

The phased approach rewards improved sanitation and hygiene behaviour. Communities that graduate to higher levels receive greater support and finance, providing incentives to work towards higher levels of service, and encouraging other communities to follow suit. In contrast, conventional approaches tend to reward harmful sanitation behaviour. Subsidies are usually provided only to households that do not have toilets, or do not practise improved sanitation behaviour, with little effort to distinguish those who can afford toilets but choose not to build them, and nothing provided to poor households or communities that have already invested in improved sanitation and hygiene.

The phased approach makes becoming ODF a more attractive proposition. Thus, it should increase the speed and success rate of both ODF and sanitation marketing processes, while also encouraging communities to go beyond ODF and achieve higher and more sustainable levels of service. These higher levels of service are also more attractive to government, which greatly increases both local support of the approach, and the likelihood of attracting local government finance for the scaling up and sustainability of the interventions.

The phased approach in action

A phased approach to rural sanitation development has been used in the Philippines since late 2013 through several UNICEF supported sanitation programmes in both development and post-emergency contexts, and it is planned in Timor-Leste, through the Australian Government-supported BESIK rural water supply and sanitation programme.

In the Philippines, the phased approach has been entitled the Philippines Approach to Total Sanitation (PhATS). It encourages barangay[10]-wide sanitation improvement with incremental rewards and incentives on attainment of each of the three grades (G1, G2, and G3) (see Figure 9.1).

The criteria for the G1 ODF grade (known as Zero Open Defecation in the Philippines) are simple: toilets must meet the minimum requirements for a hygienic toilet; the use of shared toilets is allowed; all households must have soap and water available at or nearby the toilet; and infant and child excreta must be disposed safely. These conditions are verified by a district (municipality) ZOD verification team, which always includes a third party verifier, and certified by a provincial ZOD verification team, following a well-agreed national protocol.

The G2 Sustainable Sanitation grade requires private toilets, with a higher level of service that includes the potential for safe emptying or replacement of pits and septic tanks. Handwashing facilities with soap and water are required at each household and 'sustainable toilets' must be verified in all institutions (schools, health posts, and government offices). The verification of school toilets includes specific criteria for child-friendly, functional, and clean boys' and girls' toilets, including menstrual hygiene management. The second phase also requires that the community has instituted some form of sustainability

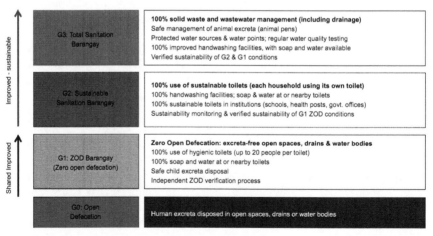

Figure 9.1 Philippines Approach to Total Sanitation (PhATS)

Source: Adapted from Robinson (2014)

monitoring, including monitoring of what happens to toilet pits and tanks when they fill, and re-verification of the conditions for the G1 ZOD phase.

The third and final grade, known as G3 Total Sanitation, requires that solid and liquid wastes are safely managed, including animal excreta; that water sources and water points are protected; and that regular water quality testing is undertaken. Handwashing facilities now have to be 'improved', which means that they limit re-contamination from dirty hands, and the G1 and G2 conditions have to be re-verified.

Incentives for graduation

The PhATS approach is supported by a sanitation finance framework (see Robinson and Gnilo, 2016, Chapter 14 of this book). Communities that are verified as G1 ZOD Barangays qualify for additional sanitation finance – usually provided by local government – and technical support to help ODF households and communities upgrade from simple sanitation facilities to more durable and sustainable ones, and reinforce the improved behaviours developed during the first phase. Communities that are verified as G2 Sustainable Sanitation Barangays receive additional finance for improvement of the public services required to achieve G3 Total Sanitation Barangay status.

The graduation incentives are designed to encourage sanitation improvement and the achievement of collective sanitation outcomes. In the Philippines, a number of new financing approaches are being tested in the post-ODF phase, including toilet vouchers for the poorest (to be redeemed with local suppliers or sanitation marketing producers) and toilet rebates for the poor, which reimburse part of the toilet upgrading costs to poor households if the toilet is verified to meet the 'sustainable toilet' criteria by the agreed verification date. Conditional grants are then provided to communities that are verified as G2 Sustainable Sanitation barangays, which requires that everyone in the community meets the higher G2 criteria.

Importantly, the phased incentive framework protects the ODF process. No finance is provided to the community until after ODF verification, in order to be more confident that behaviour change has taken place, and that the households and community will use the sanitation finance more effectively. The toilet vouchers and toilet rebates are designed to provide choice to the beneficiary households, and encourage them to make sanitation investments that might otherwise have been delayed until after other household spending priorities. Wherever possible, these household payments (vouchers and rebates) are financed by local government, in order to minimize the level of subsidy (through the constrained local budget), with central government and external agencies providing technical assistance, and conditional grants for the higher levels of service (once the G2 outcome has been verified).

Evidence base

The phased approach has been implemented in the Philippines since early 2014, with more than 600 communities now verified as G1 ZOD Barangays, five entirely ZOD municipalities verified, and a number of communities being verified for G2 Sustainable Sanitation Barangay status at the time of writing. Only 50 ZOD Barangays were achieved across the Philippines in the previous six years, so in its two years the phased approach has already resulted in a rapid acceleration of ODF progress.

The initial findings are promising. Both the implementing agencies (partner NGOs) and local governments appear to understand and like the phased approach, with evidence that local governments in the development programme are allocating significantly higher amounts[11] to their sanitation budgets since adopting this approach.

A Municipal Acceleration Program for Sanitation (MAPS), which is based on a similar phased development and financing approach to that adopted in the Philippines, is planned in Timor-Leste. The phased approach was built into the 2012 Timor-Leste National Basic Sanitation Policy, and forms the basis for the draft National Strategic Plan for Rural Sanitation, but it has not yet been tested at scale. There is already significant support for the approach from key CLTS and sanitation marketing stakeholders, in recognition of the help it will provide to accelerate and scale up sanitation progress in Timor-Leste.

A two-stage total sanitation approach has also been adopted in Nepal (see Regmi, 2016, this book). The first ODF stage is followed by a second 'totally sanitized' Village Development Committee (VDC) stage, in which every household has to have a toilet, and a broad range of other collective sanitation and hygiene criteria are verified.

Challenges

One of the key challenges is the risk that the introduction of targeted subsidies during the post-ODF phases will lead to more supply-driven and target-oriented implementation, with the tendency to want to use the subsidies earlier to accelerate ODF achievement. The experiences in the Philippines suggest that this can be resisted once evidence of ODF achievement without subsidies is available, and that there are substantial benefits to using the ODF phase to ensure genuine behaviour change before introducing toilet subsidies.

Joint WSP-IFC (IFC, 2013) work suggested that many households in developing countries prefer to build toilets in one effort (rather than multiple efforts, or through a process of upgrading), with the aim of having a 'toilet that will last forever'. Multiple phases of support and upgrading are also likely to require more time, effort, and resources, as some simple sanitation facilities have to be largely rebuilt at a later stage resulting in a potential waste of scarce materials and resources. For these reasons, some projects have combined CLTS efforts with microfinance support or up-front hardware subsidies from the start, with the aim of building more durable and sustainable toilets in one intervention.

While possible, the higher and more difficult objectives of this 'one-hit' approach make it likely that success rates will be lower, with higher entry barriers for poor households, which tend to reduce the demonstration and incentive effects. In addition, there is a greater risk of effectiveness and sustainability problems, as households that take toilet subsidies or loans may not be fully committed to sanitation improvements, with the risk that significant sanitation finance is wasted.

Conclusion

The phased approach centres on the importance of achieving collective sanitation outcomes (because of the higher health and other benefits from collective sanitation improvements), and of breaking down the huge challenge of improving sanitation in poor rural communities into a series of well-defined and easily monitored steps. Households and communities can move to the higher levels of service in one step where they prefer more rapid development, but several different levels of verification will still take place. The verification requirements of the phased approach encourage better long-term monitoring of both progress and outcomes, and ensure that monitoring does not stop when ODF status is achieved.

This approach draws on evidence that complex development interventions are more difficult to implement, and that behaviour change communication tends to be more successful when limited to a handful of clear messages. It also encourages good behaviour, by providing more support to communities that exhibit positive sanitation behaviour change, and by recognizing and rewarding progress at regular intervals (rather than setting the bar too high for many households or communities).

The incentive system built into the phased approach has the potential to drive higher ODF success rates, as we are already seeing in the Philippines. Non-ODF communities begin to understand that ODF achievement is rewarded with support to achieve higher levels of sanitation and hygiene improvement (which are often more attractive to both communities and local governments than the relatively simple CLTS outcomes).

Further work is required to produce evidence that the phased approach can work at scale. However, the feedback to date is promising. Local governments in Masbate in the Philippines allocated three times as much budget to rural sanitation in 2015 as in previous years, having seen that the phased approach generated much better and more sustainable outcomes than previous sanitation investments.

Similarly, sanitation stakeholders in the typhoon-affected areas of the Central Visayas region have seen more than 300 ODF communities verified in 2015, despite the catastrophic damage caused to local communities and institutions by the super typhoon. This rapid and highly visible progress has created significant enthusiasm and interest by government, in a region that previously lacked any significant government investment in rural sanitation.

Further progress in 2016 should greatly enhance the prospects that the phased approach can be scaled up into a nationwide government programme for sanitation and hygiene improvement.

There is also growing sector convergence around the idea. Nepal recently introduced a two-stage sanitation improvement process, with ODF VDCs supported to become 'Total Sanitation' VDCs. The national sanitation policies in Pakistan and Timor-Leste advocate a phased approach to sanitation development, starting with an ODF outcome and progressing to higher collective sanitation outcomes; and a number of sector agencies (UNICEF, WSP, and international NGOs) are working on post-ODF strategies and approaches.

CLTS has transformed rural sanitation improvement by demonstrating that poor rural communities can build simple toilets, change their social norms, and achieve impressive collective sanitation and hygiene outcomes. However, in 2015, some 15 years after CLTS was first implemented in Bangladesh, we are now aware that real sustainability problems exist, that the risk of reversion to OD is highest among the poorest and most vulnerable households, and that other sanitation and hygiene issues (beyond ODF) are also important to health and well-being.

The phased approach to sanitation development aims to strengthen the gains from CLTS interventions, and encourage progressive achievements beyond ODF. It provides a practical framework for developing and monitoring the sustainability of community sanitation and hygiene improvements and most importantly makes sure that the poorest and most vulnerable households, those whose children are at the highest risk of stunting and diseases related to inadequate sanitation, do not get left behind. While the early results of the phased approach are promising, further work is required to build on this early promise and develop evidence of what has worked and what has not. One of the strengths of the approach is that it sets collective outcomes with well-defined verification processes, rather than defining in detail how to get to these outcomes. The intention is to encourage innovation and flexibility and an evidence-based process to share the lessons learned in the process.

About the authors

Andrew Robinson is an independent WASH consultant based in France. Since 1987, Andrew has designed, worked on, evaluated, and researched WASH programmes in 27 countries in Africa and Asia, including both regional and national reviews of CLTS effectiveness, sustainability, and impact.

Michael Gnilo is a sanitation and hygiene specialist based in UNICEF headquarters in New York. Michael has designed and implemented community-based health, nutrition, and WASH programmes since 2003 in both development and emergency contexts. He has a particular interest in strengthening linkages among community, civil society, and government systems for sustained delivery of services.

Endnotes

1. Personal experience of the author from reviews and evaluations of CLTS and other rural sanitation programmes in Angola, Bangladesh, Burkina Faso, Cambodia, Ethiopia, Ghana, Kenya, India, Indonesia, Mozambique, Nepal, Niger, Nigeria, Pakistan, Philippines, Sri Lanka, Tanzania, Timor-Leste, Uganda, Yemen, and Zambia.
2. Although some subsidy has been used to support rebuilding and rapid ODF achievement in the post-emergency context in the super typhoon-affected areas of central Philippines.
3. Improved sanitation facilities in schools, health posts, markets, government buildings, and other public spaces.
4. Made from 'one-gallon' plastic containers, which were sliced to create a simple pan with an outlet that could be connected to a bamboo pipe. Many households built this sort of low-cost design during the CLTS phase, and some upgraded them with help from ACF.
5. Personal communication from Michael Gnilo, UNICEF WASH specialist.
6. Village (with each Barangay comprising 4–8 sub-villages).
7. One of the municipalities in Masbate province tripled its sanitation budget after the first year, and increased it by another 600 per cent in the second year.

References

Hanchett, S., Krieger, L., Kahn, M.H., Kullmann, C. and Ahmed, R. (2011) *Long-Term Sustainability of Improved Sanitation in Rural Bangladesh*, World Bank, Washington, DC, https://openknowledge.worldbank.org/handle/10986/17347 [accessed 29 January 2016].

IFC (2013) *Selling Sanitation: Formative Research in Kenya*, Report, International Finance Corporation, Washington DC.

Kunthy, S. and Catalla, R. (2009) *Community-Led Total Sanitation (CLTS) in Cambodia: A Formative Evaluation Report*, UNICEF and Ministry of Rural Development, Department of Rural Health Care, Bangkok.

Regmi, A. (2016) 'Tools for embedding post-ODF sustainability: experiences from SNV Nepal', in P. Bongartz, N. Vernon and J. Fox (eds.) *Sustainable Sanitation for All: Experiences, Challenges, and Innovations*, Practical Action Publishing, Rugby.

Robinson, A. (2009) *Sustainability and Equity Aspects of Total Sanitation Programmes: A Study of Recent WaterAid-Supported Programmes in Nigeria*, WaterAid UK, London.

Robinson, A. (2012) *Enabling Environment Endline Assessment: Himachal Pradesh and Madhya Pradesh, India*, Working Paper, World Bank, Water and Sanitation Program, Washington, DC.

Robinson, A. (2013) *Development of a Multi-Stakeholder Implementation Strategy for Scaling Up Rural Sanitation*, Final Report, UNICEF, Manila.

Robinson, A. (2014) *Use of Targeted Sanitation Subsidies to Support Early Recovery*, Program Guidelines, UNICEF, Manila.

Robinson, A. (2015) *Community Led Total Sanitation Review*, Final Report, UNICEF Angola, Luanda.

Robinson, A. and Gnilo, M. (2016) 'Promoting choice: smart finance for rural sanitation development', in P. Bongartz, N. Vernon and J. Fox (eds.) *Sustainable Sanitation for All: Experiences, Challenges, and Innovations*, Practical Action Publishing, Rugby.

Tyndale-Biscoe, P., Bond, M. and Kidd, R. (2013) *ODF Sustainability Study*, FH Designs and Plan International, Melbourne, http://www.communityledtotalsanitation. org/sites/communityledtotalsanitation.org/files/Plan_International_ODF_ Sustainability_Study.pdf [accessed 30 January 2016].

UNICEF (2013) *Community-Led Total Sanitation in East Asia and Pacific: Progress, Lessons and Directions*, Report, UNICEF East Asia and Pacific Regional Office, Bangkok.

CHAPTER 10

Roles and responsibilities for post-ODF engagement: building an enabling institutional environment for CLTS sustainability

Samuel Musembi Musyoki

Abstract

Sustainable Development Goal (SDG) 6 aims for sanitation activities and programmes which succeed at creating sustainable, community-owned, and managed sanitation for all. It is becoming more and more apparent that post-open defecation free (ODF) support is often necessary to ensure sustainable outcomes for Community-Led Total Sanitation (CLTS). This chapter argues for the need for governments to play the leading role in these activities. Drawing on experience from Kenya and Zambia, this chapter outlines the roles and responsibilities of different government levels (national, local, and community-based institutions) and the actions that will be necessary for them to take. At all three levels the role of the development community is considered and suggestions given on how they can support governments to take the reins of CLTS programmes and post-ODF activities. This will be essential if we are to commit to the ethos of the SDGs and fulfil goal 6.

Keywords: Sustainable Development Goals (SDGs), Kenya, Zambia, Government, Development community, Community-based organizations, Open defecation

Introduction

Community-Led Total Sanitation (CLTS) is practised in over 30 countries in the African continent, and it has been adopted in many government sanitation policies and strategies.[1] We are now in a different phase in most countries, with second and third generation problems emerging, and many governments taking a leading role in CLTS. The goalposts are moving from achieving open defecation free (ODF) communities to post-ODF sustainability. Alongside this, it has become imperative to 'think more boldly about how to position ODF in the context of broader public health and national development initiatives' (Wijesekera and Thomas, 2015: 208).

Ensuring government leadership, developing capacities of institutions and other stakeholders, and working towards sector harmonization have been

http://dx.doi.org/10.3362/9781780449272.010

identified as major bottlenecks for achieving the Sustainable Development Goal (SDG) sanitation target of universal access by 2030 (Hueso, 2015). The roles and responsibilities of central and local government, as well as local community-level institutions, will vary (Mukherjee, 2016, this book). They may differ according to the country and the specific government structures, policies, and institutional relationships that are in place. However, ownership of the process is needed at all levels. This chapter looks at the different actions national and local governments, community groups, and local institutions can take to sustain CLTS outcomes. This chapter, drawing on the experience in Kenya and Zambia, also proposes actions the development community – bilateral and multilateral donors, UN agencies, and international and national NGOs such as Plan International – can take to support these different governance levels.

National governments and CLTS

Government leadership is now widely regarded as essential to the scaling-up and sustainability of CLTS (Bongartz, 2014). There is political will and support for CLTS by many governments in Africa. This was in part influenced by international NGOs such as Plan International, WaterAid, the Water and Sanitation Program (WSP), and the United Nations International Children's Emergency Fund (UNICEF) United Nations International Children's Emergency Fund. Zambia, Malawi, Kenya, and Ethiopia, among others, have integrated CLTS as a core area within their interagency coordination mechanisms[2] to guide different stakeholders in implementation. They have embarked on programmes to scale-up CLTS and developed national ODF roadmaps for accelerating the coverage and use of improved sanitation facilities.

ODF road maps

Governments that developed ODF road maps seem to have been reading from the same script, inspired by the urgency to accelerate the attainment of Millennium Development Goal (MDG) 7c, to halve the number of people without access to basic sanitation by 2015. However, the timeframes for the road maps were unrealistic and defied all development planning logic. For example, while the ODF Rural Kenya by 2013 campaign was launched in May 2011, the road map itself was launched only in May 2012 and maintained the end date of December 2013 (Ministry of Health, 2012). Out of a targeted 269 districts, only one had been declared ODF by the end of 2013. Kenya was not alone in this. The only difference is that other countries were somewhat less ambitious with the timing of their ODF road maps.

Many countries were fixated on rapid scaling-up and reaching as many people as possible, counting the number of villages, communities, chiefdoms, districts, and counties to be declared ODF. For example, in Zambia the target was to reach 3 million people, while for Kenya it was to deliver 30,000 ODF villages (Government of Zambia, 2012). Malawi had a target of complete elimination of open defecation (OD) in rural Malawi by 2015 (Ministry of

Health, 2011). The question is whether the national ODF road maps were unduly motivated by MDG hurry and the funding opportunities that came with it. Certainly, under such self-imposed pressure, CLTS was seen to hold the key. All the road maps became short-term CLTS scaling-up projects. They all stopped at ODF and had very little focus on post-ODF sustainability. Now, countries have had to confront their failures and review their road maps.

The Sustainable Development Goal 6.2 to 'achieve access to adequate and equitable sanitation and hygiene for all and end open defecation, paying special attention to the needs of women and girls and those in vulnerable situations' offers a new opportunity to go beyond short-term ODF targets. Extending strategies to include sustainability and post-ODF plans is vital. Ensuring that everyone is included is also crucial; the needs of the poorest and least able must be integrated into national strategies (Chambers, 2012; Patkar, 2014; Patkar and Gosling, 2014; Wilbur and Jones, 2014; Cavill et al., 2016, this book). The enthusiasm and support that can be generated by setting short-term targets to achieve ODF needs to be balanced by establishing and embedding strong institutional frameworks, building adequate capacity, and securing finance to ensure long-term sustainability (Wijesekera and Thomas, 2015).

National level strategies on sanitation should provide:

- The country's aspiration or vision for change;
- A policy direction and institutional framework that creates an enabling environment for devolved structures of government, partners and communities, to drive the change process;
- Channelled resources to local government authorities, NGOs, the private sector, and other capable stakeholders in order for them to implement programmes and projects;
- Facilitation and support for knowledge management processes, including monitoring evaluation and research and post-ODF activities, as these are critical for learning and improvement (Government of Zambia, 2012; Ministry of Health, 2011 and 2012).

More information can be found in Table 10.2.

Central financing

Most CLTS programmes are externally funded. However, the government, as the duty bearer,[3] has a mandate to ensure universal sanitation access. It is important not only to establish coordination mechanisms but also to ensure adequate resources (both financial and human) are allocated and equitably distributed at different levels and phases of CLTS (pre- to post-triggering and post-ODF) to actualize this mandate. But, even if self-financed, for CLTS to be implemented effectively and post-ODF maintained sustainably, resources need to be where the shit is! There is a need to interrogate where, and for what, CLTS resources are being invested, and to consider whether shifting more resources from the centre to the frontline would have a positive impact on outcomes and their sustainability.

Since the adoption of Kenya's new constitution, sanitation is now a county government matter. Previously, a large proportion of resources were committed to national level activities for inter-agency coordination meetings, workshops, travel, national ODF celebrations, capacity building, and knowledge management (see Table 10.1). Activities at the national level can be very expensive, as they often involve technocrats who require high allowances, expensive accommodation, and transport.

Table 10.1 National ODF Rural Kenya by 2013 budget breakdown

	Dec 2012 (KES in millions)	Jun 2013 (KES in millions)	Dec 2013 (KES in millions)	Total (KES in millions)	Total (US$ m)
National support services	348.83	678.55	555.69	1,583.08	18.63
Provincial/district and village level investments	325	648	648	1,620.9	19.07

Source: ODF Rural Kenya by 2013 Campaign Roadmap (Ministry of Health)

So far, there are no studies that have been carried out to show levels of funding at different institutional levels: national, sub-national, or community. In Kenya, however, the ODF road map revealed that nearly 50 per cent of the budgets were going to national level activities. The balance is shared between sub-national, district, and village level activities. Resources earmarked for the community level are minimal, even for activities up to ODF, let alone post-ODF.

While the situation in Kenya is beginning to change, national governments need not compete for the limited resources with devolved structures that are at the frontline, where the core business of ending and sustaining ODF status happens. Rather, there is need to mobilize and disburse resources that are required to support the devolved structures for their effective implementation and sustaining of CLTS processes. Financing mechanisms need to be well coordinated within government departmental budgets and also within NGO budgets. The integration of CLTS (including post-ODF) programming into existing public health systems is another important role for national government, establishing the link between health and sanitation (Chambers and von Medeazza, 2014), and ensuring continuing government involvement. Wijesekera and Thomas (2015) identified the lack of political will at local and national levels to integrate CLTS programming with health care strategies as one of three reasons for slippage post-ODF. CLTS training could also be integrated into public health courses and training at university and training colleges, which would be a cost-effective way of creating the needed capacity for CLTS. Such mainstreaming efforts would also make it easier to integrate CLTS into public health programmes, as well as into the broader community development discourse and practice.

Development community supporting national government[4]

SDG 6.a. focuses on the importance of supporting national sanitation programming: 'expand international cooperation and capacity-building support to developing countries in water and sanitation-related activities and programmes'. Changing the focus from supporting individual and short-term projects to supporting national programming will be an important shift in helping to achieve universal access as well as sustainable outcomes. Supporting the establishment of strong government frameworks for implementing CLTS and incorporating post-ODF activities, coaching, capacity-building, and networking, is an important role that the development community should be playing (Raeside, 2010; Soublière, 2010; Bongartz, 2014).

Leveraging adequate funding and resources for CLTS and post-ODF work is a key function of national governments in order to ensure sustainability. But there are only limited mechanisms for holding governments to account, in terms of where and how resources are invested, as well as for ensuring that there is increased budgetary allocation and deployment of staff to support CLTS processes post-ODF. The development community can support and strengthen institutional mechanisms such as participatory budgeting and citizens' social accountability platforms that can be used at national, sub-national, and local government levels to ensure adequate budget allocation and strengthened mutual accountability. So far there has been only a limited effort on the part of the development community to push governments to be transparent and accountable or to match cooperating partners' contributions. The development community can support the establishment of conditional grants and demand-driven technical support for sub-national governments, NGOs, and entrepreneurs.

In countries with devolved structures, such as Kenya, emphasis will need to be put on advocacy for funding at the county level, and funding and human resource gaps need to be honestly acknowledged by policy-makers within the national government. Equity issues across the whole country will need to be considered, based on the assessments of the rates of OD, to avoid situations where one county or district is better funded and resourced than another. Convincing governments, especially finance ministries, of the cost-effectiveness of funding CLTS post-ODF, and also the cost-effectiveness of carrying out CLTS activities, is critical in securing budgets within a context of limited funds and competing interests.[5]

The development community can also support capacity building related to leadership in, and the management of, CLTS processes. Training for CLTS so far has focused on 'how to' aspects of CLTS. This is why even sub-national staff should be providing strategic leadership, and having a long-term vision that sees CLTS beyond ODF. They have instead focused on short-term goals of delivering ODF villages and, at best, chiefdoms or districts. To this end, as part of research undertaken by the Water Institute at the University of North Carolina, together with Plan International USA and Kenya, a CLTS Management Resource Pack (Fox et al., 2013) has been developed. The research project 'Testing CLTS Approaches for Scalability' in Kenya means local government staff can significantly influence the success of CLTS (Crocker and Rowe, 2015) and are therefore now evaluating whether strengthening the management capacity of sub-national government personnel actually influences CLTS outcomes (Crocker and Venkataramanan, 2014).[6]

Members of the development community have written about the potential for NGOs to play a convening and brokering role (Green, 2015) and for donors to support collaboration and coordination between government levels and departments (Hueso, 2015). A stronger focus on learning and sharing in order to influence decision-making could help strengthen these relationships and help to avoid duplication, as is being done through the Kenya Interagency Coordination Committee and thematic working task forces, and in Zambia through the WASH Alliance.

Local governments and CLTS

The significant role of local government should be implementation. A recent study shows that, at local government levels, CLTS programmes are largely supported and implemented by non-governmental actors (Crocker et al., 2015). However, in a number of countries with well-established decentralized structures of government, CLTS is being implemented through public health officers at the sub-national level (Crocker et al., 2015). At local or village levels, community health workers (CHWs) and volunteer Natural Leaders play central roles. However, local governments' capacity is limited. There is a lack of personnel and funding, even with support from national governments and other cooperating partners. The areas covered are vast, and few frontline officers have transport to facilitate their movement to carry out follow-up and monitoring post-ODF activities. CHWs in some countries have become so overloaded that it is difficult for them to complete all their duties to a satisfactory standard. Meanwhile, Natural Leaders, who are passionate and committed, can only cover areas not far from their neighbourhoods. For them to cover wider areas, they would require transport and additional support, either from the government or from NGOs. There are also questions regarding how to ensure Natural Leaders stay motivated and what incentives should be in place (see Wamera, 2016, this book).

Local government financing

Adequate funding is needed to support the new responsibilities and activities devolved to the local government level (McCollum et al., 2015), and it is important that funding is distributed among counties in an equitable way. It is important that the devolved governments prioritize post-ODF CLTS processes and budget for them. This way, the central government budgets will take into account priorities and budget proposals from local or devolved government when allocating resources. Devolved governments have a significant role in influencing budget allocations, and they can engage in budget advocacy to ensure increased allocation for CLTS activities, including post-ODF sustainability initiatives. Kenya, for instance, has participatory budgeting guidelines.[7] If these are utilized properly, it will be possible to take into account community action plans for attaining and sustaining ODF, thus ensuring adequate allocations at the national government level. In Zambia, the District Water, Sanitation and Hygiene Education Committees are involved in the development of CLTS work plans geared towards attaining ODF chiefdoms. This could be extended to include post-ODF activities. In Kenya, ODF road maps are being developed at the county level, meaning that the maps are rooted in local realities (Wijesekera and Thomas, 2015). While this is a promising practice, guidance will be necessary to ensure post-ODF sustainability activities are included in the devolved government road maps.

Local government supporting community action

Sub-national or local governments should organize volunteers and provide resources to support them in undertaking follow-up, monitoring, and reporting post-ODF. It could be possible to outsource or fund community-based organizations (CBOs) that demonstrate that they have the necessary competence and commitment to lead different aspects of CLTS at the local level. Such CBOs can be trained and linked to the sub-national management teams for periodic review and reporting. Initiatives such as the micro planning processes recently tried out in Kenya by UNICEF and the Ministry of Health (Singh and Balfour, 2015) can aid the process of identifying potential groups and Natural Leaders who can be engaged throughout the CLTS process, from pre-triggering to post-ODF.

Devolved governments can play an important role in facilitating relationships and interactions between community-based groups and the national government, as well as facilitating learning opportunities, strengthening CBOs' capacity to attain and sustain ODF. It is a matter of accompanying and coaching community-level facilitators and local leaders to manage CLTS at scale and engage in post-ODF activities.

In Zambia, the District Water, Sanitation and Hygiene Education (D-WSHE) committees are working with chiefs and the village elders to follow up and monitor CLTS activities. This is done together with CHWs and the Natural Leaders or 'CLTS champions'. Post-ODF follow-up can be integrated into existing local government primary health care systems and strategies, such as in Kenya, where CHWs carry out post-ODF follow-up within the community and are accountable to the county government (see Wamera, 2016, this book).

Development community supporting local government

Assisting local governments in establishing systems for local planning and monitoring of CLTS programming is something the development community can do, particularly where sanitation service delivery is devolved to county-level, as in Kenya. UNICEF, in consultation with the Ministry of Health, developed a micro-planning tool (a data collection template and database) which was rolled out across all 47 counties in Kenya. It mapped out the steps and costs of reaching ODF status (Singh and Balfour, 2015). Initiatives such as this need to be extended to include post-ODF activities and follow-up, mapping the costs involved, so that sufficient budgets are allocated to ensure sustainability.

Community structures and CLTS

SDG 6.b focuses on supporting and strengthening the participation of local communities in improving sanitation and water management. There are various influential local institutions and structures that should be engaged to ensure sustainability and help to embed new social norms. But these critical institutions and key influencers within the community have first to be identified. Dooley et al. (2016, this book) show how social network analysis can be used to identify key influencers from all sections of the community as part of the pre-triggering process. These local individuals and institutions need to be supported before ODF – and after – if we want to ensure ODF is sustained (Wamera, 2016, this book). What their role might be, and the support they need from local government and development partners, is explored below.

Community institutions and structures such as schools, religious institutions, CBOs, women's groups, existing health promotion groups, and local media are important in mobilizing, particularly for post-ODF activities and follow-up (Wamera, 2016, this book). They need to be identified in the pre-triggering phase. For example, respected religious and spiritual leaders can be encouraged to preach and trigger their congregations and followers to abandon OD and adopt appropriate sanitation and hygiene behaviour (Balfour et al., 2014; WSSCC, 2015). In Zambia, the roles of Safe Motherhood Action Groups (SMAG), CHWs, and volunteers, are being redefined (Wiscot Mwanza, personal communication). The decentralized structures are recognizing the important part those closer to the communities can play, not only during triggering but also in ensuring sustainability post-ODF. They are building cooperative relationships between government frontline staff in health service provision and other community-level players. The joint work of CHWs and compensated volunteers[8] is having a significant impact on the management of diseases, strengthening service provision, and increasing the capacities of communities (Wiscot Mwanza, personal communication).

In Zambia, the traditional leadership structure has counteracted weaknesses in local government, strengthening ODF actions. Chiefs, village elders, and Natural Leaders are champions for CLTS. Chiefs trigger sanitation behaviour change in their chiefdoms. Headmen and women follow-up and monitor in their own villages and also in neighbouring villages. When chiefs 'buy in' to the concept and process of CLTS they ensure that all the village elders in their chiefdoms join in the movement and include it within their daily work routines, without requiring external resources. Investing in building a movement of traditional and Natural Leaders or champions can contribute significantly to ensuring the sustainability of CLTS. The traditional leadership structure is particularly strong in Zambia. Similarly respected community leaders may be more difficult to find in other contexts. It is also important not to assume traditional leaders will always be suitable Natural Leaders (Bardosh, 2015). Selecting solely people with power within a community can reinforce existing social inequalities, and could lead to the exclusion of poor and marginalized sections of the community.

Devolved government can leverage resources from the development community to support existing local institutions that in turn support post-ODF engagement. As of now, very little money goes to local level efforts, for example, to facilitate natural and local leaders and grassroots champions who play a critical role in sustaining ODF. With appropriate support from local governments and from the development community, they could gain confidence, and be very effective.

Post-ODF activities

We should be cautious when prescribing specific post-ODF activities; formative research is essential when designing or selecting the most effective activities. However, some ideas for post-ODF activities are presented below:

- Folk media, particularly participatory education theatre is a powerful tool in working for community-led behaviour change. In order to ingrain good hygiene practices in the daily lives of the community, frontline government workers, teachers, and community leaders can be encouraged and supported in engaging in folk theatre groups that perform skits on sanitation themes.
- In Kenya's Siaya County, the TACI youth group, working with Plan International Kenya, has been engaging with their communities in using drama, poetry, songs, and traditional dances for continued awareness creation. They were doing this even before they came across CLTS, but after learning about CLTS they came up with plays that are performed to communities during triggering and after ODF.
- Plan International Kenya also engaged a local comedy group 'Vitimbi' who produced a series of plays that were shown on TV and reached over 4 million viewers nationwide. The focus was on ending OD and maintaining good hygiene (Bongartz et al., 2010). Sustained reflections and reinforcement of new norms help to change behaviour and practice.
- Writers can be supported in composing popular poems and songs, based on their understanding of the local context; these can be performed at meetings, special occasions, and celebrations. Champions from among youth and children can also be identified and involved in public activities, such as special rallies.

- In Kenya and Zambia, working with local TV and radio stations, talk shows have been carried out to engage the public in dialogue around CLTS behaviours and norms. Explicit documentaries can be important triggers for discussions on hygiene and promoting behaviour change. Those investing in CLTS beyond ODF could also consider equipping Natural Leaders and youths with photography and video skills so that they can producing similar trigger materials for use during monitoring exercises.

Table 10.2 summarizes the roles and responsibilities at different levels regarding capacity building, financing, and advocacy for post-ODF engagement. It also shows the support the development community could provide to national and local government and community institutions.

Table 10.2 Summary of the role of different government levels and the role of the development community

National government / Devolved government / Community	Development community support:
National government (Through mandated line ministry and supportive ministries, e.g. finance and planning): • Creating vision and policy guidance; • Ensuring inter-agency coordination; • Providing budget support and disbursement; • Linking devolved governments to funding opportunities; • Defining what post-ODF means; • Connecting post-ODF activities with the larger development agenda; • Supporting knowledge management.	• Support local and national governments in planning and monitoring of programming including post-ODF activities; • Convening and brokering relationships between different government levels and stakeholders;
Devolved government (Province, county, district): • Micro-level visioning, operational planning and budgeting for post-ODF activities; • Implementation oversight and guidance; • Capacity building; • Monitoring and supervision; • Administering post-ODF grants for CBOs and NGOs; • Reporting against plans and targets.	• Supporting and strengthening the development of accountability mechanisms; • Policy and budget advocacy to ensure favourable institutional environment and adequate budget support post-ODF;
Community (Community institutions and structures at ward, chiefdom, location, and village levels): • Formulating community action plans post-ODF; • Implementing projects; • Following up and monitoring situation post-ODF at the local level; • Facilitating sharing and reflection meetings within and between communities; • Reporting to devolved governments on findings; • Linking with public health technicians, government frontline staff, artisans, entrepreneurs, to improve facilities.	• Supporting evidence-based research for instance on the cost-effectiveness of post-ODF activities; • Support capacity building of staff at different government levels on management of CLTS post-ODF; • Supporting local solutions and initiatives that support post-ODF sustainability; for example participatory design of sanitation solutions.

Conclusion

The SDGs are an opportunity to define the roles and responsibilities of the key actors and institutions to achieve sustainable sanitation for all. As described in this chapter, post-ODF processes to ensure sustainability need to be embedded in government processes and systems from the national to the community level. This is a complex challenge, and will involve different levels of government taking on clearly defined roles alongside working and interacting closely together to ensure they support and reinforce each other. The development community can play a central role in supporting governments to establish their roles, in facilitating relationships and strengthening capacity of governance and accountability at all levels. Ensuring meaningful participation of communities and engaging all members within a community is also key.

There is a significant task ahead through capacity building and effecting institutional change. This requires more than training in skills. A lot is required in terms of power dynamics, attitudes, mind-sets, and behaviours of the individuals who make up the institutions. And the institutions themselves might be resistant and take more time to change. We need to know more about how to effect this institutional change, and what incentives are needed to ensure the change is sustained. Experiences and learning need to be documented. Hosting or attending events which bring key actors at different levels together for sharing and learning would be one way to begin exploring the possibilities.[9] Exposing people to the realities of challenges being faced at the frontline might be another way of adding value to such events. Experiential learning such as 'immersions' and reflection on such realities might move them to taking radical decisions that can support and sustain change.

About the author

Samuel Musembi Musyoki is the Country Director at Plan International Zambia. He holds a BA in anthropology from the University of Nairobi and an MA in Development Studies from the International Institute of Social Studies, The Hague, Netherlands. He previously worked as Strategic Director of Programmes at Plan International Kenya and at the Institute of Development Studies, UK. He is a co-editor of *Tales of Shit: CLTS in Africa*.

Endnotes

1. Countries that have CLTS within their national strategies include Benin, Cameroon, Cambodia, Cote d'Ivoire, Ethiopia, Gambia, Ghana, Guinea, Guinea Bissau, Indonesia, Kenya, Liberia, Mali, Mauritania, Niger, Nigeria, Pakistan, Philippines, Senegal, Sierra Leone, Togo, Uganda, and Zambia. Many countries have now written national verification and certification guidelines, some of which are available here http://www.communityledtotalsanitation. org/resource/national-protocols-and-guidelines-verification-and-certification [accessed 4 September 2015].

2. Inter-agency coordinating committees oversee sector-specific implementation, for instance water, sanitation, and hygiene (WASH), Education, and Health. CLTS has become a sub-theme with a dedicated working group.

3. 'Duty bearer' in relation to sanitation means that 'governments have an obligation to respect, protect and fulfil the right to sanitation, using the maximum of available resources to progressively realize the right' (COHRE et al., 2008: 2).

4. These include international NGOs, local civil society organizations, UN agencies. and donor agencies.

5. In the context of Community Health Worker (CHW) programmes, which potentially could be involved in post-ODF follow-up (see Wamera, 2016, this book), a cost-effectiveness study conducted in Kenya, Indonesia, and Ethiopia indicated that 'CHW programmes in contexts where they work with an integrated team supported by the health system have a high likelihood of being cost-effective' (McCollum et al., 2015: 8).

6. http://waterinstitute.unc.edu/clts/

7. Participatory Budgeting is a process through which citizens have an unprecedented opportunity to set development priorities, decide on the agenda, and monitor spending in their communities. Beyond budgetary tracking, participatory budgeting is a process through which the population decides on the destination of all or part of the available public resources. See http://www.fahamu.org/Participatory-Budgeting

8. Volunteers are given bicycles to enable them to move around, they are linked to income generating opportunities and economic empowerment, and given the opportunity to participate in exchange visits and training.

9. This is occurring in a number of countries, for example in Ghana (www.communityledtotalsanitation.org/resource/taking-stock-clts-implementation-ghana) and Nigeria (www.communityledtotalsanitation.org/country/nigeria). In Indonesia, TSSM introduced annual inter-district Stakeholder Learning Reviews for comparing progress across districts, participatory learning analysis of implementation experiences, and sharing of lessons, knowledge resources, and expertise developed between districts (Mukherjee, 2016, this book). On the regional and global level, the CLTS Knowledge Hub (www.communityledtotalsanitation.org) convenes sharing and learning events and workshops throughout the year to enable people engaged and interested in CLTS to share experiences, challenges, and innovations.

References

Balfour, N., Otieno, P., Mutai, C. and Thomas, A. (2014) 'CLTS in Fragile and Insecure Contexts: Experience from Somalia and South Sudan', *Eastern and Southern Africa Sanitation and Hygiene Learning Series*, UNICEF, New York NY, http://www.unicef.org/esaro/WASH-Field-CLTS-low-res.pdf [accessed 1 February 2016].

Bardosh, K. (2015) 'Achieving "total sanitation" in rural African geographies: poverty, participation and pit latrines in Eastern Zambia', *Geoforum*, 66: 53–63 <http://dx.doi.org/10.1016/j.geoforum.2015.09.004>.

Bongartz, P. (2014) 'CLTS in Africa: trajectories, challenges and moving to scale', in P. Cross and Y. Coombes (eds) *Sanitation and Hygiene in Africa: Where do We Stand?*, IWA Publishing, London and New York, www.iwaponline.com/wio/2013/wio2013RF9781780405421.pdf [accessed 11 September 2015].

Bongartz, P., Musyoki, S.M., Milligan, A. and Ashley, H. (2010) *Tales of Shit: Community-Led Total Sanitation in Africa*, Participatory Learning and Action Notes 61, Institute for Environment and Development, London.

Cavill, S., Roose, S., Stephen, C. and Wilbur, J. (2016) 'Putting the hardest to reach at the heart of the SDGs', in P. Bongartz, N. Vernon and J. Fox (eds.) *Sustainable Sanitation for All: Experiences, Challenges, and Innovations*, Practical Action Publishing, Rugby.

Chambers, R. (2012) 'Discrimination, duties and low hanging fruit: Reflections on equity', blog on CLTS website, 12 January, www.communityledtotalsanitation.org/blog/discrimination-duties-and-low-hanging-fruitreflections-equity [accessed 15 September 2015].

Chambers, R. and von Medeazza, G. (2014) *Reframing Undernutrition: Faecally-Transmitted Infections and the 5 As*, IDS Working Paper 450, Institute of Development Studies, Brighton.

COHRE, SDC, UN-HABITAT and WaterAid (2008) *Sanitation: A Human Rights Imperative* http://www.sswm.info/sites/default/files/reference_attachments/COHRE%202008%20Sanitation%20a%20human%20rights%20imperative.pdf [accessed 1 February 2016].

Crocker, J. and Rowe, E. (2015) *Community-led Total Sanitation in Kenya: Findings from a Situational Assessment*, The Water Institute, University of North Carolina, Chapel Hill, http://www.communityledtotalsanitation.org/sites/communityledtotalsanitation.org/files/SituationalAssessmentKenya.pdf [accessed 1 February 2016].

Crocker, J. and Venkataramanan, V. (2014) *Testing CLTS Approaches for Scalability: Project Briefing*, 37th WEDC International Conference, Hanoi, Vietnam.

Crocker, J., Bogle, J. and Rowe, E. (2015) *Community-led Total Sanitation Research Brief: Implementation Context in Kenya, Ghana and Ethiopia*, The Water Institute, University of North Carolina, Chapel Hill.

Dooley, T., Maule, L. and Gnilo, M. (2016) 'Using social norms theory to strengthen CATS impact and sustainability', in P. Bongartz, N. Vernon and J. Fox (eds.) *Sustainable Sanitation for All: Experiences, Challenges, and Innovations*, Practical Action Publishing, Rugby.

Fox, J., Chepleting, S. and Owuor, D. (2013) *Managing CLTS: A Facilitator's Resource Pack*, Plan International, www.communityledtotalsanitation.org/resource/managing-clts-facilitator-resource-pack [accessed 1 February 2016].

Government of Zambia (2012) *3 Million People Sanitation Programme*, Ministry of Local Government and Housing, Government of Zambia, http://www.unicef.org/zambia/washe_12210.html [accessed 1 February 2013].

Green, D. (2015) *Fit for Future? Development Trends and the Role of International NGOs*, Oxfam Discussion Paper, http://policy-practice.oxfam.org.uk/publications/fit-for-the-future-development-trends-and-the-role-of-international-ngos-556585 [accessed 27 November 2015].

Hueso, A. (2015) 'Opportunities, challenges and priorities on the road towards universal access to sanitation by 2030: Summary of evidence from an expert consultation', presented at the 2015 World Water Week in Stockholm, http://programme.worldwaterweek.org/sites/default/files/summary_sanitation_sector_2030.pdf [accessed 4 September 2015].

McCollum, R., Otiso, L., Mireku, M., Theobald, S., de Koning, K., Hussein, S. and Taegtmeyer, M. (2015) 'Exploring perceptions of community health policy in Kenya and identifying implications for policy change', *Health Policy and Planning*, 31(1): 10–20 <http://dx.doi.org/10.1093/heapol/czv007>.

Ministry of Health (2011) National ODF Malawi 2015 Strategy, National ODF Task Force, Malawi, Government of Malawi, http://www.communityledtotalsanitation.org/sites/communityledtotalsanitation.org/files/ODF_Launch_Leaflet.pdf [accessed 24 February 2016].

Ministry of Health (2012) *ODF Rural Kenya by 2013 Campaign Roadmap*, Ministry of Health, Government of Kenya, Nairobi.

Mukherjee, N. (2016) 'Building environments to support sustainability of improved sanitation behaviours at scale: levers of change in East Africa', in P. Bongartz, N. Vernon and J. Fox (eds.) *Sustainable Sanitation for All: Experiences, Challenges, and Innovations*, Practical Action Publishing, Rugby.

Patkar, A. (2014) 'Getting to everyone, everywhere: New operating principles for an old reality', speech at Brisbane WASH Conference, 25 March, www.communityledtotalsanitation.org/resource/getting-everyone-everywhere-new-operating-principles-old-reality [accessed 15 September 2015].

Patkar, A. and Gosling, L. (2014) 'Equity and inclusion in sanitation and hygiene in Africa', in P. Cross and Y. Coombes (eds) *Sanitation and Hygiene in Africa: Where do We Stand?* IWA Publishing, London and New York.

Raeside, A. (2010) 'Participatory development approaches need participatory management!' *PLA Notes*, 61, 109–118.

Singh, S. and Balfour, N. (2015) *WASH Field Note: Micro-Planning for CLTS: Experience from Kenya*, UNICEF Eastern and Southern Africa Sanitation and Hygiene Learning Series, UNICEF, www.unicef.org/esaro/WASH-Field-Microplanning-low-res.pdf [accessed 14 September 2015].

Soublière, J-F. (2010) 'Adopting CLTS. Is your organisation ready? Analysing organisational requirements', *PLA Notes*, 61, 119–128.

Wamera, E. (2016) 'Who is managing the post-ODF process in the community? A case study of Nambale District in Western Kenya', in P. Bongartz, N. Vernon and J. Fox (eds.) *Sustainable Sanitation for All: Experiences Challenges and Innovations*, Practical Action Publishing, Rugby.

Wijesekera, S. and Thomas, A. (2015) 'Taking stock: reaching the bottom billion – beyond open defecation', *Waterlines*, 34.3: 206–9 <http://dx.doi.org/10.3362/1756-3488.2015.020>.

Wilbur, J. and Jones, H. (2014) 'Disability: Making CLTS Fully Inclusive', *Frontiers of CLTS: Innovations and Insights* 3, Institute of Development Studies, Brighton, www.communityledtotalsanitation.org/sites/communityledtotalsanitation.org/files/media/Frontiers_of_CLTS_Issue3_Disabilities.pdf [accessed 15 September 2015].

WSSCC (2015) *Global Sanitation Fund: Progress Report 2014*, WSSCC, Geneva, http://wsscc.org/wp-content/uploads/2015/06/global_sanitation_fund_progress_report_2014_web.pdf [accessed 14 September 2015].

CHAPTER 11

Who is managing the post-ODF process in the community? A case study of Nambale sub-county in western Kenya[1]

Elizabeth Wamera

Abstract

Post-ODF follow-up is central to sustaining open defecation free (ODF) status, and needs to be integrated into CLTS programming from the outset. This chapter explores who is to carry out these activities, and how they might be motivated and financed. It argues for the importance of identifying existing administrative and social structures prior to implementation. Looking at reasons for success in Nambale sub-county, which was declared ODF in 2012, the chapter discusses the role of Community Health Workers (CHWs), who, under the Kenyan Community Health Strategy Approach (CHSA) have an expanded remit that includes CLTS, in follow-up and in reaching the poorest and most marginalized within communities. The chapter highlights challenges which have arisen, such as incentives to motivate CHWs, as well as the risk that devolved government structures lead to inequity among districts and varying levels of funding for the same activities, thereby threatening ODF achievement and sustainability.

Keywords: ODF sustainability, ODF custodians, Community Health Workers (CHWs), Post-ODF, Follow-up, Kenya

Introduction

Post-ODF follow-up in communities is critical for the long-term sustainability of open defecation free (ODF) behaviour (Bevan, 2011; WSP, 2011; UNICEF, 2014; Cavill et al., 2015). However, this is something that has been widely neglected until recently. Implementing agencies and their funders do not typically have a strategy for continued improvements post-ODF (including their financing), capacity building, or for counteracting slippage (Venkataramanen, 2012). After an ODF declaration, the majority of implementing organizations will leave, or massively cut down on their community support, particularly when budgets are time-limited and there are pressures to achieve targets, unless the CLTS programme activities are integrated in other community initiatives. However, recently, more long-term support is being trialled in several places (see Table 11.1). Working with local government from the start has been documented to be the most feasible and effective way to ensure

http://dx.doi.org/10.3362/9781780449272.011

sustainability for scaling-up (Perez et al., 2012). But a key challenge is that the strong partnerships developed between governments (central and local), NGOs, and other implementing agencies, are usually focused on the initial stages of the CLTS process leading up to ODF declaration, certification, and ODF celebrations, but not post-ODF.

Post-ODF plans that do exist often focus on sanitation marketing and assisting communities to climb up the sanitation ladder (Verhagen and Carrasco, 2013), and they do not usually consider how behaviour change will be embedded and become a new social norm (see Dooley et al., 2016, this book). Post-ODF follow-up is assumed to take care of itself through volunteer Natural Leaders who live within the communities. They are left to figure out how to continue working after the support they once enjoyed has been withdrawn by the NGO or government.[2] However, recent studies have highlighted that external support, follow-up, and encouragement to communities, is critical for sustaining behaviour change (Hanchett et al., 2011; WSP, 2011; Tyndale-Biscoe et al., 2013; Thomas and Bevan, 2013; UNICEF, 2014).

Key questions are:

- What happens post-ODF? Is ODF behaviour sustained? Who carries out post-ODF activities?
- Who finances the post-ODF activities when projects finish?
- What happens to the unpaid volunteer Natural Leaders?

This last question is raised in relation to those individuals or groups that become *de facto* ODF sustainability managers in the communities that have achieved ODF. It is assumed that, after the ODF declaration, Natural Leaders will continue with enthusiasm and work without payment as they live within the community. It is also assumed that the work is mainly completed and whatever work is left to be done is minimal. But the role of Natural Leaders in sustaining behaviour is critical, time consuming, and has financial implications too. Recent systematic reviews of performance for Community Health Workers (CHWs) have revealed the importance of providing motivation and remuneration for performance (Glenton et al., 2013; Kok et al., 2014).

This chapter argues that identifying existing social and administrative structures and groups within communities and government prior to CLTS implementation, and embedding them within the CLTS process from the start, is critical in sustaining ODF status. Post-ODF follow-up needs support, commitment, and action from many players (for example, communities, local and national governments, project implementers), and getting the balance between them right is a complex challenge. Expanding the remit of existing structures to include follow-up could help counter the funding and time pressures that many governments and communities face. It also creates a direct entry point to the community, providing access to members of the community who may otherwise be marginalized or excluded. The chapter outlines how the Kenyan Government's Community Health Strategy Approach (CHSA) has been expanded to include CLTS, and the CHW's remit extended to incorporate CLTS follow-up activities within the community. The case of Nambale sub-county, in Busia County, Kenya is used to illustrate how this has been done.

Nambale sub-county case study

In 2006, the Ministry of Health in Kenya developed the Community Health Strategy Approach (CHSA) (MOH, 2006). It focuses on increasing the capacity of households to take care of their health matters and supporting equitable community access to health care and services across the country. The design of this approach includes capacity building for non-professionals in health and in specific community approaches at the community level. A new national constitution was introduced in 2010, and under the new decentralized system, counties are responsible for delivering health services and implementing health programmes (National Coordinating Agency for Population and Development et al., 2010). Counties now, 'have authority for decision-making, adapting the policy to their local context, finance, implementation and management' (McCollum et al., 2015: 2). Community Units (CUs) have been created that support the discussions, implementation, and monitoring of the various initiatives. Each unit consists of 5,000 people. Community Health Committees (CHCs) have been established to manage the day-to-day running of the CUs. CHC members are elected at the Assistant Chief's meeting (*baraza*). The committee itself is chaired by a respected member of the community. There should be nine members that may include representatives of: youth groups; faith groups; women's groups; NGOs; people living with AIDS; and people with a disability. At least one-third of the committee members should be female (MOH, 2009a).

The CUs are facilitated mainly by volunteer CHWs that in Busia County chiefly comprise members of existing women's groups.[3] Table 11.1 outlines their key roles and responsibilities and the selection process. The CHWs collect health data that is relayed to the county headquarters to indicate the health status of the county. CHWs differ from Community Health Extension Workers (CHEWs) who are government-selected paid workers, stationed in local health facilities (government clinics/dispensaries). CHEWs supervise approximately 25 CHWs each (MOH, 2012), although in practice, the number is often many more. After 2011, when CLTS was introduced in Kenya, sanitation indicators were included in the data collection, and the CHW job description was amended to include CLTS activities. These included 'monitoring progress toward latrine construction, collecting sanitation, hygiene, and CLTS indicators (e.g. villages triggered and ODF status), and reporting data on a quarterly basis' (Crocker and Rowe, 2015: 2).[4]

Table 11.1 Community Health Worker roles and responsibilities according to current Community Health Strategy Approach in Kenya

Staffing per community unit	Selection and recruitment	Training	Tasks	Supervision
50	Nominated by community but selection facilitated by community representatives	Initial 10 day training followed by refreshers	Community entry, organization, sensitization for 100 people	Supervision by CHEW and community health committee
			Registering households, data gathering	
	Must be able to read and write		Collation of data on chalkboards	
	Permanent resident within the community		Community dialogue for change	
	Demonstrate attitudes valued by community		Record keeping and report writing	
			Health promotion	
			Recognition and classification of common conditions and decision for action	
			Home visiting	
			Training and supporting home caregivers	

Source: McCollum et al., 2015

Busia County is home to Nambale; the first sub-county in Kenya to be declared ODF in 2012 – and it has remained so (MOH/UNICEF, 2015). The total percentage of open defecation (OD) in Busia County was recently assessed at 8 per cent (MOH, 2013a, b; WSP, 2014; Kenya Open Data). Busia is ranked as third best in the country out of 47 counties in the county sanitation benchmarking by the Ministry of Health. This has prompted exchange visits to Nambale from other implementers to come and learn by listening to the residents of these communities. The visits have created opportunities for others to understand how they have sustained ODF status and the way they have managed households that slipped back to OD. One key reason for success is the integration of CLTS with the CHSA and use of CHWs for follow-up. Another reason is the close working relationship between the public health unit and the Community Unit at the sub-county and county levels that ensures coordinated support at the community level. Nambale also has full coverage of CUs, which is not the case across Kenya.

The Community Health Extension Workers (CHEWs) assign 15–20 households each to CHWs, these are households that are relatively easily accessible to the CHWs, depending on the size of the village and how many group members are available. They are well respected within the community and are able to reach every member, regardless of their situation. They access all homes, whether very poor, child headed, homes of single women, homes with disabled or elderly people. These are households that may not ordinarily attend triggering sessions and are often among the first to revert to OD (see Robinson and Gnilo, 2016, this book). CHWs can represent these marginalized groups in meetings and in the CHC meetings. Continued behaviour monitoring can ensure the retention of behaviour acquired at ODF (MOH, 2014a). Accessing these households ensures that everyone is reached and, in cases of slippages, they are dealt with contextually (Milward et al., 2014). Further research is needed to better understand the role of CHWs in ensuring sustained behaviour change.

Actions taken to ensure behaviour change is sustained

Community dialogue days are held to discuss health and sanitation matters, facilitated by the CHEW or CHWs. These are meant to take place on a monthly basis and are most vibrant in areas where there are active CHCs. Health data is considered, and the community discusses ways to provide support to sustain the newly acquired behaviour, and monitor progress. This information is relayed to the sub-county health team that provide follow-up and support to ensure that the behaviour is sustained.

The assumption that existing groups will indefinitely continue the follow-up work within the community soon came under pressure, with volunteers becoming demotivated, competing priorities for limited household funds, or in cases of slippages, for example collapsing latrines due to flooding or loose soil formation (MOH, 2014a). Lack of financial support to continue post-ODF follow-up in Nambale led the CHWs to rethink their strategy. They fell back on their original purpose of coming together, to support each other socially and economically, and initiated income-generating activities (IGAs) to raise the extra money needed for the promotion of hygiene and sanitation work (e.g. facilitation and coordination of follow-up, and home visits) (Ochieng, 2014). IGAs include kitchen gardens, breeding of small animals, selling of health products such as water treatment products, producing and selling sanitary towels. Communities are able to access these products through credit, to ensure that they are available when needed.

The CHWs are considered role models to encourage sustained behaviour change within the community. They have in place group sanctions about the kind of latrines they can have. For example, if a member's latrine is not up to the expected standards, the other members would not attend meetings at the person's home until the latrine is well constructed and maintained. There are also sanctions for other members of the community. For example, those who are considered to have a source of income are expected to have better latrines than the rest of the community. If their latrines are not in good condition, the CHWs write to them saying that if no corrective/upgrading action is taken within a period of time, then further action would be taken. They also write letters to the employers to request provision of loan facilities to their employees to improve their latrines. These kinds of community initiated social sanctions have ensured that Nambale sub-county has households with latrines that they can comfortably afford and access.

Challenges

One of the weaknesses identified in the CHSA is that there are no sustainability mechanisms and incentives in place. Irregularity, inconsistency, and inadequacy of remuneration have stifled CHW motivation (MOH, 2014b). There has been limited financial backing or commitment of funds for community health and sanitation from within the government. According to McCollum (2015), lack of funds to pay salaries for CHWs was identified as a threat to the sustainability of the CHSA in Kenya and their volunteer status has resulted in high CHW attrition and lack of accountability. CHEWs have limited supervision capacities for CHWs (MOH, 2014b). Lack of structure and supervision generally has also been identified as a problem. Workload is high and can put stress on family life, especially if CHWs are mainly women, as is the case in Busia County.

Revision of the CHSA is now under way to address some of these issues. One key element proposed was to increase the number and clarify the role of county government salaried CHEWs working at the community level, and decrease the number of unpaid CHWs. The recommendation was that there should be five employed CHEWS per CU (MOH, 2014b; see Figure 11.1). The move by CHW groups to establish IGAs was also identified by the government as a factor that would contribute to sustaining CHW work, and was integrated into the strategy (MOH, 2014b). In the newly devolved system, counties can now determine whether to provide a stipend to CHWs (MOH, 2014b). The stipends are consolidated to create capital to initiate the IGAs, or, in some cases, CLTS implementers provide money for follow-up. While a good initiative, the fact that it is left to counties to decide the degree of investment for this (and the CHSA as a whole) may lead to inequity within the country, with some counties prioritizing other activities, and not allocating a sufficient budget. This would limit the success of the CHSA and have a knock-on effect on ODF sustainability. Funding gaps need to be acknowledged and addressed by counties; the increase in salaried CHEWs means they will need to budget for greater costs.

There are additional equity implications which need to be considered. Within Kenya, the establishment of CUs has often been supported by NGOs and donors, rather than by the government, which has resulted in geographical inequity in their distribution. This is changing in some counties following devolution in 2010; however it is still a challenge. Devolution brings decision-making closer to the communities, which is an opportunity to ensure on-the-ground context-specific realities are integrated into the CHSA and post-ODF follow-up plans (Ochieng et al., 2014). However, it also can result in inequity between counties. Some counties have good coverage, whereas other counties

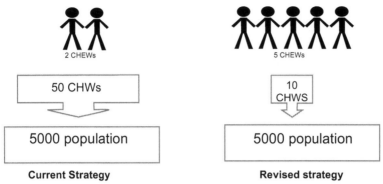

Figure 11.1 Current and revised CHWs structure
Source: McCollum et al., 2015

often have very few CUs or none at all, and people have to travel long distances to reach them (McCollum et al., 2015). This has a direct impact on the ability of CHWs to carry out post-ODF follow-up. Areas which do not have a CU, or where the county decides not to fund the CHSA sufficiently, will not be reached, which could lead to slippage. Often, these areas will be the most remote or poorest (see Cavill et al., 2016, this book).

Embedding behaviour change post-ODF achievement: lessons learned

Identifying and integrating existing social groups into the CLTS process

As has been described in the case study, understanding the social dynamics of the community before introducing a CLTS programme is important to sustainability. When the CLTS process is designed to rely on established administrative and social structures at the village level, this can help ensure proper triggering, inclusion of marginalized groups, ODF attainment, and sustainability post-ODF, while reducing the amount of extra work needed to carry out activities to support these in the long term. Existing social groupings or key influencers in communities such as CHWs or women's groups should be identified at the pre-triggering stage (for example through mapping exercises) and then included in the CLTS process from the outset so that they internalize the CLTS approach and become the custodians of the attained behaviour change within the community (Maule, 2013; Dooley et al., 2016, this book). The women's groups in Nambale sub-county originally came together to support each other socially and economically; they are now noted as a force to be reckoned with in the community as they are respected, trusted, and influential, and have access to various households, including the poorest and marginalized. The engagement of these groups can facilitate an enabling environment to sustain behaviour change.

Building capacity and incentives

In Nambale sub-county, building capacity within existing community groups, ensuring good management, commitment, and continuity of community officials and other champions, have been critical factors to sustained reinforcement of behaviour (see Box 11.1). To achieve this, external support is necessary. One example is a formalized system of support to Natural Leaders as a group or official organization, which will continue post-ODF (Rao, 2015; Cavill et al., 2015). Ongoing training of Natural Leaders or community groups, and subsequent financial reimbursement, (e.g. for time and expenses when they visit other communities) would be a way of making them more accountable to the local government for following-up and reporting. It would build sustainable capacity within the community and help counter the problem of over-reliance on individuals who may leave or move on. But care needs to be taken to avoid undermining volunteerism. However, currently there are only a few cases where there are clear plans[5] designed to support the CHWs or Natural Leaders in their work post-ODF (see Box 11.1).

Box 11.1 Capacity building taking place in different African countries

- Nigeria organizes a national annual CLTS roundtable to review progress, discuss challenges and lessons learned, and recognize different actors by giving awards to the Natural Leaders, the best performing local government area, and so on. This strengthens relationships between stakeholders and also creates a sense of healthy competition to sustain ODF status (Schouten and Smits, 2015). The annual meeting is a culmination of a series of CLTS regional consultative meetings that have provided insights on what is happening at the local level.
- Plan International in Ethiopia has supported Natural Leaders in forming an association that is set up like a business and trained them in business skills to make the group sustainable and profitable. The association focuses on ODF sustainability and moving communities up the sanitation ladder, for example, through various sanitation economic activities such as slab production and other hygiene materials and solid waste management (Cavill et al., 2015).
- Plan International in Malawi has supported Natural Leaders in forming networks at regional, district, and village levels in order to exchange information and to validate monitoring data from other districts (Kapatuka, 2013).
- The Ministry of Health in Kenya initiated a programme in 2013 to train Natural Leaders in 40 districts that received funding from the Dutch Government (MOH, 2014b). The Natural Leaders are given training in hosting community dialogues, reflection meetings, and exchange visits. They are also exposed to the process of consolidating lessons learned. This has built the capacity of Natural Leaders, motivating them to work as community consultants on sanitation matters. It has also provided them with some form of income. For example, they are given a stipend when they accompany the Public Health Teams in ODF verification and certification visits to villages (not their own). It has also motivated them to ensure that their own villages remain ODF as their villages are considered a point of reference when ODF verification is happening elsewhere. Some of the Natural Leaders are also trained in institutional triggering in cases where there are challenges with ODF attainment or large-scale slippage.
- Community coaches in Madagascar are trained in the construction of durable latrines, which means that they are assured of income if they carry on with sanitation work post-ODF, and emerge as sanitation entrepreneurs in the community (Venkataramanan, 2012; Milward et al., 2014).

Encouragement for community groups and understanding the motivations for long-term sustained behaviour change is important. In Nambale sub-county, as with all the sub-counties in Kenya, CHWs are working on a voluntary basis and some are investing the little money and time they have to ensure that ODF is sustained once attained. We should not assume they will be willing and able to do this voluntarily, and without payment on a long-term basis without support and incentives. Incentives can cover many different aspects, both financial and professional, performance contracts for health staff, mentoring and supervision, regular refresher training, and professional development to maintain the quality of interventions for behaviour change. McCollum et al. (2015: 7) found that non-financial incentives were important, with 'CHWs drawing on a sense of pride from being a role model, achievement from seeing community behaviours change, recognition from supervisors, community and peer support'. But they also found that absence of a salary was a de-motivator, and has influenced community provider performance, attrition, and accountability (McCollum et al., 2015).

Government commitment

Long-term government engagement and commitment is critical (Musyoki, 2016, this book). Incorporating CLTS indicators in the national or sector strategy, and integrating them into existing administrative structures supports ODF sustainability (see Table 11.2; MOH, 2014b; Wijesekera and Thomas, 2015). At this point, ODF becomes the first step in a longer-term process towards the main outcomes of health interventions and behaviour change. National ODF roadmaps should be extended to incorporate post-ODF follow-up (MOH, 2011; MOH/UNICEF, 2015; Musyoki, 2016, this book). This ensures that follow-up visits or continued monitoring needs are considered, included, and budgeted for. A structured follow-up process can highly improve reliability and effectiveness of monitoring post-ODF. This includes identifying the financial implications of support required for community-level monitoring going forward so that it is factored into the programme at the onset while engaging with the eventual custodian unit of the CLTS process post-ODF.

Table 11.2 Examples of where post-ODF follow-up has been integrated into government systems

Madagascar	Community consultants and champions work closely with the government, through the traditional and cultural leadership structures in the lowest units known as Tangalamena or Ampjanka (Milward et al., 2014). These leaders were identified at pre-triggering, post-triggering, and during follow-up and have taken up the work of carrying out follow-up on sanitation matters in the communities in addition to their leadership responsibilities.

(*Continue*)

Table 11.2 Examples of where post-ODF follow-up has been integrated into government systems (*Continue*)

Malawi	CHWs in Malawi are accountable to local government through the Extension Health Teams that are headed by the Assistant Environmental Health Officer, who reports to the District Coordination Teams that provide further support to facilitate their work in ensuring ODF is sustained. Engineers without Borders Canada worked very closely with local government staff in two districts in Malawi on 'extension agent re-organization' for CLTS implementation and monitoring through an approach called 'block monitoring'. This approach ensures CLTS and hygiene promotion activities are integrated directly into everyday health centre work. This is done without specific project funding but using the existing resources of health extension services. CHWs are assigned to blocks of villages and carry out CLTS work in addition to their daily work. This has proven successful so far, but there is a risk, as the system is designed to be championed by one person at the health centre. If the champion leaves or fails to report to work, the entire system could stall (Kennedy and Meek, 2013).
Ethiopia	Health Extension Workers are part of a structured government system and are trained in advance in various health matters such as family planning and nutrition, as well as sanitation.
Somalia	Somalia is fast learning from other countries and is now working at integrating ODF indicators as part of routine health monitoring, thus entrenching sanitation as part of basic health programming. Sanitation monitoring is now appearing in the job description of health workers (Thomas and Bevan, 2013).
Mauritania	In Mauritania, CLTS has been integrated with existing Essential Family Practices programmes, that carry out triggering and post-ODF follow-up for at least two more years after ODF achievement. Bonuses are given to facilitators for each new village certified ODF (Weddady and Sandoz, 2011).

Looking ahead: recommendations and challenges

To achieve long-term sustainability of ODF behaviour and embed a new social norm, CLTS has to become a way of life and not a project (see also Dooley et al., 2016, this book). Ways to realize this include the following:

- Existing social and administrative structures should be identified within communities and government prior to CLTS implementation, and embedded within the CLTS process from the beginning. This ensures that beyond ODF, the community is well-placed to continue with follow-up, verification, and monitoring with minimal strain and financial burden. These groups should be well-placed to access the poorest and most marginalized people within the community, and ensure they are included in the CLTS process.
- Self-financing initiatives like IGAs to support follow-up costs can in some instances be possible within communities, but this should not be relied on. Long-term institutional commitment and financial and other resources for follow-up and capacity building need to be factored into

programming (both government and NGO) from the outset to support community groups (Venkataramanan, 2012). In the revised CHSA in Kenya, the focus is on the use of the popular IGAs, as well as provision for sustainable funding mechanisms and incentives through the use of the devolved governments' resources (MOH, 2014b).

- Formalized structures to support capacity development and ongoing activities of Natural Leader and community organizations need to be established.

The challenges are great. As the case of Nambale sub-county shows, balancing the tension between community engagement, enthusiasm, and commitment to sustaining the ODF status and health of their community against the simultaneous need for government (local and national) responsibility and engagement and support of communities' post-ODF can be difficult. Post-ODF activities and long-term monitoring and engagement need to be prioritized by governments and implementing agencies, and appropriate institutional arrangements (MOH, 2009b; see also Musyoki, 2016, this book) and resources embedded to support community groups and initiatives through structures which enable and do not undermine existing groups. Devolution in Kenya and the increase in power for the counties is an opportunity to bring communities closer to decision-making processes, but with this opportunity comes the potential for inequity; efforts must be made to ensure even distribution and financing of CLTS processes throughout the country.

Further research is needed to understand the extent to which ODF behaviour is maintained beyond the end of projects, and also to understand how this can be realized in practice. The revised CHSA has taken into consideration some of the lessons learned over the past years and integrated them. The revised implementation framework of the CHSA provides support for coordination, sharing, and learning through participation in relevant interagency coordination committees (ICCs) and stakeholder forums. It also seeks to strengthen health financing through promoting entrepreneurial/livelihoods activities at CU level; these include IGAs (MOH, 2014b). These activities have been provided with clear indicators[6] to ensure there are ways to measure the achievements made. The integration of CLTS into the CHSA in Kenya presents an opportunity to strengthen community leadership and governance in the health sector and give sanitation practitioners impetus to sustain gains made.

About the author

Elizabeth Wamera is Programme Officer, Water Supply and Sanitation Collaborative Council. Elizabeth worked in Kenya, in the Ministry of Health, Department of Environmental Health as a Knowledge Management Specialist in the CLTS Knowledge Hub 2012–2013.

Endnotes

1. Thanks are due to Rosalind McCollum for reviewing a draft of this chapter, and for valuable comments and suggestions.
2. For example, they would sometimes be provided with facilitation for travel, either by bicycle, motorbike, or by receiving a transport allowance (Wamera, 2015).
3. For example, traditional birth attendants, church women's groups (Mothers' Guild, Mothers' Union), and merry-go-round groups.
4. There are still problems with the system, for example, a recent assessment has shown that monitoring data is not consistently reported and project costs are not tracked (Crocker and Rowe, 2015).
5. For example, in Sierra Leone the following training manual has been developed by the Ministry of Health and Sanitation, UNICEF and GOAL, www.communityledtotalsanitation.org/resource/clts-training-manual-natural-leaders. See also examples from Sierra Leone and Ethiopia, www.communityledtotalsanitation.org/resource/natural-leaders-networks.
6. The indicators in the revised CHSA of 2015 clearly outline what would be considered as entrepreneurial/livelihood activities and how they would be managed and measured.

References

Bevan, J. (2011) *Review of the UNICEF Roll-Out of the CLTS Approach in West and Central Africa*, Briefing Paper 1247, 35th WEDC International Conference, Loughborough, UK, http://wedc.lboro.ac.uk/resources/conference/35/Bevan-J-1247.pdf [accessed 2 February 2016].

Cavill, S. with Chambers, R. and Vernon, N. (2015) 'Sustainability and CLTS: Taking Stock', *Frontiers of CLTS: Innovations and Insights*, Issue 4, Institute of Development Studies, Brighton, http://www.ids.ac.uk/publication/sustainability-and-clts-taking-stock, [accessed 2 February 2016].

Cavill, S., Roose, S., Stephen, C. and Wilbur, J. (2016) 'Putting the hardest to reach at the heart of the SDGs', in P. Bongartz, N. Vernon and J. Fox (eds.) *Sustainable Sanitation for All: Experiences, Challenges, and Innovations*, Practical Action Publishing, Rugby.

Crocker, J. and Rowe, E. (2015) *Community-led Total Sanitation in Kenya: Findings from a Situational Assessment*, The Water Institute, University of North Carolina, Chapel Hill, http://www.communityledtotalsanitation.org/sites/communityledtotalsanitation.org/files/SituationalAssessmentKenya.pdf [accessed 2 February 2016].

Dooley, T., Maule, L. and Gnilo, M.E. (2016) 'Using social norms theory to strengthen CATS impact and sustainability', in P. Bongartz, N.Vernon and J. Fox (eds.) *Sustainable Sanitation for All: Experiences, Challenges, and Innovations*, Practical Action Publishing, Rugby.

Glenton, C., Colvin, C.J., Carlsen, B., Swartz, A., Lewin, S., Noyes, J. and Rashidian, A. (2013) 'Barriers and facilitators to the implementation of lay health worker programmes to improve access to maternal and child health: qualitative evidence synthesis', *The Cochrane Database of Systematic Reviews*, 10 (10): CD010414 <http://dx.doi.org/10.1002/14651858.CD010414.pub2>.

Hanchett, S., Krieger, L., Kahn, M.H., Kullmann, C. and Ahmed, R. (2011) *Long-Term Sustainability of Improved Sanitation in Rural Bangladesh*, World Bank, Washington, DC, https://openknowledge.worldbank.org/handle/10986/17347 [accessed 2 February 2016].

Kapatuka, D. (2013) 'Natural leaders energizing change in villages to attain and sustain ODF status: A case study of Plan Malawi impact areas – Mulanje and Lilongwe districts', IRC Symposium, Ethiopia.

Kennedy, M. and Meek, A. (2013) *Extension Agent Reorganization into a 'Block' system for CLTS – Implementation and Monitoring in Salima and Zomba Districts, Malawi*, paper presented at IRC Symposium on Monitoring Sustainable WASH Delivery, Addis Ababa, Engineers Without Borders Canada, www.communityledtotalsanitation.org/resource/extension-agent-reorganization-block-system-clts-implementation-and-monitoring-salima-and [accessed 14 September 2015].

Kok, M.C., Dieleman, M., Taegtmeyer, M., Broerse, J.E., Kane, S.S., Ormel, H., and de Koning, K. A. (2014) 'Which intervention design factors influence performance of community health workers in low- and middle-income countries? A systematic review', *Health Policy and Planning*, 30(9): 1207–27 <http://dx.doi.org/10.1093/heapol/czu126>.

Maule, L. (2013) *Using Social Norms Theory to Strengthen UNICEF's CATS Programmes*, UNICEF, New York.

McCollum, R. (2015) 'Implications of the community health policy change in Kenya in light of world health worker week', *REACHOUT*, 10 April, www.reachoutconsortium.org/news/identifying-implications-of-community-health-policy-change-in-kenya-in-light-of-world-health-worker-week-whwweek/ [accessed 2 February 2016].

McCollum, R., Otiso, L., Mireku, M. Theobald, S., de Koning, K., Hussein, S. and Taegtmeyer, M. (2015) 'Exploring perceptions of community health policy in Kenya and identifying implications for policy change', *Health Policy and Planning*, 31(1): 10–20 <http://dx.doi.org/10.1093/heapol/czv007>.

Milward, K., Pradhan, S., and Pasteur, K. (2014) *Promising Pathways. Innovations and Best Practices in CLTS at Scale in Madagascar*, CLTS Foundation, Kolkata.

Ministry of Health (MOH) (2006) *Taking the Kenya Essential Package for Health to the Community: A Strategy for the Delivery of Level One Services*, MOH, Government of Kenya, Nairobi.

MOH (2009a) *The Kenya Community Health Strategy Manual*, Department of Community Health, MOH, Government of Kenya, Nairobi.

MOH (2009b) *The Kenya Environmental And Sanitation Hygiene Policy*. MOH, Government of Kenya, Nairobi.

MOH (2011) *The Rural Kenya Open Defecation Free Roadmap*, Government of Kenya, Nairobi.

MOH (2012) *The Rural Kenya Open Defecation Free Reporting Framework*. Government of Kenya, Nairobi.

MOH (2013a) *WASH Annual Report 2012-2013*, MOH, Government of Kenya, Nairobi, http://www.communityledtotalsanitation.org/sites/communityledtotalsanitation.org/files/media/DEH_Annual_Report_2012_2013.pdf [accessed 2 February 2016].

MOH (2013b) *The Status of Sanitation in Busia County*, Government of Kenya, Nairobi.

MOH (2014a) *The Annual Report 2012–2013*, The Department of Environmental Health, WASH Unit, MOH, Government of Kenya, Nairobi.

MOH (2014b) *Strategy for Community Health 2014–2019: Transforming Health: Accelerating the Attainment of Health Goals*. USAID, PEPFAR and FANIKISHA.

MOH/UNICEF (2015) *Realizing Open Defecation Free Rural Kenya; Achievements and Road Ahead. A Synthesized Analysis of Village Micro-Planning for Community Led Total Sanitation*, Government of Kenya, Nairobi.

Musyoki, S. (2016) 'Roles and responsibilities for post-ODF engagement: building an enabling institutional environment for CLTS sustainability', in P. Bongartz, N. Vernon and J. Fox (eds.) *Sustainable Sanitation for All: Experiences, Challenges, and Innovations*, Practical Action Publishing, Rugby.

National Coordinating Agency for Population and Development, Ministry of Medical Services, Ministry of Public Health and Sanitation, Kenya National Bureau of Statistics, ICF Macro (2010) *Kenya Service Provision Assessment Survey 2010*, http://dhsprogram.com/pubs/pdf/SPA17/SPA17.pdf [accessed 2 February 2016].

Ochieng, B., Akunja, E., Edwards, N. Mombo, D., Marende, L. and Kaseje, D.C.O. (2014) 'Perceptions of health stakeholders on task shifting and motivation of community health workers in different socio demographic contexts in Kenya (nomadic, per-urban and rural agrarian)', *BMC Health Services Research*, 14(1): S4 <http://dx.doi.org/10.1186/1472-6963-14-S1-S4>.

Ochieng, G. (2014) *CHVs and CLTS Promoters Exchange Visit Report to Nambale Sub-County in Busia County*, WSP/MOH partnership.

Perez, E. with Cardosi, J., Coombes, Y., Devine, J., Grossman, A., Kullmann, C., Kumar, A., Mukherjee, N., Prakash, M., Robiarto, A., Setiawan, D., Singh, U. and Wartono D. (2012) *What Does It Take to Scale Up Rural Sanitation?* Water and Sanitation Program Working Paper, World Bank, Washington DC, www.wsp.org/sites/wsp.org/files/publications/WSP-What-does-it-take-to-scale-up-rural-sanitation.pdf [accessed 2 February 2016].

Rao, V. (2015) *A Study of Two Natural Leaders' Organisations in India*, CLTS Knowledge Hub, www.communityledtotalsanitation.org/resource/study-natural-leaders-networks-chhattisgarh-and-madhya-pradesh [accessed 2 February 2016].

Robinson, A. and Gnilo, M. (2016) 'Promoting choice: smart finance for rural sanitation development', in P. Bongartz, N. Vernon and J. Fox (eds.) *Sustainable Sanitation for All: Experiences, Challenges, and Innovations*, Practical Action Publishing, Rugby.

Schouten, T. and Smits, S. (2015) *A State of the Art of Strengthening Monitoring Water Supply and Sanitation in Developing Countries*, IRC/ Practical Action Publishing, Rugby.

Thomas, A. and Bevan, J. (2013) *Developing and Monitoring Protocol for the Elimination of Open Defecation in sub-Saharan Africa*, UNICEF, New York, www.communityledtotalsanitation.org/sites/communityledtotalsanitation.org/files/Thomas_and_Bevan_Elimination_of_open_defecation_SSA.pdf [accessed 2 February 2016].

Tyndale-Biscoe, P., Bond, M. and Kidd, R. (2013) *ODF Sustainability Study*, FH Designs and Plan International, www.communityledtotalsanitation.org/resource/odf-sustainability-study-plan [accessed 2 February 2016].

UNICEF (2014) *Evaluation of the WASH Sector Strategy 'Community Approaches to Total Sanitation' (CATS)*, UNICEF, New York NY, www.unicef.org/evaluation/files/Evaluation_of_the_WASH_Sector_Strategy_FINAL_VERSION_March_2014.pdf [accessed 2 February 2016].

Venkataramanan, V. (2012) *Testing CLTS Approaches for Scalability Systematic Literature Review*, University of North Carolina and Plan International USA, Chapel Hill NC and Washington DC.

Verhagen, J. and Carrasco, M. (2013) *Full Chain Sanitation Services That Last: Non Sewered Sanitation Services*, IRC, The Hague.

Wamera, E. (2015) *Natural Leaders Training Report in Uasin Gishu County, Kenya*, WSSCC, Geneva.

Weddady, A. and Sandoz, S. (2011) *Gradual Progression of Mixed CLTS-EFP Programme and Using Performance Bonus to Improve Facilitators' and Natural Leaders' Effectiveness*, UNICEF, Mauritania, www.communityledtotalsanitation.org/resource/combining-clts-essential-family-practices-programme-and-using-performance-bonus [accessed 2 November 2015].

Wijesekera, S. and Thomas, A. (2015) 'Taking stock: Reaching the bottom billion – beyond open defecation', *Waterlines*, 34(3) <http://dx.doi.org/10.3362/1756-3488.2015.020>.

Water and Sanitation Program (WSP) (2011) *Factors Associated with Achieving and Sustaining Open Defecation Free Communities: Learning from East Java*, Research Brief, Water and Sanitation Program, Washington DC, www.wsp.org/sites/wsp.org/files/publications/WSP-Factors-Achieving-ODF-East-Java.pdf [accessed 2 February 2016].

WSP (2014) *State of Sanitation in Busia County*, Water and Sanitation Program, World Bank: Washington DC.

CHAPTER 12

Tools for embedding post-ODF sustainability: experiences from SNV Nepal

Anup Kumar Regmi

Abstract

In 2008, SNV introduced the Sustainable Sanitation and Hygiene for All (SSH4A) Programme that aims to build the capacity of local governments, the private sector, and other local stakeholders, for more effective service delivery in sanitation and hygiene – and also to sustain it. This chapter presents SNV Nepal's experiences in post-ODF interventions as part of this integrated approach, in particular, the tools and processes applied for monitoring ODF and ensuring its sustainability. These tools and processes include the drafting and endorsement of a district post-ODF strategy which encompassed existing post-ODF tools, such as the introduction of early detection tools to enable the identification of poorly maintained toilets, maintaining ODF, and sustainable hygiene behaviour. A behaviour change communication campaign was developed, based on formative research to identify the barriers and motivating factors to toilet use and handwashing with soap; and a process to re-verify ODF status was also created. These tools are presented in the context of Nepal's sanitation movement and SNV Nepal's experience in Kalikot (the first ODF district in the Mid-Western Region in Nepal).

Keywords: Total sanitation, Post-ODF tools and process, Post-ODF strategy, ODF re-verification and monitoring Nepal

The ODF and post-ODF scenario in Nepal

For a long time, sanitation in Nepal was viewed as part of water supply initiatives. Toilets in most cases were subsidized, and access and usage remained low. The introduction of the National Sanitation and Hygiene Master Plan in 2011 (Government of Nepal, 2011) brought change to the sector in many ways: local government has become more responsible for sanitation, while communities have become more responsive. In the Mid-Western Region, repeated cholera outbreaks pushed the government to take the lead, improve collaboration with stakeholders, and in the process create a sanitation movement. The extensive use of Community-Led Total Sanitation (CLTS) triggering as part of this led to open defecation free (ODF) declarations and by the end of 2015, 29 districts (out of 75), over 1,500 Village Development Committees (VDCs) (out of 3,900),

http://dx.doi.org/10.3362/9781780449272.012

and 77 municipalities (out of 192) had been declared ODF. ODF is now the new norm, which in turn presents new challenges for the sector. While recent government data (NMIP, 2014) shows national coverage has reached 70 per cent from 43 per cent in 2010, issues with slippage and concerns with the quality of ODF verification and monitoring processes cannot be ignored.

The Interim Constitution of Nepal (Government of Nepal, 2007) and the 2015 Constitution of Nepal (Government of Nepal, 2015) identified access to sanitation as a fundamental right and, to support this, the country set a target to provide all Nepalese with access to basic sanitation services by 2017. Almost all districts have now prepared sanitation strategies. In general, the district sanitation strategy includes the current sanitation scenario in the districts (coverage, status), analysis of opportunities, barriers, and gaps (resource, policy, capacity), vision and objectives of the strategy, and strategic actions to reach the ODF targets (VDC and district targets), pro-poor support mechanisms, and the ODF declaration protocol, among others.[1] Furthermore, the sanitation movement has created a competitive environment resulting in districts achieving ODF ahead of their targeted time (year or months). This movement has been led by local government, involving the different sectoral actors (water, sanitation, and hygiene (WASH), health and education sectors) and also private entrepreneurs, local organizations, children, school teachers, and development agencies. Thus, sanitation is not left as a government's or development agency's agenda. Importantly, it has become a shared agenda for stakeholders supported though government-led coordination mechanisms and owned by communities and different actors through sensitization campaigns, rallies, debates, drama, or community-led triggering.

Within this context of harmonization, national plans and policies have been developed, for example the National Sanitation and Hygiene Master Plan (Government of Nepal, 2011), which indicated that ODF is a minimum condition of total sanitation,[2] and the Joint Sector Review on WASH (Ministry of Urban Development, 2011) which proposed looking at both rural and urban sanitation contexts. Gaps in capacity are also identified and acknowledged; for example, the second Joint Sector Review on WASH (Ministry of Urban Development, 2014) recognized a huge resource shortfall and a capacity gap in sanitation service delivery, especially in relation to reaching the remoter populations. It highlighted the need for developing a more precise and coherent strategy, and consistent implementation of post-ODF/total sanitation interventions. Moreover, the second Joint Sector Review has indicated an allocation of 20 per cent of district budget for water and sanitation, but the budgetary provision and mechanism has not been clarified. The Sector Development Plan (SDP) being drafted in 2015[3] is expected to bring uniformity in concepts and approaches of total sanitation and beyond (post-post-ODF) and needed clarity on sector financing.

In 2008, SNV, with the International Water and Sanitation Centre (IRC), developed the Sustainable Sanitation and Hygiene for All (SSH4A) programme, an integrated package that combines sanitation demand creation, sanitation supply chain, behavioural change communication, and strengthening governance (Halcrow et al., 2014). SSH4A aims to strengthen the capacity of local government to lead and accelerate the progress while tailoring the solutions. Building on the successful intervention in the seven districts of the Mid-Western Region, and satisfactory scaling up in lowland areas in Nepal, SNV continued building capacity for sustainable service provision and sustainable behaviour change, for which ODF is the first milestone. After Kalikot District (one of the most remote and underdeveloped districts in Nepal) was officially declared ODF in 2012,[4] SNV supported the development of a district post-ODF strategy, incorporating a number of post-ODF tools to monitor and assess if ODF status was being sustained, and to discover if households were moving up the sanitation ladder.[5]

Initial results prove promising, with noticeably better outcomes in Kalikot than in other districts. In an ODF re-verification exercise,[6] the SNV annual monitoring in 2013 sampled 2,466 households across the seven districts in the Mid-Western Region and found 85 per cent sanitation coverage in SNV-engaged VDCs (SNV, 2013). If ODF status is equated with access to sanitation for individual households, then, on average the study revealed 15 per cent households reverted back to open defecation (OD). Ending OD is not only demonstrated by the building and retaining of toilets, it is whether those facilities are used in a proper way and by all. According to this data then, 73 per cent of households not only own but also use hygienic toilets in the Mid-Western Region (SNV, 2013), leaving 27 per cent of the population who either do not use their latrines for defecation or use them improperly.[7] Similar results were observed in a subsequent baseline survey conducted by SNV in further VDCs across six districts in the Mid-Western Region (SNV, 2014). Of the 85 per cent of households who owned a toilet, 72 per cent were using them in a hygienic way and 13 per cent of households had reverted back to OD. A difference is observable in the case of Kalikot District, in which the same annual performance monitoring (SNV, 2013) confirmed that only 2 per cent of households defecated openly – indicating sustainability even after nearly two years of ODF – and 89 per cent owned improved toilets (as per the JMP definition, WHO/UNICEF, n.d.).

In Kalikot District, the baseline survey of 2014 indicated that 96 per cent of toilets were functioning as intended and were also well maintained (SNV, 2014). However, some lacked privacy (13 per cent) due to issues with the lock and/or door. Further, not only was ODF consistently maintained in Kalikot, there was a tendency for toilets to be continuously upgraded over time. Figure 12.1 compares the figure from the 2010 baseline, the annual monitoring in three consecutive years 2011, 2012, and 2013, the baseline survey in a new area in 2014, and government data (NMIP, 2014).[8] It seems 90 per cent or more people owned improved toilets (as per the JMP definition) and had upgraded to a large extent since the declaration of ODF in 2012 (from 63 per cent to above 90 per cent).

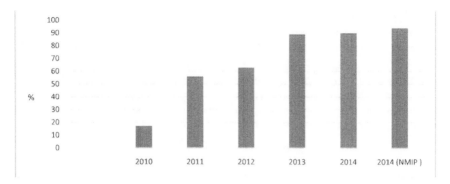

Figure 12.1 Progress in improved latrines in Kalikot (% in the vertical axis refers to the sanitation coverage)

Source: Original figure based on data from baseline survey and end year monitoring reports, SNV Nepal

What led to this success is discussed below.

Post-ODF strategy development

SNV engaged in developing a post-ODF strategy through a multi-stakeholder process in Kalikot District in 2012, integrating existing successful post-ODF tools such as early detection processes, and a behaviour change communication campaign, both of which are discussed later in this chapter. The strategy aimed to achieve a target of total sanitation for the district by 2017, while 50 per cent of VDCs were targeted to attain a total sanitized village status by 2015.[9] Total sanitation is measured against six behaviours: safe drinking water; hygienic use of toilets; handwashing with soap; food hygiene; environmental hygiene; and household hygiene. The District WASH Coordination Committee (D-WASH-CC)[10] monitors and confirms the achievement for each VDC and likewise Village WASH-CC (V-WASH-CC) confirms the achievement for the villages or community.

Apart from monitoring ODF, the strategy includes an evidence-based behaviour change process, with specific targets to attain total sanitation, re-verification of ODF, changing key behaviours for all (mainly two key behaviours, handwashing with soap and hygienic use of toilets), building capacity at district and village levels to implement and monitor the total sanitation activities, and institutionalizing a multi-stakeholder process. As a result of the strategy and its effective implementation, ODF is being sustained in Kalikot District with very few reversions. The strategy and related actions at different levels of government are outlined in Figure 12.2.

The post-ODF strategy for Kalikot District has been developed in a coordinated manner with collaboration of all district stakeholders, led by the D-WASH-CC. SNV, as a key player, provides technical advisory support to develop or to review the strategy. The strategy describes key actions to be taken, identifies available

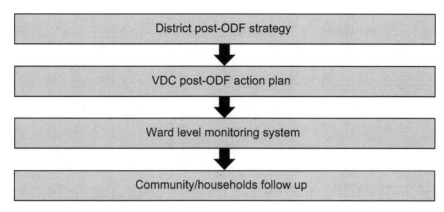

Figure 12.2 Post-ODF strategy process and actions in Kalikot
Source: SNV Nepal

resources, assesses the capacity of implementers, and identifies resource gaps, all towards achieving the agreed targets. The strategy documents highlight the six behavioural indicators, the implementation modalities, joint monitoring and total sanitation declaration process and protocols, and the ODF re-verification process (see also Mukherjee, 2016, this book).

Based on the district strategy, the VDCs' post-ODF plans are developed with the V-WASH-CCs taking the lead. These plans include the village-level targets and actions to be taken, who are responsible for these actions, the timelines, the monitoring activities, and resource mobilization. The ward-level monitoring complements the VDC plans and is supportive in monitoring community-level progress and achievements. This is more to do with detecting any shortfalls in implementation.

Three villages in Kalikot District have attained Model Village (total sanitized village) status since SNV started the post-ODF activities. They have been officially confirmed by the D-WASH-CC monitoring team and endorsed by the D-WASH-CC meeting.

Moreover, enabling equal participation of people living with disabilities, females, and households living in poverty is of concern, particularly in the post-ODF scenario, if access for all is to be sustained (see also Patkar, 2016, this book; Roose et al., 2016, this book). SNV advocates for inclusive wash in its working districts and has signed a tripartite agreement with the Women and Child Office and Water Supply and Sanitation Division Office (WSSDO) in each district to prioritize this issue. Within the district total sanitation strategy in Kalikot and Rukum, space has been given for gender and social inclusion.

Early detection processes to strengthen community assessment, household level monitoring, and to retain ODF status

At the village level, SNV emphasizes institutionalizing community monitoring and early detection to retain ODF status (see also Wamera, 2016, this book). Adding to the recommendation of the *Community-Led Total Sanitation Handbook* (Kar with Chambers, 2008) for community participatory monitoring, districts are developing post-ODF 'early detection tools' to enable the identification of poorly maintained toilets and to ensure the quality of ODF processes and sustainable hygiene behaviour. The early detection process includes a community-wide assessment and observation using a self-assessment checklist (see Box 12.1); focus group discussions; key informant interviews; and triangulation of the data collected.

The early detection process is used at the community (ward) level. The V-WASH-CC is responsible for identifying gaps or slippage in the ODF process and for recommending effective remedial measures for maintaining ODF status and climbing up the sanitation ladder. The VDC secretary is the key person who owns the process and motivates the community. This process supports the identification of issues or problems, as well as supplementing the village-level database on a regular basis (the frequency is dependent on the V-WASH-CC's decision, but ideally every three months). This new surveillance system became very effective in Kalikot, and is still being used.

Detection tools (described in Box 12.1) were developed in cooperation with SNV and its local NGO partner, after ODF declaration, and used by the V-WASH-CCs. Initially, Lalu, Kotbada, and Malkot VDCs in Kalikot were assessed by the concerned V-WASH-CC a year after ODF. It was found that there had been about 10 per cent slippage due to the construction of new houses without toilets, and affordability constraints for the poor and single female-headed families. The details were confirmed by the V-WASH-CC, and a campaign was organized involving self-help and pro-poor support mechanisms. These are outlined in the National Sanitation and Hygiene Master Plan (Government of Nepal, 2011), and they have authorized the concerned V-WASH-CC to identify the poor[11] and provide necessary support if required.

Later, the piloted tool was adopted by the D-WASH-CC, and it is now being applied in all VDCs across the districts. Every surveillance report has helped to prepare and update the district sanitation status, and it has enabled the

---

Box 12.1 The checklist used in the early detection process to retain ODF status

√ Details of the house owner, family size, and composition of the family (male, female and children).
√ Access to a toilet (yes/no).
√ Type of toilet (simple pit, pour flush with pan, VIP, etc.).
√ Type of containment (double pit, single pit, biogas, septic tank with soak pit or simple holding tank, or a soak-away pit only).
√ Date toilet was constructed.
√ Status of hygienic use and maintenance (not in use, used for other purposes, used but unhygienic, used in hygienic way with no visibility of faecal smears around the pan, wall and lid, availability of cleansing materials, etc.).
√ Availability of handwashing facilities (designated place for handwashing, distance of handwashing facility from the toilet, availability of soap, etc.).

identification of possible remedial measures (for instance, the households which had built the temporary toilets, upgraded their sub-structures as committed). Similarly, they could identify householders who did not use the toilets and were in need of being sensitized again. The recent household-level monitoring[12] (blanket survey) in three VDCs of Kalikot shows only 2 per cent slippage and, as stated by VDC Secretaries, the early detection tools have become instrumental in illustrating the on-the-ground reality, the need for re-sensitizing communities, and making everyone accountable. Now, this is an integral part of the VDC WASH plan.[13]

Moreover, the early detection tools were replicated in adjoining districts. In early 2015, SNV, through its implementing partners (local capacity builders or the local NGOs), applied the early detection tool in a VDC in Rukum (a new ODF district)[14] and found 20 per cent of people were not using their toilets, and another 10 per cent had toilets under construction. Some other key findings of this rapid assessment were:

- There had been a weak sanitation and behavioural change campaign; some communities had not been triggered;
- Some toilet adopters had built their toilets to 'show off' to other people, others had done so only to count towards the targets rather than to commit to a behaviour change;
- There had been poor monitoring at the community level;
- A number of V-WASH-CCs had not met for a long time.

After detecting and diagnosing the problem in Rukum District, SNV, through its local partner, started a post-ODF and behaviour change communication (BCC) campaign, while focusing on ODF retention and the proper use and maintenance of toilets. The following observations were made at the household monitoring in February 2015:

- 15 per cent more households started to use their toilets;
- 5 per cent more households completed their toilets and started using them;
- Community monitoring mechanisms were strengthened by the Women Citizens' Awareness Centre; they had conducted campaigns on their own while developing a revolving fund;
- The V-WASH-CC was active and had started to meet on a regular basis.

A strength of the early detection mechanism at the community level is that it is not only helping to sustain ODF and diagnosing problems, it is also instrumental in continuously engaging the community and local authorities for moving up the sanitation ladder (up to the six behaviours and beyond), where ODF is seen as only the bottom rung (see also Robinson and Gnilo, 2016a, this book). Thus, the process of community action is also being sustained and institutionalized.

In general, the following broader outputs were observed with the strengthening of community surveillance through early detection tools:

- Maps were made of the sanitation status in the community and displayed for all to see.

- Communities and individuals were providing follow-up on a regular basis, as planned and agreed in the community or village (D-WASH-CC level).
- At the ward level, or V-WASH-CC level, reviewing of progress was being carried out.
- The VDC-level data base was maintained and updated by the VDC Secretary.
- Participatory monitoring and action planning was carried out.
- Ideas were provided for reviewing and developing the sanitation and behaviour change campaign.
- Help was given for tailoring the pro-poor approaches or the implementation of sanctions.
- Technological options were being offered so that people could make informed choices about sanitation improvements.
- Whole-community responses were considered, while also the specific constraints of individual households.

Thus, the early detection and community surveillance has proved itself as effective, not only in ascertaining the ODF status but also in updating the situation for a wider dissemination of issues to community members. Inspired by the successful examples of Kalikot and Rukum districts, SNV is encouraging all district stakeholders to include community surveillance as an integral part of their post-ODF strategies.

Evidence-based behaviour change communication campaign

Post-ODF activities in Kalikot and other districts have been reinforced through a BCC campaign, designed by SNV on the basis of formative research (SNV Nepal, 2012). SNV Nepal carried out research on sanitation and hygiene behaviour in Kalikot in 2012 in order to identify the key barriers and motivators for hygienic toilet use. The major findings of the qualitative study were:

- Women had less voice and choice in the sanitation campaign; since there was less consultation with women, they had less knowledge about the benefits of a hygienic toilet;
- Poor access to water meant people did not use enough water to flush their toilets;
- People believed that maintenance of toilets was a personal matter and not a social concern;
- There was a general lack of knowledge about toilet hygiene and benefits of hygienic use;
- Affordability and availability of cleansing materials were big concerns;
- There was a general belief that the ODF environment, in particular the access to toilets, was enough to give dignity and good health.

Moreover, the research showed that disgust, embarrassment, avoidance of sanctions, and fear of illness were the key motivators for sustained behaviour change in mid-western Nepal. On the basis of the research outcomes, BCC activities were intensified by SNV and its partners to ensure that the toilet adopters used their toilets on a regular basis and maintained their functionality and hygienic use.

The campaign focused on advocating at the district and VDC levels, creating pressure through different stakeholders, including D-WASH-CC or V-WASH-CC platforms, political parties, cross-sectoral actors, and social activists, to maintain the district or VDC ODF status and to raise awareness in the community about the reversion of ODF and how and why the continuation of the ODF environment was needed. A BCC activity plan was developed at the district and VDC levels (VDC role defined in BCC strategy), developing communication objectives, identifying the audience or target groups, developing the messages and identifying the effective disseminating channels and tools, mobilizing the communities through local partners, and monitoring the progress through V-WASH-CCs and or D-WASH-CCs.

In the community level campaign, activities included street drama, debates in schools and VDCs, mobilizing the teachers' and children's club, and mobilizing the local level health volunteers (see Figure 12.3). A mass gathering led by V-WASH-CC brought together health workers, female community health volunteers, social mobilizers, school teachers, students, and members of the community, to raise awareness on handwashing and hygienic use of toilets (see also Musyoki, 2016, this book; Wamera, 2016, this book). Regular, follow-up door-to-door visits were carried out by SNV partners, to identify

Figure 12.3 Student rally, Mid-Western Region, 2013; placard reads:'Make a toilet. Is not an expense of wealth, it is the protection, promotion and preservation of community health'
Source: SNV Nepal

whether the community had received the message or not. Poster and wall painting campaigns were carried out, and the media engaged to broadcast behaviour change messages.

At the district level, key activities or strategic actions to sustain behaviour change were discussed by stakeholders and agreed. Activities in the district campaign included celebration of key events (such as Global Handwashing Day, International Women's Day, and World Environment Day) and organization of mass gatherings. These celebrations were usually focused on delivering key behaviour change messages, with a special focus on handwashing and use of toilets. Health workers were mobilized through District Public Health Offices, and education sectors (teachers and students) were mobilized through District Education Offices. Broader media, poster, and wall painting campaigns were also carried out at the district level.

Re-verification of ODF

SNV has supported the district government in developing an ODF verification protocol and a joint monitoring protocol, which has now been integrated into the post-ODF strategy. It has applied various tools to verify not only the ODF status but also the wider aspects of sustainable sanitation and hygiene behaviour change.

Re-verification in households and at the community level is done by the community through the Ward WASH-CC or V-WASH-CC. SNV through its partner provides technical support, establishing indicators of verification, the process of verification, and representation of the outcomes after verification to the V-WASH-CC and later on to the D-WASH-CC. Re-verification of the entire village or VDC is conducted by the V-WASH-CC, VDC level stakeholders, and, occasionally, a D-WASH-CC representative. Technical support is again provided by SNV through its partner, for example in mobilizing the Social Mobilizers[15] and other actors with the tools and templates to assist the re-verification team.

In order to have the final endorsement of the re-verification, a monitoring visit is also carried out by the D-WASH-CC, which officially formulates a monitoring team comprising key district stakeholders. SNV mobilizes staff and partner organizations with the tools and templates to assist the re-verification and the finalizing of the re-verification process or protocols. It also funds the monitoring visits and organization of the endorsement meetings. This re-verification exercise has been applied in some VDCs in Kalikot and Rukum districts. The recently updated total sanitation strategies in both districts acknowledge this and have agreed to reassess the ODF on an annual basis as far as possible.

Conclusions and ways forward

Post-ODF is a longer-term process of behavioural and social change and sustainable service provision, rather than a short-term, results-driven campaign. It is not limited to retaining ODF status alone. Its effectiveness is measured against the achievement of clean and healthy communities and equitable access to improved sanitation for all. The integrated capacity building process used as part of the SSH4A programme has been effective in terms of first supporting area-wide ODF, then encouraging and monitoring progress up the sanitation ladder. This in turn is sustained through behaviour change aligned with the six focus behaviours of total sanitation (see also Robinson and Gnilo, 2016a, this book).

Replication of post-ODF tools in non-SNV engaged areas is relatively challenging; however, as a member of National Sanitation and Hygiene Coordination Committee SNV can play a significant role to achieve buy-in from all. The next big challenge is to ensure no slippage in ODF from the first day of ODF and effective implementation of various tools including early detection.

In order to develop an enabling environment and achieve sustainable ODF communities the following points are important:

- A clear and consistent national policy and achievable district and village-level plans should be formulated to ensure that the voiceless, and people with particular needs, are included in the total sanitation scenario (see also Patkar, 2016, this book).
- Monitoring ODF should be institutionalized and owned by WASH-CCs. Harmonization of the different sectors and ownership of the process is important, so the responsibility of embedding ODF status is not left as a government's or development agency's agenda, and is adopted by communities and multiple actors (see also Musyoki, 2016, this book).
- Evidence-based monitoring tools should be introduced in multi-stakeholder platforms and owned by all.
- Approaches and tools should be continuously adapted and revised based on what is found on the ground. Problems need to be detected and diagnosed, and approaches designed with the information gathered.
- The government should institutionalize ODF re-verification at certain intervals (ideally on an annual basis) and consider suspending ODF status after verification and monitoring if any VDC or district fails to comply. Re-verification processes should incorporate different actors, including community, local, and district level committees.
- The creation of an enabling environment and continuous support and guidance from government agencies and development activists are key motivators for ensuring people use and maintain their toilets. Hence, the government agencies should continuously steer the post-ODF movement, as they did for ODF (see also Thomas, 2016, this book; Wamera, 2016, this book; Musyoki, 2016, this book).
- Early detection and community surveillance has proved effective, not only in ascertaining the ODF status, but also in updating the situation for a wider dissemination of issues to community members.

- Access to sanitation for all and for all the time is still not perceived well by all the actors, hence the needs of all people should be taken seriously into account (see also Patkar, 2016, this book; Cavill et al., 2016, this book; and Robinson and Gnilo, 2016b, this book).

About the author

Anup Kumar Regmi leads the Sustainable Sanitation and Hygiene for All (SSH4A) project currently being implemented by SNV in eight districts in Nepal. He holds a Master's degree from Ghent University and has worked on both professional and academic assignments in the WASH sector in Nepal and abroad for 15 years.

Endnotes

1. See also Mukherjee (2016, this book) for discussion on national sanitation strategies in Laos PDR, Vietnam, and Indonesia.
2. Total sanitation is the state where ODF status is retained and a village or community achieves six additional key behavioural indicators: personal hygiene; safe drinking water; safe food; use of latrine; household sanitation; and environmental sanitation.
3. This is due to be published later in 2016.
4. Kalikot had only 3 per cent sanitation coverage in 2008, where SNV piloted its first WASH project together with another four districts.
5. See Robinson and Gnilo (2016a, this book) for an alternative phased approach to achieving sustainable sanitation and hygiene behaviour change being trialled in the Philippines, which goes beyond the achievement of ODF status.
6. ODF re-verification is to assess how far ODF status is being retained; this exercise was led by the D-WASH-CC and SNV through its partner supported to carry out the assessment and set the process of re-verification.
7. Where faecal smears are visible around the pan, rodents can enter the toilet and come out easily, and there is no water seal or lid covering the squatting hole.
8. These reports are not published yet and are the internal products of SNV.
9. A total sanitized village is a village which is verified to have achieved all six key behavioural indicators mentioned earlier.
10. District WASH Coordination Committees (D-WASH-CCs) and Village WASH Coordination Committees (V-WASH-CCs) are the WASH coordination structures formulated in line with the recommendation of the National Sanitation and Hygiene Master Plan 2011, and they are responsible for on-the-ground implementation, monitoring, and sector harmonization.
11. The generic criteria outlined in the Master Plan define poor as having for example a female-headed household, a household which has had a food deficiency for more than six months, and indigenous or low caste people.
12. The local partner of SNV conducts regular monitoring and follow-up and updates the status.

13. The VDC WASH plan is usually a village-level strategic plan developed to support the district strategy. Each VDC prepares its WASH or sanitation plan, indicating resources for ODF and post-ODF activities, with clear targets and responsibilities assigned.
14. Rukum is a new ODF district in the Mid-Western Region, declared ODF in December 2014.
15. Community members who work on a voluntary basis and are usually hired and mobilized by the District Development Office.

References

Cavill, S., Roose, S., Stephen, C. and Wilbur, J. (2016) 'Putting the hardest to reach at the heart of the SDGs', in P. Bongarz, N. Vernon and J. Fox (eds.) *Sustainable Sanitation for All: Experiences, Challenges, and Innovations*, Practical Action Publishing, Rugby.

Government of Nepal (2007) *The Interim Constitution of Nepal*, www.lawcommission.gov.np

Government of Nepal (2011) *National Sanitation and Hygiene Master Plan*, Government of Nepal, Kathmandu.

Government of Nepal (2015) *Constitution of Federal Republic of Nepal*, www.lawcommission.gov.np

Halcrow, G. with Krukkkert, I., Kome, A. and Baetings, E. (2014) 'Developing capacity for an integrated rural sanitation service delivery model at scale', 37th WEDC International Conference, Hanoi, Vietnam.

Kar, K. with Chambers, R. (2008) *Handbook on Community-Led Total Sanitation*, Plan International and Institute of Development Studies, London and Brighton.

Ministry of Urban Development (2011) *First Joint Sector Review on WASH*, Technical Report, Sector Efficiency Improvement Unit, Ministry of Urban Development, Kathmandu.

Ministry of Urban Development (2014) *Second Joint Sector Review on WASH*, Technical Report, Sector Efficiency Improvement Unit, Ministry of Urban Development, Kathmandu.

Mukherjee, N. (2016) 'Building environments to support sustainability of improved sanitation behaviours at scale: levers of change in East Asia', in P. Bongartz, N. Vernon and J. Fox (eds.) *Sustainable Sanitation for All: Experiences, Challenges, and Innovations*, Practical Action Publishing, Rugby.

Musyoki, S. (2016) 'Roles and responsibilities for post-ODF engagement: building an enabling institutional environment for CLTS sustainability', in P. Bongarz, N. Vernon and J. Fox (eds.) *Sustainable Sanitation for All: Experiences, Challenges, and Innovations*, Practical Action Publishing, Rugby.

NMIP (2014) *Nationwide Coverage and Functionality Status of Water Supply and Sanitation in Nepal*, National Management and Information Project (NMIP), Department of Water Supply and Sewerage, Panipokahri, Kathmandu, www.dwss.gov.np [accessed 2 February 2016].

Patkar, A. (2016) 'Equality and non-discrimination in sanitation and hygiene: ensuring the "one" in everyone', in P. Bongarz, N. Vernon and J. Fox (eds.) *Sustainable Sanitation for All: Experiences, Challenges, and Innovations*, Practical Action Publishing, Rugby.

Robinson, A. and Gnilo, M. E. (2016a) 'A phased approach to rural sanitation development', in P. Bongartz, N. Vernon and J. Fox (eds.) *Sustainable Sanitation for All: Experiences, Challenges, and Innovations*, Practical Action Publishing, Rugby.

Robinson, A. and Gnilo, M. E. (2016b) 'Financing for the poorest', in P. Bongartz, N. Vernon and J. Fox (eds.) *Sustainable Sanitation for All: Experiences, Challenges, and Innovations*, Practical Action Publishing, Rugby.

SNV Nepal (2012) 'Formative Research on Sanitation and hygiene behaviour in Kalikot, 2012/2013', SNV Nepal, Kathmandu.

SNV Nepal (2013) 'End Year Monitoring of SSH4A program in 7 districts in Mid-Western Region', unpublished internal report, SNV Nepal, Kathmandu.

SNV Nepal (2014) 'Baseline survey of SSH4A program in 8 Districts in Mid-Western Region', unpublished internal report, SNV Nepal, Kathmandu.

Thomas, A. (2016) 'Strengthening post-ODF programming: reviewing lessons from sub-Saharan Africa', in P. Bongarz, N. Vernon and J. Fox (eds.) *Sustainable Sanitation for All: Experiences, Challenges, and Innovations*, Practical Action Publishing, Rugby.

Wamera, E. (2016) 'Who is managing the post-ODF process in the community? A case study of Nambale District in Western Kenya', in P. Bongartz, N. Vernon and J. Fox (eds.) *Sustainable Sanitation for All: Experiences, Challenges, and Innovations*, Practical Action Publishing, Rugby.

WHO/UNICEF (n.d.) 'Improved and unimproved water sources and sanitation facilities', Joint Monitoring Programme (JMP) for Water Supply and Sanitation, Geneva, http://www.wssinfo.org/definitions-methods/watsan-categories [accessed 2 February 2016].

CHAPTER 13

Certification of open defecation free status: emerging lessons from Kenya

Lewnida Sara

Abstract

This chapter is a case study of the certification processes related to establishing the open defecation free (ODF) status of communities. It identifies the key indicators for appraising ODF status as set out in the 'Protocol for Implementing CLTS in Kenya'. It traces and assesses the changes in certification processes as Kenya has moved to a devolved system of governance – processes that seek to achieve standardization and improve efficiency and cost-effectiveness while maintaining independence and objectivity. In particular, it analyses the strengths and challenges involved in implementing a decentralized and diversified third-party system of certification.

Keywords: Verification, Kenya, Third party certification, Devolution

Introduction

Since the introduction of Community-Led Total Sanitation (CLTS) in Bangladesh in 1999 and its adoption in many countries around the world, the verification of outcomes and certification of open defecation free (ODF) status remain important elements of the process. However, ensuring quality, maintaining independence, operating with efficiency as well as at scale, and achieving sustainability in relation to verification and certification, a key consequence of effective post-ODF monitoring, continue to pose significant challenges. This chapter focuses on verification and certification, in particular on emerging lessons, with a special focus on Kenya in its shift from a centralized, 'contracted' system of third party certification, to a more 'devolved' system, nearer to the people.

Verification

Verification is the process of assessing ODF claims made by a community. It is based on agreed criteria. In the interests of upholding principles of transparency and credibility what is preferred is a multi-stage, multi-stakeholder verification process, based on objective criteria. Of course, different countries have developed different verification guidelines, but their shared purpose is to harmonize approaches in field verification and to streamline the process for all actors involved.[1] What is also shared is the recognition that appropriate

http://dx.doi.org/10.3362/9781780449272.013

and rigorous verification processes can help in ensuring that CLTS gains will be sustained.

Kenya has a robust verification process. It starts with a community assessing itself to be ODF. The community then makes a claim to the local public health team, which in turn carries out its own assessment. If the team makes a positive assessment, this results in an escalation of the claim for third-party certification.

The *Protocol for Implementing CLTS in Kenya* (MoH, 2014) has seven non-negotiable key indicators for achieving ODF status:

- No exposed human excreta within the community/households.
- All households have access to a toilet (individual or shared) which should not facilitate faecal-oral transmission.
- The squat hole is covered.
- The floor is free of faeces and urine.
- The superstructure provides privacy.
- All households have a handwashing facility near the latrine with soap/ash and water.
- There is continued use of the toilet by the household owner.

However, there are a number of challenges in operating this verification system:

- The remoteness of some villages hinders timely verification of ODF status once a claim has been made, and this can result in frustration for villages who have worked hard to reach ODF status.
- There are only limited resources for monitoring and evaluation, including CLTS follow-up.
- In a number of areas there is a constrained capacity for verification exercises, the consequence of few training opportunities and insufficient deployment of personnel.
- The standardization of verification exercises is needed, to ensure that it is neither too lax in some areas nor too strict in others.
- With sanitation service delivery now a responsibility of the county governments, there are likely to be differences in priorities and consequent disparities in performance.

Certification

Certification is the official confirmation and recognition of the ODF status of a community after verification. It might actually go beyond ODF by including other agreed-upon conditions related to sanitation and hygiene.[2] In some countries, the certification process is undertaken by the same agencies that had carried out the verification exercise. In Kenya, an independent, third-party agency carried it out, the Kenya Water for Health Organization (KWAHO).

Third-party certification is an independent confirmation of ODF claims made by communities. As the name third party implies, it is conducted by agencies (organizations, government agencies, community organizations, consultants) that are not directly involved in the implementation of the CLTS activities. This involvement of a third party should bring in a fresh outlook, ensure the credibility of the certification process, make the community realize their potential, and trigger enthusiasm in neighbouring communities. However, it should also be acknowledged that, though they are not involved in programme implementation, the third party agencies are being paid to do a job, so there might sometimes be pressure put upon them by their funders to produce results they want to see. And the same might be true for those who carry out the verification exercises, in that government staff might wish to get good results and so become lenient during verification.

In Africa, third-party certification using such an independent organization is said to have been tested only in Kenya (KWAHO, 2012). Zambia considered, but eventually dropped, an approach similar to Kenya's, on grounds related to affordability, speed, and scale-up. In Ghana, the government's lead ministry is involved in the certification, while in Nigeria the task forces, at state and national levels, comprise various sanitation stakeholders responsible for the certification. They carry out random unannounced spot checks on the list of villages claiming to be ODF.

Certification in Kenya: the old model

While ODF verification in Kenya has been the mandate of the Ministry of Health through the deployment of sub-county public health officers, certification, for the period 2010 to 2014, was carried out solely by a third party, KWAHO, a local NGO (see Figure 13.1).

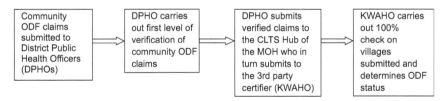

Figure 13.1 Verification and certification of ODF status in Kenya – the old model
Source: KWAHO.

With the financial support of UNICEF, the third-party certification was carried out in Nyanza and Western regions from late 2010. In July 2012, Nambale District in Busia County was certified as the first ODF district in Kenya.

However, many villages that claimed ODF status remained uncertified. Some of the reasons proffered for the slow rate were:

- The high cost of certification. It was estimated that certification was costing, on average, far more than the cost of triggering of a village. The cost of certifying one village was estimated at US$85, compared with US$60 required per village for triggering.
- The human resources capacity of a single NGO to carry out the certification process nationally was also a focus of discussion, as triggering and claims of ODF were happening quicker than they could be certified.
- The efficiency and sustainability of managing third-party certification centrally came into question.

Significantly, between 2010 and 2011 this initiative registered impressive results with over 1,000 villages (571,231 people) attaining ODF status (KWAHO, 2012). However, due to the expense involved, the third-party certification exercise remained part of a project contract with UNICEF Kenya and it was, in the main, carried out only in the GoK/ UNICEF CLTS programmes. Consequently, the sanitation sector, through its coordinating mechanism known as the Inter-Agency Coordinating Committee (ICC) and its sanitation working sub-group, the Sanitation Technical Working Group (TWG), reviewed the whole issue of third-party certification in Kenya. The TWG was convinced of the need to continue with a third-party system, but questions remained about scale-up, quality, and cost-effectiveness, particularly in the context of Kenya's devolution of powers, where the mandate for sanitation service delivery is no longer at the national level, but is instead at county level. The TWG resolved to create a new model more aligned to the new constitution and which would take into account the issues related to scale, quality, sustainability, and cost-effectiveness.

The new certification model

In 2010, Kenya had promulgated a new constitution (Government of Kenya, 2010), which, along with that of South Africa, is acclaimed as one of the world's most progressive. In it, Article 43(1) (b) guarantees the right of every person to 'reasonable standards of sanitation' and, further, in Articles 22 and 70, gives every person the right to institute court proceedings claiming that his or her rights to sanitation and clean and healthy environment have been denied, violated, infringed, or threatened. So the significance of the new constitution for sanitation is twofold:

- Sanitation has been enshrined as a constitutional right and one that is actionable.
- The responsibility for service delivery in health and sanitation was moved from the national government to the 47 county governments.

This has had far-reaching effects and important implications for the sanitation sector in Kenya in that the constitution promotes the devolution of systems and processes to bring them closer to the people and ensure service delivery. It also provides a rationale for devolving third-party certification.

In scaling up CLTS in Kenya, it was agreed that a well-defined process of independently assessing, confirming, and certifying claims made by communities about their ODF status needed to be established and maintained. The sector needed to explore options and establish a system that would be:

- Able to speed up the certification process to cope with the large number of anticipated ODF claims.
- Cost-effective.
- Independent and therefore objective.
- Acceptable and therefore able to be adopted by all stakeholders.

With these key prerequisites in mind, Kenya has moved towards a hybrid approach to certification, comprising an independent organization/institution at the national level and trained teams at county levels. County-level teams ensure that the harmonized approach developed by the Sanitation Technical Working Group and the CLTS National Steering Committee, among other key stakeholders, was accepted and used by all. The model is designed to address issues related to the need to establish a sustainable institutional framework, ensure efficient organization, secure funding, and promote objectivity in the certification process (MoH, 2014).

Development partners supported the rolling out of the new model. KWAHO was still engaged, with a role of supporting and training counties on the required third-party certification processes and establishing a pool of trained Master Certifiers who were recruited for training based on the affiliation they had with their own counties. In line with the TWG recommendations, local-level actors, Natural Leaders, and community-based organizations (CBOs) are directly involved in the process. KWAHO, as well as building the capacity of the county teams, provides quality control through spot checks in certified villages. And this will help to standardize the certification process across the counties.

So, essentially, one step was added to the sequence set out in Figure 13.1, the certification of ODF claims carried out at the local level by what are called 'Third-Party Master Certifiers', and KWAHO's role changed to that of trainer and quality assurer. In setting up county teams in 11 pilot counties, KWAHO took the steps outlined in Figure 13.2.

By the end of 2015, 11 counties had fully established and trained teams, with 108 Master Certifiers. The criteria for the selection of these Master Certifiers are given in Annex A. Their Certification Tool is given in Annex B. The goal was to have 470 Master Certifiers trained around the country (10 per county) and their contacts made available within a national database based at the CLTS Hub of the Ministry of Health.

Figure 13.2 Establishing the county ODF certification teams
Source: KWAHO

Some emerging issues and questions

Following the initial roll-out of the new Master Certification process in Kenya, a number of challenges were faced and some early lessons can be drawn from the experience of the 11 counties.

Low response to the call for Master Certifiers

Despite the requirement that there should be a minimum of 10 Master Certifiers per county, some counties had less than half this number of applicants and, of course, the number retained was reduced after the interviews. It emerged that a number of the applicants expected that they were being interviewed for a regular paid position, rather than being only 'on call' for undertaking certification. The only obligatory payment they receive is when they are required to carry out certification, and this is limited to the cost of transport and meals. However, KWAHO recommends a daily 'allowance' of KES5,000

(US$50 in December 2015) that would cover transportation, meals, and have something left over that would be considered 'payment'. Nakuru County is the only county (among the 11 counties that have so far adopted the devolved system of certification) that has been able to pay a figure close to this, which was KES3,500. For Nakuru County, this payment was made possible by the fact that the county has a budget line for sanitation that is well funded. There are however other counties that have no funding at all for sanitation activities and thus would not be able to pay the Master Certifiers.

This was a particular concern of the Executive Director of KWAHO when she was asked for her thoughts on the revised certification system. 'As I see it, a main challenge will be that we are setting up large teams,' she said. 'We should have accredited fewer people at the county level rather than a large team. If certification work is not forthcoming mainly due to lack of agencies to fund certification, they will be idle and discouraged.'[3] Another possible inhibiting factor was the requirement that in order to cut down on the cost of certification, Master Certifiers should be from, or residing within, the county calling for applications.

As a consequence, some of the pilot counties had to lower the academic qualifications for their Master Certifiers. There was a concern, then, about how this will affect reporting standards, and whether the tools will need to be simplified. The tools are given in Annex B.

Standardization of CLTS indicators

Under the new CLTS protocol and guidelines (MoH, 2014), a number of non-negotiable indicators were introduced, including that there should be a nearby handwashing facility and a drop-hole cover. Previously, these two indicators had been encouraged but not listed as non-negotiable; thus, triggering teams had not emphasized them, but focused rather on a community being ODF. So a new communication issue has emerged, the need to clarify for communities, well in advance, the range of criteria being used in the certification process.

Potential conflict of interest

There was concern in some sub-counties about potential conflict of interest, when it seemed that some Public Health Officers (PHO) wanted to influence the recruitment of peer reviewers/enumerators (KWAHO, 2015). There is a possibility that they might influence the process of certification. So the question remains as to whether the objectivity of the third-party certification will be compromised by engaging local level reviewers.

This question of objectivity was also a concern of KWAHO's Executive Director, who in an interview with the author, wondered how impartial the Master Certifiers could be if, after recruitment by their county, they were required to certify within their own county. If they are accountable to the county, what assurance and quality control would there be?

Another conflict of interest challenge emerged in areas where Public Health Officials demanded to be accredited as Master Certifiers, which would have had potentially serious negative impacts on objectivity and independence of the certification process.

Uniformity

The maintenance of a quality standard for verification and certification throughout the country will be key to upholding the integrity of the process, and in ensuring the sustainability of ODF status. Will there be worrying disparities in the way counties apply the defined standards?

Equity

Different budgetary allocations per county for the same process might well distort the certification system. Will the counties recognize the importance of post-ODF monitoring and evaluation in working for sustainability? Will they provide sufficient budgets for verification and certification? How best can they be persuaded to do so?

Conclusion

Perhaps the key problem, then, in relation to verification and certification in countries such as Kenya where devolution of responsibilities is taking place, is how to ensure that there are equitable processes across the country, when there will be a tendency for county governments to identify different priorities and allocate different budgets. In 2015 there were efforts to finalize guidelines for achieving an ODF Kenya and advocating for budget allocations for sanitation. Additionally, there was a push for integration with other sectors, including nutrition, for better health outcomes. On the issue of inclusion, there is still a need to review policies and establish mechanisms for assisting the most vulnerable members of the community, bearing in mind that the country has a no-subsidy policy for households.

A main challenge related to budget is the lack of hard and fast rules/guidelines on the level of payment of Master Certifiers. What will be the effect on quality of certification in counties where Master Certifiers are not paid at all, and in other counties where they are paid? Can a county retain a Master Certifier who they cannot pay and who needs to be able to have a source of income?

The other main challenge will be in addressing issues of impartiality and conflict of interest, especially when the Master Certifiers come under pressure because targets have to be reached. Only if it upholds values of honesty, equity, and transparency can a system for verification and certification be said to be trusted and effective.

As with all other sectors, the health sector in Kenya continues to grapple with various challenges occasioned by devolution and the shift of service provision responsibility from the national level to the county levels. Sanitation-related challenges, in particular, have had a significant and very visible effect both on the health and the economy of the country. Throughout 2015, nearly half of the counties had breakouts of cholera with many casualties reported. Early feedback from some of the counties showed that villages that were ODF escaped the recurrent waves of cholera, even as villages around them were continuously affected. This makes it even more imperative for the sector to speed up the ODF campaign and resolve the questions that still arise on how to ensure a robust, efficient, and cost-effective certification process that counties can trust, adopt, and execute.

About the author

Lewnida Sara, World Bank Water and Sanitation Program (WSP). Lewnida led WSP's implementation of the new Ministry of Health guidelines for third party certification of ODF status following the devolution of health services in Kenya from central to county governments.

Endnotes

1. See CLTS website, www.communityledtotalsanitation.org/resource/national-protocols-and-guidelines-verification-and-certification
2. Other conditions in Kenya include a clothes line, a rubbish pit, and a dish rack.
3. Phone interview with the Executive Director of KWAHO, Catherine Mwango, on 28 September 2015.

References

Government of Kenya (2010) *Constitution of Kenya 2010*, Government of Kenya, Nairobi, http://www.kenyalaw.org:8181/exist/kenyalex/actview.xql?actid=const2010 [accessed 5 February 2016].

Kenya Water for Health Organization (KWAHO) (2012) *Third Party ODF Certification* Concept, KWAHO, Nairobi.

Kenya Water for Health Organization (KWAHO) (2015) *Report of Capacity Building of 7 Counties in 3rd Party ODF Certification*, KWAHO, Nairobi.

Ministry of Health (MoH) (2014) *Protocol for Implementing CLTS in Kenya*, MoH, Government of Kenya. Nairobi.

Annex A

Re-advertisement: capacity development (training) opportunity for third party open defecation free Master Certifiers

Kenya Water for Health Organization (KWAHO) in collaboration with the Ministry of Health plans to establish County Level systems for Third

Party Certification of Open Defecation Free (ODF) villages. This will be done by developing a responsive capacity building Strategy through one week's training that not only will impart skills, but will also promote local ownership of the ODF Third Party Certification process at the County level in the following Counties: Migori, Kisii, Kisumu, Busia, Nakuru, Nyeri and Kajiado.

KWAHO is mandated by the Ministry of Health to carry out Third Party Certification of ODF villages. In response to and in the spirit of supporting the Devolution Governance Structure for sanitation, KWAHO will train Master Certifiers to play this role in their respective Counties.

The training aims at building local capacities of 10 Master Third Party ODF Certifiers per County by adaptation of Community Led Total Sanitation (CLTS) principles for the purpose of scaling up sanitation uptake by communities. The 10 Master certifiers will form a pool from which Organizations/stakeholders at their County level can contract them to lead in the certification of villages that will have been verified using local peer review teams.

KWAHO therefore invites qualified individuals and/or local Organizations from the 7 Counties above to send in their applications to be considered for selection as Master Certifiers.

Criteria and Qualifications:

Individuals

- CLTS experience or exposure both through training and triggering.
- Demonstrated 4 years' experience with community development approaches with a bias to WASH implementation both in rural and urban set-ups
- Evidenced experience in conducting participatory qualitative and quantitative studies
- Evidenced advanced report writing (English) and documentation skills for internal and external sharing (with partners and donors)
- Has a minimum first degree in Public/Environmental Health, social and other related sciences

For Organizations:

They must submit CV of at least 2 employees with all the above qualifications
Have a permanent physical address
Meets and provides proof of legal status of registration (PIN, VAT)

| All interested parties to send their hard or soft application indicating the County you are applying for by 12th January 2015 to: The Executive Director, Kenya Water for Health Organization, P.O 61470-00200, Nairobi / info@kwaho.org | Hard copies to be delivered to KWAHO offices: Industrial area- off Dunga Road, within National Water Conservation & pipeline Corporation compound |

Annex B

Certification tools

FGD ODF Certification Tool

Please remember the climate setting protocol, and ensure you have at least 7 people, write their names, mobile No at the back of this form and fill in a precise and concise manner

County..   Sub-County..

Location.....................................   Village Name..

No of House Holds   Water point Name.....................   Date................................

Full Name/s of Assessors..

This is intended for a small community team who should include, natural leaders, community health worker and community administration

1. What was the date of the triggering / Health Education & Sanitation training........................... Who & How was it done? (if not, Skip Question 2 & 3)

2. How many '**Natural Leaders**' from the triggering are still active?, any drop outs & why

3. How many households have **built a new latrine** since the triggering? (additional)

4. How many households are **in the process of building a latrine**? (e.g. pits dug)

5. How many households **IN TOTAL have a completed, functional latrine**?

6. How many households **HAVE NO LATRINE**?

7. For all existing latrines (old & new), how many have **hand-washing facilities**?

8. For all existing latrines (old & new), how many have **drop hole covers**?

9. Would you rank your village as ODF or not yet? OR Would you confidently say that your village is free of all human excreta in the open?

10. Go in the bush and check the Open Defecation (OD) areas. **Do you find any shit?** (Don't ask only fill at the end of transect walk)

11. Is it time to inform the authorities that your village is ODF i.e. free of human excreta in the open

VILLAGE ODF CERTIFICATION REPORT

County		Sub-County	
Location		Village Name	
Total No of Households		Total No of Households With Latrine	
Total No. of Households Visited		Total no of Latrines with Drop/Squat hole covers	
No of Households with Individual Latrine	No of Households with Shared Latrine within Homestead	No of Households sharing latrines with neighbors	No of households with improved latrine- VIP or toilets
Open defecation site/s status		Active	**Not Active**
Total No. of Households with Hand washing facility		Total No. Latrines with anal cleansing materials	Total No. of Households which Had latrine before triggering
Open Defecation Free Village Status		**ODF**	**Not ODF**

ODF Certification Team Composition (plse tick box and indicator number)

KWAHO Staff/Enumerator	Natural Leader(s)	CBO	Local Administrator	Other

We the undersigned having carried out a complete certification process which included Focus Group Discussions, observations in the village (streets, fields, schools, health center, playgrounds, market area) and a certification of all households certifying that each has **access** to a latrine(s), have drop hole covers & hand washing facilities including transect walk of the entire village. We have today satisfied ourselves that **THE VILLAGE IS OPEN DEFECATION FREE (ODF)/ NOT ODF (OD)**

We the undersigned confirm this as a true record of the ODF state of our village

Full Name of Enumerator, & Mobile No	Profession (natural leader, Village Headman, Teacher, KWAHO, Master certifier, peer reviewers.	Signature & Date

PART IV: How to ensure equity and inclusion

CHAPTER 14

Promoting choice: smart finance for rural sanitation development

Andrew Robinson and Michael Gnilo

Abstract

Effective sanitation finance is a key factor in the success of a phased approach to rural sanitation development: creating incentives for rural communities and households to invest in sanitation and hygiene improvement, and encouraging more rapid and sustainable progress to higher levels of service. Smart sanitation finance should be carefully designed and targeted to reach the least able, those who are most at risk of reverting to open defecation (OD) over time, and to encourage upgrading and improvement of sanitation services across the entire community. Critically, this finance should provide choice to the households targeted – choice of options and suppliers, and choices around installation – to improve the likelihood of sustained sanitation behaviour change. This chapter proposes a range of sanitation solutions, including targeted toilet vouchers and toilet rebates that can be used to reward certified open defecation free (ODF) communities for their improved sanitation behaviour, and assist poor and vulnerable households to upgrade and improve their sanitation facilities. Conditional grants are also recommended to encourage the achievement of higher level collective sanitation outcomes, including 100 per cent use of improved sanitation facilities, improved institutional sanitation services, handwashing with soap, and effective sustainability monitoring.

Keywords: Sanitation finance, Phased approach, Sustainability, Subsidy, Incentives, Targeting

Why is smart finance relevant to rural sanitation development?

This chapter outlines a framework for rural sanitation finance, which derives from a phased approach to rural sanitation development that has been implemented by UNICEF in the Philippines since late 2013, and from earlier work for the World Bank Water and Sanitation Program and the Asian Development Bank on sanitation finance in Cambodia (Robinson, 2012; UNICEF, 2013). Chapter 9 in this book outlines the phased approach, known as PhATS (Philippines Approach to Total Sanitation), while this chapter provides complementary details on the sanitation finance that supported and incentivized the phased approach.

http://dx.doi.org/10.3362/9781780449272.014

This chapter pulls together some best practice on the financing of household and community sanitation and hygiene outcomes, and presents it alongside the adaptations introduced in the PhATS programme. The financing approach was developed explicitly to improve the effectiveness, equity, and sustainability of the sanitation and hygiene outcomes targeted by the phased approach. A key issue is that the poorest often suffer the highest sustainability losses in post-ODF (open defecation free) communities, thus the sanitation finance framework was designed to encourage upgrading and improvement to more durable and resilient toilets, and other higher sanitation and hygiene outcomes, without undermining demand creation and sanitation marketing activities that rely on household commitment and investment.

Why do we need public finance for rural sanitation?

The case for the public finance of sanitation rests on the consequence of individual sanitation behaviour on the health and well-being of other people. The polluter rarely pays for bad sanitation practice, which means that the practice is more widespread than it would be if the individual had to account for the external costs of his or her behaviour. Furthermore, those who suffer from these external costs do so involuntarily, leading to non-optimal social and economic outcomes (Robinson, 2012).

Sanitation improvement is a significant development challenge due to the difficulty of generating private demand for sanitation facilities. Awareness of the private and external costs of inadequate sanitation is generally low in developing countries. Despite widespread diarrhoeal disease and high child mortality rates, health costs are rarely ascribed to unhygienic sanitation practices, toilets are often perceived to be unaffordable, and demand for improved sanitation remains low (Robinson, 2005, 2012).

Everyone without an improved sanitation facility is 'sanitation poor' and, therefore, will benefit from public support to improve sanitation. Furthermore, each new improved sanitation facility that is used will reduce the number of pathogens in the environment, thus providing societal as well as private benefits (Robinson, 2012). In a context of low demand for sanitation, this understanding suggests that there is little need for targeting (among those not using improved sanitation facilities) as any new toilet will be beneficial.

The best welfare-enhancing approaches target the poorest first, due to the higher benefit per dollar gained by assisting the poorest. In contrast, sanitation programmes often target the 'low-hanging fruit', those without improved sanitation facilities that are more willing to invest, more responsive to promotional programmes, and easier to reach (Robinson, 2012). The intention of this self-selected targeting approach is that, in addition to the benefits from the additional sanitation facilities, the supply of sanitation goods and services to these responsive households will build a larger sanitation market, developing the economies of scale and common good practice that will be needed to change sanitation behaviour and spending priorities among the poorest households (Robinson, 2012).

In practice, these benefits rarely trickle down to the poor, with many sanitation subsidies captured by the non-poor households who respond first to interventions, or who are better connected to local leaders tasked with allocating project resources. A 2009 ADB-WSP review of a toilet subsidy programme in Cambodia (Robinson, 2012) found that, despite explicit targeting of poor communities and households, 90 per cent of the toilet subsidies were received by non-poor households building relatively expensive toilets.

The benefits of public investment in improved sanitation will be limited by an approach that fails to reach the poor, due to the lower disease and mortality burden found among non-poor households. The exact relationship between health outcomes and sanitation status remains uncertain, but children from poor households have significantly higher mortality, morbidity, and malnutrition rates than those from non-poor households.[1] Children from poor households, particularly those who are malnourished, are likely to contribute more pathogens to the environment through unsafe excreta disposal than children from non-poor households (Robinson, 2012).

As a result, sanitation strategies and investments that fail to enable improved sanitation to poor households are likely to have sub-optimal outcomes, with fewer health and economic benefits, than those that succeed in reaching the poor (Robinson, 2012). Ensuring that sanitation programmes reach the poorest and most vulnerable, where the disease burden is highly concentrated, is therefore critical to the benefits generated by these programmes.

CLTS and sanitation finance

The spread and success of Community-Led Total Sanitation (CLTS) has challenged conventional thinking on sanitation finance, demonstrating that hardware subsidies are not required for the construction of low-cost household toilets, and that community-wide improvements in sanitation behaviour can be achieved without external financial assistance.

Nevertheless, close examination of successful ODF achievement sometimes reveals that the poorest and most vulnerable have been assisted in the construction of their toilets, through the donation of materials by other households in the community, or by the village government, and sometimes through the provision of assistance to vulnerable households that lack the labour or technical capacity to build their own toilets.[2] These 'internal subsidies' are considered acceptable because they are designed, targeted, and monitored by the community, which usually means that they are low-cost (within the means of the community) and well targeted (restricted to only those whom the community discern to be genuinely in need of assistance). Other times, ODF status is verified even though some disadvantaged households still do not have or use toilets, due to ineffective verification processes and inattention to the sanitation practices of these marginal groups (Tyndale-Biscoe et al., 2013; Robinson, 2015).

Over the last decade, evidence has emerged of sustainability problems in previously ODF communities. CLTS sustainability studies (Kunthy and Catalla, 2009; Hanchett et al., 2011; Tyndale-Biscoe et al., 2013; UNICEF, 2013) have found that a proportion of the community reverts to OD over time, although with considerable variation from project to project. The quality of the CLTS process, including triggering, follow-up, and the long-term support provided, and the local enabling environment for sanitation improvement, have been suggested as major factors influencing the proportion of the community that reverts to OD (UNICEF, 2013).

The poorest and most vulnerable households are often the first to revert to OD, perhaps because their limited resources and capacity tend to result in less well-built, less durable, and less well-located toilets.[3] These toilets are more likely to collapse, face problems, and discourage use, than those built by better-off households living in less marginal conditions (see Coombes, 2016, this book; Munkhondia et al., 2016, this book). Vulnerable and time-poor households can also be marginalized by CLTS processes that require attendance at multiple triggering activities, or that are led by more prosperous or political community members. Disadvantaged households are sometimes less convinced about the ODF movement, and can be pressured into toilet construction that lacks the conviction or investment made by others. The drive to achieve ODF status can leave these poor households with sanitation facilities that they do not like or want, and are not willing to use or maintain.

The CLTS process does not provide any ready-made solution to these sustainability problems, other than to re-trigger renewed collective pressure against OD, or to encourage and support reconstruction of collapsed toilets. Households and communities who face periodic floods and tropical storms that destroy toilets, or rapid degradation of simple toilets due to termite problems, collapsible soils, or other durability issues, sometimes struggle to maintain their enthusiasm and commitment to ODF status (see Munkhondia et al., 2016, this book; Hanchett et al., 2011). Where the households that revert to OD include the poorest and most vulnerable, those with the highest disease burden, it is likely that the benefits of CLTS are greatly diminished.

Therefore, there is a need to re-examine the use of sanitation finance and how more effective use could encourage sustainability, with an emphasis on how best to provide targeted finance to sustain improved sanitation practices among the poorest and most vulnerable, without undermining the CLTS process or other sanitation improvement processes such as sanitation marketing that are reliant on household investment and self-sufficiency.

Sanitation subsidies for equity and inclusion

The social protection sector has significant experience with effective benefit transfers (through unemployment, pension, disability, food stamps, and a wide variety of other social welfare schemes). One of the central principles of social protection theory is that the poorest should be targeted first for optimal benefits. Hence, that some form of targeting is required. Another is that cash transfers provide the optimal form of transfer, as they allow household choice (recognizing that different households have different needs, priorities, and preferences at different times). In the past, cash transfers were difficult and expensive to distribute or monitor and thus, in-kind subsidies were often preferred. Today, cash transfers are increasingly simple and efficient (using mobile banking, electronic bank transfers, and so on).

Sanitation transfers are often provided as in-kind subsidies, such as concrete slabs or toilet pans, to ensure that the finance is used for sanitation improvement. Where in-kind subsidies are preferred, the social protection theory notes that the goods provided should be those preferred and commonly utilized by the poor, otherwise there is a significant risk of capture by non-poor households.

This principle is important for the sanitation sub-sector, where many previous projects have subsidized relatively expensive toilets in the understanding that poor households often prefer facilities similar to those used by non-poor households, even though cheaper hygienic toilet options could have been provided. As a result, these subsidies become attractive to non-poor households, who often use their greater influence to capture the toilet subsidies. In contrast, the subsidy of cheaper toilet options is more likely to be self-targeting (as fewer non-poor households will find them attractive), and also means that more people can be reached for the same investment, reducing the targeting problem caused by rationing.

The lesson from the social protection sector is that greater attention is required to the size of subsidy provided, and the nature of the subsidy, in order to improve the targeting and effective use of the public finance. The problem is not with the toilet subsidy – as other sectors use targeted subsidies effectively to reach the poor, and households tend to under-value sanitation investments – but the way in which sanitation subsidies have been designed, targeted, and delivered.

Key financing issues

Weaknesses of in-kind hardware subsidies

Few attempts to subsidize the provision of sanitation hardware to the poor have been successful. The design of any sanitation subsidy scheme needs to recognize and address the problems with subsidies for sanitation hardware that have already been identified, including the following:

- Hardware subsidies often encourage supply-driven approaches, which limit the sense of 'ownership' and lower the chances of sustainability.
- Cost sharing approaches may require higher household contributions than poor households can (or are willing to) afford.

- Over-designed project toilets encourage high hardware subsidies, rationing of subsidized facilities, and capture of these attractive facilities by non-poor households.
- Hardware subsidies are often targeted to those without toilets, which penalizes poor households who have invested in private toilets (and rewards households that favour other spending priorities over sanitation), which is a perverse incentive in the long term.
- Ineffective targeting (90 per cent inclusion error[4] found in some projects) (Robinson, 2012).
- Inefficient project supply and distribution of in-kind hardware subsidies (75 per cent reduction in toilet costs achieved by private sector production and distribution in Cambodia) (Robinson, 2012).
- Lower response to CLTS and sanitation marketing interventions in communities nearby previous or current toilet subsidy programmes.
- Potential distortion of markets due to external decisions on priority products and services.
- Crowding out of household investments in sanitation (possibility of receiving hardware subsidies in future lowers household willingness to pay for toilets).

While none of these problems is insurmountable, or sufficient to recommend the discontinuation of sanitation hardware subsidies, it is critical that any sanitation finance framework is designed to minimize these problems.

ODF rewards

There has been significant debate within the rural sanitation sub-sector over how best to reward ODF achievement by a community (or other collective sanitation achievements). Several countries, notably India with its Nirmal Gram Puraskar (NGP) 'Clean Village Award', bestowed financial awards and political recognition for the achievement of collective sanitation outcomes. The results have been mixed, with some researchers (Robinson, 2005, 2011) finding significant benefits from these incentive systems (including much higher government and development partner interest in community sanitation), and others (TARU, 2008; Kar and Milward, 2011) reporting that the incentives encouraged target-driven approaches, fraudulent verification processes (to gain the awards), and short-term interventions with low sustainability.

Nonetheless, many sanitation stakeholders agree that incentives in their broadest sense, which include non-financial incentives (such as political recognition, media coverage, banners, celebrations) and indirect financial incentives (qualification for grants, projects, discounts, and other forms of support), can be useful tools for sanitation development.

Incentive systems require verification of sanitation outcomes to trigger the award of the incentive. Given frequent problems in developing sustainable monitoring systems for rural sanitation, well-designed and phased incentive systems offer a mechanism that encourages more reliable and regular monitoring of sanitation outcomes by both communities and local governments.

The future benefits of ODF rewards, and the opportunity to protect the ODF process from the potentially detrimental effects of hardware subsidies, argue for their inclusion in any sanitation finance framework. Careful attention must be paid to the risk that these awards lead to target-driven implementation and short-term gains, to the detriment of sustainability, but this risk can be mitigated by integrating the ODF rewards into a larger phased approach to sanitation development, with the aim of nudging rural communities towards gradually higher sanitation goals over time. The problem with one-time ODF rewards has been that there is rarely an effective check of the sustainability of ODF outcomes over time, whereas a more phased approach (see Robinson and Gnilo, 2016, this book) encourages regular checks of these collective outcomes.

Size of transfer

The size of any subsidy or transfer needs to be appropriate to the target audience, and at a level that can be sustained by the sanitation financing agency. The lowest acceptable level of service should be ensured, which in most cases is a simple hygienic toilet, in recognition that the provision of subsidies or transfers for a higher level of service would risk capture from non-poor households. Any subsidy or transfer should aim to help poor households to construct the minimum level of service, with the option to upgrade to higher levels of service if they are willing to contribute more to the toilet cost, or want to upgrade at a later date.

Household choice

Sanitation finance should promote household choice, because of the strong links to effective use and sustainability, and encourage the use and development of sustainable local supply chains (rather than temporary project procurement) (Robinson, 2012).

Rural households and communities vary significantly in their socio-economic status, alignment with social and cultural norms, willingness to invest in sanitation and hygiene improvement, and personal preferences. Despite this diversity of demand and context, most projects promote only a few standard toilet designs, notably when construction materials are provided as an up-front toilet subsidy.

There are five main elements of choice related to toilet construction:

- Toilet design;
- Toilet location;

- Toilet suppliers (who supply materials, transport, installation services);
- Amount invested in the toilet;
- Toilet installation timing.

The best way to provide household choice in toilet construction or upgrading is to encourage the user households to make the decisions and build the toilet themselves. However, in many cases, particularly among households who have never previously owned or used toilets, sanitation demand is low, awareness of technical options is limited, and the information and services available through the market may not be suitable for low-cost or affordable solutions.

Therefore, sanitation programmes must include effective demand creation for household toilets; provide information and advice on a range of affordable toilet designs and options; recognize that toilet owners and users will have a range of preferences and requirements; and strengthen local sanitation supply chains to ensure that toilet goods and services are readily available (see also Coombes, 2016, this book; Munkhondia et al., 2016, this book).

Toilet subsidy mechanisms

A number of new financing options are being piloted and used in development programmes, but few of these options have been adopted by the sanitation sub-sector. One of the most popular options is the use of Conditional Cash Transfers (CCTs), where cash transfers are conditioned on the consumption of a particular good, usually pre-specified investments in the human capital of children. For instance, regular payments to poor mothers conditional on the use of health or education services by her child or children (Robinson, 2012).

CCTs recognize that the timing, nature, and recipient of the transfer are important to its effectiveness. The payment of CCTs to mothers (rather than fathers) has been found to increase the chances that the payments are invested in the children (Fiszbein and Schady, 2009), and better monitoring has highlighted the importance of tackling the underlying causes of disease and poverty rather than the symptoms of these problems. For instance, that supplementary feeding does not solve under-nutrition when the children suffer from persistent diarrhoea, enteropathy, and helminth infections (Bassett, 2008; Manley et al., 2012).

Few existing sanitation finance mechanisms recognize that, because the main benefits of sanitation improvement lie in reducing stunting and diarrhoeal disease (and other sanitation-related health issues) in young children in poor households, sanitation interventions need to target the carers of children, and ensure that young children in poor households use and benefit from any sanitation improvements.

Two of the elements within the Cambodia CCT plan (see Box 14.1) provide relatively straightforward mechanisms for sanitation improvement, which

---

Box 14.1 Grow-up-with-a-toilet plan, Cambodia

A 2010 ADB-WSP working paper on sanitation finance (Robinson, 2012) in Cambodia proposed a 'Grow-Up-With-A-Toilet-Plan' based on a CCT design that would ensure that every poor child born in Cambodia would grow up using a hygienic toilet through the provision of finance for toilet construction and improvement to poor households during the first five years after their first child was born.

The five-year plan targeted poor mothers on the birth of their first child, in the understanding that poor children under five years old are the highest risk group for diarrhoea, malnutrition, worms, and other sanitation-related illnesses;[5] that a number of life habits are engrained by the age of five (after which they become more difficult to change); and that the majority of stunting associated with inadequate sanitation takes place during the first two years of the child's life.

The idea is that once poor mothers have been supported to build a simple sanitation facility for their first child (and themselves), further payments are made to encourage the sustained use and improvement of this facility over time. When additional children are born, the family should already be in the habit of using a hygienic toilet and washing their hands with soap, so that all future children in the family adopt the same improved sanitation and hygiene practices as a matter of course.

Plan: 5-year cycle for each family with a newborn

Year 0:   US$15 toilet voucher (redeemable by local toilet producers).

Plus: US$5 rebate on construction of a second toilet pit.

Years 1–5:   US$0–10 annual payment on verification of:

a) Hygienic toilet usage;

b) Village ODF status;

c) Completion of hygiene course;

d) Presence of handwashing facility and soap.

The CCT approach encourages a process of sanitation development over several years, through providing incentives for the upgrading and improvement of facilities, and the adoption of improved behaviours over time. The CCT approach also promotes more efficient demand-side financing through vouchers, rebates, and cash transfers, which in turn encourage the development of sustainable local supply chains for sanitation goods and services.

The Grow-Up-With-A-Toilet plan garnered attention from key sector stakeholders (with a notable reference in a 2011 WSP working paper;Trémolet, 2011) and it was presented to the Advisory Committee of the Global Sanitation Fund in 2009 but has yet to be implemented due to the challenges associated with setting up this new and relatively complex form of sanitation finance.

---

have already been tried and tested by large-scale sanitation programmes (see below for examples):

- Toilet vouchers: fixed value paper that entitles the holder to goods and services of the stated value from a choice of approved suppliers.
- Toilet rebates: fixed value cash payment made on verification that a qualifying household is using a hygienic toilet (according to agreed criteria).

The concept that sanitation finance should support a medium-term programme designed to inculcate improved sanitation habits in young children and their families during the first five years of the children's lives, rather than just finance household infrastructure such as toilets, is an important one. It can be further developed and explored through a phased approach to sanitation development that allows several different financing and incentive mechanisms to operate within the same programme.

Finance options

Toilet vouchers

Toilet vouchers are printed (or electronic) entitlements that can be exchanged for sanitation goods or services, or for discounts against these goods and services, with approved suppliers. Vouchers allow careful targeting of sanitation finance, with household choice (of options, supplier, and timing), and direct the targeted subsidies through local supply chains, thus helping to strengthen and sustain local production and supply. Vouchers are sometimes sold or fraudulently obtained, but provide ready opportunities for monitoring, and give useful information on local preferences.

The value of the toilet voucher should be set at the minimum cost of the lowest level of service deemed acceptable within the service area, with some proportion of the cost to be financed by the household as a demonstration of commitment (although this amount can also be refunded through a toilet rebate, see below). Any higher level of service or additional goods and services should be financed by the household. The intention is to encourage the household to build its preferred facility, while only providing public finance for the minimum required to meet public health standards.

There should be local competition among the approved suppliers, with beneficiaries encouraged to reward the more reputable, reliable and cost-efficient suppliers. A range of suppliers, from project-initiated to private providers, should be encouraged, providing that all suppliers receive the same level of subsidy and support.

BRAC, the largest development NGO in the world, provided toilet vouchers through its water, sanitation, and hygiene (WASH) programme in Bangladesh to enable 6.6 million people to benefit from hygienic toilets (Castalia Strategic Advisors, 2015). BRAC provided vouchers to poor households (and loans to non-poor households) whose value covered part of the cost of toilet materials from a local supplier. The supplier then used the voucher, and other supporting documentation, to prove that the materials had been distributed to eligible households, and BRAC reimbursed the voucher value to the supplier.

Toilet rebates

Toilet rebates provide a partial refund of the household investment in a hygienic toilet subject to verification on a fixed date (see example in Box 14.2). The aim is to encourage household freedom of choice in the design and implementation of the toilet, within a window of opportunity before the agreed date of the rebate verification process. The rebate verification process

---

Box 14.2 Toilet rebates in action in Vietnam

The East Meets West Foundation (EMWF) has implemented a community WASH project in Vietnam since 2007, which included sanitation and hygiene promotion, a sanitation credit programme (bank loans facilitated by the Vietnam Women's Union), but no support for toilet hardware. Instead, the project offered the incentive of a toilet rebate to any household from a project community that both met the poverty criteria and was verified to be using a hygienic toilet (at a fixed time 6–9 months after the intervention).

   The intention of the rebate was to recognize that the government's new sanitation policy made it difficult for poor households to construct a toilet that met the minimum technical requirements. The toilet rebate was set at US$24, which many onlookers felt was too low to have much effect on demand for sanitation in a context where many households spent US$60–100 to construct a household toilet (Jenkins et al., 2011).

   More than 50,000 poor households have now been paid the rebate within the project area, illustrating both that poor households can often find the money to build hygienic toilets, and that a small incentive can be significant in persuading these households to invest in sanitation. Further research is required to determine the significance of the rebate in influencing these households to build their toilets, but it seems likely that ongoing and project promotion has increased awareness of the importance of improved sanitation, and households require only a small nudge to persuade them to invest now rather than later.

   One of the weaknesses of the toilet rebate is that it doesn't encourage ODF status or 100 per cent toilet coverage across the community. The EMWF is now working on an Output Based Aid (OBA) system that will combine the rebates with other finance designed to encourage collective sanitation outcomes.

Source: Jenkins et al. (2011)

---

checks that the household meets the rebate qualification criteria (e.g. the household is either poor, previously had no toilet, or was the owner of a toilet that was damaged or destroyed).

   Toilet voucher beneficiaries should also qualify for the toilet rebate, with the toilet voucher designed to help the poorest households build an adequate sanitation facility, and the toilet rebate designed to reward the successful construction and use of a hygienic toilet. Poor and vulnerable households that were already using hygienic toilets before the intervention should also qualify for the toilet rebate, in the understanding that these households are the main target group for the sanitation finance. Hence, that sustainable use of hygienic toilets by this primary target group should be encouraged and rewarded.

   Toilet rebates are generally set at around 25–33 per cent of toilet cost, in the understanding that these rebates are not refunding the entire toilet cost (and that the neediest may already have received toilet vouchers to cover the majority of the costs). The toilet rebate is designed to provide a nudge for unserved households to invest in sanitation improvement earlier than they would otherwise have done.

Relevance of sanitation microfinance

The finance gap (between what rural households are currently willing to pay and the cost of a well-built and hygienic toilet) argues for the introduction of credit systems, mechanisms to allow rural households to take loans against sanitation investments, or to pay for toilets in instalments. Significant efforts and innovations are under way in sanitation microfinance, but few large-scale programmes have yet been successful in increasing sanitation coverage among poor rural households. Key constraints include the reluctance of rural households to borrow against a non-productive investment, the high transaction costs associated with the numerous small loans required, and the reluctance of rural banks and microfinance institutions to lend to poor households with no credit history, no collateral, and no formal identification papers.

Microfinance has not yet been widely adopted or accepted in some countries, with sanitation microfinance, in particular, proving hard to scale-up. Some rural households are reluctant to take on formal debt, local banking systems are sometimes under-developed, and few previous microfinance initiatives for sanitation have been successful in reaching poor and disadvantaged households.

Sanitation microfinance, perhaps through less formal savings and credit groups, should still be considered an option (particularly for assisting better off households, who are more likely to meet MFI credit requirements, to construct their own toilets), but the thrust of the sanitation finance framework, with the emphasis on reaching the poorest, has been developed around other financial tools.

Putting it all together: sanitation finance framework

Three critical principles need to be considered in the development of a sanitation finance framework (and implementation strategy). The first is the importance of choice to the sustainability of sanitation outcomes: the beneficiary household must be provided with some choice over the type and location of the toilet, even if from a limited menu of technical options, and within the constraints created by the need for a hygienic outcome. Without this choice, the lower ownership and commitment felt by the household greatly increases the risk of reversion to OD.

The second principle recognizes that rapid demand generation processes such as CLTS can result in poor households building simple, homemade facilities that lack durability in the face of adverse weather conditions like storms and floods. Good technical support and follow-up monitoring can improve the durability and sustainability of these facilities, but it is also important that upgrading options are made available so that households that now place a greater value on their facilities can easily upgrade and improve their facilities (see also Coombes, 2016, this book; Munkhondia et al., 2016, this book).

The third principle is that any transfer provided to poor and vulnerable households does not undermine other sanitation improvement processes, in particular any CLTS-based approaches that encourage the rest of the community to build, use, and maintain their own sanitation facilities. This means that transfers need to be carefully targeted to those perceived by the community to be most in need of assistance; and that the transfers are provided in a way that complements and supports the wider process of sanitation improvement within the community.

Phase 1: ODF achievement

A sanitation finance framework should seek to encourage ODF achievement, and to recognize that many households can build adequate toilets without external assistance, while recognizing that few of the poorest and most vulnerable households, particularly those that lack labour or resources, are likely to build durable and hygienic toilets without some assistance or incentive.

In the past, the prospect of the provision of hardware subsidies has led to some households and communities waiting for assistance rather than building simple toilets that would immediately improve sanitation conditions. However, large-scale ODF achievements confirm that most rural households are capable of building simple toilets, albeit sometimes with community assistance when they lack labour or basic resources. But some of these simple toilets do not last long. The challenge for these disadvantaged households is to upgrade to more durable and hygienic toilets that will provide benefits over several years, as this may require resources and skills that are beyond the capacity of the community.

ODF achievement provides evidence of community commitment and sanitation behaviour change, thus provides a solid entry requirement for the sanitation finance framework. Financial assistance should be provided to communities verified as ODF to assist the poor to upgrade and improve their facilities and hygiene practices so that the community can achieve 'sustainable sanitation' status. The intention is to reward communities that demonstrate improved sanitation behaviour in becoming ODF, to assist them to move up to the next level of phased sanitation development, and to provide incentives that encourage other communities to work towards ODF achievement.

Phase 2: upgrading toilets

The sanitation finance framework should provide support for ODF communities to upgrade and improve their toilets. This support can take several forms:

- Supply strengthening (increased sanitation marketing efforts to ensure that affordable goods and services for toilet upgrading and improvement are available).
- Development of toilet loan schemes (piloting of simple credit schemes to encourage the purchase of new toilets and upgrade packages).
- Provision of toilet vouchers to the poorest and most vulnerable households.
- Provision of toilet rebates to poor households that build durable toilets.

Where national poverty identification systems exist, these should be used to identify the poorest and most vulnerable households for toilet voucher distribution. In their absence, it is important to use objective targeting systems with clear and verifiable criteria that can be checked, as there is a significant risk that the targeted subsidies will be diverted to non-poor households where local power relations influence the targeting. The intention is to assist the poorest and most vulnerable, those with little or no cash to purchase sanitation materials and services from local markets for the upgrading and improvement of the toilets that they have already built as part of the ODF process.

The toilet vouchers should be redeemed through approved local toilet producers and material suppliers. The toilet vouchers should allow the beneficiary households to choose from a selection of toilet packages, toilet upgrade materials, and toilet installation services, up to the voucher value, with any additional costs to be financed by the household. Households who are not eligible for the toilet vouchers are encouraged to upgrade and improve their toilets as part of the government drive to achieve sustainable sanitation status. No financial support is provided to these households, except in particularly remote or poor areas where time-limited toilet discounts should be considered to encourage non-poor households to improve their toilets.

In addition, a toilet rebate should be provided to poor households that are verified to be using a hygienic toilet within a 6–12 month period after the upgrading campaign is launched. The intention is to reward poor households that demonstrate good sanitation practice. The rebate should also be available to poor households that had built a toilet before the ODF or upgrading campaigns started, providing that this toilet meets the minimum standards required and is verified to be in use.

Phase 3: conditional grant to local government

The missing element from the proposed toilet voucher and rebate system is a mechanism that encourages community-level sanitation improvement beyond ODF status. While all of the elements (sanitation supply strengthening, credit options, toilet vouchers, toilet rebates, increased monitoring and follow-up) will encourage toilet upgrading and sanitation improvement, there is no guarantee that this will lead to 100 per cent hygienic toilet coverage, or that every poor household will respond to the voucher and rebate opportunities. Therefore, the sanitation finance framework should also include a conditional grant, which is awarded to each village government on verification and declaration of sustainable sanitation status, and which can be used to assist the community to work towards achievement of Phase 3: Total Sanitation.

Minimum criteria for sustainable sanitation status should include the following:

- Verification of continued ODF status;
- 100 per cent use of hygienic toilets (no sharing, hygienic toilets in all institutions);
- 100 per cent handwashing stations with soap and water at or nearby all toilets;
- 100 per cent safe disposal of infant and child excreta.

Special finance: grow-up-with-a-toilet plan

First-time mothers in poor households (either pregnant or with a first child that is less than one year old) should be identified during a community poverty and vulnerability mapping process at the start of the campaign. First-time mothers in poor households in other ODF communities should also be able to apply to join the grow-up-with-a-toilet plan. Subsequent verification and payment of the annual plan benefits will be the responsibility of the local governments, with finance being provided from central government.

Special finance: sanitation for the disabled

Additional finance should also be provided to assist poor households with at least one disabled member to build a hygienic toilet that can be easily used by the disabled family member, as these facilities can be more expensive and difficult to build than other toilets. Where available, a toilet voucher can be provided to poor households containing at least one disabled member. The voucher should be the same as those provided to the households ranked as the poorest and most vulnerable, hence will be redeemed through approved local toilet sellers for sanitation goods and services suitable for upgrading and improving the household toilet so that it can be easily used by the disabled family member.

Evidence: smart sanitation finance in action

Most elements of the sanitation finance framework described above are now being implemented through UNICEF programmes in the Philippines. UNICEF partners with a number of international and local NGOs in its development and emergency programmes, which are being implemented within the PhATS phased approach to sanitation development described in Chapter 9. These partners were provided with guidelines on sanitation finance, which encouraged them to utilize toilet vouchers, rebates, and some of the other innovative financing approaches described above, in combination with Direct Cash Transfers to local governments (to ensure that the local governments had some funding that could be used for sanitation and hygiene improvement).

The UNICEF partners in the Philippines were set outcome targets in their contracts, to achieve a number of ODF communities and a number of (Phase 2) Sustainable Sanitation communities, but were given the freedom to decide how best to use their finance to achieve these outcomes. The intention was to encourage innovation and flexibility, and to recognize that different approaches were likely to be required in the different contexts and capacities found across the large implementation area.

As a result, a wide range of different approaches have been used, with varying degrees of success. But we are already seeing the effective use of toilet vouchers, which have achieved a 100 per cent redemption rate when implemented by Action Contre la Faim (ACF) in the Masbate region; the development of a range of post-ODF targeted toilet subsidies for different poor groups by the International Medical Corps (IMC) in Leyte; and the use of post-ODF sanitation microfinance and toilet vouchers linked to toilets sold by sanitation marketing entrepreneurs trained by Samaritan's Purse (Robinson, 2013; UNICEF, 2015a, 2015b).

Importantly, the UNICEF partners note that WASH governance strengthening, which has included explaining to local governments how the PhATS approach and sanitation finance are intended to work, has been critical in generating buy-in and commitment to these new approaches from local officials and stakeholders.

The alignment of sanitation finance with local government WASH plans has avoided subsidy policies and mechanisms undermining each other in the same area. Local governments now understand that sanitation demand can be utilized as an indicator of potential sustainability, and that significant investment should be delayed until households and communities have demonstrated demand and commitment to sanitation behaviour change through their efforts to achieve ODF status.

Five municipalities within the UNICEF implementation area have now been verified as 100 per cent Zero Open Defecation (ZOD = ODF), and more than 600 ZOD communities have been verified, which has generated significant political capital for the municipal mayors in the successful municipalities. These high profile achievements have encouraged efforts to verify the first batch of G2 Sustainable Sanitation Barangays, as well as greatly increased the funding provided by local governments to sanitation improvement. Growing understanding of the phased approach, combined with the tangible benefits in the completely ZOD areas, are now raising hopes that the first 100 per cent Sustainable Sanitation municipality in the Philippines may not be far away!

Conclusion

The demand for smarter sanitation finance, which can provide more effective and targeted financial assistance to poor and vulnerable households without undermining demand creation or sustainability, has been growing steadily with the rise of CLTS and sanitation marketing. The key challenge is to provide public finance for sanitation that reaches the poorest and most vulnerable population; that encourages household choice and ownership of the improved facilities; and that rewards good sanitation and hygiene behaviour, thus generating incentives for other households and communities to invest in improved sanitation and hygiene behaviour.

Smart sanitation finance should recognize the varying needs and priorities of different market segments within rural communities and across programme areas, and provide a range of financial instruments to serve these different segments. Current sanitation finance initiatives often focus on a single approach, such as the provision of toilet loans, which rarely reaches a broad enough cross-section of the community to impact either the sanitation practices or disease burden of the poorest.

Wherever possible, smart sanitation finance should also be provided by local governments, with technical assistance from development partners, in order to ensure sustainable finance of these sanitation incentives, and strengthen accountability to the rural households and communities receiving the finance.

Context is often the critical element in development practice, with too many sanitation projects failing because a standardized approach was unable to adapt to the diverse needs, priorities, and practices found across a large project area. Smarter sanitation finance should encourage the achievement of easily verifiable sanitation outcomes, using a toolbox of financing mechanisms and implementation approaches that can be adapted to fit local contexts and capacities. More visible sanitation progress, achieved through the more effective and targeted use of limited sanitation finance and capacity, is the surest way to convince decision-makers to strengthen and enlarge the support provided to large-scale sanitation and hygiene improvement.

About the authors

Andrew Robinson is an independent WASH consultant based in France. Since 1987, Andrew has designed, worked on, evaluated, and researched WASH programmes in 27 countries in Africa and Asia, including both regional and national reviews of CLTS effectiveness, sustainability, and impact.

Michael Gnilo is a sanitation and hygiene specialist based in UNICEF headquarters in New York. Michael has designed and implemented community-based health, nutrition, and WASH programmes since 2003 in both development and emergency contexts. He has a particular interest in strengthening linkages among community, civil society, and government systems for sustained delivery of services.

Endnotes

1. 2005 DHS household survey data in Cambodia reports under-five mortality rates 39 per cent higher across the bottom two wealth quintiles than in the fourth quintile. Similarly, the proportion of severely underweight children was 76 per cent higher in the bottom two wealth quintiles than in the fourth quintile. UNICEF research in Laos (2012) indicated that severely underweight children aged 0 to 4 years had 2.8 times higher likelihood of diarrhoea than children with normal weight-for-age status, with 3.6 times higher likelihood of diarrhoea found in severely underweight children aged 0 to 11 months.
2. Personal experience of the author from reviews and evaluations of CLTS and other rural sanitation programmes in: Angola; Bangladesh; Burkina Faso; Cambodia; Ethiopia; Ghana; Kenya; India; Indonesia; Mozambique;

Nepal; Niger; Nigeria; Pakistan; Philippines; Sri Lanka; Tanzania; Timor-Leste; Uganda; Yemen; and Zambia.

3. Personal experience of the author from reviews and evaluations of CLTS and other rural sanitation programmes in: Angola; Bangladesh; Burkina Faso; Cambodia; Ethiopia; Ghana; Kenya; India; Indonesia; Mozambique; Nepal; Niger; Nigeria; Pakistan; Philippines; Sri Lanka; Tanzania; Timor-Leste; Uganda; Yemen; and Zambia.

4. Inclusion error: proportion of non-eligible households that received the subsidy.

5. Diarrhoeal disease and mortality in children peak between the age of six months and two years, often linked to the age of weaning.

6. East Meets West Foundation is now renamed: Thrive Networks.

References

Bassett, L. (2008) *Can Conditional Cash Transfer Programs Play a Greater Role in Reducing Child Undernutrition*, SP Discussion Paper No. 835, World Bank, Washington, DC.

Castalia Strategic Advisors (2015) *Review of Results-Based Financing (RBF) Schemes in WASH*, Report to Bill & Melinda Gates Foundation, Castalia Strategic Advisors, Washington, DC.

Coombes, Y. (2016) 'User centred latrine guidelines. Integrating CLTS with sanitation marketing: a case study from Kenya to promote informed choice', in P. Bongartz, N. Vernon and J. Fox (eds.) *Sustainable Sanitation for All: Experiences, Challenges, and Innovations*, Practical Action Publishing, Rugby.

Fiszbein, A. and Schady, N. (2009) *Conditional Cash Transfers: Reducing Present and Future Poverty*, Report, World Bank, Washington, DC.

Hanchett, S., Krieger, L., Kahn, M.H., Kullmann, C. and Ahmed, R. (2011) *Long-Term Sustainability of Improved Sanitation in Rural Bangladesh*, World Bank, Washington, DC, https://openknowledge.worldbank.org/handle/10986/17347 [accessed 5 February 2016].

Jenkins, M., Hien, V., Canada, H., Brown, J. and Sobsey, M. (2011) *Household Participation, Satisfaction, Usage and Investment in an OBA Sanitation Program to Increase the Uptake of Hygienic Facilities Among the Rural Poor in Central Vietnam*, UNC Water and Health Conference, poster, Chapel Hill, NC.

Kar, K. and Milward, K. (2011) *Digging In, Spreading Out and Growing Up: Introducing CLTS in Africa*, IDS Practice Paper 8, Institute of Development Studies, Brighton.

Kunthy, S. and Catalla, R. (2009) *Community-Led Total Sanitation (CLTS) in Cambodia: A Formative Evaluation Report*, UNICEF and Ministry of Rural Development, Department of Rural Health Care.

Manley, J., Mitter, S. and Slavchevska, V. (2012) *How Effective are Cash Transfer Programmes at Improving Nutritional Status?* EPPI-Centre, Social Science Research Unit, University of London, London.

Munkhondia, T., Simangolwa, W. and Zapico, A. (2016) 'CLTS and sanitation marketing: aspects to consider for a better integrated approach', in P.

Bongartz, N. Vernon and J. Fox (eds.) *Sustainable Sanitation for All: Experiences, Challenges, and Innovations*, Practical Action Publishing, Rugby.

Robinson, A. (2005) *Scaling Up Rural Sanitation in South Asia: Lessons Learned From Bangladesh, India and Pakistan*, Report, Water and Sanitation Program, World Bank, Washington, DC.

Robinson, A. (2011) *Enabling Environment Endline Assessment: Indonesia*, Working Paper, Water and Sanitation Program, World Bank, Washington, DC.

Robinson, A. (2012) *Sanitation Finance in Rural Cambodia*, Water and Sanitation Program, World Bank, Washington, DC.

Robinson, A. (2013) *Development of a Multi-Stakeholder Implementation Strategy for Scaling Up Rural Sanitation*, Final Report, UNICEF, Manila.

Robinson, A. (2015) *Community-Led Total Sanitation Review*, Final Report, UNICEF Angola, Luanda.

Robinson, A. and Gnilo, M. (2016) 'Beyond ODF: a phased approach to rural sanitation development', in P. Bongartz, N. Vernon and J. Fox (eds.) *Sustainable Sanitation for All: Experiences, Challenges, and Innovations*, Practical Action Publishing, Rugby.

TARU (2008) *Impact Assessment of Nirmal Gram Puraskar Awarded Panchayats*, Final Report Volume 1, UNICEF, New York.

Trémolet, S. (2011) *Identifying the Potential for Results-Based Financing for Sanitation*, Water and Sanitation Program, World Bank, Washington, DC, https://www.wsp.org/sites/wsp.org/files/publications/WSP-Tremolet-Results-Based-Financing.pdf [accessed 5 February 2016].

Tyndale-Biscoe, P., Bond, M. and Kidd, R. (2013) *ODF Sustainability Study*, FH Designs and Plan International, www.communityledtotalsanitation.org/resource/odf-sustainability-study-plan [accessed 5 February 2016].

UNICEF (2013) *Community-Led Total Sanitation in East Asia and Pacific: Progress, Lessons and Directions*, Report, UNICEF East Asia and Pacific Regional Office, Bangkok.

UNICEF (2015a) *PhATS Field Note 05/2015 - IMC: Two-level toilet subsidies for G2 barangays*, UNICEF Philippines, Field Note, Manila.

UNICEF (2015b) *PhATS Field Note 04/2015 - Samaritan's Purse: Sanitation Supply Chain Development*, UNICEF Philippines, Field Note, Manila.

CHAPTER 15

Putting the hardest to reach at the heart of the Sustainable Development Goals

Sue Cavill, Sharon Roose, Cathy Stephen, and Jane Wilbur

Abstract

Universal access to improved sanitation by 2030 with an emphasis on the rights of all excluded groups is one of the Sustainable Development Goals (SDGs). This chapter argues that Community-Led Total Sanitation (CLTS) can support the achievement of this goal. However open defecation free (ODF) status can be put at risk by just one person. It will be unachievable and unsustainable unless people who are marginalized and vulnerable are actively and meaningfully included, consulted, and considered in all aspects of CLTS programming. Without this, there is a risk of inappropriate design or location of facilities, overlooking the needs of people who are marginalized, which can limit or deny their access to sanitation. This chapter outlines the dimensions of equality and non-discrimination and barriers to access, and suggests practical entry points for inclusive and sustainable CLTS programming.

Keywords: Equity, Inclusion, Exclusion, Non-discrimination, Gender, Disability, Rights, Sustainable Development Goals (SDGs)

Introduction

The Sustainable Development Goals (SDGs) provide an opportunity to go beyond the ambitions of the Millennium Development Goals (MDGs) and ensure universal access to improved sanitation. Over the lifetime of the MDGs, 2.1 billion people gained access to improved sanitation between 1990 and 2015. However, 2.4 billion people still use unimproved sanitation facilities, of which 1 billion practise open defecation (OD). Nine out of 10 people defecating in the open live in rural areas (WHO/UNICEF, 2015). There are stark disparities across regions, between urban and rural areas, and between the rich and the poor or people who are marginalized. Progress among the poorest wealth quintiles has been the slowest. The 2015 Joint Monitoring Programme report predicts, 'At current rates of reduction, open defecation will not be eliminated among the poorest in rural areas by 2030' (WHO/ UNICEF, 2015: 24). Recent data from Uganda and Zambia indicates that a person who is older, disabled, or chronically ill is more likely to defecate in the open (Wilbur and Danquah, 2015).[1]

http://dx.doi.org/10.3362/9781780449272.015

The post-2015 agenda aims to eradicate poverty in all its forms by 2030. The commitment to 'leave no one behind', together with the idea that 'no goal should be met unless it is met for everyone' is already well established in the rhetoric around the SDGs. This directly links to issues around equality and non-discrimination. Community-Led Total Sanitation (CLTS) can help ensure that the human rights to water[2] and sanitation expressed in the SDGs are realized, and this will require an inclusive approach for total sanitation. The *CLTS Handbook* promotes community self-help and cooperation, and social solidarity between the rich and poor to ensure consideration of the needs of marginalized people (Kar with Chambers, 2008). However, this cannot be relied upon in all communities; some form of external assistance for poor and marginalized people may be needed (see Robinson and Gnilo, 2016a and b, this book). The right to sanitation places an obligation on states to ensure access to sanitation is progressively available to all, without discrimination (González, 2013).

Open defecation free (ODF) status for all is the first step towards realizing the right to sanitation. However, ODF status will be unachievable and unsustainable unless the poorest and marginalized groups are included, consulted, and considered in aspects of CLTS programming. Lack of consultation and active, free, and meaningful participation can lead to inappropriate design or location of facilities, overlooking the needs of marginalized people, and limiting or denying their access to sanitation (Wilbur et al., 2013). Arguably, if these barriers are not addressed, the CLTS process may cause discrimination of people who already experience marginalization. Addressing these barriers is crucial throughout the processes of CLTS: while OD continues, all are affected. This may include regulating service delivery and potentially targeting support to people who are marginalized.

Discrimination on the grounds of race, colour, caste, sex, language, or religion is prohibited under the right to sanitation (de Alburqerque, 2014). It also recognizes that particular attention may need to be given to people who are often marginalized or excluded including older persons, people with disabilities, people with serious or chronic illnesses, children, and women (de Alburqerque, 2014). These are complex challenges which need to be tackled if the ambitious targets of the SDGs are to be met and sustained in the future. This chapter will highlight the dimensions of equality and non-discrimination at play in sanitation and will give examples of how CLTS has contributed, and can contribute, to universal access to sanitation.

SDGs and equality and non-discrimination ambitions for sanitation

SDG 6: *Ensure availability and sustainable management of water and sanitation for all* demands adequate and equitable access to sanitation and hygiene for all, and an end to OD. The target refers to water, sanitation, and hygiene (WASH) for all women and girls in vulnerable situations and to improving their participation. It also contributes towards other SDGs. For instance, investing in school WASH services with Menstrual Hygiene Management (MHM) contributes to SDG 4: *Ensure inclusive and equitable quality education and promote lifelong learning opportunities for all*, as well as SDG 5: *Achieve gender equality and empower all women and girls.* Having access to safe WASH services is also directly linked to reducing chronic malnutrition or stunting under SDG 2: *Ending hunger and improved nutrition; Ending poverty in all its forms everywhere* (SDG 1); and *Reducing inequalities within and among countries* (SDG 10).

With inadequate access to clean water, safe sanitation, and handwashing facilities with soap, people's living standards are impacted in various different but mutually reinforcing parts of their lives: education; health; nutrition; reproductive health; privacy and dignity; economic opportunities; safety and security; as well as personal development (Alkire et al., 2013). Measuring mechanisms like the Multidimensional Poverty Index can support the monitoring of progress made. It complements traditional income-based poverty measures by capturing the severe deprivations that each person faces at the same time with respect to education, health, and living standards (OPHI, 2015). In order for the SDGs to really 'leave no one behind' and to create a sustainable impact for people from marginalized groups (WHO/ UNICEF, 2015; see also Thomas, 2016, this book), issues related to inequality and discrimination need to be taken into account at all levels of interventions.

What is equality and non-discrimination?

Equality refers to the legally binding obligation to ensure that all can enjoy their rights equally. Human rights law requires equal access to water and sanitation services, but it does not assume identical treatment in all cases. It does not mean that everyone should have the same type of service, such as flush toilets. Equality does not imply treating what is unequal equally. People who are not equal may require different treatment in order to achieve substantive equality. States may need to adopt affirmative measures, giving preference to certain groups and individuals in order to redress past discrimination (de Albuquerque, 2014).

Non-discrimination is the legal principle that prohibits any distinction, exclusion, or restriction that results in individuals or groups not being able to enjoy, or recognize their human rights on an equal basis with others based on 'prohibited grounds'. These include race, colour, sex, language, religion, political or other opinion, national or social origin, property, birth, disability, age, health status, or economic and social situation (de Albuquerque, 2014).

Poverty and social exclusion is multidimensional, made up of several factors that constitute poor people's experience of deprivation (Alkire et al., 2013). The situation is often made worse by discrimination, stigma, and existing inequalities that occur at all levels (WHO/UNICEF, 2012), including:

- *Physical and geographical inequalities* such as those experienced by communities in remote and inaccessible rural areas, and slum-dwellers in urban and peri-urban areas.

- *Group-related inequalities* that vary across countries such as those based on ethnicity, race, nationality, language, religion, and caste. Often, CLTS practitioners target communities that face such inequalities.
- *Individual-related inequalities* that are relevant in every country of the globe, such as those based on sex/gender, age, disability, and health conditions, which impose constraints on access to water and sanitation. For instance:
    - Globally, an estimated 1 billion people have an impairment (WHO and World Bank, 2011).
    - More than 700 million people are aged 60 and over (UN, 2011). Within ten years there will be over a billion older people worldwide (UN, 2011; HAI Global Age Watch, 2013).
    - An estimated 35 million people are living with HIV (UNAIDS, 2014).

There are limited studies that have looked at the conditions of individual household members, who are not using a household toilet, and why.

The dimensions of equality and non-discrimination in practice

CLTS is a participatory and community-driven approach to rural sanitation that can powerfully contribute towards reaching universal access to rural sanitation. However, equality and non-discrimination are not guaranteed in the process of striving for and achieving ODF and sustainable sanitation. CLTS can actually reinforce inequalities for people with disabilities, older people, children, and women and girls if facilitators do not have explicit objectives for inclusion (Adeyeye, 2011; Wilbur and Jones, 2014). This has a direct impact on sustainability. It is also a violation of human rights.

Some critics have argued that the focus on community rights comes at a loss to individual rights (Bartram et al., 2012). However, rights do not exist in isolation; individual behaviour has a community-wide impact, and conflict can arise between individual and community rights. For example, when a person refuses to build a toilet and/or chooses to continue practising OD they have exercised their right to choose whether and where to invest their labour, but this has a direct impact on the health and related rights of other community members (see House and Cavill, 2015; Musembi and Musyoki, 2016).

During triggering, strong emotions such as disgust, shame, and shock are often experienced (along with positive emotions such as pride, self-respect, and dignity). The perceived use of shame has attracted criticism from a human rights perspective (Engel and Susilo, 2014; Galvin, 2015); however in CLTS stigmatization of individuals is not the intention. Rather it is to make the practice of OD shameful, and embed a new social norm (House and Cavill, 2015; Musembi and Musyoki, 2016). Shame may be experienced, but the primary motivator for behaviour change, which comes from the realization that, 'we are eating each other's shit', is usually disgust (Bongartz, 2012). The use of sanctions has also been controversial, with anecdotal evidence of encouraging people to throw rocks at those practising OD near water sources, threats of fines, and threats to withhold government subsidies (Bartram et al., 2012; O'Reilly and Louis, 2014). Sanctions must never take the form of rights abuses. Throwing rocks would be a criminal offence and CLTS should not be used as an excuse to break the law. Such human rights abuses obviously must be challenged and condemned wherever they are found. Sanctions against the poorest or most marginalized people who are unable to build toilets without support from either within or outside the community must not happen (Myers, 2015a; Musembi and Musyoki, 2016). People should be encouraged and supported, not harassed and bullied into changing their behaviour. However, the use of sanctions *per se* should not be dismissed. Where sanctions are needed, they should target households who can change (e.g. have the means, both in terms of money and time) but are refusing.

Care must be taken when implementing CLTS to understand and analyse the context and culture in which CLTS is being implemented, and integrate practical ways to reduce or avoid the risk of abuses taking place into programming. This section documents and explores some experiences, with reference to key elements used for effective intervention, and suggests entry points for inclusive and sustainable CLTS programming.

Gender

Women and girls are disproportionally affected by a lack of access to adequate WASH (WHO/UNICEF, 2010: 13). Gender-related power dynamics and discrimination determine women and girls' ability to access these basic services, as well as the multiple impacts of living without them. WASH is core to dignity and wellbeing. It is important that existing gender issues and power dynamics within communities are consistently considered and addressed before and during implementation of CLTS activities (Adeyeye, 2011). Without this, problems will quickly arise that can threaten the sustainability of ODF status and, ultimately, sustainable sanitation achievements:

> CLTS recognizes the importance of women in creating sustainable sanitation and hygiene systems, but CLTS projects are often designed without gender considerations. CLTS facilitators do not often ensure gender balance while facilitating triggering sessions, thus compromising the equal participation of men and women and limiting the emergence of both female and male natural leaders. Hence, the entire process is gender unaware. By not explicitly focusing on gender relations, CLTS processes are more likely to overburden women, rather than making them agents of change. (Plan International, 2012: 8)

WASH development staff need to be trained in gender relations to ensure they have the knowledge and capacity to address these issues. Care must also be taken not to reinforce patriarchal norms within societies when implementing CLTS or other WASH programmes, for example through toilet promotion campaigns that appeal to patriarchal notions of women's seclusion to the household, modest behaviour, and practice of veiling (Coffey et al., 2014; Srivastav and Gupta, 2015; Gupta et al., 2016, this book).

Research in Sierra Leone noted that Natural Leaders are not often trained in gender issues and that gender inequality can be heightened when the majority of Natural Leaders who 'emerge' are men, often due to existing power dynamics (Africa Ahead, 2013). Recent research in Zambia has found implementation of CLTS more successful when Natural Leaders are inspired community members from all sections of the community, including those from marginalized or stigmatized groups, not just the chiefs and headmen:

> The three villages with positive outcomes had more community volunteers, active and empowered women and support to vulnerable social groups such as widows and the elderly. They had, as one leader stated, 'the spirit of togetherness'. Again, this was well shown in Chaata where motivations to improve health were not driven by the headman – an unassuming who had 'owned the village' (as he stated) for two decades but himself had no latrine! Rather, a group of young men and women associated with the local school across the road ... were the main catalysts (Bardosh, 2015: 61).

Encouraging and supporting women from marginalized groups to become leaders can also raise awareness of their rights to water and sanitation as seen by WaterAid in Nepal.

> Though I am *Dalit* and uneducated, the community people selected me as a Water and Sanitation User Committee member. In the training I learnt about the rights of both men and women in terms of labour and decision-making. Now I can help people with these issues regardless of their education or economic status, which I couldn't do before (female Water and Sanitation User Committee member, Mahattori) (WaterAid, 2009).

Plan International's research on the impact of gender on CLTS processes in Uganda aimed to establish the participation and inclusion of men and women, boys and girls, and disadvantaged groups, in decision-making processes and assesses the degree of collective action towards ODF (Plan International, 2012). One of the research findings was that, while most children were said to be active, adolescent girls were reported to be most active, as they often encouraged – and sometimes forced – their parents to install toilets in households. Both parents and girls acknowledged the importance of toilet use in protecting the dignity and integrity of women. The study also revealed that gender issues were not consciously and consistently addressed during the introduction and implementation of CLTS activities. Where gender was addressed, it was not by design (Plan International, 2012).

Integrating gender strategies into WASH programmes and monitoring their progress towards change can be a challenge. To assist this process, Plan International piloted a Gender WASH and Monitoring Tool in Vietnam to enable practitioners to explore and monitor gender relations in WASH projects. It was found that the effectiveness and sustainability of WASH programmes is enhanced when there is an explicit focus on gender equality (Plan International, 2014).

In Timor-Leste, WaterAid and partners have developed a facilitator's manual to guide gender dialogue sessions with communities as part of CLTS activities. Using the manual, gender focal point persons/staff carry out practical activities which explore gender aspects during each stage of CLTS. The idea for the manual grew out of the challenge that WASH actors faced in talking about power relations and engaging women in decision-making processes during CLTS. The manual has been piloted and tested in Timor-Leste, and the process of developing it has been an action learning approach. The gender manual is now an annex to the Timorese Government's national CLTS Guidelines (Government of Timor-Leste, forthcoming).

In Malawi, dialogue circles were used to identify problems and barriers experienced by disabled, older, and sick people with an outcome of action planning (Jones, 2015a). The circles worked best with small groups of around 20 people, targeted to encourage active participation of the most vulnerable people. It was found that dialogue circles were very effective in creating practice action plans agreed by the village and follow-up meetings.

Violence against women and girls

Open defecation can be especially degrading and dangerous for girls and women. The evidence that a lack of WASH can increase vulnerability to violence against women and girls is growing. For example, research carried out in an urban township in Cape Town revealed 635 sexual assaults of women travelling to and from toilets were reported between 2003 and 2012 (Gonsalves et al., 2015). The study stated that providing sanitation close to homes in South Africa's townships could reduce vulnerability to sexual violence by up to 30 per cent. Reaching the nearest toilet may require a circuitous route through the alleyways of the township. The nearest toilet may be in disrepair, and individuals may visit a toilet as part of a longer trip to other destinations. Locations such as alcohol serving establishments and the home are important loci of risk for women in urban settlements. Other research shows the psychological impact of lack of sanitation on women who openly defecate (Steinmann et al., 2015). Coping mechanisms used by women and girls include reducing the consumption of food and drink to limit the need to relieve themselves in daylight. These have obvious health implications (House et al., 2014).

There are a number of practical ways to reduce vulnerabilities to WASH-related violence (House and Cavill, 2015). For example, privacy, safety, and dignity can be increased through toilet design.[3] CLTS mapping combined with Safety Mapping can be a tool for women and girls to map out their community/surroundings and show the areas where they feel safe or unsafe. The map shown in Figure 15.1 was developed by women from Bhalswa slum in Delhi, who identified places in their local environment where violence had occurred (Lennon, 2011). While the map was developed in a low-income urban context, the same principles apply to the rural context.

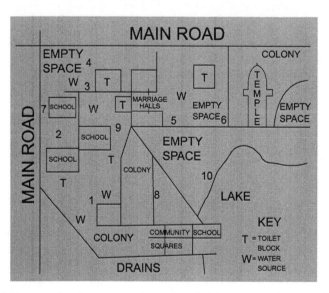

Figure 15.1 Map showing frequency and severity of violence against women in Bhalswa slum, Delhi)
Source: Based on original from Shirley Lennon/SHARE, 2011

Menstrual hygiene management

Menstruation is a natural process, but menstrual hygiene (how to manage menstruation safely and with dignity) has in the past been largely neglected by the WASH sector (Roose et al., 2015). This makes the menstrual hygiene challenges faced by women and girls even more difficult. Without menstrual hygiene services at school and in homes, girls may skip school or drop out altogether if there are no private toilets and hygiene supplies in their place of education. In Ethiopia, 50 per cent of girls in one school missed between one and four days of school per month due to menstruation (WaterAid, 2012). In India, inadequate menstrual hygiene services lead adolescent girls to miss five days of school a month (Nielsen and Plan India, 2010). Approximately 23 per cent of these girls drop out of school after they begin menstruating (Nielsen and Plan India, 2010). This limits their opportunity for education, income generation, and societal participation, all of which hamper self-worth and confidence. CLTS programmes can be expanded to address menstrual hygiene in schools and communities to alleviate these stresses on women and girls, as well as challenging the myths, silence, and negativity which often surround menstruation.

- In Uganda, Plan International has used a range of approaches to engage school children as peer educators of menstrual hygiene, sharing poems and 'change' stories with other girls. Village Health Teams, and other community members, have performed drama sessions on the myths and taboos of menstruation, demonstrated effective use of pads, and included MHM in the hygiene awareness sessions held in CLTS post-triggering (Roose et al., 2015).
- WaterAid Zambia and partners have supported menstrual hygiene awareness-raising in schools through School Health and Nutrition Coordinators, School Health Clubs, Mother's Support Groups, Parent Teachers Associations, peer learning, and focus group discussions, to provide a supportive environment for girls and boys to learn about menstrual hygiene (Roose et al., 2015).
- In Mulanje, Malawi, Plan International has been encouraging school-based Mothers' Groups to engage village leaders to organize community-level discussions (involving men, women, boys, and girls) on menstrual hygiene to break down existing taboos and myths. Existing school Sanitation Clubs, strengthened through School-Led Total Sanitation (SLTS), have also proved receptive and motivated to engage with menstrual hygiene management (Roose et al., 2015).
- WaterAid Bangladesh established cultural groups for adolescent girls and boys in the schools and communities where they spoke about menstrual hygiene (or just menstruation). The outcomes have been impressive: negative myths, taboos, and restrictions during menstruation for girls and women have reduced. For instance, families no longer expected girls to bathe in secret or restrict food, and girls were able to wash sanitary cloths in the spring and hang them out in the sunlight to dry. Adolescent girls described no longer feeling ashamed of menstruation or trying to hide it. They described how this change in attitudes and improved hygienic practices had occurred slowly, over the course of several years. They saw themselves as change agents for both older and younger generations. Adolescent boys saw themselves as champions of menstrual hygiene among their peers and the broader community and had carried out advocacy activities with senior community members. Adolescent girls described how they felt listened to by their male peers and how boys came to them for help and listened to their opinions (Wilbur and Huggett, 2015).

Children and ageing

Almost half of all schools in low-income countries still lack water and sanitation facilities (UNICEF, 2015). Providing adequate WASH in schools significantly reduces preventable diseases. It can increase student attendance and learning achievement, and help promote dignity, inclusion, and equality. This establishes an important foundation for ongoing development and economic growth (UNICEF, 2012).

Children can, and often do, play a key role in CLTS. They can be very enthusiastic in motivational activities and preventing people from practising OD. In Ethiopia, Plan International uses teachers as community facilitators in the promotion of hygiene and sanitation. Students play active roles by initiating families to go to triggering sites, to construct toilets, and to report on developments after communities have been triggered. After a village has decided to stop OD, a village 'shit eradication team' is created, which includes adults, boys, and girls (Plan International, 2011). Plan International also uses sanitation and hygiene games to empower children to influence their parents to improve their sanitation. The purpose is to imprint the concept of hygiene and sanitation in the minds of children, so that using the toilet and washing their hands with soap becomes their daily routine (Plan International, 2010).

In Tanzania, SNV are harmonizing school WASH and improving sanitation access for school children, including those with disabilities. SNV engaged with four government ministries, development partners, local authorities, village councils, and school committees, all of whom had key roles to play in improving the WASH situation in Tanzanian schools. The intervention involved: improved coordination; financial arrangements; operation and maintenance; development of School WASH Guidelines and toolkits; and a pilot of the toolkit. As a result of the interventions, school children, including those with disabilities, now have access to improved and gender-friendly WASH facilities in schools. The intervention will be up-scaled in order to help more schools improve their facilities (SNV, 2012).

Recent research in Uganda and Zambia revealed that older people consistently face difficulties accessing toilets, especially at night, as they may find it hard to find the toilet and maintain balance inside without any support structures (Danquah, 2014). Older people in these communities faced the most discrimination in the community and within the household, because of decreased mobility and ill health (Wilbur and Danquah, 2015).

People with disabilities

An estimated 15 per cent of the world's population have an impairment, and 80 per cent of those reside in developing countries (WHO and World Bank, 2011), where as many as one in five individuals living in the lowest wealth quintile are likely to be disabled (Jones and Reed, 2005). Poverty is both a cause and a consequence of disability. Disabled people are more likely to be poor and if you are poor you are more likely to be disabled (Jones and Reed, 2005: 6–7). The lowest wealth quintile are 5.5 times more likely to lack improved water access and 3.3 times more likely to lack adequate sanitation, compared with households in the highest wealth quintile in the same country (Moe and Reingans, 2006).

People with disabilities in poor communities often lack WASH services because:

- Facilities are not inclusive, meaning that some physically disabled people have to crawl on the floor to use a toilet or defecate in the open (Wilbur and Jones, 2014).
- There is limited information on inclusive WASH options, so people with disabilities and their families are often unaware of the options available (Wilbur et al., 2013).
- A lack of information about the cause of disability leads to stigma and discrimination. In Uganda, 19 per cent of people with disabilities in a research sample were stopped from touching water points because they were considered 'dirty' (Wilbur and Danquah, 2015).
- They are rarely meaningfully consulted or involved in decisions about WASH policy and programmes.
- Policies and standards are often not enforced, or do not adequately include the needs of older people, people with disabilities, and children (WaterAid, 2011).

A WaterAid research project, 'Undoing Inequity – water, sanitation and hygiene services that deliver for all in Uganda and Zambia', aimed to understand the barriers to WASH services and opportunities faced by disabled, chronically sick, and older people; to develop and test an inclusive WASH approach that addresses the barriers; and to assess the impact that improved access to safe WASH has on the lives of people from excluded groups (Wilbur et al., 2013). The project has found ways in which CLTS can address many of the barriers that people with disabilities face and make each stage of CLTS more inclusive, accessible, and sustainable.

A study on social inclusion in Malawi, by Plan International and the Water, Engineering and Development Centre (WEDC) (Jones, 2015a) found that the use of accessibility and safety audits was especially useful. Some key findings included the importance of:

- Men, women, and people with disabilities being part of the audit team.
- Consulting with a range of different users, not just committee members or community leaders, in a range of different locations: for example, women working at the market had a different approach to managing menstrual rags from that of other women.
- Considering multiple issues at a time: for example, a person living with disability is also a woman who experiences menstruation and gender discrimination.

During implementation of a number of Plan's CLTS projects in Indonesia it was found that people with disabilities needed special attention to enable them to have full access to the toilets. Training sessions were held, based on WaterAid's and WEDC's awareness raising materials (WEDC, 2014), to increase awareness of disability inclusion and disability rights among field staff who were responsible for implementing the activities at the community level.

Sub-district officials who participated in the training were 'triggered' to adopt a disability inclusive approach in their sub-district. Project staff members and government counterparts are working together with communities to achieve universal access to toilets at the village level, the scale at which ODF is declared. However, the most promising result has been the effort to link sanitation marketing and disability inclusion. Local entrepreneurs have been encouraged to focus on sanitation options for people with disabilities and include them in design processes to address their specific needs (Triwahyudi and Setiawan, 2014). Despite all these efforts, there is limited evidence of sanitation marketing being led by people with disabilities and the sector lacks evidence on how successful sanitation marketing is in meeting the needs of the poorest and excluded.

How can CLTS contribute to universal access to sanitation in the SDGs?

CLTS aims for ODF, but it does not automatically equate to adequate sanitation. ODF is an important, but intermediate step to sustainable sanitation.

The initial rung on the sanitation ladder (ODF) can be jeopardized by just one person. It is essential to ensure that everyone's needs are being considered and that accessible facilities are available (Wilbur and Jones, 2014). This can be made a reality if we move beyond the assumption that the basic CLTS tool is always inclusive and equitable, and if we actively build-in equality and non-discrimination considerations at every stage of the approach, to ensure ODF status is sustained as well as to move sustainably beyond ODF. Unless explicitly included, equality and non-discrimination risk being omitted by implementers in their rush to simply reach ODF.

Research is under way to discover how to do this in practice. The London School of Hygiene and Tropical Medicine (LSHTM), WEDC, Mzuzu University, and the Centre for Social Research at the University of Malawi are collaborating on a research study in northern Malawi. The purpose is to see whether it's possible for CLTS implementers to make small adaptations to the usual CLTS implementation process that would result in improved participation by vulnerable people in the process, and improved access to sanitation for vulnerable people in the community (Jones, 2015b). So far this research has indicated that integrating inclusive WASH training in CLTS has effectively increased awareness of communities about the needs of people with disabilities, older people, and those with chronic illnesses and has resulted in some structures being modified and adapted to help people move towards improved sanitation.

However, it is clear that more effort is needed to include the perspectives of all toilet users when designing and constructing toilets and handwashing facilities and evidence is still to be gathered (in the end line evaluation) on whether there has been a resulting increase in access to sanitation and hygiene for disabled people, older people, and those with chronic illness in Rumphi district in northern Malawi.

The voices, views, and needs of those who have low status, minorities, those who are very poor, women, girls, and children are relevant in deciding technical options for toilets, their location, and accessibility. Their empowerment throughout CLTS and WASH processes can be enhanced by the following actions:

Training and capacity development for pre-triggering. Without adequate facilitator training, aspects of equality and non-discrimination may be omitted. Pre-triggering is the most important stage of CLTS to bring in components of equality and non-discrimination.

Triggering. The more inclusive attendance at triggering, the better. A target of 80 per cent of community members present is cited as a rule of thumb. The Plan International ODF sustainability study found that women's attendance at triggering was more important than men's (Tyndale-Biscoe et al., 2013). All community members, including people with disabilities, older people, and the marginalized, should be encouraged and supported to participate by a supportive facilitator (Wilbur and Jones, 2014).

Post-triggering, monitoring, and follow-up. Post-triggering, there may be some households that are unable to construct a toilet (either from lack of time or resources). Ideally, support will come from within the community (Kar with Chambers, 2008). However, we need to understand the extent to which this actually happens (Robinson and Gnilo, 2016a, this book; Musembi and Musyoki, 2016). In addition, it is possible that members of the community getting assistance may be provided with facilities they do not want or that do not meet their needs, and subsequently they will not use. This could leave them vulnerable to abuse or sanctions from other community members.

Post-ODF towards sustainable sanitation. Post-ODF follow-up is critical for sustainability (see Robinson and Gnilo, 2016a, this book; Regmi 2016, this book; Wamera, 2016, this book; Musyoki, 2016, this book). To ensure the new social norm is embedded and sustained, everyone has to be included and not revert to the existing practice of OD. Ideally, households will climb the sanitation ladder over time and improve their toilets; however, this does not always happen, particularly among poor and marginalized households. Reversion to OD is also a problem.

Practical steps to integrate inclusion

To avoid reinforcing inequalities, and to ensure behaviour change is sustained, there are a number of practical steps that can be taken within CLTS programmes. The suggestions outlined in Table 15.1 should help ensure meaningful participation of excluded groups, and integrate measures to support sustainability from the start of the process.

Table 15.1 Practical steps to integrate inclusion into CLTS processes

Activity	Purpose	CLTS stage
Equality and inclusion integrated into training of facilitators	Equip facilitators with the mind-sets and skills to avoid shaming poor or marginalized people. Training should include the issue of stigma and mentor schemes, and groups could be set up to ensure facilitators receive adequate support and advice, and are able to discuss ways to address any problems (Musembi and Musyoki, 2016). Marginalized people, such as people living with disabilities, can also be trained as facilitators to improve participation of people from excluded groups and raise awareness of the experiences of marginalized people. It also demonstrates that people from excluded groups can take leadership positions.	• Training and capacity development for pre-triggering
Situational analysis, scoping studies, or wealth ranking	Understand power dynamics and resource (time and money) burdens faced by men, women, the poorest, marginalized individuals and groups, people with disabilities, older people, children, and youth, in CLTS programmes.	• Training and capacity development for pre-triggering
Analysis of key influencers	Identify people within the community who can become Natural Leaders and help drive the process (see Dooley et al., 2016, this book). Identify people who may be marginalized, bearing in mind that they may be 'hidden' in the household due to stigma and discrimination. Ensure inclusion of marginalized people. People who have faced social exclusion often feel disempowered, so appropriate support is vital in order that they can effectively deliver their roles and responsibilities. Guard against unintentionally putting additional economic and domestic burdens on marginalized people, otherwise the process will be extractive rather than mutually beneficial and empowering.	• Pre-triggering
Mapping of community groups	Identify those who have access to all sections of the community to carry out pre- and post-ODF activities (see Dooley et al., 2016, this book; and Wamera, 2016, this book). Involving excluded groups, such as transgender groups, can help to ensure they are not only participants, but also leaders in the process of change (Tiwari, 2015). Identification of people with disabilities can be helped by including disability organizations who are more aware of this issue.	• Pre-triggering
Accessibility and safety audits	Raise awareness of the barriers to access that different people face; highlight designs that are not accessible, and jointly propose solutions for greater access. Auditing teams should be made up of CLTS implementers, sanitation masons, women and men, older people, girls and boys, including disabled people with different impairments. The team should not be too large and there should be a strong coordination role. If the team attempts to use facilities and encounter challenges, they can discuss how to make them more accessible (WEDC and WaterAid, 2014; Jones, 2015a).	• Pre-triggering • Triggering • Post-triggering, monitoring, and follow-up

(Continued)

Table 15.1 Practical steps to integrate inclusion into CLTS processes (*Continued*)

Activity	Purpose	CLTS stage
Timing of triggering	Ensure as many people as possible can attend the triggering sessions. This means considering the place, timing, and pace for triggering carefully (Wilbur and Jones, 2014). Consider the possibility of separate discussions with women and with children, and home visits for disabled or older persons who may not be very mobile.	• Pre-triggering
Separate meetings and dialogue circles for different groups	Hold separate meetings for people or groups who may feel unable to speak in community meetings, or those unable to leave their homes such as older people and disabled people. Discuss specific needs of people with disability and women/girls with regard to WASH. WEDC (2014) have developed tools and activities that can be incorporated into CLTS monitoring and follow up, to encourage a reflection on barriers to inclusion (WEDC, 2014). There is a revised guidance note on how to conduct effective dialogue circles developed by WEDC and Plan International (Jones, 2015a).	• Pre-triggering • Triggering • Post-triggering
Identification of those unable to build toilets	The CLTS process can facilitate the linkages between people, encouraging local actions and innovations to provide what is needed (Kar with Chambers, 2008; Chambers, 2012).	• Triggering • Post-triggering
Information on menstrual hygiene, disability, and communicable diseases	Reinforce the need to provide access to all, and challenge false beliefs that result in discrimination. Information should be available in local languages and accessible formats, with pictures for people who cannot read or hear, and audio for people who cannot see.	• Triggering
Information about accessible technology options for household toilets	Ensure materials to inform choice are available, as well as practical support on low-cost, low-tech inclusive designs (e.g. Jones and Wilbur, 2014).	• Post-triggering
Inclusive monitoring and evaluation indicators	Indicators should reflect targets for: facilities with a specified level of accessibility; reduced numbers of people who are marginalized lacking access to facilities; increased participation of marginalized community members, not only as users but also in active roles with responsibilities and payment where possible. Participation monitoring can be carried out to include a range of excluded groups. This can also be carried out using dialogue circles (Jones 2015a).	• Post-triggering
Data collection	Capture data on sanitation for people with additional access requirements. Population data should be disaggregated by sex, age, disability; questions about menstrual hygiene, safety, security, accessibility of facilities for disabled persons, and traditional attitudes about gender, disability, and age, in relation to WASH. Surveys collect views of women, children, older people, disabled people and their households, and any groups living in the area whose needs are likely to be neglected (low caste, pastoralists, migrant workers, displaced people, sex workers, prisoners).	• Post-triggering

(*Continue*)

Table 15.1 Practical steps to integrate inclusion into CLTS processes (*Continued*)

Activity	Purpose	CLTS stage
Review of progress up the sanitation ladder	Identify households who are stuck on the bottom rung of the sanitation ladder. Consider options that encourage communities to gradually improve (Robinson and Gnilo, 2016b, this book).	• Post-ODF
Post-ODF follow-up	Maintain ODF status especially when, e.g. the pit is full or the infrastructure collapses during flooding. User committees have a role in post-ODF follow-up, alongside follow-up by programmes or government, and should be facilitated to ensure meaningful participation by marginalized groups. It is important that these groups receive adequate support and encouragement to ensure they are not overburdened (Wamera, 2016, this book).	• Post-ODF
Availability of financing options	Consider financing options such as vouchers, rebates, and rewards to ensure poor and marginalized people are able to retain ODF status and climb the sanitation ladder (Myers, 2015b; Robinson and Gnilo, 2016b, this book).	• Post-ODF
Toilets in public places	Public or institutional toilets (in markets, schools, health centres) should include separate facilities for males and females, with accessible cubicles, and water provided inside the women's cubicles for MHM.	• Post-triggering
Cross-sector collaboration	Establish links with relevant agencies (e.g. health, rehabilitation) to address issues or needs that are beyond the scope of the WASH sector.	• All phases

Institutional enabling environment

Realization of the human rights to water and sanitation is both the duty of the state and the responsibility of the individual. CLTS actively promotes community and individual responsibility. However, attention to government and institutional strengthening for inclusive rural sanitation is also critical. Successful approaches to ensure a supportive enabling environment include:

- Active involvement of national and district governments (including traditional leaders) in barrier analysis, accessibility, and safety audits, community meetings, training for implementing officers on inclusion, triggering, and follow-up.
- Creation of institutions that can support CLTS processes and integration into the broader systems that provide sanitation delivery options.
- Where there is high turnover of government and local partner staff, follow-up training and support for monitoring.
- Collection of baseline data on people who may face barriers to accessing sanitation during CLTS household registration, which is included in ODF criteria (Wilbur and Jones, 2014).
- Providing financial support where necessary, in terms of subsidies or other support for those households that cannot afford to construct an adequate toilet that complies with the standards set out in the human right to sanitation (see Robinson and Gnilo, 2016b, this book).

Conclusion

The local approach and global reach of CLTS makes it an ideal methodology for promoting equality and non-discrimination in communities. CLTS can lay the ground for active community ownership of new behaviours and habits, and ensure that all community members are involved in the process of change, especially those who were previously ignored or excluded. This can support the achievement of the ambitious SDGs on sanitation and their emphasis on the rights of all excluded groups to achieve sustained access to sanitation and hygiene. It is important to recognize, however, that CLTS cannot solve existing social inequalities and structural problems by itself, and should not be expected to. Unless implemented with care and inclusion in mind, CLTS can actually reinforce or exacerbate existing problems. Currently, many programmes are run and financed with a focus on scale and speed, which are key to achieving universal access. However, there is also a critical need for ensuring quality CLTS programmes that lead to long-term sustainable change; incorporating concerns for equality and inclusion may mean that it will take longer to reach everyone and reach targets, but this approach might be the only way to achieve sustainability. Wide societal shifts in terms of awareness about, and establishment of, social norms will be needed. While the imperative for equality and non-discrimination is widely recognized in the WASH sector, we still have a lot to learn about how to turn these binding principles into reality through programme implementation.

About the authors

Sue Cavill is a water supply, sanitation, and hygiene specialist. Her experience includes implementation of water supply and sanitation programmes, policy and programme-relevant research, analysis and dissemination, as well as programme evaluation.

Sharon Roose (MSc) previously worked as a WASH Adviser for Plan International Netherlands, and now works as a WASH Senior Advocacy Officer for SNV. She is a WASH specialist with experience in the management and implementation of WASH projects, with a specific interest in social development and community empowerment.

Cathy Stephen (MSc, Dipl) currently works as WASH Adviser for Plan International UK. She has previously worked as WASH technical adviser for the Liberia WASH Consortium and for the World Vision Southern Africa WASH learning centre, based in Malawi.

Jane Wilbur is a social inclusion specialist currently working at WaterAid. She has experience in developing and implementing inclusive WASH projects and project evaluation, as well as conducting, analysing, and disseminating research to influence policy and practice.

Endnotes

1. However, this research did not investigate if every household member defecates in the open, or if it is just the person who is marginalized. Nor did it examine reasons for practising OD. More research is required to understand these specific conditions.
2. UN General Assembly resolution (2015) defines water and sanitation as two separate rights for the first time.
3. For example, facilities are well lit, or women and girls have access to torches or other forms of light; the facility has a solid door and a lock on the inside of the door. Toilets have roofs. Facilities are accessible for family members with limited mobility (House and Cavill, 2015).

References

Adeyeye, A. (2011) 'Gender and Community-Led Total Sanitation: A case study of Ekiti State, Nigeria', *Tropical Resources*, Bulletin of the Yale Tropical Resources Institute, 30: 18–27.

Africa Ahead (2013) 'A scoping study to consider options to strengthen integration, sustainability, institutionalisation & self-reliance (ISIS) of the environmental health sector in Sierra Leone', *Africa Ahead*, Sierra Leone.

de Albuquerque, C. (2014) *Realising the Human Rights to Water and Sanitation: A Handbook by the UN Special Rapporteur*, Office of the United Nations High Commissioner for Human Rights, Geneva.

Alkire, S., Roche, J.M. and Seth, S. (2013) *Multidimensional Poverty Index 2013*, Oxford Poverty & Human Development Initiative, University of Oxford, Oxford, http://www.ophi.org.uk/wp-content/uploads/Multidimensional-Poverty-Index-2013-Alkire-Roche-and-Seth.pdf [accessed 15 February 2016].

Bardosh, K. (2015) 'Achieving "total sanitation" in rural african geographies: poverty, participation and pit latrines in eastern Zambia', *Geoforum*, 66: 53–63 <http://dx.doi.org/10.1016/j.geoforum.2015.09.004>.

Bartram J., Charles, C., Evans, B., O'Hanlon, L. and Pedley, S. (2012) 'Commentary on community-led total sanitation and human rights: should the right to community-wide health be won at the cost of individual rights?' *Journal of Water and Health* 10.4: 499–503 <http://dx.doi.org/10.2166/wh.2012.205>.

Bongartz, P. (2012) *Emotional triggers: Shame? Or Shock, Disgust and Dignity*, CLTS website blog, www.communityledtotalsanitation.org/blog/emotional-triggers-shame-or-shock-disgust-and-dignity [accessed 15 February 2016].

Chambers, R. (2012) *Discrimination, Duties and Low-Hanging Fruit: Reflections on Equity*, CLTS website blog, http://www.communityledtotalsanitation.org/blog/discrimination-duties-and-low-hanging-fruitreflections-equity [accessed 15 February 2016].

Coffey, D., Gupta, A., Hathi, P., Spears, D. and Vyas, S. (2014) 'Toilets are urgently needed in rural India, but don't imagine they will reduce rape', *Scroll.in*, June 7.

Danquah, D. (2014) *Mid-term Review: Undoing Inequity: Inclusive Water, Sanitation and Hygiene Programmes that Deliver for All in Uganda and Zambia*, WaterAid,

London, http://www.wateraid.org/uk/what-we-do/policy-practice-and-advocacy/research-and-publications/view-publication?id=25633f29-8f85-4f0e-9a54-ffe2ca085fce [accessed 16 February 2016].

Dooley, T., Maule, L. and Gnilo, M. (2016) 'Using social norms theory to strengthen CATS impact and sustainability', in P. Bongartz, N. Vernon and J. Fox (eds.) *Sustainable Sanitation for All: Experiences, Challenges, and Innovations*, Practical Action Publishing, Rugby.

Engel, S. and Susilo, A. (2014) 'Shaming and sanitation in Indonesia: a return to colonial public health practices', *Development and Change*, 45.1: 157–178 <http://dx.doi.org/10.1111/dech.12075>.

Galvin, M. (2015) 'Talking shit: is Community-Led Total Sanitation a radical and revolutionary approach to sanitation?' *WIREs Water*, 2.

Gonsalves, G., Kaplan, E. and Paltiel, A. (2015) 'Reducing sexual violence by increasing the supply of toilets in Khayelitsha, South Africa: a mathematical model', *PLoS ONE*, 10.4: e0122244 <http://dx.doi.org/10.1371/journal.pone.0122244>.

González, A.H. (2013) *Report on the IRC Symposium 2013: Monitoring Sustainable WASH Service Delivery*, April 2013, Addis Ababa http://www.communityledtotalsanitation.org/sites/communityledtotalsanitation.org/files/Report_IRCAddiSymposium_AHG.pdf [accessed 15 February 2016].

Government of Timor-Leste (forthcoming) *National Community Led Total Sanitation Guideline*, Government of Timor-Leste, Dili.

Gupta, A., Coffey, D. and Spears, D. (2016) 'Purity, pollution, and untouchability: challenges affecting the adoption, use, and sustainability of sanitation programmes in rural India', in P. Bongartz, N. Vernon and J. Fox (eds.) *Sustainable Sanitation for All: Experiences, Challenges, and Innovations*, Practical Action Publishing, Rugby.

HAI Global Age Watch (2013) *Global Age Watch* 2015, HelpAge International, London, http://www.helpage.org/global-agewatch/ [accessed 15 February 2016].

House, S. and Cavill, S. (2015) 'Making Sanitation and hygiene safer: Reducing vulnerabilities to violence' *Frontiers of CLTS: Innovations and Insights* 5, Institute of Development Studies, Brighton.

House, S., Ferron, S., Sommer, M. and Cavill, S. (2014) *Violence, Gender and WASH: A Practitioner's Toolkit*, Loughborough University, Loughborough, http://violence-wash.lboro.ac.uk/ [accessed 15 February 2016].

Jones, H. (2015a) *Social Inclusion in Malawi WASH Project*, Research Report, Loughborough University, Loughborough.

Jones, H. (2015b) *CLTS+ triggering Rumphi District Malawi*, Unpublished Research Report.

Jones, H. and Reed, R.A. (2005) *Water and Sanitation for Disabled People and Other Vulnerable Groups: Designing Services to Improve Accessibility*, WEDC, Loughborough University, Loughborough, https://wedc-knowledge.lboro.ac.uk/details.html?id=16357 [accessed 15 February 2016].

Jones, H. and Wilbur, J. (2014) *Compendium of Accessible WASH Technologies*, WEDC, WaterAid and SHARE, Loughborough and London.

Kar, K. with Chambers, R. (2008) *Handbook on Community-Led Total Sanitation*, Plan International and Institute of Development Studies, London and Brighton.

Lennon, S. (2011) 'Fear and anger: Perceptions of risks related to sexual violence against women linked to water and sanitation in Delhi, India', Briefing Note, SHARE (Sanitation and Hygiene Applied Research for Equity) and WaterAid, London.

Moe, C.L. and Reingans, R.D. (2006) 'Global challenges in water, sanitation and health', *Journal of Water and Health*, 4.1: 41–57 <http://dx.doi.org/10.2166/wh.2005.039>.

Musembi, C. and Musyoki, S. (2016) 'CLTS and the right to sanitation', *Frontiers of CLTS: Innovations and Insights* 8, Institute of Development Studies, Brighton.

Musyoki, S. (2016) 'Roles and responsibilities for post-ODF engagement: building an enabling institutional environment for CLTS sustainability', in P. Bongartz, N. Vernon and J. Fox (eds.) *Sustainable Sanitation for All: Experiences, Challenges, and Innovations*, Practical Action Publishing, Rugby.

Myers, J. (2015a) 'Take-aways from the UNC Water and Health Conference', CLTS website blog, http://www.communityledtotalsanitation.org/blog/take-aways-unc-water-and-health-conference [accessed 6 November 2015].

Myers, J. (2015b) 'Lessons from Pakistan', CLTS website blog, www.communityledtotalsanitation.org/blog/lessons-pakistan [accessed 6 November 2015].

Nielsen, A.C. and Plan India (2010) *Sanitation Protection: Every Women's Health Right*, Plan International, New Delhi.

Oxford Poverty and Human Development Initiative (OPHI) (2015) *Global Multidimensional Poverty Index*, http://www.ophi.org.uk/multidimensional-poverty-index/ [accessed 6 April 2016].

O'Reilly, K. and Louis, E. (2014) 'The Toilet Tripod: understanding successful sanitation in rural India', *Health and Place*, 29: 43–51 <http://dx.doi.org/10.1016/j.healthplace.2014.05.007>.

Plan International (2010) *Annual Report Pan African CLTS Programme*, Plan Nederland, Amsterdam, http://www.communityledtotalsanitation.org/sites/communityledtotalsanitation.org/files/Plan_Trigger.pdf [accessed 15 February 2016].

Plan International (2011) *Annual Report Pan African CLTS Programme*, Plan Nederland, Amsterdam, http://www.communityledtotalsanitation.org/sites/communityledtotalsanitation.org/files/Annual_report_2011_PanAfrica.pdf [accessed 15 February 2016].

Plan International (2012) *Research on the Impact of Gender on Community-Led Total Sanitation Processes*, Final Report, Plan Uganda, http://www.communityledtotalsanitation.org/sites/communityledtotalsanitation.org/files/Gender%20and%20CLTS%20report%20final.pdf [accessed 15 February 2016].

Plan International (2014) *Gender and WASH Monitoring Tool*, Plan International Australia, Melbourne.

Regmi, A. (2016) 'Tools for embedding post-ODF sustainability: experiences from SNV Nepal', in P. Bongartz, N. Vernon and J. Fox (eds.) *Sustainable Sanitation for All: Experiences, Challenges, and Innovations*, Practical Action Publishing, Rugby.

Robinson, M. and Gnilo, M.E. (2016a) 'Beyond ODF: a phased approach to rural sanitation development', in P Bongartz, N. Vernon and J. Fox (eds.)

Sustainable Sanitation for All: Experiences, Challenges, and Innovations, Practical Action Publishing, Rugby.

Robinson, M. and Gnilo, M.E. (2016b) 'Financing for the poorest', in P. Bongartz, N. Vernon and J. Fox (eds.) *Sustainable Sanitation for All: Experiences, Challenges, and Innovations*, Practical Action Publishing, Rugby.

Roose, S., Rankin, T. and Cavill, S. (2015) 'Breaking the next taboo: Menstrual hygiene within CLTS', *Frontiers of CLTS: Innovations and Insights* 6, Institute of Development Studies, Brighton.

SNV (2012) *Harmonising School WASH in Tanzania: Improving Sanitation Access for Schoolchildren Including those with Disabilities*, Corporate Annual Report – Case Studies, SNV, The Hague.

Srivastav, N. and Gupta, A. (2015) 'Why using patriarchal messaging to promote toilets is a bad idea', *TheWire.in*, 7 June.

Steinmann, P., Juvekar S., Hirve S. and Weiss M.G. (2015) *Coping Strategies to Deal with Inadequate WASH Facilities and Related Health Risks*, Research Briefing Note, SHARE, LSHTM, London, http://wsscc.org/wp-content/uploads/2015/09/Briefing_Note_1_2015_LoRes.pdf [accessed 15 February 2016].

Thomas, A. (2016) 'Strengthening post ODF programming: reviewing lessons from sub-Saharan Africa', in P. Bongartz, N. Vernon and J. Fox (eds.) *Sustainable Sanitation for All: Experiences, Challenges, and Innovations*, Practical Action, Rugby.

Tiwari, A. (2015) *Involvement of Transgender People in Sanitation Campaigns: An Initiative in Madhya Pradesh*, CLTS website, http://www.communityledtotalsanitation.org/resource/involvement-transgender-people-sanitation-campaigns-initiative-madhya-pradesh [accessed 16 February 2016].

Triwahyudi, W. and Setiawan, E. (2014) *Disability Inclusion on WASH: What Has Been Achieved and How Can This Help Other Practitioners?* Briefing paper, 37th WEDC International Conference, Hanoi.

Tyndale-Biscoe, P., Bond, M. and Kidd, R. (2013) *ODF Sustainability Study*, FH Designs and Plan International, http://www.communityledtotalsanitation.org/sites/communityledtotalsanitation.org/files/Plan_International_ODF_Sustainability_Study.pdf [accessed 15 February 2016].

UN (2011) *Follow Up on the Second World Assembly on Ageing, Report of the Secretary-General*, http://www.un.org/en/ga/search/view_doc.asp?symbol=A/66/173 [accessed 4 April 2016].

UNAIDS (2014) *Factsheet 2014, Global Statistics*, UNAIDS, Geneva, http://www.unaids.org/sites/default/files/en/media/unaids/contentassets/documents/factsheet/2014/20140716_FactSheet_en.pdf [accessed 15 February 2016].

UNICEF (2012) *Raising Even More Clean Hands: Advancing Health, Learning and Equity through WASH in Schools*, UNICEF: New York, http://www.unicef.org/wash/schools/files/Raising_Even_More_Clean_Hands_Web_17_October_2012(1).pdf [accessed 15 February 2016].

UNICEF (2015) *Advancing WASH in Schools Monitoring*, UNICEF: New York, http://www.unicef.org/wash/schools/files/Advancing_WASH_in_Schools_Monitoring(1).pdf [accessed 15 February 2016].

Wamera, E. (2016) 'Who is managing the post-ODF process in the community? A case study of Nambale sub-county in Western Kenya', in P. Bongartz, N. Vernon and J. Fox (eds.) *Sustainable Sanitation for All: Experiences, Challenges, and Innovations*, Practical Action, Rugby.

WaterAid (2009) *Seen but not heard? A Review of the Effectiveness of Gender Approaches in Water and Sanitation Service Provision*, WaterAid, London, http://www.wateraid.org/~/media/Publications/gender-approach-water-sanitation-provision.pdf [accessed 15 February 2016].

WaterAid (2011) *What the Global Report on Disability Means for the WASH Sector*, Briefing Note, WaterAid, London.

WaterAid (2012) *Menstrual Hygiene Matters*, WaterAid, London, http://www.wateraid.org/what-we-do/our-approach/research-and-publications/view-publication?id=02309d73-8e41-4d04-b2ef-6641f6616a4f [accessed 15 February 2016].

WEDC (2014) *Equity and Inclusion in WASH: Learning Materials*, Loughborough University Loughborough, https://wedc-knowledge.lboro.ac.uk/collections/equity-inclusion/general.html [accessed 15 February 2016].

WEDC and WaterAid (2014) *Accessibility and Safety Audit: Latrine*, WEDC and WaterAid, Loughborough and London, http://wedc.lboro.ac.uk/resources/learning/EI_FN2_Accessibility_Safety_Audit_v2.pdf [accessed 15 February 2016].

WHO/UNICEF (2010) *Progress on Sanitation and Drinking-Water: 2010 Update*, WHO and UNICEF, Geneva.

WHO/UNICEF (2012) *Process for Drinking Water and Sanitation on Post-2015 Global Monitoring of Water, Sanitation and Hygiene*, Summary of the Final Report of the Working Group on Equity and Non-Discrimination, Joint Monitoring Programme (JMP), WHO and UNICEF, Geneva, http://www.wssinfo.org/fileadmin/user_upload/resources/JMP-END-WG-Summary-2-pager.pdf [accessed 15 February 2016].

WHO/UNICEF (2015) *Progress on Drinking Water and Sanitation: 2015 Update and MDG Assessment*, Joint Monitoring Programme (JMP), WHO and UNICEF, Geneva, www.wssinfo.org/fileadmin/user_upload/resources/JMP-Update-report-2015_English.pdf [accessed 27 October 2015.]

WHO/World Bank (2011) *World Report on Disability*, WHO, Geneva, http://www.who.int/disabilities/world_report/2011/report.pdf [accessed 15 February 2016].

Wilbur, J. and Danquah, L. (2015) *Undoing Inequity: Water, Sanitation and Hygiene Programmes That Deliver for All in Uganda and Zambia – An Early Indication of Trends*, Briefing Paper, 38th WEDC International Conference, Loughborough University, Loughborough, http://wedc.lboro.ac.uk/resources/conference/38/Wilbur-2191.pdf [accessed 15 February 2016].

Wilbur, J. and Huggett, C. (2015) *WaterAid Bangladesh Equity and Inclusion Review Report*, WaterAid, London, file:///C:/Users/janboyes/Downloads/WaterAid%20Bangladesh%20Equity%20and%20Inclusion%20Report%20(2).pdf [accessed 16 February 2016].

Wilbur, J. and Jones, H. (2014) 'Disability: Making CLTS fully inclusive', *Frontiers of CLTS: Innovations and Insights* 3, Institute of Development Studies, Brighton, http://www.communityledtotalsanitation.org/resources/frontiers/disability-making-clts-fully-inclusive [accessed 15 February 2016].

Wilbur, J., Jones, H., Gosling, L., Groce, N. and Challenger, E. (2013) *Undoing Inequity: Inclusive Water, Sanitation and Hygiene Programmes That Deliver for All in Uganda and Zambia*, Briefing Paper, 36th WEDC International Conference, Nakuru.

CHAPTER 16

Leave no one behind: equality and non-discrimination in sanitation and hygiene

Archana Patkar

Abstract

Sustainable Development Goal Target 6.2 aims, by 2030, to achieve access to adequate and equitable sanitation and hygiene for all and end open defecation (OD), paying special attention to the needs of women and girls and those in vulnerable situations. If we are serious about leaving no one behind, we will need to put human beings first, and infrastructure designed to serve them second. Many individuals and groups cannot use sanitation and hygiene facilities due to physical or societal restrictions placed on them by their gender, disability, age, caste, religion, gender, or poverty. Non-discrimination should be embedded into policy and practice, so that people's realities, needs, and demands are clearly articulated and matched with budgets, adapted public facilities on the ground, more equitable sharing of water, sanitation, and hygiene (WASH) burdens, and systematic, meaningful participation in decision-making and monitoring. This chapter summarizes the testimonies and aspirations of individuals across a number of Asian countries who were never asked what they need and who are excluded from services. They remind us that in order to leave no one behind we will need to listen to them, involve them fully at all key stages, and forge true partnerships to achieve shared goals.

Keywords: Equity, Inclusion, Lifecycle, Sustainable Development Goals (SDGs), Non-discrimination, Menstrual hygiene, the elderly, Disability, Gender

Introduction

Open defecation (OD) is the single biggest indignity for billions of people worldwide. It also endangers the safety, normal growth, health, and wellbeing of all communities within which it continues to be practised. To eliminate this forever, all people must be able to have access to convenient, affordable, and comfortable sanitation and hygiene inside and outside the home, from childhood to old age, through good and ill-health, including permanent or temporary impairments.

On 17 December 2015, the United Nations General Assembly adopted, by consensus, Resolution 70/169, presented by Spain and Germany and supported by 95 nations, to differentiate, for the first time, the human rights to water and to sanitation. The separate recognition of the rights to water and to sanitation

http://dx.doi.org/10.3362/9781780449272.016

responds to the need to highlight their individual features, as well as to step up the right to sanitation.[1] It also finally elevates sanitation and its corollary, hygiene, to the list of human obligations along with dignity, safety, non-discrimination, education and health, water, and decent conditions of shelter and work (UN Water, 2013). The right to sanitation was implicit in most other rights that preceded it, but much remains to be done so that every human being is able to defecate safely and without discrimination, wash oneself and one's hands after defecation, bathe, and manage one's menstruation with safety, dignity, and privacy.

For universal realization of this right we must systematically address the universal patterns and factors for discrimination that deny people sanitation and hygiene access and use. For simplicity let us divide these factors into those that are universal, age, gender, and physical ability including temporary or long-term mental, intellectual, and sensory impairment; and more context-specific discriminators such as occupation, location, economic condition, sexual preference, ethnicity, or geopolitical situation. These factors are pervasive and deeply embedded. We just have to visualize the male and female human lifecycle and superimpose specific discriminators at various stages of the life course to see these play out. A poor, blind adolescent girl faces many more challenges at menarche than her poor girlfriend across the street without a visual impairment. A young pregnant waste picker endangers her own health and that of her baby because of her work and life conditions, while also being stigmatized for the work she does. An older man with cataracts is doubly challenged, negotiating the slopes to go out and defecate and wash himself every day. He will very often be unable and unwilling to make the extra effort to also wash his hands. Age, context, and gender heavily shape and influence sanitation and hygiene access and the user experience itself, with direct impacts on sustainability.

This chapter will focus on:

- Listening to users: transforming sanitation and hygiene services in partnership with them.

- Putting non-discrimination into policy and practice: West and Central Africa and India.

Listening to users: transforming services with them

When we think of food, healthcare, or learning for children, we design these services with some physical and cognitive life stage attributes in mind. On reaching puberty, children are perceived to have crossed over to the world of adults. Adulthood is then seldom differentiated to reflect differing physical ability, changed access to and control of resources that once again diminish with menopause and older age for women and men. Adolescence is a particular point of real vulnerability, when hormonal changes affect boys and girls so that semenarche[2] and menarche[3] are in different but equally important ways, traumatic experiences shrouded in silence and stigma. If all people, everywhere, all of the time are to use and maintain sanitation and hygiene facilities, we must take account of the natural human life course across which all human beings embark, with differing impairments and needs at different stages of their life. How much more complex and nuanced is this journey across the female life course which includes menarche, menstruation, pregnancy, childbirth, and menopause (see Figure 16.1)!

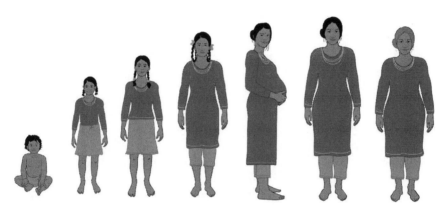

Figure 16.1. The female lifecycle
Source: © WSSCC, 2015. Design by ACW, London

The global quest to rid the planet of faeces in the environment will only succeed if services are available for a dynamic and diverse clientele. But this remains a distant dream for almost half the world's people. The Water Supply and Sanitation Collaborative Council (WSSCC), in collaboration with the Fresh Water Action Network-South Asia (FANSA), conducted consultations across eight countries[4] in the run up to SACOSAN VI[5] and asked a few questions of communities and their local governments interested in achieving open defecation free (ODF) environments (WSSCC and FANSA, 2016). This is what we heard:

- **Not systematically asked or included**: Adolescent girls and boys, older men (ill, disabled), women (young, pregnant, disabled, ill, older), lesbian, gay, bisexual, and transgender groups (ill, disabled, young, and older) are not separately consulted or asked about their daily sanitation and hygiene experience, how they cope and what solutions they can offer. Asking them what they need and want and resourcing them to partner in the design and development of inclusive services is a prerequisite for sustainable behaviour change.

- **Discriminated against**: Transgender community members in South India[6] reported discrimination at all levels from other family members and society in general. Everyone, without exception, treats them with disdain and suspicion. They are seen as unclean and polluting and are ridiculed and denied access to public toilets. Worse still, it is assumed that they want to access public facilities only to engage in paid sex. In addition to the post castration or sex reassignment surgery complications which lead to difficulties in urinating, incontinence, and kidney problems, they are denied all basic services including safe shelter. In fact they are barely considered human, and therefore the question of responding to basic sanitation and hygiene needs is absent from the water, sanitation, and hygiene (WASH) discourse.

- **Stigmatized and shunned**: Sanitation workers and waste pickers who clean drains, empty pits, and segregate and sort garbage, remain the most invisible and unheard in discussions on WASH (see Figure 16.2). Their own needs, safety, and dignity are ignored. Doubly discriminated, because of the work they do and the poor unsanitary conditions of their habitat, they are often denied use of the very services they maintain. This is particularly serious in South Asia where caste and class complexities make it unacceptable for a sweeper or cleaner to use the same toilet as others in the community, or worse where it is seen as demeaning to clean one's own toilet. In violation of basic human respect, dignity, and safety, these workers try to eke out a living in precarious conditions, without any protection. They are deeply stigmatized and their kin after them for the work they do. There will be no universal access or sustainability without their voice, full participation, and access to the very services they help maintain.

Figure 16.2 Waste picker on Delhi landfill
Source: WSSCC, Javier Acebal, 2015

- **Vulnerable and violated:** Women and girls defecating in the open, talk with pain about the daily stress of trying to ensure that no one sees them while also trying to avoid sexual harassment. Users of public toilets are no happier, reporting unsafe locations, peeping, touching, revealing, together with dirty, smelly conditions (Kulkarni and O'Reilly, 2015). Women of all ages try to complete their bathing, washing, and defecation tasks quickly for fear of being seen, watched, or interrupted by men. So how does this affect their daily routine? Since most women lacked the ability and/or agency to modify their sanitation environments, they were forced to adapt their behaviour in response to stressors. Figure 16.3 shows that the methods employed to minimize sanitation-related psychosocial stress included seeking social support, changing the timing of sanitation activities to minimize confrontation and exposure, and employing physiological regulation such as withholding food or withholding urination or defecation (Sahoo et al., 2015). Adolescents and newly married women are particularly vulnerable and resorted to defecating in plastic bags in their backyard when faced with insufficient social support.

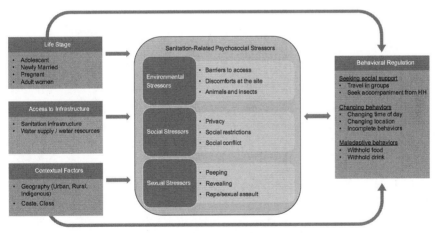

Figure 16.3 Sanitation-related psychosocial stress (SRPS): a conceptual framework
Source: Sahoo et al., 2015

- **Invisible, embarrassed and ashamed:** In South Asia, the sanctity of food, prayer, and celebrations are all considered at risk when a girl or woman is menstruating. At other times too, she must make every effort to hide this fact from the world lest she endanger the purity of the family and community. What does this mean for those five days a month without enough water, privacy, and affordable access to convenient sanitary protection while menstruating? Twelve thousand women and girls consulted in the Nirmal Bharat Yatra across five states in northern India in 2012 welcomed the rare opportunity to discuss menstruation, its safe and hygienic management, and the destruction of taboos and superstitions among family, friends, and society. They pledged to break the silence at home, at school, and at work (Patkar, 2014). Three years later, across South Asia, girls and women echoed the same relief at being asked, shed tears at the pain and stigma, and resolved to speak up and act when provided the space to do so (WSSCC and FANSA, 2016).

The taboos and perceptions may vary by geography, from menstruating blood spoiling pickles in South Asia, to curdling milk in West Africa (WSSCC and UN Women, 2015a). But the fact remains that decades of taps and toilets have neglected this most basic biological phenomenon affecting half of humanity. This is a violation of women's rights on multiple fronts (Winkler and Roaf, 2015). As a girl progresses from puberty to womanhood, reproductive tract infections potentially triggered by poor Menstrual Hygiene Management (MHM) could affect her reproductive health (Das et al., 2015). Women and girls must be able to demand with confidence what services and support they need to manage menstruation, post-partum bleeding, fibroids, or other abnormal uterine bleeding at home, school, and work. This includes but is not limited to safe spaces for changing, washing, use of the right materials in the right quantity, safe disposal, pain medication, and counselling (WSSCC, 2013).

- **Forgotten and isolated**: Consultations with elderly people (aged 70 years or over) across South Asia revealed that this is a completely invisible, neglected group for whom defecation, washing, and bathing are the biggest daily challenge surrounded with risks, fear, discomfort, and indignity. Men whose wives had passed away said that their biggest problem was collecting, storing, and carrying water. Older women reported struggling with water collection and carrying. Falls and spills were common including serious injuries. After defecation, older men and women often walk home first and then wash properly as they are unable to do all this while holding onto a stick (see Figure 16.4).

  Nobody speaks to us or asks us what we need. We do not exist for the 'community' – our children do not visit us, they are just waiting for us to die. We defecate in the open half standing as we cannot squat. We use a stick for support all through. It is difficult to defecate, wash, bathe with poor eye sight, hearing, weak limbs, long distances and no water.[7]

Figure 16.4 We defecate in the open as we cannot squat: consultations with elderly men and women, Nepal, 2015

Source: Javier Acebal

Putting non-discrimination into policy and practice: West and Central Africa and India

The WSSCC UN Women Joint Programme in Senegal, Niger, and Cameroon[8] and WSSCC's policy and learning partnerships with the Government of India both illustrate the power of breaking the silence with visionary and practical government counterparts for the twin goals of inclusion and sustainability.

The Joint Programme on Gender, Hygiene and Sanitation was launched on 8 March 2014 by WSSCC and UN Women with the aim of establishing a framework nationally and regionally by which all women and girls in West and Central Africa will benefit in a sustained manner from appropriate WASH services. The strategic ambition of the programme is to transform policies in Senegal, Cameroon, and Niger so that women and girl's realities, needs, and demands are clearly articulated and to match these with budgets, adapted public facilities on the ground, more equitable sharing of WASH burdens, and women and girls' systematic participation in decision-making and monitoring. MHM is the programme's entry point for breaking the silence and opening the door to the realization of a host of women's rights in participation, WASH, health, education, work, and shelter.

Building the evidence

Existing national policies including Senegal's development plan, sectoral strategies on health, education, WASH, budgets and monitoring frameworks, hygiene code, and gender strategies were analysed while formative research documented people's perceptions of actual conditions in Louga and Kedougou Senegal (WSSCC and UN Women, 2015c), Kye-ossi and Bafoussam in Cameroon (WSSCC and UN Women, 2015b). The studies confirm the complete exclusion of women and girls from design, planning, and decision-making in WASH, the absence of adequate and appropriate sanitation facilities in private dwellings, workplaces and markets (where women are present in large numbers), health centres, prisons, and educational establishments.

Menstruation itself is a taboo shrouded in silence and surrounded by religious restrictions (no fasting, praying, visiting holy sites), forbidden foods (ice cream, peanuts, lemon, sugar in Senegal; pistachio, mackerel and sugarcane in Cameroon), forbidden tasks (doing laundry, fishing, picking ripe fruit or vegetables (WSSCC and UN Women, 2015b), or braiding hair) or sexual restrictions (sharing the conjugal bed) (WSSCC and UN Women, 2015c) during this period. Girls are poorly prepared for their periods; over 70 per cent in Kye-ossi and Bamoungoum (WSSCC and UN Women, 2015b) did not know what was happening to them at the onset of menarche. Girls and women stayed away from school and work during their periods due to poorly maintained facilities. These findings completely corroborate WSSCC's findings during focus group discussions and surveys in schools with 12,000 women and girls during the 51 day journey with the Menstrual Hygiene Lab across five states in 2011.[9]

Building demand and capacity

WSSCC's MHM tools[10] were first developed in 2011 through an elaborate process of formative research that reviewed existing tools and their acceptability in local contexts, adapted through wide consultations in the 2012 Yatra and published in partnership with the Government of India as a simple toolbox for WASH, health, and education practitioners across the country. These have been subsequently adapted in West Africa through research and training for use in the MHM lab,[11] training of trainers events, and national and regional training for policy-makers.

Policy change

As a result of sustained, evidence-based advocacy reinforced by training of government practitioners across the country, the Ministry of Water and Sanitation amended the national policy to include menstrual hygiene management in December 2013.[12] With a change of government and the launch of the Swachh Bharat Mission on 2 October 2014, MHM was maintained as a key focus together with priority to children, adolescents, older people, and persons with disabilities (Swachh Bharat Mission guidelines, 5.9: 17).[13] In Senegal, the national strategies and policies are being amended to integrate these aspects.

Advocacy and partnership at the highest levels of government

At the 59th Commission on the Status of Women in New York, the permanent missions of Singapore and Senegal co-hosted an event in partnership with WSSCC and UN Women on 'Unlocking multiple benefits for women and girls through sanitation and hygiene in the post 2015 era'. The Minister of Drinking Water and Sanitation spoke eloquently about Senegal's commitment to integrating the needs of women and girls, disabled people, and HIV positive users into WASH services. This was repeated at AfricaSan IV in Dakar when the Ministers from Senegal and Niger reiterated commitments and practical steps to put this into action.[14] Today, Senegal boasts an inter-ministerial committee of the Ministries of Environment, Education, Health, and Gender chaired by the Ministry of Water and Sanitation to address MHM across sectors.

Changing how services look and feel on the ground

The high level advocacy above has led to systematic integration of MHM into all government coordinated project financing of WASH infrastructure in Senegal. To meet the growing demand for practical solutions on safe MHM, WSSCC has deployed an engineer in the Ministry of Water and Sanitation tasked with listening to women and girls to pilot and test practical solutions on the ground.[15] WSSCC is also facilitating learning exchanges between India and Kenya (December 2015) Senegal, Togo, and Madagascar (February 2016) so that these practical experiences can be shared with policy-makers and practitioners to accelerate change.

Measuring what we treasure

Integrating simple indicators into the national monitoring system to reflect the needs of women and girls in WASH inside and outside the home is key to ensuring that we redefine achievement. In April 2015, WSSCC in partnership with the Government of India held the first verification workshop on what constitutes ODF and how will it be measured in the long term. The outcomes of the workshop which consulted with local government at all levels from across India, divided the process of ODF achievement and consolidation into two or three phases. It was agreed that the first phase would include a basic definition[16] that ensures everyone is living in a safe environment as announced in the official government circular issued following the workshop:

> ODF is the termination of faecal-oral transmission. This is defined by:
> a) no visible faeces found in the environment/village; and b) every household as well as public/community institutions is using a safe technology option for disposal of faeces. Since ODF is not a one-time process, at least two verifications may be carried out. The first verification may be carried out within three months of the declaration to verify the ODF status. Thereafter, in order to ensure sustainability of ODF, one

more verification may be carried out after around six months of first verification (Government of India, 2015).

However, communities reproduce societal inequalities, and the planned second phase of ODF verification will discuss how states and local governments can integrate age, gender, and varying physical impairments across public toilets and WASH facilities in health centres, educational establishments, government buildings, marketplaces, transport hubs, and other public spaces.

Conclusion: redefining how and what we measure – treasuring the 'one' in everyone

Water, sanitation, and hygiene are more than services – they are human rights. It is our collective and individual duty and obligation to make them universally accessible. Staying clean, smelling good, relieving yourself every day in decent surroundings, and not suffering from thirst or the risk of drinking dirty water is about being human. Every human being has a right to live a full and productive life with safety and dignity, no matter what they look like or where they come from and regardless of their gender or sexual identity. Lack of access to basic WASH is a denial of these rights and an invisible form of discrimination. The following actions, perspectives, and attitudes will help ensure we really do leave no one behind in our efforts to achieve sanitation for all.

1. **Sustainability and equity/equal access and use** are two sides of the same coin: Ensuring that WASH services, their use, and maintenance are guaranteed for generations to come is impossible without a recognition of the diversity and needs of the clientele who will use and maintain these services. Human beings change across their life course. Services that ignore this will *not* be sustainable.
2. **Universal access and use is about the '*one* in *everyone*'**: The billions of people with poor WASH are made up of myriad individuals, from infants and their caregivers to grandparents with impairments. Each one has specific needs depending on age, gender identity, physical strength, health, and ability.
3. **Situate, contextualize and localize**: Everywhere is specific, particular, different – based on ethnicity, homelessness, occupation, culture, tradition, climate, conflict, and natural disasters.
4. **Salute the feminine and give it true voice, space, and power in WASH**: Long suffering, silent managers of WASH services on the ground – women, adolescent girls and boys, need to be accorded their due voice, resources, and defining roles. There is no better formula for sustainability with empowerment.
5. **Seek out and vanquish taboos**: Menstruation, menopause, incontinence, sexual preference, occupation, location, and status of dwelling –

sanitation is a human right – its denial is a violation of many rights but also a threat to universal sustainability of services. The first step is to break the silence at home, with those who are near and dear and empowering them in turn to spread the word. This will require spaces and platforms for users traditionally not asked and listened to followed by mechanisms for their continued involvement in design, maintenance, and upgrading. Focusing on toilets and handwashing stations without these essential steps to break the silence and eliminate stigma will result in continued exclusion and non-use.

6. **Keep services relevant, attractive, and user-friendly**: Maintenance, cleaning, upgradation, and sludge management are the bedrock of sustainability. Slipping back into old, bad habits is so much easier when facilities are blocked, smelly, unclean, locked, too far away, or too difficult to use safely. Recognizing sanitation workers of all types with good working conditions and remuneration is a first step to removing the stigma around this valuable work and achieving universal sanitation and hygiene for everyone, everywhere, all of the time.

About the author

Archana Patkar is a Programme Manager for the Water Supply and Sanitation Collaborative Council (WSSCC). Archana has been working on MHM, disability, and age-related inequalities in WASH in India, Senegal, and Niger since 2011.

Endnotes

1. Press Release 327, 'United Nations General Assembly decides to separate human rights to water and to sanitation', http://www.exteriores.gob.es/Portal/en/SalaDePrensa/NotasdePrensa/Paginas/2015_NOTAS_P/20151218_NOTA327.aspx
2. Semenarche or spermarche, refers to the beginning of development of sperm in boys' testicles at puberty. It contrasts with menarche in girls. Depending on their upbringing, cultural differences, and prior sexual knowledge, boys may have different reactions to spermarche, ranging from fear to excitement, https://en.wikipedia.org/wiki/Spermarche
3. Menarche (from the Greek for 'month' and 'beginning') is the first menstrual cycle, or first menstrual bleeding, in female humans. From both social and medical perspectives, it is often considered the central event of female puberty, as it signals the possibility of fertility, https://en.wikipedia.org/wiki/Menarche
4. Afghanistan, Bangladesh, Bhutan, India, Maldives, Nepal, Pakistan, and Sri Lanka.
5. Sixth South Asian Conference on Sanitation 'Better Sanitation Better Life', 11–13 January 2016, Dhaka, Bangladesh, http://www.sacosanvi.gov.bd/
6. FANSA-WSSCC consultation with 36 members of the transgender community India in partnership with the HIV/AIDS Alliance and Avagahana,

a community-based organization working with the transgender community, 12 November 2015, Telengana, India.

7. FANSA/WSSCC consultations with elderly men and women in Warangal District, Telangana State, India, October, 2015.
8. *WSSCC/UNWomen Joint Programme on Gender, Hygiene and Sanitation*, Information Letter No 6 (2015) http://wsscc.org/resources-feed/the-wssccun-women-joint-programme-on-gender-hygiene-and-sanitation-information-letter-no-6/, [accessed 12 February 2016]. All programme resources are available on the WSSCC website.
9. *The Nirmal Bharat Yatra - Goodwill on Wheels!* http://www.indiawaterportal.org/articles/nirmal-bharat-yatra-goodwill-wheels; Indian Girls Break Taboos on Menstrual Hygiene http://www.ipsnews.net/2014/05/indian-girls-break-taboos-menstrual-hygiene/
10. WSSCC MHM Tools are available on: http://wsscc.org/resources-feed/menstrual-wheel/?_sf_s=menstrual+wheel (English, French, Hindi, and Chinese) and 'As We Grow Up' flipbook http://wsscc.org/resources-feed/as-we-grow-up-flipbook/?_sf_s=as+we+grow+up (English, French, Hindi, and Chinese).
11. WSSCC MHM Lab http://wsscc.org/wp-content/uploads/2015/10/MHM-lab-manual-EN-LowRes.pdf
12. Modification in national policy to include MHM: http://hptsc.nic.in/M3.pdf
13. Swachh Bharat Mission guidelines, http://www.and.nic.in/archives/rdpri/downloads/guidelines_Swachh_Bharat_Mission_Gramin.pdf
14. Menstrual Hygiene Management (MHM): Possible solutions for breaking taboos, https://wssccafricasan4.wordpress.com/2015/05/27/menstrual-hygiene-management-mhm-possible-solutions-for-breaking-taboos/
15. Terms of Reference for the Engineer by the Government of Senegal http://wsscc.org/wp-content/uploads/2015/12/Avis_Recruit_Expert_GHM_SEN.pdf
16. Guidelines for ODF verification http://mdws.gov.in/sites/default/files/R_274_1441280478318.pdf

References

Das, P., Baker, K.K., Dutta, A., Swain, T., Sahoo, S., Das, B.S., Panda, B., Nayak, A., Bara, M., Bilung B., Mishra, P.R., Panigrahi, P., Cairncross, S. and Torondel, B. (2015) 'Menstrual hygiene practices, WASH access and the risk of urogenital infection in women from Odisha, India', *PLoS ONE* 10(6): e0130777 <http://dx.doi.org/10.1371/journal.pone.0130777>.
Government of India (2015) 'Guidelines for ODF verification', Ministry of Water and Sanitation, New Delhi, http://mdws.gov.in/sites/default/files/R_274_1441280478318.pdf [accessed 12 February 2016].
Kulkarni, S. and O'Reilly, K. (2015) *Sanitation Vulnerabilities: Women's Stresses and Struggles For Violence-Free Sanitation*, Research Briefing Note, Water Supply and Sanitation Collaborative Council and London School of

Hygiene and Tropical Medicine, Geneva and London, http://wsscc.org/wp-content/uploads/2015/09/Briefing_Note_2_2015_LoRes-Copy.pdf [accessed 12 February 2016].

Patkar, A. (2014) 'Menstrual hygiene management and the red thread movement', in *Sanitation for Improved Lives of Women and Children*, Report from a Seminar Organized by Sida and WaterAid, World Toilet Day, 19 November 2014, Stockholm, http://www.sida.se/globalassets/global/about-sida/vara-amnesomraden/vatten/helpdesk-report-from-world-toilet-day-1411212.pdf [accessed 12 February 2016].

Sahoo, K.C., Hulland, K.R., Caruso, B.A., Swain, R., Freeman, M.C., Panigrahi, P. and Dreibelbis, R. (2015) 'Sanitation-related psychosocial stress: a grounded theory study of women across the life-course in Odisha, India', *Social Science & Medicine* 139: 80–9 <http://dx.doi.org/10.1016/j.socscimed.2015.06.031>.

UN Water (2013) *Eliminating Discrimination and Inequalities in Access to Water and Sanitation*, UN Water, Geneva, http://www.unwater.org/fileadmin/user_upload/unwater_new/docs/UN-Water_Policy_Brief_Anti-Discrimination.pdf [accessed 12 February 2016].

Winkler, I.T. and Roaf, V. (2015) *Taking the Bloody Linen out of the Closet: Menstrual Hygiene as a Priority for Achieving Gender Equality*, Cardozo Journal of Law & Gender, http://ingawinkler.weebly.com/uploads/4/8/6/0/48601803/winkler_&_roaf_-_menstrual_hygiene.pdf [accessed 12 February 2016].

WSSCC (2013) *Training of Trainers Manual – WASH and Health for Menstrual Hygiene Management*, WSSCC Learning Series, Menstrual Health Management, Geneva, http://wsscc.org/resources-feed/training-of-trainers-manual-wash-and-health-for-menstrual-hygiene-management/ [accessed 12 February 2016].

WSSCC and FANSA (2016) *Sanitation and Hygiene in South Asia. Leave No One Behind: Voices of Women, Adolescent Girls, Elderly, Persons with Disabilities and Sanitation Workforce*, FANSA and WSSCC, Hyderabad, https://sanitationupdates.files.wordpress.com/2016/01/leave-no-one-behind-report-2016-wsscc-fansa.pdf [accessed 12 February 2016].

WSSCC/UN Women (2015a) *Menstrual Hygiene Management: Behaviours and Practices in the Louga Region, Senegal*, WSSCC and UN Women, Geneva and Dakar, http://wsscc.org/wp-content/uploads/2015/09/Louga-Study-EN-LoRes.pdf (English and French) [accessed 12 February 2016].

WSSCC/UN Women (2015b) *Menstrual Hygiene Management: Behaviour and Practices in Kye-Ossi and Bamoungoum, Cameroon*, WSSCC and UN Women, Geneva and Dakar, http://wsscc.org/resources-feed/study-menstrual-hygiene-management-behaviour-and-practices-in-kye-ossi-and-bamoungoum-cameroon/ [accessed 12 February 2016].

WSSCC/UN Women (2015c) *Menstrual Hygiene Management: Behaviour and Practices in Kedougou Region, Senegal*, http://wsscc.org/wp-content/uploads/2015/05/kedougou_study_en_lores.pdf [accessed 12 February 2016].

MHM tools

Menstrual Wheel, WSSCC, Geneva, http://wsscc.org/resources-feed/menstrual-wheel/?_sf_s=menstrual+wheel [accessed 12 February 2016] (English, French, Hindi, and Chinese).

As We Grow Up, flipbook, WSSCC, Geneva, http://wsscc.org/resources-feed/as-we-grow-up-flipbook/?_sf_s=as+we+grow+up [accessed 12 February 2016] (English, French, Hindi, and Chinese).

MHM Lab Convenor's Manual, WSSCC, Geneva, http://wsscc.org/wp-content/uploads/2015/10/MHM-lab-manual-EN-LowRes.pdf [accessed 12 February 2016].

Manual: Training of Trainers. Menstrual Hygiene Management, WSSCC, Geneva, http://wsscc.org/resources-feed/training-of-trainers-manual-wash-and-health-for-menstrual-hygiene-management/ [accessed 12 February 2016].

PART V: How to transform social norms

CHAPTER 17

Purity, pollution, and untouchability: challenges affecting the adoption, use, and sustainability of sanitation programmes in rural India

Aashish Gupta, Diane Coffey, and Dean Spears

Abstract

Despite decades of toilet construction, open defecation (OD) remains stubbornly common in rural India. The three authors, all associated with the Research Institute for Compassionate Economics (RICE), explore one of the reasons for this: the rejection of affordable pit latrines – particularly the emptying of them – because they are considered ritually polluting. The research for this chapter was conducted as part of the Sanitation Quality Use Access and Trends (SQUAT) survey with Sangita Vyas, Nikhil Srivastav, and Payal Hathi; it was an initiative supported by the Bill & Melinda Gates Foundation and the International Growth Centre. SQUAT set out to answer the question: why is OD so widespread in India? People were interviewed in 3,235 households in the rural 'Hindi Heartland' – Rajasthan, Madhya Pradesh, Haryana, Uttar Pradesh, and Bihar. A parallel qualitative study involved in-depth interviews with 100 individuals in Nepal, Haryana, Uttar Pradesh, and Gujarat (see Coffey et al., 2014a and b). This chapter draws heavily on these two studies. It goes on to suggest some ways in which the restrictive social norms related to the use and maintenance of low-cost sanitation facilities can be challenged.

Keywords: Open defecation, Latrine pits, India, Caste, Untouchability

Introduction

Sanitation is widely recognized as an important determinant of early child health, especially where population density is high (Cutler and Miller, 2005; Hathi et al., 2014). Poor sanitation spreads bacterial, viral, and parasitic infections, including diarrhoea, polio, cholera, and hookworm (Feachem et al., 1983; Chambers and von Medeazza, 2014). Recent research highlights the continuing importance of improving sanitation in developing countries for sustaining reductions in mortality and morbidity (Humphrey, 2009; Spears, 2013).

http://dx.doi.org/10.3362/9781780449272.017

Yet, India, home to 60 per cent of the people who defecate in the open, stubbornly resists efforts to eliminate open defecation (OD), even as this behaviour becomes less common in the rest of the world. Why does OD persist in India? Why is the use and sustainability of two-pit Indian government latrines, which cost about US$200, so low? And what challenges do behaviour change campaigns, in particular Community-Led Total Sanitation (CLTS), face in India?

This chapter limits itself to a discussion of the role played by caste and untouchability in severely constraining the sustainability of sanitation programmes in India. We are not arguing that this is the only challenge facing programmes such as CLTS in India, but reducing OD in India would be impossible without understanding and challenging notions of purity and pollution which prevent Indians from adopting and using latrines.

Many people resist sanitation behaviour change because they see benefits from OD. This is true in India. OD is socially acceptable behaviour in rural India (Coffey et al., 2014a), while using a simple toilet might be considered a sign of weakness, infirmity, or old-age. Using a toilet might be socially acceptable for a young newly-wed daughter-in-law, and might even be encouraged, but is certainly not desirable behaviour for many other people in rural areas of India.

An important reason why people in rural India do not use pit toilets is anxieties related to filling of the pit and the need for its subsequent cleaning once the pit fills up. These anxieties are driven by beliefs in practices of purity and pollution, rooted in India's centuries-old caste system (Coffey et al., 2014b), and are explored in this article.[1]

Contexts and comparisons

Of all the countries in the world, sanitation challenges are the gravest in India. Most of the world's OD occurs in India, and most Indians defecate in the open. As Figure 17.1 shows, Africa is nine times as large as India in land area, but the number of people without latrines in India is more than three times that of Africa. The total number of rural people without a toilet in the whole of Africa was 182.5 million in 2012 (WHO and UNICEF, 2014). Considering a household size of 5.4 persons per household (Government of India, 2012) and that more than 116 million households did not own a toilet in India, at least 626 million people defecated in the open in 2011.

India has, by far, the highest density of OD, which means that babies growing up in India are exposed to the worst faecal disease environment in the world. This disease environment is worsening over time. From 108 million households defecating in the open in 2001, India had 116 million households doing this in its rural areas in 2011 (Government of India, 2012).

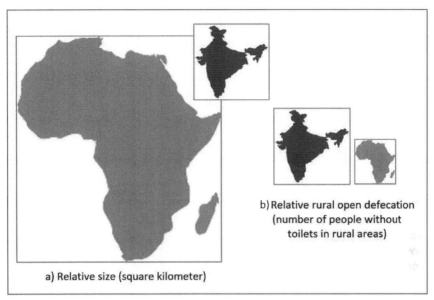

Figure 17.1 Comparison of India and Africa, by size and OD in rural areas
Source: Authors' calculations from WHO and UNICEF (2014)

Over the past two decades, India has had many sanitation programmes, and millions of latrines have been constructed by the government. Starting from the Central Rural Sanitation Programme in 1986, Indian governments have advocated using a 'demand-driven' approach but, in practice, they continue to prioritize the top-down construction of toilets (Hueso and Bell, 2013; Srivastav and Gupta, 2015a).[2] While the guidelines of the Total Sanitation Campaign (started in 1999), the Nirmal Bharat Abhiyan (started in 2012), and the Swachh Bharat (Clean India) Mission (started in 2014) advocate behaviour change campaigns and use CLTS approaches such as 'triggering', in practice most funds are devoted to the construction of toilets and, with few staff knowledgeable about behaviour change approaches, the consequence is that behaviour change strategies are weak and limited in scope (Sanan, 2011).[3]

Between 2001 and 2011, the Indian Government claimed to have built 78 million toilets in rural areas (Government of India, 2015). In the period between 2001 and 2011, the number of rural households increased by about 30 million. So by 2011 the number of households not owning a toilet should have declined by 48 million (from 78 million to 30 million). Yet, when the results of the 2011 census related to household assets were published, it was revealed that the number of households not owning a toilet had actually increased to 116 million (see Figure 17.2).

Most of the toilets constructed by the government were not in use in 2011, and many were not actually constructed in the first place because of corruption or a lack of demand (Hueso and Bell, 2013). Construction programmes in India

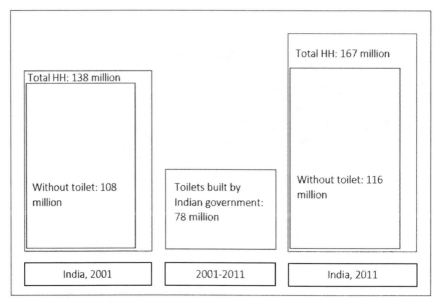

Figure 17.2 OD and toilet construction in rural India, 2001–2011

Note: HH = households

Source: Author's calculations from Census 2011 (Government of India, 2012) and NBA administrative data (Government of India, 2015)

are known to be corrupt and, in this case, the government was constructing something many if not most people did not want.[4] A lot of toilets that were constructed were repurposed into walls or roofs.

Across the world, more than 1.7 billion people are estimated to own some kind of a pit latrine (Graham and Polizotto, 2013). It is because of the ownership and use of simple pit toilets that OD is just 3 per cent in Bangladesh, 13 per cent in Kenya, 15 per cent in Afghanistan, and 23 per cent in neighbouring Pakistan. In countries defined as 'low-income' by the World Bank, OD is about 21 per cent. In sub-Saharan countries, about 25 per cent of the population defecates in the open.

Figure 17.3, which presents UNICEF-WHO Joint Monitoring Programme data on the types of toilets used in different countries, illustrates this point. The population is split into two categories, OD and unimproved or shared sanitation. The rest of the population, not shown in Figure 17.3, has access to improved sanitation – more expensive toilets, such as septic tanks.[5]

All countries listed in the figure have a lower per capita GDP than India. The data for India show that, even though India is richer than all other countries, no country listed has a smaller fraction of unimproved or shared sanitation.

Many countries, in contrast, have both a lower fraction of the population defecating in the open and a lower fraction with improved sanitation. In India, only 16 per cent of the population uses inexpensive toilets, compared with 40

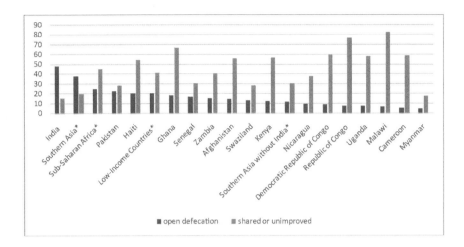

Figure 17.3 Indians do not use simple toilets

*Categories as defined by the World Bank in WDI 2015.

Source: Authors' calculations from WHO and UNICEF (2014)

per cent in Bangladesh, and 45 per cent for sub-Saharan Africa overall. Although Figure 17.3 only presents country-level statistics, the contrast for rural India is even starker: only 6 per cent of rural Indians use a simple toilet.

As for the sustainability of its sanitation programmes, and as stated above, India's record is probably the worst in the world. No other country that has invested as much as India in toilet construction has such a high rate of OD.[6] However, it is only recently that the scale of the failure has been recognized. Even in 2010 the Secretary of the Ministry of Drinking Water and Sanitation could say in a foreword to a World Bank Water and Sanitation Program review of India's Total Sanitation Campaign:

> The TSC can be considered one of the most effective programmes in rural sanitation across the world for its focus on a community-led, demand-driven approach in reaching total sanitation to villages across the country, resulting in rural populations living in a clean, healthy environment (WSP, 2011).

The following year, the release of the 2011 census (Government of India, 2012) made such optimistic judgements far less tenable, giving credence to studies which criticized the implementation of the Total Sanitation Campaign, such as those by Hueso and Bell (2013) and Barnard et al. (2013).

So why, given the extensive sanitation construction programmes in India, does OD persist on such a large scale? The following section focuses on the views people have about the government-promoted pit latrines, as revealed in the surveys carried out in rural northern India.

Caste matters

A small but growing amount of literature documents the importance of caste and purity and pollution for sanitation campaigns in India. Coffey et al. (2014c) and Lyla Mehta in her introductory chapter to Mehta and Movik (2011) discuss the implications of fragmentation along caste and gender lines in rural India for community-led approaches in particular and participative approaches in general. Mehta and Movik (2011) say: 'It is true that CLTS discourses draw on a rather idealized notion of "community" which in reality may be conflict ridden and moulded by gender, power, and patron/client relations and inequalities'.

Recent articles have argued that the use of patriarchal notions of veiling, women's modesty, and sexual violence faced by women may reinforce patriarchal social norms while harming the use of toilets by men (Srivastav and Gupta, 2015b; Coffey et al., 2014d).[7]

As for caste, there is a long tradition of research on caste and its role in undermining cooperation, development interventions, and programmes in rural India (a point originally made by Ambedkar 1979). Recent literature on its role in undermining sanitation programmes is also emerging. For instance, Coffey et al. (2014c) and Spears and Lamba (2013) discuss the implications of village conflict in India for caste campaigns. Ending OD is a public good and requires social cooperation, but most villages in India are affected by caste hierarchy, social distance, and adversarial caste relations. Both these papers find that OD is more common in villages with more caste conflict. They argue that community approaches emphasize cooperation among villagers, which might be hard to generate because of caste hierarchy.

We submit that there is a critical need for all sanitation programmes to address the challenges posed by attitudes related to purity and pollution – attitudes that deepen social inequalities and reinforce the inflexibility of power structures. Sanitation programmes in India need to promote a contrary social norm, where OD is no longer considered acceptable, and where there is an appreciation of the benefits of sustainable sanitation.[8]

For rural Indians, size matters

The World Health Organization promotes the use of inexpensive toilets with pits of about 50 cubic feet (1.4 m³) that interrupt the spread of disease by safely containing faeces underground (WHO, 1996). These toilets can be simple pit latrines, or what are called 'pour-flush' latrines. Those that were provided by the government under the Nirmal Bharat Abhiyan, and those which are proposed under the Swachh Bharat Mission, are slightly fancier versions of the WHO recommended toilets, because they have brick and mortar superstructures and ceramic sub-structures.

During our survey, one man interviewed in rural Uttar Pradesh had received one of the government toilets. Rather than using it as a toilet, his wife used it as a place to wash clothes. This is what he said:

> See, all these latrines that have been built, they are just for show. I am telling you openly. They are just for show. Is the government blind? These pits, which are four feet deep, how long are people going to use them? When someone makes a pit that is 10 feet by 10 feet, he obviously applies some logic in wanting to construct such a deep pit. He puts a cement slab on it, attaches a pipe [...] What will he do in these small latrines? These are to be used if it's dark and you have a problem. The government blind; it's giving so much money [...] for people to eat it away.

So this man suspects that the pits the government are providing are small because those constructing them are embezzling some of the money. It seems, then, that the government programmes have done little to inform the public about the specifications and use of the toilets.

But we found that people's aversion to small pit latrines was common, even for people who you would expect to have a better understanding. In one village we visited the home of an Accredited Social and Health Activist (ASHA), a person who assists in organizing health promotion activities in her neighbourhood. Her village was one where the government had recently constructed toilets for all the households in the village. She herself had a newly constructed two-pit latrine, just outside the house. When we asked her about it, she told us without hesitation that sometimes her three children use it, but she and her husband go in the open. When we asked her why, she said, 'The toilet outside is fake!'

Very often the people we interviewed described the government-provided toilets as *nakli*, which means 'fake'. They also use the English word 'temporary'. Or they say the latrine is *keval emergency ke liye*, 'only for use in an emergency'. They sometimes call them *khilona* ('toy') or refer to them as *dikhavati* ('just for show'). As for the superstructure, this is much appreciated. The brick-and-mortar construction is better than the *kachha* (mud) houses that many rural Indians live in. But they do strongly resist the idea of defecating in a toilet in which the faeces are confined in, what they perceive as, a small pit.

As another man said, 'The pit of the latrine is small, and so it fills up very quickly. That's why, I mean, we don't go, so that women in the household can go, and men can go outside. That's why a lot of people don't prefer going inside the latrine.'

In reaction to these responses, in the SQUAT survey and in-depth interviews, we asked respondents about the kinds of toilets they would find acceptable, and about ones they would like to have. Figure 17.4 shows the size of pits recommended by the WHO (1996); those recommended by the Indian Government in its 2012 guidelines; and the median pit size among toilets owned by households interviewed for the SQUAT survey. Among toilets that were being used by at least one member of the household, less than 4 per cent had pits that were 60 cubic feet (1.7 m^3) or less.

The median pit size of a private toilet that is being used by at least one household member is 250 cubic feet (7.1 m^3). Figure 17.4 also plots a 10 ft by 10 ft by 10 ft pit (28.3 m³), the ideal pit size as described by many of the respondents in the interviews.

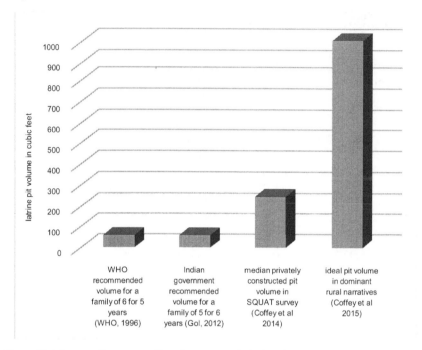

Figure 17.4 Comparative perspective of recommended pit volumes and actual and ideal pit volumes in rural India

Source: Coffey et al., 2014b

Why size matters

It is clear that the main reason why people reject small pits is that they believe they fill up quickly and that they have to be cleaned manually. Many people wrongly believe that these pits fill up in a matter of months, rather than years, and that they require frequent manual emptying.

It is true that mechanical emptying of small pits is impractical, because it is excessively costly to pump small quantities of sewage, and because simple toilets are often built in places that are difficult for vacuum trucks to access. Emptying service providers, whether public or private, are uncommon and hard to find. For these reasons, mechanical emptying services are uncommon in rural India. Therefore, in order to avoid emptying latrine pits, many people make septic tanks so large that they do not need to be emptied in their lifetimes.

A man in Uttar Pradesh who defecates in the open and does not own a toilet explained, 'pit emptying does not happen here [...] You would get a new pit dug so deep that it would never fill up'. A woman with a 450 cubic foot (12.7 m³) toilet in Gujarat explained why her household had invested so much money in the pit, 'if we made [the pit] less expensively, it would not last a lifetime.'

Still, why do rural Indians resist the idea of cleaning a pit, even if they are offered the explanation that the contents of the pit, if left to dry, turn into manure after a few months, and even when they are told that the government-provided toilets take much longer to fill than they think?

Caste and untouchability in rural India

To answer this question, we need to understand notions of purity and pollution rooted in the caste system in India. Especially in rural India, faeces are seen to be ritually polluting. Toilets with pits are seen as places which hold faeces near the house. The house is a place which is supposed to remain pure. And leach pit latrines,[9] as opposed to septic tanks, are particularly polluting because they allow water contained in faeces to seep into the ground.

Although some conservative rural Hindus find toilets of any sort distasteful (on this, see Rukmini, 2015), most people feel that expensive toilets with large pits or septic tanks are not polluting, but rather are a useful addition to a wealthy person's home. Expensive toilets with large pits or septic tanks help their owners avoid pollution, particularly because they help avoid the problem of pit emptying.

Rural Indians abhor the idea of emptying out a latrine pit themselves. Dealing with faeces is considered the responsibility of *Bhangis* (also referred to as the *Mehtar/Valmiki/Jamadar* caste in rural north India), the lowest caste in the caste system. Members of other castes think that they would become like *Bhangis,* or the lowest caste even within the untouchable castes, if they empty out a latrine pit themselves. Although most intense among higher caste Hindus, these attitudes are prevalent among 'lower' caste Hindus, including *Dalits,* as well as Muslims.

Bhangis are a historically marginalized caste, who had the responsibility of dealing with collecting faeces from latrines that require daily servicing, sweeping streets, and collecting used plates in weddings and other rural functions. They are among the lowest in the caste hierarchy. Indeed, *Bhangis* often face discrimination by other discriminated castes such as *Chamars* (leather-workers). *Bhangis* and other low castes, while still facing discrimination, have improved their bargaining power over the years, helped in part by local struggles, democratic voting rights, and basic legal protections.

Even so, this change has come slowly and, while there has been an improvement in their lot, marginalization continues. Today, untouchability and caste-based social exclusion are slowly being renegotiated in rural India (Jaffrelot, 2005). The exclusion of Dalits from schools and water sources is less common than it once was, but it is still common for high caste Hindus to refuse to eat food or take water from the houses of Dalits and to exclude untouchables from temples (Shah et al., 2006).

The fact that Dalits perform 'dirty' work is often used as evidence of their permanent ritual pollution, and it has been used as a justification for excluding them from schools, public water sources, and more dignified employment (Ambedkar, 1979). An important part of *Dalits'* struggle for equality has been through resistance to performing the kinds of degrading tasks that are associated with untouchability (Zelliot, 1992; Valmiki, 2003).

Because of historical and continued discrimination and oppression, *Bhangis*, justifiably, do not want to clean faeces and do other 'degrading' work. Other castes can see this, and now think that they would have to either pay a larger sum for a *Bhangi* to clean pits, or that *Bhangis* are no longer available to do this work. In some cases *Bhangis* do continue to do such work, but the feudal relationships of the past have weakened and upper-castes find it harder to command them to do their bidding (Desai and Dubey, 2012). In rural India, these three factors combine to create the situation that the minimally accepted toilet that a rural Indian would use without worry of pollution would have to fulfil at least two requirements: it will need a very large septic tank, so that it need not be emptied-out for decades; and if the pit is near the house, then it would need to be *pakka* (permanent) and cemented, so that faeces and their 'pollution' could be contained.

We asked a young and educated Brahmin (high-caste) man in rural north India if he would be willing to clean his latrine pit. His response was what we expected it to be. 'We will not be able to do it. I mean, this depends on your thinking and your strength. People can do it, but we can't do it [...] because of the 'gandagi' we cannot do it.'

In rural India, *gandagi* can mean many things. It can refer to faeces, or anything that is dirty, either ritually or physically. It is derived from the word *ganda*, which could mean dirty, impure, or ethically wrong. Our follow-up question to him was, 'Why do some people clean it then?' 'This is because it is their work,' he said. 'They belong to the Bhangi caste, the caste which is for doing this work [...] No one from any other caste will do this work. It's their sole responsibility [...] We won't be able to do it, why should we lie to you.'

Rural Indians, even if they want to empty out the pit themselves, worry about the social consequences of such an action. A man who belonged to a caste that was low but higher than the *Bhangis* told us that if he emptied his own pit, he would be considered a *Bhangi* by his village. He also worried about being ostracized, 'of course, they will throw one out of the village, whether they be Hindu or Muslim'.

Implications for sanitation policies and actions

Forces of social inequality, such as caste, patriarchy, or for that matter racism, are difficult to tackle through the available tools of public policy, even if governments are committed to tackling them. Public policies designed to reduce discrimination, social hierarchy, or inequality are likely to take a long time to bring results. In India, governments have a limited capacity and interest in ending this discrimination and hierarchy, despite constitutional commitments to do so. While caste and hierarchy are likely to remain important inhibiting influences on behaviour for many years, interventions can be proposed to accelerate change in behaviour and social norms relating to sanitation and hygiene.

These interventions fall into three categories:

Interventions related to pits and their emptying:

- *Pit size.* Deeper and larger pits can be recommended by the government. Except where there is endemic flooding, the water table is very close to the ground, or rock close to the surface, pits can be deeper than 4 feet (1.2 m). These pits can also be built cheaply, for instance, by using rings instead of bricks. The government can explicitly communicate that deeper pits built using private investments are welcome.[10]
- *Pit emptying.* One potentially important idea would be to correct misinformation among villagers about how simple twin-pit latrines work. Such awareness campaigns through mass and local media would also have to explicitly address the mistaken idea that these pits 'fill quickly'. Dispelling misinformation might involve demonstrating that latrine pits actually last a long time. Pit emptying can be a service provided or commercialized:
  - Search for, innovate with, and introduce light, cheap pit-emptying technology like the Oxfam gulper that does not require manual contact with shit. Learning from Bangladesh could be useful here.[11] Perhaps subsidizing pit-emptying hardware for local entrepreneurs will be needed.
  - Search for Indian entrepreneurs who have already started emptying pits and give them prominent recognition.
- *Popularizing harmless fertilizer.* Search for households with twin pits which have emptied their second pit and found it harmless and a valuable fertilizer.[12] Exploit and publicize positive deviance in this respect. Encourage members of such households to become natural leaders and demonstrate to others (with consent from the families). Those who empty their pits themselves can be given rewards, and celebrated.

Rapid action learning and sharing

Rapid Action Learning Units (RALUs) at national, state, and district levels, are proposed in the Swachh Bharat Mission (Gramin) Guidelines (Ministry of Drinking Water and Sanitation, 2014). Rapid action learning includes searching for and sharing innovations and good practices, and initiating and learning from others. These approaches can be applied to the interventions listed above, with rapid and extensive sharing of lessons learned and successful practices (Government of India and Institute of Development Studies, 2015).[13]

Social norms of purity and pollution

- *Confront notions of purity and pollution.* Potential areas for experimentation include teaching people about the germ theory of disease (which in itself might tackle some notions of purity and pollution) and communicating that emptying a pit in which faeces have decomposed is not manual scavenging.
- *Political leadership.* The Indian Prime Minister has raised the profile of sanitation. There is potential for deepening this commitment through the national campaign of the Swachh Bharat Mission (Gramin), with political leaders confronting behavioural norms as well as notions of purity and pollution. These efforts can also include spiritual and other natural leaders. Ground level government functionaries, such as ASHAs and village heads, can also be used to dispel misinformation, while they can be required to use a toilet themselves.
- *Shit stunts all castes.* Pilot information, education, and communication (IEC) approaches which stress how faecally transmitted infections inhibit growth and stunt children, and how this affects their life prospects with poorer performance and lower attendance in school, impaired cognitive development, and lower earnings later in life.

Along with piloting these ideas, it would be vital not to reinforce existing inequalities of gender and caste in sanitation campaigns. This is not just a theoretical problem, sanitation campaigns in India have often relied on promoting the construction of toilets while appealing to patriarchal notions of women's seclusion to the household and veiling (on this, see Srivastav and Gupta, 2015b). India is by far the biggest hurdle in achieving a world free of OD, and solutions to the problem aren't obvious. Given the scope of India's sanitation problem, it will be important to experiment with these and other ideas that take seriously rural Indians' reasons for continuing to defecate in the open.

About the authors

Aashish Gupta is a PhD Student in Demography at the University of Pennsylvania. Aashish Gupta was a research fellow at the Research Institute for Compassionate Economics, 2013–2015.
Diane Coffey is a Visiting Economist at the Indian Statistical Institute and Executive Director at the Research Institute for Compassionate Economics.
Dean Spears is a Visiting Economist at the Indian Statistical Institute and Executive Director at the Research Institute for Compassionate Economics.

Notes

1. The caste system is a system of hereditary social stratification prevalent in South Asia, primarily in Hindu society, in which members of society are divided into castes or *jatis*. Amebdkar (1979) calls it a system of 'graded inequality' with castes considered high or low based on relative degrees of ritual purity or

pollution and of social status. In the caste system, a large number of castes are considered 'untouchable' and permanently polluted because of their hereditary menial occupations. These untouchable castes call themselves *Dalits*, and the caste associated with dealing with faeces, the *Balmikis*, faces discrimination from higher castes as well as *Dalit* castes considered less polluting than them.

2. Srivastav and Gupta (2015a) also provide figures on spending and budgetary allocation towards sanitation.

3. Also on the Swachh Bharat Mission see Vyas (2015) and Srivastav and Gupta (2015a).

4. On corruption in the construction business in India, see KPMG (2011). For reporting on missing or 'ghost' toilets, see *Economic Times* (2013).

5. For definitions of 'improved' and 'unimproved' toilets see UNICEF and WHO (2014).

6. It has been argued that even if the Indian Government constructed a toilet for every household that doesn't have one, most Indians would still defecate in the open.

7. On this topic also see Chatterjee (2014). This is a long report from Katra Sadatganj, a village which made international headlines after two girls were found hanging from a tree after they had gone to defecate in the open. Chatterjee reports that in the village, many people had received toilets from the government but did not use them because they thought that their pits were too small.

8. On designing interventions that change social norms see Bicchieri (2006).

9. When we say leach pit latrines, we mean the two-pit latrines built by the government of India as part of its sanitation programmes, and which allow water to seep into the soil but keep faecal matter within the pit.

10. This recommendation would go well with giving people a bouquet of toilet options and designs to choose from, which is already a part of government sanitation programme guidelines (Ministry of Drinking Water and Sanitation, 2014) and which have shown promising results in some areas (Sethuraman, 2015).

11. For a review of pit emptying technologies in developing countries see Thye et al. (2011). Technologies that are not seen as 'polluting' by rural Indians or help avoid contact with faeces may have a higher likelihood of adoption.

12. It would have to be explicitly mentioned in this publicity that the fertilizer is harmless.

13. Government of India and the Institute of Development Studies (2015) compiled the report and proceedings of a recent workshop on rapid learning, and included insights from several case studies, http://www.communityledtotalsanitation.org/resource/getting-swachh-bharat-gramin-faster-through-rapid-action-learning-and-sharing-workshop

References

Ambedkar, B.R. (1979) *Annihilation of Caste: Dr. Babasaheb Ambedkar Writings and Speeches*, compiled by Vasant Moon, Education Department, Government of Maharashtra.

Barnard, S., Routray, P., Majorin, F., Peletz, R., Boisson, S., Sinha, A., and Clas-
sen, T. (2013) 'Impact of Indian Total Sanitation Campaign on latrine
coverage and use: a cross-sectional study in Orissa three years following programme implementation', *PLoS ONE* 8(8): e71438 <http://dx.doi.
org/10.1371/journal.pone.0071438>.

Bicchieri, C. (2006) *The Grammar of Society: the Nature and Dynamics of Social
Norms*, Cambridge University Press, Cambridge.

Chambers, R. and von Medeazza, G. (2014) *Reframing Undernutrition: Faecally-
Transmitted Infections and the 5 As*, IDS Working Paper 450, Institute of
Development Studies, Brighton.

Chatterjee, P. (2014) 'Going to toilet in Katra Sadatganj', *Indian Express*, 8 June
2014.

Coffey, D., Gupta, A., Hathi, P., Khurana, D., Spears, D., Srivastav, N. and Vyas,
S. (2014a) 'Revealed preference for open defecation: evidence from a new
survey in rural North India', *Economic & Political Weekly* 49(38): 43–55.

Coffey, D., Gupta, A., Hathi, P., Spears, D., Srivastav, N. and Vyas, S. (2014b)
*The Puzzle of Widespread Open Defecation in Rural India: Evidence from New
Qualitative and Quantitative Data'*, r.i.c.e. Working Paper, Research Institute
for Compassionate Economics.

Coffey, D., Hathi, P. and Spears, D. (2014c) *What's So Communal About
Communities in India? 'Social Distance, Village Conflict and Open Defecation
in India'*, poster, Research Institute for Compassionate Economics, http://
riceinstitute.org/presentation/social-distance-village-conflict-and-open-
defecation/ [accessed 18 February 2016].

Coffey, D., Gupta, A., Hathi, P., Spears, D. and Vyas, S. (2014d) 'Toilets are
urgently needed in rural India, but don't imagine they will reduce rape',
Scroll.in, 7 June 2014.

Cutler, D.M. and Miller, G. (2005) 'The role of public health improvements in
health advances: the twentieth-century United States', *Demography* 42(1):
1–22 <http://dx.doi.org/10.1353/dem.2005.0002>.

Desai, S., and Dubey, A. (2012) 'Caste in 21st century India: competing
narratives', *Economic and Political Weekly*, 46(11): 40.

Economic Times (2013) 'India "missing" 3.75 crore toilets: sanitation activists',
The Economic Times, 19 November 2013, http://articles.economictimes.
indiatimes.com/2013-11-19/news/44242708_1_toilets-open-defecation-
sanitation [accessed 18 February 2016].

Feachem, R., Mara, D. and Bradley, D. (1983) *Sanitation and Disease: Health
Aspects of Excreta and Wastewater Management*, World Bank Studies in Water
Supply and Sanitation 3, World Bank/John Wiley & Sons, Washington DC.

Government of India (2012) *Availability and Type of Latrine Facility: 2001–2011*,
ORGI, New Delhi, http://www.censusindia.gov.in/2011census/Hlo-series/
HH08.html [accessed 26 February 2016].

Government of India (2015) *[Format A7] All India Figures of Physical Achievement*,
Ministry of Drinking Water and Sanitation, New Delhi, http://sbm.gov.
in/TSC/Report/Physical/RptYearWiseCountryLevelAch.aspx?id=Home
[accessed 18 February 2016].

Government of India and Institute of Development Studies (2015) *Getting to
Swachh Bharat Gramin Faster Through Rapid Action Learning and Sharing: A
Rapid Action Learning and Sharing Workshop on Innovations in Rural Sanita-
tion*, Workshop Report, http://www.communityledtotalsanitation.org/

sites/communityledtotalsanitation.org/files/Full_Report_Rapid_Action_ Learning_Sharing_Workshop.pdf [accessed 18 February 2016].

Graham, J.P. and Polizzotto, M.L. (2013) 'Pit latrines and their impacts on groundwater quality: a systematic review', *Environmental Health Perspectives* 121: 521–30 <http://dx.doi.org/10.1289/ehp.1206028>.

Hathi, P., Haque, S., Pant, L., Coffey, D. and Spears, D. (2014) *Place and Child Health: The Interaction of Population Density and Sanitation in Developing Countries*, Policy Research Working Paper 7124, World Bank, Washington, DC.

Hueso, A. and Bell, B. (2013) 'An untold story of policy failure: the Total Sanitation Campaign in India', *Water Policy*, 15(6): 1001–17 <http://dx.doi. org/10.2166/wp.2013.032>.

Humphrey, J.H. (2009) 'Child undernutrition, tropical enteropathy, toilets, and handwashing', *The Lancet* 374: 1032–5 <http://dx.doi.org/10.1016/ S0140-6736(09)60950-8>.

Jaffrelot, C. (2005) *Dr. Ambedkar and Untouchability: Fighting the Indian Caste System*, Columbia University Press, Cambridge.

KPMG (2011) *Survey on Bribery and Corruption: Impact on Economy and Business Environment*, KPMG, New Delhi, http://www.kpmg.com/IN/en/ IssuesAndInsights/ThoughtLeadership/KPMG_Bribery_Survey_Report_ new.pdf [accessed 18 February 2016].

Mehta, L. and Movik, S. (2011) *Shit Matters: The Potential of Community Led Total Sanitation*, Practical Action Publishing, Rugby.

Ministry of Drinking Water and Sanitation (2014) *Guidelines for Swachh Bharat Mission (Gramin)*, Government of India, New Delhi.

Rukmini, S. (2015) 'The battle for toilets and minds', *The Hindu*, 4 April 2015.

Sanan, D. (2011) 'The CLTS story in India: the sanitation story of the millennium', in L. Mehta and S. Movik, *Shit Matters: The Potential of Community Led Total Sanitation*, Practical Action Publishing, Rugby.

Sethuraman, S. (2015) 'Here's the secret behind Rajasthan's sanitation revolution', *TheWire.in*, 19 May 2015.

Shah, G., Mander, H., Thorat, S., Deshpande, S. and Baviskar, A. (2006) *Untouchability in Rural India*, Sage, New Delhi.

Spears, D. (2013) *How Much International Variation in Child Height can Sanitation Explain?* World Bank Policy Research Working Paper 6351, World Bank, Washington, DC.

Spears, D. and Lamba, S. (2013) 'Caste, cleanliness and cash: effects of caste based political reservations in Rajasthan on a Sanitation prize', *Journal of Development Studies* 49(3): 1592–1606 <http://dx.doi.org/10.1080/0022038 8.2013.828835>.

Srivastav, N. and Gupta, A. (2015a) 'Like its predecessors, Modi's sanitation programme is struggling', *LiveMint*, 4 June 2015.

Srivastav, N. and Gupta, A. (2015b) 'Why using patriarchal messaging to promote toilets is a bad idea', *TheWire.in*, 7 June 2015.

Thye, Y.P., Templeton, M.R. and Ali, M. (2011) 'A critical review of technologies for pit latrine emptying in developing countries', *Critical Reviews in Environmental Science and Technology* 41(20): 1793–819 <http://dx.doi.org/1 0.1080/10643389.2010.481593>.

Valmiki, O. (2003) *Joothan: A Dalit's Life*, Columbia University Press, New York.

Vyas, S. (2015) 'Not a clean sweep', *Indian Express*, 21 January 2015.

Water and Sanitation Program (WSP) (2011) *A Decade of the Total Sanitation Campaign Rapid Assessment of Processes and Outcomes*, WSP, New Delhi, http://www.sswm.info/sites/default/files/reference_attachments/WSP%20 2011%20A%20Decade%20of%20the%20Total%20Sanitation%20 Campaign.pdf [accessed 4 April 2016].
WHO (1996) *Simple Pit Latrines*, Technical Report, World Health Organization, Geneva.
WHO and UNICEF (2014) *Joint Monitoring Programme (JMP) for Water Supply and Sanitation*, WHO/UNICEF, New York and Geneva, http://www.wssinfo. org/ [accessed 18 February 2016].
Zelliot, E. (1992) *From Untouchable to Dalit: Essays on the Ambedkar Movement*, Manohar, New Delhi.

CHAPTER 18

Using social norms theory to strengthen CATS impact and sustainability

Therese Dooley, Louise Maule, and Michael Gnilo

Abstract

Significant strides have been made through programmes such as Community Approaches to Total Sanitation (CATS), which focus on eliminating open defecation (OD) by working with communities to change their beliefs and expectations around sanitation. However, challenges of effectiveness and slippage remain which can limit longer-term sustainability. Social Norms Theory (SNT) is a framework which can be used to explain why CATS works, and help us improve both the effectiveness and sustainability of our sanitation interventions. Achieving ODF is about creating a new social norm, and in order to do this, not only do we require a change in beliefs and attitudes, but we also need to create new social expectations. In this chapter we explain SNT and discuss how the achievement of ODF is not an end point but just one step along the way to stabilizing a new social norm.

Keywords: Social norms, Behaviour change, Open defecation, CATS, Factual beliefs, Normative expectations, Phased approach, Collective action

Background

Over the past decade significant strides have been made through programmes such as Community Approaches to Total Sanitation (CATS),[1] in which the traditional model of building toilets has been replaced with a focus on eliminating open defecation (OD) by working with communities to change their beliefs and expectations around sanitation. CATS has been successful in achieving open defecation free (ODF) communities, but challenges of effectiveness and slippage can limit longer-term sustainability. What can be done to strengthen what has already been achieved and ensure the sustainability of future achievements? Can the answer be as simple as having a better understanding of social norms and of how practitioners can use that knowledge in development work?

Within UNICEF, work on health, nutrition, education, and child protection has been greatly strengthened over the last few decades by a better understanding of behaviour and social change. The WASH sector has also embraced various behavioural/social change models from the use of participatory approaches such as Self Esteem, Associative Strengths, Resourcefulness, Action Planning and Responsibility (SARAR),[2] and Participatory Hygiene and Sanitation Transformation (PHAST) in the 1980s and 1990s, to the use of Community-Led Total Sanitation

http://dx.doi.org/10.3362/9781780449272.018

(CLTS) and the socio-ecological model (Parvanta, 2011) in the 2000s to design its behaviour and social change programmes. CATS builds on and successfully uses many of the tools, methods, and theories behind these models, but we realized that in order to improve the sustainability of our interventions there was a need for us to better appreciate and understand the broader issue of social norms – what factors change, stabilize, or even create new norms within a social group?

This chapter outlines Social Norms Theory (SNT) and explains how it can be used to strengthen CATS programmes. Using a SNT framework to assess UNICEF's work on CATS critically, a number of areas of potential refinement will be highlighted which would improve ODF success rates and sustainability.

Understanding social norms

Some people identify social norms with observable, recurrent patterns of behaviour. Norms, however, cannot be identified with observable behaviour alone as social norms also express social approval or disapproval of such behaviours; they tell us how we 'ought' to act (Bicchieri and Muldoon, 2011; Rivis and Sheeran, 2003). Our preference for obeying social norms is conditional, and depends on our expectations of collective compliance. Bicchieri (2006) defines a social norm as follows (see Figure 18.1):

> A social norm is a rule of behaviour such that individuals prefer to conform to it on condition that they believe that, (a) most people in their reference network[4] conform to it (empirical[5] expectations), and (b) that most people in their reference network believe they ought to conform to it (normative[6] expectations).

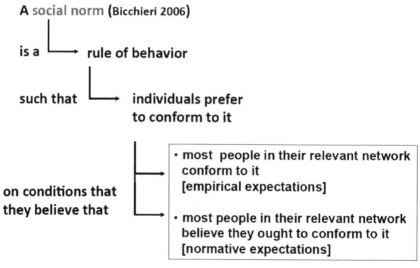

Figure 18.1 Definition of a social norm
Source: Bicchieri, 2006

In other words, people choose to follow a social norm not necessarily because they like to but because they believe people ought to behave a certain way. Because they can see that most people are behaving in that way, and they believe that they themselves ought to behave the same way. They believe people important to them expect them to behave that way too. Social norms are all about social expectations: empirical expectations (how I expect others to behave based on what I see everyone else doing), and normative expectations (how I think others think that I ought to behave).

So how does this relate to OD and CATS? The authors originally assumed that OD was a social norm in many communities. However, upon studying and analysing OD with the support of colleagues from the University of Pennsylvania[7] we realized that, in the majority of communities where OD is currently practised, it is not a social norm (Dooley, 2010). This was a very important starting point, as the authors sought to better strengthen and sustain the impact of CATS programmes on the ground and guide and support UNICEF colleagues throughout the world.

If one lives in a community where toilets do not exist, people simply defecate in the open to satisfy their bodily needs. Because this action meets their needs, it will likely be repeated. This repetition creates a habit and eventually a custom. So OD is in fact a tradition or custom[8] (see Figure 18.2), it is the easiest way to relieve oneself. In most cases, practising OD is not dependent on social expectations. A person openly defecates simply because it is an acceptable and convenient solution to the need to defecate, hence, that person prefers to continue this practice (Dooley, 2010).

copyright@Cristina Bicchieri

Figure 18.2 Diagnostic framework for behaviours
Source: Bicchieri, Penn-UNICEF Lectures on Social Norms, 2015

The main difference between a custom and a norm lies in the reasons why people follow one or the other. An important factor to understand in the context of OD is that a custom is a pattern of independent actions, but for a village to become ODF, it entails changing beliefs from 'OD is personal business' to recognizing that 'OD is everyone's business'. People need to realize that OD produces negative externalities and one person's action can result in everyone's suffering. The only way this will end is for the community to take a collective decision to stop OD together and take collective action. And in order to sustain this new behaviour over time, the decision to change also needs to be supported by both empirical and normative expectations.

In creating a new social norm we need to create a new behavioural rule – often this means using a toilet – which people choose to follow. Not necessarily because they want to or like to, or because they think it's right or it's wrong, but because they can see that everyone is conforming, and they believe that they are expected by everyone else to conform to the new behavioural rule (Dooley, 2010). Where there is a social norm, individual behaviour is influenced not just by personal knowledge or likes and dislikes, but also by social expectations and social pressure to behave in a certain way. So there has to be a collective understanding of how people are expected to behave, empirical reminders that people are conforming to these expectations, and rewards and sanctions for maintaining the right behaviour. CATS needs to address all of these issues if OD is to move from a custom/tradition to the introduction and establishment of a new social norm of ODF which is sustained over time.

Social norms theory and CATS

Bicchieri (2010–15, 2016) proposes that it is possible to create new social norms using the following five steps:

1) Changes in beliefs and attitudes;
2) Collective decision to change;
3) Coordinated action to enforce change (positive and negative sanctions);
4) Creation of a normative expectation; and
5) Reinforcement by a change in empirical expectations.

If we look at the steps within a typical CLTS programme (Kar with Chambers, 2008), we can examine how many of these support the process for creating a new social norm under Bicchieri's proposal (Dooley, 2010):

1) *Step 1.* CLTS triggering is used to facilitate the development of new beliefs and attitudes. Through this process, new factual beliefs[9] become apparent. OD has health, social, and economic costs, it is disgusting because if it is done I end up *eating my neighbour's shit*. Through this process, people develop personal beliefs around OD and feel that people should clean up their shit, use a toilet, wash their hands with soap, and dispose of their children's faeces appropriately.

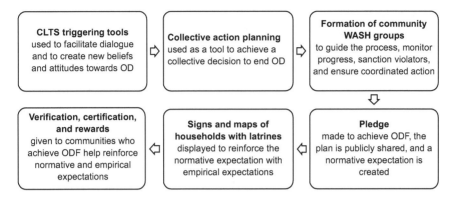

Figure 18.3 Steps towards creating new social norms in CLTS
Source: Gnilo, 2014

2) *Step 2*. Collective action planning involves group discussion. It provides an opportunity to come to a common understanding of what the problem is and what needs to be achieved. It is also used to inform a collective decision on how (and how soon) they would like to solve their issue of OD.

3) *Step 3*. Community coordination is required and is usually done through the formation of WASH committees or groups (formal or informal) that monitor progress via house-to-house visits and creation of positive and negative sanctions. This mechanism reinforces expectations to follow what was collectively decided.

4) *Step 4*. The plan is shared or a pledge is made. The public commitment creates a normative expectation. People believe that their neighbours and leaders expect them to end OD and manage their excreta appropriately (e.g. in Mali the pledge is videotaped and rebroadcast at certain points in the process).

5) *Step 5*. Signs and maps of households and latrines are put up to reinforce the normative expectation. People who start doing things are recognized. Empirical expectations reinforce the normative expectation and people see that others are disposing of shit properly, and those who do gain social rewards. Celebrations are conducted to publicize good practice. Collective rewards may be given to reinforce positive practice. A declaration is made that their village is ODF.

6) *Step 6*. Verification and certification of ODF status recognizes the achievement. This supports both the normative and empirical expectations and, in a sense, serves as the stamp of commitment by the village.

Although CLTS wasn't developed around the concepts of SNT, CLTS addresses the key elements required to create social norms: the introduction of a new behavioural rule supported by empirical and normative expectations – *I will build and use a toilet, not because I am alone in understanding its importance to me and my family, but because everyone else in the community has committed to and is using a toilet and everyone in the community thinks I ought to use one too.* However, the degree to which these components are addressed varies. A better understanding of the dynamics of social norms, and more particularly of empirical and normative expectations, would greatly enhance the process and better sustain the norm.

The process of adapting a new social norm

While many of these steps are addressed through the current CATS process, a number of areas could be reinforced to strengthen and sustain the new social norm. Without a reinforced social norms approach, we often see real change only in innovators and early adopters; and even these changes will be fragile over time, due to the absence of normative expectations within the target community and networks (Gaya, 2013; Gnilo, 2014; Maule, 2013).

It is the opinion of the authors that the weakest points in the current CATS interventions are Steps 4 and 5, particularly creating new expectations. Activities that support the creation of new expectations are alluded to by Kar and Chambers (2008) in the post-triggering component of the *CLTS Handbook*, for example, reminding the community of the target dates. Many of the activities suggested in the community action follow-up section, whether it was messaging national leaders to follow up in the community, developing spot maps, formation of committees, and even visiting other villages who are progressing faster, reinforce expectations; however these are not consistently applied across all programmes.

During the global CATS evaluation (UNICEF, 2014), we saw that where these activities were properly implemented, CATS programmes succeeded in creating normative and empirical expectations. In these programmes the creation of social norms was evidenced by genuine adoption and enforcement of community-level rules and by-laws which were accepted by all community members and cannot be transgressed without consequences. For example, fees between US$0.67 and US$1.12 were being enforced for those that openly defecated, that didn't have handwashing facilities, were not using a 'potty' for small children, or even not reporting broken toilets.

But changing expectations is an intricate process, involving trust, public pressure, meaningful collective deliberation, common pledges, and common knowledge of what the group is going to do and expects others to do. Most importantly, it has to be intentional. In the CATS evaluation, it was noted that while components of the processes to create norms were in many of the CATS programmes across the globe, success or failure against these processes was rarely analysed. The evaluation also found that the social norms concept had not fully influenced all segments of CATS programming. It was highlighted that many implementers and implementing partners still did not understand or appreciate the role expectations play in creating and, more importantly, stabilizing a social norm. It was further stated in the evaluation that, 'it is expected that a better understanding and use of the social norm concept will help increase the conversion ratio of communities triggered to ODF status achieved, which would have a strong impact on the effectiveness of CATS programmes'.

Using SNT to strengthen CATS programming

As with CLTS, within CATS we divide interventions into three main processes – pre-triggering, triggering, and post-triggering – with each process containing valid and important steps. This breakdown is necessary to ensure that all steps are undertaken, monitored, and assessed. In the early days of CATS, the tendency was to focus just on triggering and certification, with limited or no attention given to pre-triggering and post-triggering, which we now understand are just as important in the development of expectations.

Pre-triggering

Pre-triggering involves selecting a community and building rapport before triggering commences; getting to know and understand the community and its leaders; and ensuring everyone is included in the process. Everyone needs to trust the facilitator before triggering can begin. Social Network Analysis can be used at the community level to map and analyse the relationships between individuals and between groups, and to think more systematically about key issues of relevance to our programming, such as how information flows within and between reference networks and communities as a whole, and to identify which individuals (opinion leaders) have most influence on what others believe and do (Dooley, 2010; Maule, 2013). Certain marginalized groups may be identified as having different circles of influence or a different set of reference networks. Identifying these in the pre-triggering stage would be important especially in places where communities are highly heterogeneous, where coming to a collective decision might be particularly challenging. This is vital to ensure equal participation of all groups within the change process at community level. Only relying on Natural Leaders to emerge is too risky to CATS effectiveness.

Mapping of the social networks across villages at the district or sub-district level can identify central villages that are well positioned to support a process of organized diffusion of positive examples. During this phase it is also possible to identify existing traditions, beliefs, customs, or even social norms which may have a negative impact on the processes. The field note from Madagascar (UNICEF, 2015) illustrates how this can be addressed within CATS (see Box 18.1).

Triggering

Engaging the whole community, or at least a critical mass and key influencers, in the triggering process, is essential to ensure that enough people go through the 'ah-ha moment' and realize the impact that OD is having on the community, creating a collective change of factual beliefs and attitudes, and resulting in a collective decision to enact change. Collective belief change and the collective decision to enact change create new normative expectations; through the public declaration and development of the community action plan, individuals now know that the people around them expect them to stop the practice of OD. During this process, communities also develop their own vision and schema[10] with autonomy and this may require some adaptations (Dooley, 2010).

Box 18.1 Using social norms theory to understand why CATS wasn't working in Madagascar

Social norms and customs are context specific and in some cases there can be existing social norms that have a negative impact on the creation of a new social norm. In such cases the existing norm needs to be addressed and abandoned or modified before work can commence on creating a new norm. For this, a similar but slightly modified series of steps needs to be followed with the main difference being the order of empirical and normative expectations:

Creating new norms	Abandoning or changing a social norm
Changes in beliefs and attitudes	Change in beliefs and attitudes
Collective decision to change	Collective decision to abandon the norm
Coordinated action to enforce change	Coordinated action
Creation of a normative expectation	New empirical expectations
Reinforcement by empirical expectations	Abandon old normative expectations

Source: Bicchieri (2015, 2016)

In Madagascar challenges were apparent with CATS in the south where progress was falling behind compared with the rest of the country. A social norms analysis of the context was undertaken and found that people believed there was no harm in openly defecating. They also believed that the ground was sacred, as this was the place where their ancestors were buried. Digging a pit and putting excrement in the ground was considered to be an insult to the ancestors, hence taboo. More importantly, the consequences of doing so might be a fine in the form of animal sacrifice to the traditional leaders, or not being allowed to bury deceased members of the family in the future or, worse, being shunned by the community. In these communities, the social norms analysis identified that it would be important to address not only the false factual beliefs and normative expectations around the practice of OD, but also to confront the sacred values upheld by the community given the role these were playing in preventing adoption of an ODF social norm.

Triggering was introduced to express the risk in OD and challenge the factual belief that it is safe to openly defecate. At the same time, values deliberations with the traditional leaders and their communities were used to discuss what it meant to honour their ancestors and to identify how these values could continue to be upheld in a way that would not interrupt the introduction of latrine use. The core groups, which were made up of influential members of their communities, were essential in helping to initiate change. Festivals were used to make public declarations and create new empirical expectations.

Understanding the difference in steps required in such communities was a key factor, as without finding ways to support important social values, while abandoning the existing normative beliefs around OD, the new process could not begin and these communities would be classified as 'difficult'. Undertaking a robust social norms analysis during the pre-triggering phase would have assisted the implementers in identifying these issues from the outset and to adjust accordingly.

Source: Gaya (2013), UNICEF (2014)

Post-triggering

Toilet construction, monitoring and follow-up, ODF verification, declaration and celebration, reinforcement, incentives, and diffusion: all of these create both internal and external incentives to achieving ODF status (Dooley, 2010). They generate a positive internal incentive, pride in the community. Negative internal incentives include shame and disgust in the act of OD. External incentives include the ODF certification process and the celebration for achieving the ODF status. Negative external incentives can include fines, as for some people, there will be a continued personal preference to practice OD rather than go to the trouble of building or using toilets. Through the celebration process, traditional and political leaders from neighbouring communities and districts are engaged. Including measurements of beliefs and social expectations in baseline assessments allows for subsequent results monitoring (Maule, 2013). Comparisons with measurements taken post-triggering may provide evidence of whether the triggering has been successful in changing personal factual beliefs and in creating new normative expectations. Comparisons with measurements taken following ODF certification and in sustainability checks may provide evidence of whether there has been a harmonization of personal normative beliefs, empirical expectations, and normative expectations. This would provide evidence of whether a social norm has been established, and if so, how 'secure' or stable the norm is. Reinforcement of the new social norm is vital; this may take the form of traditional, public, or media campaigns undertaken by either the public or the private sector to provide a reminder to individuals of what societal expectations around OD are. At the time of writing of this chapter, UNICEF is integrating social norms measures into the CATS sustainability evaluations.

As mentioned above, within CATS we categorize interventions into three major components, pre-triggering, triggering, and post-triggering, with each component having valid and important steps. Within these components, we have drawn on SNT to introduce a number of important checks, which may have previously been taken for granted as part of the process. This helps to ensure that all steps are followed, as many of these elements are vital in the creation of expectations and a new social norm. The following are some of the checks and actions we suggest are undertaken by implementers:

- *Social norm analysis.* Is OD a custom in this community, or are there existing normative expectations around OD which first need to be addressed? If there are normative expectations, do they influence in-dividual behaviours? Do other customs or social norms within the community prevent the creation of a new ODF norm (as identified in the Madagascar example in Box 18.1)?
- *Measure baseline expectations.* Do individuals currently expect others in the community to use a toilet and do they think that others expect them to use a toilet (or defecate in the open)?

- *Measure behaviour.* If such expectations exist, measure whether they influence behaviour.
- *Social Network Analysis (SNA).* Use SNA to get a better understanding of formal and informal communication channels and the key individuals (influencers) who are central or have more connection to people (both within and outside the target community). SNA also provides the facilitators with a more systematic way to analyse the reference networks in the targeted communities. Understanding who should be present in the triggering and in their networks could also provide insight on the need for more triggering in other sub-villages or who should be targeted for post-triggering activities, thereby supporting *organized diffusion.*
- *Collective belief change.* Are all the relevant people engaged in the discussions and are the discussions being led by Natural Leaders? Is there a commitment to effect change and do people agree/pledge to abide by the decisions of the group?
- *Public declaration.* Not everyone can always take part in the triggering and discussions, so how can decisions be made public? How can everyone be reached? (If the initial group was large enough, the rest of the community may follow suit, realizing that most other people will follow the new norm as their empirical expectations have been changed.)
- *Incentives/sanctions.* As people normally require incentives to follow a norm, has there been any discussion of this? Social approval or disapproval is often sufficient incentive, so have the community discussed this? Have any positive (rewards) or negative (punishments) incentives been discussed and agreed upon by the community?
- *Organized diffusion and norm reinforcement.* How is information about this change relayed to others? Has there been spontaneous diffusion internally and externally? Have meetings been held outside the community? Are certified communities and districts recognized by the media? Is there a public information campaign about sanitation and ODF which would help reinforce the norm? Is the private sector involved in promoting sanitation products?
- *Monitoring social expectations.* In the post-triggering stages, are beliefs and social expectations monitored? Is there evidence of a significant change in both personal normative beliefs and normative expectations? During sustainability checks are beliefs and social expectation measured? Has a social norm been established (is there consensus on what people believe others expect them to do)? And is it being maintained (are people conforming to the expected behaviour)?

New social norms and sustainability

What we hope to achieve, once the community has agreed to abandon OD, takes action, and declares itself ODF, is a new social norm, whereby it is best (easier) for individuals and the community as a whole to follow the norm and hygienically separate human waste from human contact through toilet use, handwashing with soap, and safe management of children's excreta. By taking these actions, we stabilize the new social norm and ensure it is sustained over time. In some instances following ODF declaration, communities have created local by-laws to prevent OD in their village, thus aligning social norms with legal norms. Such systems may be important to monitor, regulate, and sustain the social norm, as it indicates to all (including newcomers to the community) that the normative expectation in that community is that everyone uses toilets.

Once the new social norm is created, it can remain volatile until it is stabilized. A social norm finds stability when a sizable majority of community members has the right social expectations, since it can be observed that toilet use is now widespread. This is why toilets made by communities themselves and the communication of progress in the form of household maps are important; they create common knowledge about behaviour change. It is also important that people's ideas about the future contain the social norms we want to maintain. If we do not always create a vision of what comes after ODF from the start, we may find instability of the new norm in the form of OD 'slippage' or reversion.

The 2014 UNICEF global CATS evaluation concluded that 'natural erosion' (slippage) is not due to a general lack of adherence to the new social norm created by CATS, but is caused by other circumstances, such as newcomers in the community, or a deterioration of toilet function (see Figure 18.4), and suggested this was acceptable if the effort necessary to maintain ODF status over time originated within the community itself or with very light external support. However, the evaluation also found,

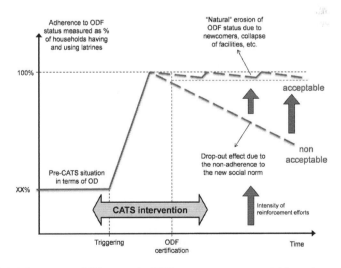

Figure 18.4 Adherence to ODF status in CATS programmes: acceptable and unacceptable slippage
Source: UNICEF (2014)

in a majority of countries, that it was not possible to assess the extent of slippage due to the lack of systematic ODF monitoring over time. We simply do not know enough about why some communities do not sustain collective behaviour change, and the role social norms play in their behaviour. This gap is mainly due to a lack of information and monitoring of social expectations. The evaluation (UNICEF, 2014) also indicated the need for adjustments to UNICEF's sanitation programme vision, as well as the immediate need to strengthen the conceptual understanding of SNT by UNICEF staff and partners.

SNT emphasizes the importance of not viewing the achievement of ODF status as the end-point – instead it is just one more step along the way to stabilizing a new social norm. SNT also offers potential tools to improve the way that we work – to allow us to be more strategic in our efforts to reinforce new social expectations (both normative and empirical) (see Box 18.2).

Box 18.2 Using a phased approach to sustainable sanitation: developing a vision or schema

CATS builds on people's existing resources and capacities to solve their open defecation challenge. A facilitator does not provide a solution but supports the community's discovery of how to end OD. When facilitation is done well, this results in a rapid change in the community. Problems sometimes arise when resources are scarce, the environment is challenging, and/or external standards are set that may be too high given the context of a specific community. This is often when programme managers feel compelled to push for subsidies or technical solutions, which undermine the core principles of CATS, creating new social norms through collective action.

Assisting communities and other stakeholders to develop a vision or schema can help them meet the challenges of resource scarcity, challenging environments, and externally imposed standards. The process of supporting a community to set the date on when they will become ODF and supporting the development of their collective action plan to end OD helps to shape that schema of the future and is a key component of the CLTS process. Often, the schema of the future ends at achieving ODF, with some link to sustainability. In the Philippines, UNICEF and partners have developed a framework whereby achieving ODF was made only the first of three phases in a longer process towards improved environmental sanitation and hygiene (see Robinson and Gnilo, 2016, this book). These distinctions allowed communities to develop a vision for change (schema or script), using their own capacities and resources to address the issues they had control over (OD), in the context of the bigger picture of achieving total sanitation.

Grade 1 (Zero Open Defecation) in the phased approach protected the behavioural and social norms change process, allowed the community to manage what was within their means, and allowed for limited sharing of latrines. A key component of the ODF verification process was to check that communities had a community action plan (schema or vision) for progression to the next grade. The vision being created for Grade 2 (Sustainable Sanitation) was universal use: toilets in all households and all public institutions, meeting the national standards for excreta management, plus a monitoring system that captures sustainability losses over time. The phased approach recognizes that there will be challenges that require intervention from outside the community in the long term, but that they can develop their own vision for actions which they have control over now.

Source: Gnilo (2014)

Conclusions

SNT is a framework which can be used to explain why CATS works, and improve both the effectiveness and sustainability of our sanitation interventions. It is not prescriptive but a set of principles and tools which we can use to enhance what we do and strengthen and sustain our overall approach. Understanding social norms is vital to how we work and the approaches we take during the pre-triggering, triggering, and post-triggering phases of the CATS process. We must ensure that everyone involved in our programmes is clear that we are creating a new social norm and that, in order to do this, not only do we require a change in beliefs and attitudes, but we also need to create new normative expectations that are reinforced by empirical expectations. This requires us to adjust some of our programming to strengthen our work in the areas of social networking, values and beliefs, monitoring expectations, developing organized diffusion and so on. Most important, however, is the need for reinforcement at community, subnational, and national levels; creating an environment where community members are able to express a clear vision to local and national governments of whether their right to sanitation is met, including how they believe it can be achieved. These changes are what will contribute most to sustainability and assist people in climbing the sanitation ladder.

CATS cannot work in isolation of other factors that directly or indirectly influence the community's ability to change, thus we need to be aware of this in our programming. What we started village by village, is rapidly progressing and expanding to larger geographic areas. With this spread, comes a strengthening of the new social norm, whereby someday it will no longer be about introducing a new social norm around OD, because by then ODF will be a global social norm.

About the authors

Therese Dooley has over 25 years of experience working on sanitation in various countries across Africa and Asia specifically focusing on community-based approaches. She is the former Senior Advisor for Sanitation and Hygiene at UNICEF.

Louise Maule is currently leading UNICEF's WASH Programme in the Philippines. Previously, Louise worked as the Sanitation and Hygiene Specialist at UNICEF's headquarters in New York, where she supported the development of organizational strategy, capacities, guidelines, and tools for UNICEF's sanitation programming globally. Louise has over 15 years of humanitarian and development experience, and has worked in a number of countries in Africa and Asia.

Michael Gnilo is a sanitation and hygiene specialist based in UNICEF headquarters in New York. Michael has designed and implemented community-based health, nutrition, and WASH programmes since 2003 in both development and emergency contexts. He has a particular interest in strengthening linkages among community, civil society, and government systems for sustained delivery of services.

Endnotes

1. CATS – Community Approaches to Total Sanitation was coined by UNICEF in 2008 to capture the variations of sanitation programming across its country offices including Community Led Total Sanitation (CLTS) in Sierra Leone, School Led Total Sanitation (SLTS) in Nepal, and the Total Sanitation Campaign (TSC) in India. Many of the programme designs were inspired by CLTS and similarly aimed for open defecation free (ODF) villages with one of the key distinct features to CLTS being government's involvement from the start.
2. SARAR is aparticipatory education/training methodology for working with stakeholders at different levels to engage their creative capacities in planning, problem solving, and evaluation.
3. Reference Network: those whose actions or approval we care about (family, clan, village members, religious authorities, co-workers, etc.) whoever has the power to influence our choice.
4. Empirical expectation: an expectation about what other people *will do*.
5. Normative expectation: an expectation about what other people *think we ought to do*
6. Penn-UNICEF 2013 Summer Program on Advances in Social Norms and Social Change course.
7. Custom: a pattern of behaviour such that individuals prefer to conform to it because it meets their basic needs.
8. Factual beliefs: based on a better knowledge and understanding of the issue often through the introduction of new information.
9. Schema or scripts are the mental representations of what you do (how you behave, who to talk with, what to expect from people) in specific social situations, e.g. tipping in a restaurant.

References

Bicchieri, C. (2006) *The Grammar of Society: The Nature and Dynamics of Social Norms*, Cambridge: Cambridge University Press.

Bicchieri, C. (2010-2015) *Penn-UNICEF Lectures on Social Norms and Social Change*, University of Pennsylvania, Philadelphia, PA, https://sites.sas.upenn.edu/?q=penn-unicef-summer/.

Bicchieri C (2016) *Norms in the Wild: How to Diagnose, Measure and Change Social Norms*, Oxford University Press, Oxford.

Bicchieri, C. and Muldoon, R. (2011) 'Social norms', in E.N. Salta (ed.) *The Stanford Encyclopedia of Philosophy*, Stanford University, Stanford, CA.

Dooley, T. (2010) *Creating a New Social Norm: Open Defecation Free Communities*, unpublished case study (Penn-UNICEF course).

Gaya, S. (2013) 'Eradicate open defecation in Madagascar: social norms theory at work to achieve behavior change', unpublished case study.

Gnilo, M.E. (2014) 'Keeping Total Sanitation from Total Reversion: The Phased Approach in the Philippines', unpublished case study (Penn-UNICEF course).

Kar, K. with Chambers, R. (2008) *Handbook on Community Led Total Sanitation*, Plan International and Institute of Development Studies, London and Brighton.

Maule, L. (2013) 'Using Social Norms Theory to strengthen UNICEF's CATS programmes', unpublished case study (Penn-UNICEF course).

Parvanta, C. (2011) 'Introduction to public health communication and informatics', in C. Parvanta, D.E. Nelson, S.A. Parvanta and R.N. Harner (eds.) *Essentials of Public Health Communication*, Joes Bartlett Learning, Sudbury, MA.

Rivis, A. and Sheeran, P. (2003) 'Descriptive norms as an additional predictor in the theory of planned behaviour: a meta-analysis', *Current Psychology: Developmental, Learning, Personality, Social* 22(3): 218–33 <http://dx.doi.org/10.1007/s12144-003-1018-2>.

Robinson, A. and Gnilo, M.E. (2016) 'A phased approach to rural sanitation development', in P. Bongartz, N. Vernon and J. Fox (eds.) *Sustainable Sanitation for All: Experiences, Challenges, and Innovations*, Practical Action Publishing, Rugby.

UNICEF (2014) *Evaluation of the WASH Sector Strategy 'Community Approaches to Total Sanitation' (CATS)*, UNICEF, New York, http://www.unicef.org/evaldatabase/index_CATS.html [accessed 25 February 2016].

UNICEF (2015) 'Application of social norms theory to strengthen CLTS in Madagascar: the case of southern Madagascar', *Eastern and Southern Africa Sanitation and Hygiene Learning Series*, UNICEF, New York.

CHAPTER 19

Conclusion: gaps in knowledge and further research needs

Naomi Vernon and Petra Bongartz

Having considered these different dimensions of sustainability of Community-Led Total Sanitation (CLTS) and water, sanitation, and hygiene (WASH) across different countries' and organization's experiences, it is clear that while there is a lot of existing experience and research that points us in the direction of how to make outcomes more sustainable and inclusive, there are many unknowns that require further investigation. Many of these have been identified by the authors in the preceding chapters. Nevertheless, below, we list some of these gaps in our current knowledge and thinking and propose the key issues that need more research.

Physical sustainability

We need:

- More data on rural sludge disposal practices, and where faecal sludge ends up once the pit is full.
- Formative research into what households do once pits fill up.
- To know what the different options for phasing and timing of CLTS and sanitation marketing are, when using them together – this will vary in different contexts.
- More knowledge on how to reach the poorest – sometimes options developed in sanitation marketing are unaffordable without assistance. Does the introduction of 'aspirational' technologies put households off choosing or building simpler toilet options?
- More formative research on identifying people's needs, financial capabilities, and what is available in the local sanitation market.

CLTS and WASH at scale

Questions include:

- How to improve advocacy for prioritization of sanitation in government policies, with adequate budgets for CLTS and post open defecation free (ODF) activities.
- How to improve routine monitoring of sanitation coverage, quality, and usage.

- How to monitor effectively and cost-efficiently. Monitoring and longer-term follow-up needs to be thorough yet simple, and be integrated as far as possible into existing government systems for it to be sustained.
- How to gather more accurate data, more effectively, and in ways that encourage and support communities.
- How to analyse and translate the collected data into improved practice.
- Does a phased approach encourage progression up the sanitation ladder by the whole community? What are the challenges? How transferable is it to different country contexts?

Research is needed on:

- The revised third party monitoring system in Kenya and whether using Master Certifiers is effective in the long-term. What is needed to incentivize them? Is the process sufficiently open, rigorous, and independent?

Equity, inclusion, the poorest: different needs

We need to know more about:

- How to go to scale without jeopardizing equity and inclusion; ambitious targets can lead to the most vulnerable and marginalized being left behind – instead, they need to be at the heart of any sanitation strategy.
- How to better/more effectively reach the poorest and most marginalized ensuring that they can access affordable sanitation options that respond to their needs.
- How to identify people in need of financial assistance when there are no national poverty identification systems available.
- How to make shared toilets work for those who need them.

We need to study:

- Whether including the perspectives of all toilet users when designing and constructing toilets and handwashing facilities is resulting in an increase in access to sanitation and hygiene for disabled people, older people, and those with chronic illness.
- How to build private sector capacity and interest in delivering products and services for the poorest.
- Reversion to OD in more detail: to what extent is reversion higher among the poorest, marginalized, or vulnerable?
- Whether devolution is resulting in inequity across counties.

Financing

We need to know:

- More about householders' willingness to pay for products and services.
- Whether it is possible to scale-up participatory design.

- What other ways there are to develop low-cost, durable local latrine options that people want.
- If the financial incentives embedded into the phased approach are effective, and reach the right people. Are any people still left behind?
- More about smart, targeted support for the poorest.
- More about the costs of post-ODF follow-up.
- How effective targeted sanitation finance is at reaching the poorest and helping them move up the sanitation ladder? Is it undermining community self-help, or encouraging fraudulent reporting and short-term incentives? Are vouchers or rebates being captured by non-poor households?

Behaviour change and social norms

We need to further investigate:

- What factors will sustain both behaviours and structures. These may go beyond CLTS and involve a combination of interventions. We need to understand what they are and apply this knowledge in programming.
- How to address and challenge social stigma and discrimination associated with pit emptying.
- The reasons why some communities do not sustain collective behaviour change, and what role social norms play.
- Whether Social Norms Theory can translate into practical steps for implementers that are different from 'standard' CLTS practice and lead to sustainable behaviour change. How can it be used to design post-triggering and post-ODF interventions?
- How to address social issues such as the challenges relating to caste and hierarchy in India. To what extent can and should sanitation programmes aim for and intervene in changes in broader social norms?
- How to motivate and incentivize (in financial and non-financial ways) different individuals and implementing units, e.g. Community Health Workers, Natural Leaders, government staff.

Final thoughts

One very important point that will help to improve knowledge and practice on all of these issues and questions is the prioritization of documentation, sharing, and learning. Programmes, projects, and institutions across the board must set up better mechanisms for, and, through providing time and capacity-building, encourage action learning. Flexibility of donors and implementing organizations alike will be crucial to ensuring that there is space for honest reflection, that learning from on the ground realities is fed back into and taken on board by programmes, and that adjustments to the course are encouraged. There are already good examples of processes, spaces, and support mechanisms for this kind of sharing and learning,[1] but we must be innovative in creating more ways of quickly learning and disseminating what works. For example, the Rapid Action Learning Units currently being established in India are a promising initiative, and we need to find out if they are leading to innovations which can be scaled-up across the country. We hope that the collection of experiences in this book will go some way to further opening up discussion about sustainability, contribute to improved practice, and thus help the millions of people around the world who are suffering the consequences of the lack of adequate sanitation.

About the authors

Naomi Vernon is the Programme Officer for the CLTS Knowledge Hub at the Institute of Development Studies, where she has worked for nine years. She is also the lead editor and designer of the CLTS Knowledge Hub publication series *Frontiers of CLTS: Innovations and Insights*, and co-authored the issue 'CLTS and Sustainability: Taking Stock'.

Petra Bongartz is the CLTS Knowledge Hub's Strategy, Communications, and Networking Officer and has been working on CLTS for almost 10 years. Together with Robert Chambers she created the CLTS Knowledge Hub at IDS in 2009. Petra leads on the Hub's communication activities including the CLTS website, (co)facilitates workshops and develops and implements the Hub's strategy with the other Hub members. She is the co-editor of *Tales of Shit: CLTS in Africa*.

Endnote

1. For example, the Sanitation Community of Practice; the SuSanA forum, the CLTS Knowledge Hub Sharing and Learning workshops and the *Frontiers of CLTS* series, the UNICEF *Eastern and Southern Africa Sanitation and Hygiene Learning Series*, and numerous webinars and learning enclaves.

Index

Action Contre le Faim (ACF) 169, 175, 249

advocacy 7, 18, 71–72, 78, 181, 183, 215, 284, 325

  role of media in 72, 73, 185–86, 216, 303

affordability, latrine 4, 11, 38, 102, 105–06, 107, 108, 135, 139, 141, 212, 214

Afghanistan 142, 287, 296

Africa 10, 57, 63, 79, 153, 167, 177, 178, 223, 282, 294–95.

See also sub-Saharan Africa

AfricaSan 7, 285

aid 33, 48, 56, 198

AIDS, *see* people living with AIDS

Angola 175, 251–2

American Standard, *see* SaTo-pan

Arborloo 155

Asia 57, 63, 79, 157, 167, 280–82

Asian Development Bank 235

Bangladesh 2–3, 10, 15, 31–52, 59, 151, 152, 155, 175, 244, 251–2, 263, 287, 296–97

  national sanitation campaign 16, 31–37, 44, 46, 48

  unions/councils (*parishad*) 32–35, 38, 39, 40, 42, 44, 45, 46, 47, 48, 49, 50, 51

behaviour change 3, 7, 12, 16, 35, 58, 85, 86, 184–85, 197, 294–95, 310, 319

  collective 35, 54, 55, 59–64, 65, 72, 167, 171, 172–73, 185, 192, 195, 210, 217, 250, 263, 315–16, 318, 320, 327

  research into 54, 195, 201, 214, 327

communication for 73, 173, 179, 209, 213–16, 303–04, 318

sustainability of 85, 95, 132–33, 195–96, 198, 214–16, 267, 271

emotional factors influencing 48, 102, 133, 198, 213, 214–15, 238, 258–59, 262,

Benin 187

Bhutan 142, 287

Bill & Melinda Gates Foundation 43

BRAC 15, 33, 34, 35, 37, 44, 45, 47, 50, 151, 155, 244

building materials 85, 102, 108, 110, 155

  availability of 104, 107, 108, 139, 146–47

  affordability of 104, 109, 141, 146–47

Burkina Faso 175, 251–2

Cambodia 16, 56, 150, 152, 175, 187, 235, 237, 242–43, 251–2

Cameroon 89, 187, 283–84

campaigns, sanitation 5, 7, 16, 31–33, 43, 46, 54, 57–59, 63, 77, 133–34, 147, 179–81, 208, 213–14, 235, 255, 295, 298, 304, 318

capacity building 70, 179, 180, 181

  local 65, 69, 71, 73, 181–82, 193, 198, 210

  institutional 46, 54–55, 57, 58, 68–71, 209–10, *see also* scaling up

CARE 31

caste hierarchy 16, 294, 298, 301–05, 327

certification of ODF 5, 170, 221–25, 227, 231, 232. *See also* verification of ODF

Community Health Strategy
Approach (CHSA) 193–97, 201,
202

Lao PDR 55–57, 61, 62, 66–70, 72,
74, 77, 78, 150, 152, 156, 251
Nam Saat (National Centre for
Environmental Health and
Water Supply) 56, 69
Latin America 79
latrines:
cleanliness 38, 48, 135–6, 138, 214
improved/hygienic 5, 10, 135,
209–10, 215–16, 218, 248
unimproved/unhygienic 14, 58,
146, 167
definition of 11, 36, 47, 50,
115, 137–38
institutional 5, 48, 170, 263, 270,
284, 286
parts:
lid 135, 138, 218
slab 20, 108, 113, 135–6, 146,
150–51
sub and superstructures 7, 13,
20, 38, 116, 135, 138, 146,
150, 157, 298–99
repair and maintenance 4, 10, 38,
41–42
shared/communal 11, 36, 43, 47,
146, 326
types:
composting 138, 155
eco-san 40, 111, 155
flushing 36, 39
hanging 36, 38, 40, 42, 57
offset 38, 45
pit 20, 34, 36, 38, 101, 134,
294, 296, 298–301
pour-flush 111, 116, 138,
156, 298
raised 38
ring-slab 38, 40, 42, 44
twin-pit 38, 40, 155, 294, 299,
303, 305

ventilated improved pit (VIP)
115, 135, 138
see also household latrine
coverage; affordability, latrines;
pit latrines
leaching 10, 13, 38–40, 152
leadership (community/local) 85–86,
93, 110, 181, 184–85, 197, 199,
260, 270
leakage, *see* leaching
learning and knowledge sharing 54,
55, 60, 68, 73–75, 114, 139, 179,
182, 187, 194, 198, 303, 327
Liberia 187
livelihoods 39, 46, 57, 74, 195–96,
200–02. *See also* entrepreneurs
local knowledge 108, 139

Madagascar 20, 86, 87, 198, 199,
285, 315–16
Malawi 85, 86, 87, 88, 89, 92, 103,
104, 107, 108, 110, 111, 178, 198,
200, 261, 263, 265–66
Accelerated Sanitation and
Hygiene Promotion
Programme (ASHPP) 103,
104, 109
Maldives 287
Mali 85, 89, 187, 313
malnutrition 2, 7, 37, 57, 72, 237,
242, 257
mapping:
key influencers 17, 86, 184, 197,
268, 314, 318
ODF roadmaps 92, 133, 178–80,
183, 199
sanitation maps 62, 213, 313
CLTS mapping and safety
mapping 261–62
marketing 7, 12, 13, 18, 39, 56–57,
59, 86, 95, 101–15, 131–2, 151,
154–55, 157, 192, 195, 236, 240,
247, 250, 266, 325; pro-poor 58,
62; hybrid 87, 104, 150; research
115, 134, 147